SAGE was founded in 1965 by Sara Miller McCune to support the dissemination of usable knowledge by publishing innovative and high-quality research and teaching content. Today, we publish over 900 journals, including those of more than 400 learned societies, more than 800 new books per year, and a growing range of library products including archives, data, case studies, reports, and video. SAGE remains majority-owned by our founder, and after Sara's lifetime will become owned by a charitable trust that secures our continued independence.

Los Angeles | London | New Delhi | Singapore | Washington DC | Melbourne

CITIZENSHIP
DEBATE
OVER NRC AND CAA

Thank you for choosing a SAGE product!
If you have any comment, observation or feedback,
I would like to personally hear from you.

Please write to me at **contactceo@sagepub.in**

Vivek Mehra, Managing Director and CEO, SAGE India.

Bulk Sales

SAGE India offers special discounts
for purchase of books in bulk.
We also make available special imprints
and excerpts from our books on demand.

For orders and enquiries, write to us at

Marketing Department
SAGE Publications India Pvt Ltd
B1/I-1, Mohan Cooperative Industrial Area
Mathura Road, Post Bag 7
New Delhi 110044, India

E-mail us at **marketing@sagepub.in**

Subscribe to our mailing list
Write to **marketing@sagepub.in**

This book is also available as an e-book.

CITIZENSHIP
DEBATE
OVER NRC AND CAA

Assam and the
Politics of History

Nani Gopal
Mahanta

Los Angeles | London | New Delhi
Singapore | Washington DC | Melbourne

First published in 2021 by

SAGE Publications India Pvt Ltd
B1/I-1 Mohan Cooperative Industrial Area
Mathura Road, New Delhi 110 044, India
www.sagepub.in

SAGE Publications Inc
2455 Teller Road
Thousand Oaks, California 91320, USA

SAGE Publications Ltd
1 Oliver's Yard, 55 City Road
London EC1Y 1SP, United Kingdom

SAGE Publications Asia-Pacific Pte Ltd
18 Cross Street #10-10/11/12
China Square Central
Singapore 048423

Published by Vivek Mehra for SAGE Publications India Pvt Ltd. Typeset in 10.5/13 pt Berkeley by Zaza Eunice, Hosur, Tamil Nadu, India.

Library of Congress Cataloging-in-Publication Data Available

ISBN: 978-93-91370-05-3 (HB)

SAGE Team: Rajesh Dey, Vandana Gupta and Rajinder Kaur

To my wife Gargi

Contents

Foreword

Assam is one of the oldest provinces of India; organized in 1874, it was the seventh. Territorial embellishment of the province went on till the geographical mass touched the international boundaries in the north, south and the east. The vastness of the province led to the issues of reorganization, immigration and insurgency. The ultimate result was the formation of an equilateral triangle based on reorganization, immigration and insurgency with immigration constituting the apex of the triangle. The hill regions were not profitable possessions for the British. Except for two hill subdivisions, as they were called, all hill districts were almost terra-incognito for most of the plainsmen. For whatever reasons, they were singularly insular and were not willing to belong to Assam, for they had an uncanny sense that to belong was to get lost. The tragic upshot of this was the successive reorganization of the province till 1972 when the province created in 1874 found its feet. It was nearly a journey of 100 years. The hill districts gained more from the British rule in Assam than the British gained from them.

The colonial government of the sprawling province needed resources to justify their own existence. The discovery of tea, petroleum and natural resources contributed enormously to British capital interest. Though the thrust of the government was on agricultural progress through better security and experiments in cash crops such as cotton and sugarcane, the fatalism of the peasants got the better of it. Ultimately, they fell upon jute, and, to cut a long story short, jute was the root cause of immigration that began in the 1890s. The land-hungry Muslim peasants of lower Bengal came rushing to take and occupy land. The census figure of 1911 revealed that the free flow of immigrants had already reached a cataclysmic climax which forced the government to sit up and take notice. The result was the counter-productive line system selectively introduced in 1920.

Men professing Islam had symbolic presence in lower Assam from the early 13th century to the end of the 15th century. The Ahom–Mughal relation entered a critical phase in the 17th century. There was no record of any Muslim settlement in the 16th century. After suffering a serious setback, the Ahom king recovered western Assam from the Mughals in 1682. A fair chunk of Mughal soldiers and their camp followers preferred to stay back in the settled condition of life where they came as aggressors in batches. Obviously, they made a choice. This, I would like to argue, has to be understood in the backdrop of the agrarian crisis of the Mughal state and the civil war in the second half of the 17th century. They lost their faith in the invincibility of the Mughal power and resolved to try their luck elsewhere. Soon, they endeared themselves to the Ahom-ruling class by their expertise in various professions. Since then, they have been an integral part of the Assamese nationality.

Assam was home to many fortune seekers coming from distant parts of undivided India, and every group of people thrived on mutual trust and goodwill. The non-stop flow of immigrants gave rise to social tensions and protest. Land was up for grabs and there was no let up. The Muslim League took their cause and broadened their social base. From the 1940s, the Muslim League worked under the illusion that Assam was on its way into their pocket. That did not happen.

After independence, the issue of Hindu Bengali refugees snow-balled into a crisis of confidence. It critically told upon the postcolonial reconstruction agenda. However, the post-partition phase of rehabilitation was completed by the state government in record time. The Bengali–Hindu refugees brought in some new elements to the nationality question.

Professor Nani Gopal Mahanta, author and political analyst, picked up the thread of his discussion from this conjuncture. From whichever angle one looks at it, the citizenship question is the kernel around which the entire politics of power moved. The question of citizenship is essentially a question of nationality, a question of holding power in one's own domain and fulfilment of the rightful aspirations without let or hindrance. Professor Mahanta has done extensive research and dissects many tendentious arguments and presents his views from the academic point of view. I see good reason in the author's view that, though it can't be stretched too far, the inward logic of partition qualifies the refugees for citizenship, but the immigrants, by their very definition, can't claim such privilege. From exuberant chaos created by small-time politicos, Professor Mahanta has produced a neat work of lasting value. Written with verve and breadth of vision, the *Citizenship Debate over NRC and CAA* is really a debate for the future of Assam and the Assamese. I warmly recommend the book to readers.

Rajen Saikia
Socio-economic Historian
Former sectional President
Indian History Congress (IHC), Delhi session

Preface

Assam is perhaps the only state in India where the issue of immigration and migration has been defining its core politics since the pre-Independence days. 'Assamese' is never a homogenous group of people. The problem with some of the inward-looking regionalist groups is that they consider Assam to be what it was before 6 February 1874, that is, the Ahom territory alone. When the Bengali-speaking district of Sylhet, with a population of nearly 2 million, was annexed to Goalpara (a largely Assamese- and Bengali-speaking district) and the hill districts, with diverse dialects, the nature and character of Assamese nationality fundamentally changed. The inclusion of Assam in Bengal, with Dhaka as its capital, further facilitated the immigration of East Bengal-origin Muslims (EBOMs) and Hindus to the hitherto under-populated virgin state of Assam. These events had fundamentally altered what was understood to be the core 'Assamese' group. The result was that the Assamese-speaking groups were reported to be a minority in all subsequent censuses until 1951. From the very beginning of the 20th century, the Assamese nationality had the fear of being outnumbered and taken over by the Bengali Muslim immigrants. Assam's Provincial Muslim League's demand to include Assam in the Pakistan scheme further exacerbated the sense of insecurity among the Assamese-speaking groups. However, the Assamese nationality attempted to overcome the numerical challenges by incorporating various other migrant groups into its fold. We have argued that since the 1920s, the Marwaris, the tea tribes, the Nepalis, the graziers and other upcountry people have been accepted as a part of greater Assamese society largely to counter the numerical, land and political challenges posed by the EBOMs and Muslim League. As we have shown in the book, the Bengali Hindus sided with the Assamese Hindus in a number of critical decision-making processes by the Assam Assembly and Council, although the challenges posed by the Bengali Hindus at the linguistic and administrative domain continued.

An attempt was also made to enlarge the Assamese fold by incorporating EBOM as the *Na-Asomiya* (neo-Assamese). The acceptance of the Assamese language by EBOMs generated a sense of confidence among the Assamese elites. Until the advent of the Assam Movement in 1979, the process of assimilation was largely smooth except ethnic assertions by the indigenous groups that occasionally challenged the hegemony of Assamese nationality. However, the post-Assam Movement period unfolded increasing assertions by EBOMs, and their increasing population strength again brought back the agonies and dilemma of Assamese nationality of being outnumbered and sidelined. The penetration and emergence of Bharatiya Janata Party (BJP) and the introduction of the Citizenship Amendment Act (CAA) and National Register of Citizens (NRC) in Assam are to be seen in this context. This book tries to analyse the growth and nature of Assamese nationality, and, in the process, questions some of the underlying assumptions as highlighted by the Leftist–Marxist scholarship. I argue that both NRC and Citizenship Amendment Act, 2019 (CAA-2019) are the unresolved legacies of Partition. Our analysis on NRC and CAA-2019 may perhaps be cited as the first academic effort to examine the twin issues from a historical perspective. The rehabilitation and resettlement of Bengali Hindus in the period from the 1950s until 1970s is a political reality which most of the contemporary scholars blissfully tend to put into oblivion. What is the extent of such rehabilitation, how were the issues of Bengali refugees and Muslim immigrants discussed and debated in the Constituent Assembly and Parliament, what is the contemporary relevance of those narratives, how has the relationship between EBOMs and Assamese Hindus unfolded in Assam in recent times, what is the connection between political Hindutva and ethnic identity—these are some of the crucial questions that this monograph tries to address and fill the vacuum left open in the study of citizenship and immigration.

Acknowledgements

I would like to express my gratitude to Gauhati University and the Centre for Southeast Asian Studies (CSEAS) for giving me the opportunity to work on the 'Immigration, Land and Identity' project, which has enabled me to look into the critical issues highlighted in the present book. I deeply acknowledge former Vice Chancellor of Gauhati University, Dr Mridul Hazarika, and current Vice Chancellor, Professor (Dr) Pratap Jyoti Handique, for their help and guidance. My colleagues in the Political Science department, Professor Alaka Sarmah, Professor Akhil Ranjan Dutta, Professor Jayanta Krishana Sharmah, Dr Dhruba Jyoti Sharma, Dr Rubul Patgiri, Dr Shbhura J. Konwer, Dr Joana Mahjebeen, Dr Barosa Deka, Dr Viaksh Tripathi and Dr Sukanya Bharadwaj have always been sources of inspiration. I have also enormously benefitted from my discussions with my friends Professor Chandan Sarmah (Tezpur University), Professor Akhil R. Dutta and Vikash Tripathi (Department of Political Science, GU). My sincere gratitude goes to Dr Rajen Saikia—one of the most celebrated historians of the state—for his views and opinion on the project. I deeply acknowledge his critical input.

I am especially grateful to my research team. Monoj Das, Coordinator of CSEAS, GU, helped to collect data and other archival materials from Delhi and Kolkata. My sincere thanks to Belina Barman, Bidyut Jyoti Kalita, Mridusmita Kalita and Shikha Rani Das for collecting archival and other library materials from Guwahati. The Assam Archive personnel, particularly Arnab Jyoti Kashyap and Abdul Rahman, deserve special kudos for their diligent work and constant help. I thank Chandan Das, Mukul Sarma and Gunajn Haloi for their logistical support all along. I am grateful to Kamal Krishna Boruah for his assistance and comments.

A special word of gratitude and thanks to Dr Rajesh Dey, Commissioning Editor, SAGE Publications, and the entire team for constantly guiding and helping me in the production process.

My five brothers, *Maa-Deti* and my children have been a constant source of encouragement throughout this journey.

Introduction

Assamese Nationality and the 'Politics of History'

Academic discourses in India are mostly confined to, what I would like to call, the trap of binaries. These binaries broadly fall in 'regionalist vs nationalist', 'communalist vs secularist', 'progressive vs regressive', 'chauvinism vs humanism', 'leftist vs rightist', 'absolutism vs universalism', 'nationalism vs internationalism', 'liberalism vs parochialism' and so on. This book makes a modest attempt to transcend these binaries and tries to look at the issues of identity and citizenry from the perspective of a marginalized, numerically smaller nationality and region, 98 per cent of which is surrounded by international borders. The book does not attempt to suggest that the issues confronting the north-east society in general and Assam, in particular, are different from all communities of the world. There are commonalities but at the same time, there are specificities. Specifics are defined from the evolution of Assamese society as a part of the greater Indian civilization, by its interaction with south-east Asian communities and as a nationality the characteristics of which have been defined from the arrival of the colonial British. I would like to argue that a society cannot be seen from one specific prism—be it leftist, liberalist or rightist. It is for the critics to decide to which category one belongs to. This is not a typical objective-neutral book; it has a position which essentially emanates from the perspective of a smaller nationality surrounded by transnational boundaries. Having said that, the perspectives or empirical deductions where I provide salience are scientifically arrived at with verifiable facts and figures. In the process, this book tries to critique some of the established perspectives on 'nationality', 'secularism' and 'citizenship debate' which are popularly prevalent among the leftist scholarship. The book also questions some of the prevalent scholarships on Assamese nationality and identity which ignores some of the historically discernible factors. I am trying to project the argument that Assamese nationality, if it wants to maintain its hegemony in Assam, has to adopt a historically inclusive nationality process. Since the beginning of the nationality process in modern history, the Assamese has never been a majority community on its own. It has been evolving by partnering with other smaller nationalities as stakeholders. The book draws the majority of its sources from archives in Assam, Delhi and Kolkata, libraries in various places of India, proceedings of legislative assembly debates and reports in Assam and the parliament.

Noted scholars writing on immigration and identity issues of Assam and the larger north-eastern region have hardly undertaken such analyses that consider the definitional parameters of Assamese nationality. Here, I would like to analyse the dimensions of identity in Assam by delving into the organic literature of specifically the former presidents of Assam Sahitya Sabha, and others, who have repeatedly highlighted the vexed issue of identity with their writings in the Assamese language. The medium of writing may be a reason why these scholars, poets and litterateurs do not find much resonance and visibility in the outside academia. This is also applicable to the scholars who are writing about the region in English or have been teaching abroad but have little exposure to primary reading materials and writings in Assamese (there are, of course, exceptions). In the process, they could hardly reflect upon the pulse of the Assamese nationality from within. In fact, in the realm of political analysis, our effort may perhaps be the first one that tries to see the question of Assamese nationality from the perspective of Assam, particularly on how it has been evolving over a long time. Scholars have talked about the conceptualization of 'nationality' or 'subnationality' as it operates in Assam, but what constitutes Assamese nationality has not received much attention so far.[1]

---

[1] Baruah's *Social Tensions in Assam* is an important contribution in this regard. The author includes a chapter on Ambikagiri Raichaudhury, a prominent nationalist of the past century. Although our ways of looking at identity formation are different, nevertheless, this is an important contribution in understanding Assamese middle class and the nationality-formation process in Assam.

Bases of Assamese Nationality: A Melange of Sankardeva's Bhakti Movement and the Indigenous Culture of Assam

It is important to ponder how the fundamentals or essentials of the Assamese society, as postulated by the scholars and doyens of Assam, have been evolving.

The journey of Assamese nationality is very old. The Assamese nationality-formation process in the modern sense of the term is a late 19th- and early 20th-century phenomenon. However, it would be wrong to trace Assamese history and nationality from the 19th century. The formation and growth of Assamese as a composite and plural community began a thousand years ago. Since time immemorial, Assam has been a part of the Indian civilizational axis. It is a continuation of a connected history of the ancient kingdom known as Pragjyotishpura and Kamarupa. In his monumental work *Early History of Kamarupa*, Rai K. L. Barua Bahadur argues that Pragjyotisha, which was then a powerful kingdom, is often mentioned in the epics and Puranas. Long before Bengal was even fit for habitation, Kamarupa underwent the process of Aryanization at an earlier time than central and lower Bengal.[2] Another book that traces Assam's long history with the Indian Aryan culture is Rajmohan Nath's book on the background of Assamese culture.[3]

In the Mahabharata, the extent of Pragjyotisha was up to the Bay of Bengal in the south and to the Karatoya (which stretches from the Tista, the Koshi to the Mahanadi) in the west. The *Kalika Purana* mentions that the temple of Kamakhya near Guwahati was the centre point of Kamarupa. The Purana deals with the story of Kamarupa and Naraka. Naraka was born from the earth through its impregnation by Vishnu (in the *Treta Yuga*) and was brought up by Janaka, the king of Videha, in present-day north Bihar. He married the daughter of the king of Vidarbha. He came under the influence of Bana Asura and as a result became irreligious and presumptuous. Bana Asura ruled over

[2] See Preface, Barua Bahadur, *Early History of Kamarupa*.

[3] See Nath, *The Background of Assamese Culture*, 25–45.

Sonitpura and is believed to have built the Mahabhairava temple that contains a huge *linga*.[4]

Naraka was eventually slain by Vishnu in his incarnation as Krishna. In present-day North Guwahati, there now stands the temple of Aswaklanta, which means jaded horses. While invading Pragjyotisha to destroy Narakasura, Lord Krishna is said to have halted there, after his horses became tired, and a large number of small holes in the rocks near the river are believed to be the footprints of his horses. Bhagadatta, the son of Naraka and the successor Pragjyotisha, took part in the Mahabharata battle on the side of the Kauravas and died in the hands of Arjuna.[5] The *Vishnu Purana* says that the country extended around the temple in all directions for 100 *yojana*s (about 450 miles). Its domain included the present-day territories of eastern Bengal, Assam and Bhutan. According to the *Yogini Tantra*, the kingdom of Kamarupa extended from the Karatoya river on the west to the Dikhou on the east, and from the mountains of Kanjagiri on the north to the confluence of Brahmaputra and Lakhya rivers on the south. It included the Brahmaputra valley, Bhutan, Rangpur, Cooch Behar, the north-east of Mymensingh and the Garo Hills.[6]

Assam's sociocultural fabric is agog with stories from the Ramayana and Mahabharata. Right from Sadiya, Manipur and Liqabali (near Silapathar) in Arunachal Pradesh to the land of Dimarajya (now known as the NC Hills), Tezpur or Sonitpur, many places in the entire region are associated with various ancient tales of Indic civilization and religion. The Kamakhya temple and several other temples dedicated to Durga, Shiva, Vishnu and Krishna are scattered in the north-eastern region, and many festivals celebrated in their honour have been glorifying and sustaining those cultural memories for generations. It is pointless to argue whether those stories from the Ramayana and Mahabharata that are supposedly based on the north-eastern region

---

[4] Barua Bahadur, *Early History of Kamrupa*, 30.

[5] Ibid., 34.

[6] Explanations on Assam's prehistory and references to Kamrupa and Pragjyotispura in various Puranas and Tantras as well as Bhagadatta's participation in the Mahabharata war could be found in Agarwala, 'Presidential Speech', 48–56.

in general and Assam in particular belong to the realm of mythology or reality. The fact is that people have believed in them for ages and imagined their reality as deeply integrated to the long-held cultural beliefs and memories. Such cultural socialization or acculturation is not just confined to the caste-Hindu people but also encompasses all communities of people, including those from the scheduled castes, scheduled tribes, autochthones and other migrant groups.

Kumar Bhaskar Burman, the last king of the Burman dynasty of Kamarupa, in the 7th century AD, was very influential. Immediately after ascending the throne, he defeated King Shashanka of Banga after forging a friendship with Harshavardhana. As per the text of the Nidhanpur copperplate, the king, along with a huge army, invaded King Shashanka's kingdom. Stories from folklore and inferences from other historical documents point that he sent a naval army from Assam via the Brahmaputra towards the Ganges to attack Shashanka's kingdom. His land army consisted of elephant, horse and foot soldiers. Attacked from two sides on both land and water, Shashanka retreated and fled to Orissa. To celebrate his victory over Karnasubarna or Banga, Kumar Bhaskar Burman ordered the issuance of the copperplate inscription of Nidhanpur.

The first Ramayana to be translated into a regional language from the main Sanskrit Ramayana, among the north Indian languages, is Madhav Kandali's *Saptakanda Ramayana* in Assamese. This was carried out in the 14th century. Madhava Kandali created his work under the patronage of Raja Mahamanikya, the Kachari king whose kingdom was situated in the present-day district of Nagaon. Acknowledging Madhava Kandali's literary prowess, Mahapurusha Sri Sankardeva later commented thus 'Seeking Rama in the works of my unchallenged predecessor, I felt like the rabbit running away in fear seeing the elephant's dung'.

Along with K. L. Barua's and Rajmohan Nath's books that we have referred above, another important work that reflects Assam's early contact with Aryan[7] India through references to the Ramayana and

---

[7] Here, we do not want to go into the 'Aryan-Dravidian' construct, as both these concepts are critiqued as misnomers. We are using the terms as used by the writers

Mahabharata is B. K. Baruah's *A Cultural History of Assam*.[8] These scholars have demonstrated that in the early Christian era, a significant number of Aryans came up to Sadiya and influenced the culture and religion of those areas. As Baruah has argued 'The Aryan influence became so widespread and penetrating that even minor Vedic customs and rituals deep rooted in the life of the common people'.[9] By citing Banikanta Kakati, Professor A. K. Baruah argues that the 'Aryanisation led to a unification of the innumerable tribal groups particularly in the Brahmaputra valley primarily through the development of a language which was a direct descendant of Magadhi Apabhramsa'.[10] There is evidence to suggest that the Assamese language, in some form or the other, developed in the middle of the 7th century.[11] Although the base of Assamese language is mainly drawn from Sanskrit, it also contains a large number of words from the Austric and Tibeto-Burman languages.[12]

Thus, Assam is a unique melange of movement of people coming from Indo-Gangetic plains in the Indian mainland and the Tibeto-Burman communities descending through the low hills of the Patkai range and the foothills of Himalayas. According to prominent litterateur and poet Harekrishna Deka:

> The physical features of the Assamese people are a mixture of the racial characteristics of both the Aryan and the Mongoloid races, with traces of the Dravidian and the Austric people as well .... The Ahoms, descendants of the Shan community from China's Yunan province, played a major role in bringing the Assamese-speaking people within a common political umbrella and gave the people the name Assamese, a derivative of the word Ahom.[13]

we are referring to.

[8] Baruah, *A Cultural History of Assam*.

[9] Ibid., 9.

[10] Baruah, *Social Tensions in Assam*, 20–21.

[11] Baruah, *A Cultural History of Assam*, 9.

[12] The most authoritative work on the Assamese language so far is Kakati, *Assamese, Its Formation and Development*.

[13] Deka, 'The Assamese Mind: Contours of a Landscape', 190.

The emergence of the Assamese language slowly gave birth to a new linguistic community that brought into its fold various other tribal communities. Professor A. K. Baruah succinctly argues that it was

> a process of Aryanisation in which even some tribes like the Kacharis, the Lalungs, the Mikirs and others were converted to a new caste, the Koch. Thus the linguistic community which took shape in Brahmaputra valley and came to be known as the Assamese underwent a process of Aryanisation and in the process brought Assam culturally so close to the rest of India that by the 15th century Sankardeva who took pride in the fact that he was born in the 'Bharatabarsha'.[14]

Role of Sankardeva and Bhakti Tradition

The character of the Assamese society is defined by the liberal and humanitarian outlook of the Sankardeva movement. The Vaisnavite philosophy, as enunciated by Sankardeva, is all about inclusiveness and democratization of 'bhakti'. The socio-religious and cultural foundation of Assamese society was laid by Srimanta Sankardeva (1449–1568) and his apostles. Venerated as the 'Mahapurusha', Srimanta Sankardeva was such a personality who heralded Assamese modernity and renaissance. He was a saint-scholar, dramatist, poet, singer, litterateur, social reformer, religious leader, sculptor, actor and danseur who laid the sociocultural and religious foundation of the then undivided Assam. At that point, Assam was a divided society, segregated into tiny kingdoms (in fact, the name 'Assam' was never used by anyone; Sankardeva used 'Bharatbarsha').

Sankardeva used Vaisnavism as a means to bring reforms to society. To popularize *ekasaran-bhagawati dharma* (monotheism with supreme devotion to Vishnu or Krishna), he democratized and simplified religious practices which hitherto were inaccessible to common masses. Sankardeva established a new institution known as the *Satra* through which he popularized his teachings among the people through his wide corpus of literary creations like dramas (*Ankiya Bhaona* or one-act plays), songs (*Borgeet*) and dance (known as *Satriya* dance). In the

---

[14] Baruah, *Social Tensions in Assam: Middle Class Politics*, 22.

process, Sankardeva ushered a new life, a new corpus of literature and a new cultural state the resonances of which still remain vibrant in all aspects of the Assamese society. His creative works include a large body of immortal verses such as the *Kirtana Ghosa, Nimi-Nava-Siddha-Samvada, Bhakti-Pradipa, Harichandra Upakhyan* and six *Ankiya bhaonas*. The *Kirtana Ghosa* is a collection of about 33 *kirtanas* (chapters), and each chapter is a description of 'bhagawata leela' of Krishna or Vasudeva or Narayana from the Bhagavata Purana.

He composed six *Ankiya Bhaonas* by creating a new language known as Brajabuli which is intelligible to all the communities of eastern India. Sankardeva used his plays as a tool to popularize his ideology to a largely illiterate society, divided on caste, communal and religious lines. He took great care to involve every section of the society in his activities. The disciples of Sankardeva were drawn from various tribes and communities of Assam. Some of them are Norottom from Naga, Damodor from Bhut, Gobindo from Garo, Narayana from Mising, Bolai from Karbi, Ram from Kachari, Sri Ram from Koibortto, Chandshai from Muslim, Ananta Kondoli and Ram Saraswati from Brahmin and Madhavdeva from the Kayastha community. He also made his religion open for all, especially women and other lower tribes in the society. He said:

Nahi-bhaktatit jaati-ajati-bichar,

Krishnaro bhakatit samastore adhikar.

(For creeds, devotion has bias for none; love for Krishna is meant for everyone.)

Samasto bhutato byapi asu moi Hari,

Sobaku janiba tumi Bishnu buddhi kari.

(In all beings as Hari I dwell; regard everyone as Vishnu in them dwell.)

Stri-Shudro kare jadi amako bhakati

Tahako janibaha gyano mahamoti.

(When on me devotion do women and folks flippant shower, then know they are in wisdom's bower.)

Sankardeva institutionalized his religion by establishing *satras* to propagate his teachings. There are more than 750 *satra* institutions today in every nook and corner of Assam. These centres became the first cooperative societies through which principles of self-help and vocational training were disseminated. It is the *satras* that subsequently became the nerve centre of the satriya dance (later recognized as the seventh form of Indian classical dance by Sangeet Natak Akademi in 2003), drama, mask-making, Vaisnavite sculpture, monograph painting, training in musical instruments like the *khol* (a two-faced drum), *taal* (a type of cymbal), etc., and, most importantly, the satriya way of life. The *naamghar* (prayer house), the epicentre of *satra* and village life in Assam, where all these activities are carried out, is a two-roofed thatched structure rectangular in shape like the *vikrsta* type of playhouse mentioned in the *Natya Shastra*. Subsequently, the *satras* and *naamghars* became the foundation of Assamese culture, spirituality and social justice. *Naamghar* was also identified as the meeting point of all sections of the society, including women. There is no discrimination of anyone based on class, caste or position, and everybody enjoys equal status as *bhakat* or *vaishnava* or as *baap* (a devotee). Although there are certain restrictions on the entry of women in certain *satras* (like in Bordowa and Barpeta), a majority of the *satras* and *naamghars* facilitate vibrant women participation in the bhakti activities along with the male bhakats. *Lakhimi naam, gopini naam, gopini sabah, pasoti, aai-sokolor naam*, etc., are some of the spiritual and cultural activities which are exclusively carried out by the women bhakats.

The philosophical foundation of Sankardeva's ideals is drawn from the Vedas, Puranas and Tantras. *Bharatabarsha* was the most revered name for him, and we find no mention of the word 'Assam' in his writings. According to Nagen Saikia and Rajen Saikia, no other saints and scholars of the Bhakti movement espoused the notion of *Bharatabarsha* so much as was done by Sankardeva. He considered *Bharatabarsha* as *punya bhumi* (holy land), *jonmo bhumi* (land of birth) and *karma bhumi* (land of toil). He considered the land of Bharatbarsha as the most revered place in the whole world.

Sankardeva is the architect for initiating modernity and renaissance in Assam. He questioned regressive social customs and religious norms, visualizing a society where all sections of the society could take part. He also talked about individuals and society, equality and freedom for all. Modernity does not mean neglect to the past rich cultural heritages; the concept of modernity is all about advancing our own practices and thoughts as well as ensuring the progress of our society in our own terms without imitating the West.[15] The reason we have provided a relatively long introduction to Sankardeva is to precisely show how he laid a liberal cultural-religious society in Assam.[16] However, it is not just *Vaisnavite dharma* and culture that had shaped the liberal outlook of Assam. A renowned scholar and historian, Surya Kumar Bhuyan, in his presidential address as the president of the Assam Sahitya Sabha in Shillong in November 1953, said that Assamese society is a unique melange of 'Aryan and non-Aryan cultures'. There were very powerful non-Aryan kings and kingdoms in Assam which not only gradually adopted Hinduism but also became its greatest proponents.[17] Besides enriching Assamese culture and civilization, such interaction, Bhuyan further argued, impacted Indian Hinduism as well. He said that many believed that the Vedic *tantric* and *shakti* cult had its strong origin in Assam and Bengal. He further said:

> It is indeed gratifying to see how at the initiative of *ekasaran bhagawati dharma* as propagated by Mahapurusha Sankardeva has brought the autochthones to the mainstream fold and in the process, they got completely merged with Assamese identity. Such liberal stories are highly educative and highly encouraging.

Another stalwart of Assamese language, culture and literature, Lakshminath Bezbarua made the following remark in his address as

---

[15] For a discussion on modernity, see Chakrabarty, 'Modernity and Ethnicity in India', 143–55.

[16] To learn more about the contribution of Sankardeva and his apostles, one may look at Neog, *Sankardeva and His Times*; Mahanta, *Satra-Sanskritir Aachar-Ritiaru Utsav-Anustan*; Sarma, *The Neo-Vaisnavite Movement and the Satra Institution of Assam*.

[17] Bhuyan, *Presidential Address*.

the president of Assam Sahitya Sabha in its seventh session held at Guwahati in December 1924:

> People from many countries and nations belonging to both Aryan and non-Aryan cultures came to Assam and lived here as Assamese. That is how we are weaving every thread of Assamese nationality. Konoujia, Hindustani, Bengali, Oriya, Nepali, Gujarati, Punjabi and many others have become part of Assamese society. The invincible Ahoms, Singphos, Morans, Nagas, Mikirs, Miris, Doflas, Garos, etc., have *Sanskritised* themselves to become Hindus and got assimilated as Assamese Hindus. In the process, they are strengthening the cultural base of Assam. Even during the invasion by the Muhammadans, many foreign Muslims became part of Assamese culture. (Bezbarua authored several books on Sankardeva and the Bhakti Movement)[18]

This is how the development of a distinct and unique character of Assamese culture and Assamese nationality took place. It is based upon a composite, plural and liberal identity, the foundation of which was laid down by Sankardeva. Another architect of modern Assamese culture, Jyoti Prasad Agarwala paid his deep tribute to Sankardeva in his various treatises and poems. He believed that Sankardeva provided a revolutionary cultural character to the Assamese society.[19] Similar tributes could also be seen in the writings of Banikanta Kakati, Bishnu Rabha, Bhupen Hazarika, Nagen Saikia and Rajen Saikia—the list is endless.

Internationally acclaimed Indologist and the first Vice-Chancellor of Gauhati University, Krishna Kanta Handique, conceptualized a platform called 'Sankar Mission' for the propagation of Assamese language and culture. In the 17th session of the Assam Sahitya Sabha in 1937 (December), Handique in his presidential address called for the expansion of Sankardeva's *naamdharma* which would act as an instrument for the expansion of Assamese language. He urged the *satras* and *satradhikars* to play a pivotal role in this regard. In other words, his argument for the expansion of Assamese language and literature

[18] Bezbarua, *Shri Sankardeva* and *Mahapurusha Sankardeva aru Madhavdeva.*

[19] See Agarwala, 'Natunar Puja', 493–97. To know about Krishna culture as conceptualised by Jyoti Prasad Agarwala and the influence of Sankardeva on him, one can read *Shilpir Prithivi*, Agarwala, 'Natunar Puja', 453–80.

is organically linked with Sankardeva's religion. It may be mentioned that even the thousands of illiterate Assamese across the state could read, recite and memorize the texts and hymns of *naamdharma* as a part of their daily ritualistic exercises. The opinion of a Marxist scholar (we shall have occasion to refer to him towards the later part of the book), Hiren Gohain is noteworthy in this context. He stated that the role played by the *mahapurusia dharma* and *dharma andolan* in enriching Assamese nation and national culture during the middle ages is acknowledged by every Assamese. However, he cautioned against the exaggeration of Sankardeva and Madhavdeva's role as the 'fathers of Assamese nation', as they did not start their journey in a vacuum. One must not forget the role of the tribes and tribal cultures of Assam. He, however, argued

> This dharma andolan had succeeded in establishing a culture which is broader, more developed and liberal than the tribal society. This dharma andolan was a broad platform for attracting many tribal people into its fold. This is how the foundation of modern Assamese nationality was laid.[20]

Thus, the vaishnavite *dharma andolan*, as enunciated by Sankardeva and his apostles and indigenous ethnic cultures, constituted the basic foundation of Assamese nationality.

We reiterate that we have just attempted to provide an outline to the nature of Assamese nationality, which was never a one-dimensional process. While tracing the organic connection with the pan-Indian cultural ethos, the chasm between the Indian nationalism and Assamese nationality gets reflected occasionally, at times the intensity is grave and sometimes negotiable.[21]

Our purpose here is not to document a very linear, simplistic straightforward nationality-formation process of the Assamese people. Various factors have contributed to the growth of a composite

[20] Gohain, *Asomiya Jatiya Jibanat Mahapurushia Parampara.*

[21] To understand such gulf between the Indian state and the Assamese nationality, one may look at the nature and functioning of ULFA—the most organised secessionist organisation fighting for separation from India. See Mahanta, *Confronting the State,* introduction and conclusion.

Assamese nationality. Assam's resolute fight against the Mughals on multiple occasions also fuelled its nationality-formation process. Noted litterateur and poet Harekrishna Deka argues:

> [A] cultural community developed into a political people with Assameseness as the core element of unity. They offered a heroic resistance to the superior force of the Mughals, who invaded the Ahom kingdom a number of times but were defeated. The finest example of this spirit was witnessed in the battle of Saraighat where a heroic leader, Lachit Borphukan, inspired the Assamese to rise as one against an alien invasion. The Mughal invasions were a litmus test for the Assamese spirit. Their unified resistance against an alien power led to the consciousness of an identity, the birth of a kind of nation-ness, without the concept of naturalism.[22]

New Entrants to Assamese Nationality: East Bengal Origin Muslims as *Na-Asomiya*

There are issues of subnational identity formation of various ethnic groups many of which are in opposition to Assamese identity.[23] Nevertheless, as a result of de-tribalization and Sanskritization, many tribal groups have given up their traditional modes of production and social behaviour to embrace Hindu religion and customs,[24] even though a few sections of the tribal groups have embraced Christianity because of the strong educational, economic and emotional role of various missionaries in the region. However, it may be categorically stated that the foundation of Assamese nationality in association with various ethnic tribal groups is very strong and constitutes an unbreakable base in the light of increasing 'immigrant-centric' polity in the state. Needless to say, with the change of time, new elements have been added with several waves of immigration. Such migrants/ immigrants or the East Bengal origin Muslims (EBOM—also known as *pomua*, *chorua* and *bhatia* or by a generic name *abhibhasi* Muslims) have

---

[22] Deka, 'The Assamese Mind: Contours of a Landscape', 190.

[23] To see the dialectics and contradictions of such an identity formation of the Assamese people, one may look at Sarmah, *Asomiya Kun*.

[24] Ibid., 32–45.

also become a part of this nationality, although the accommodation of them and their descendants to the Assamese nationality formation is not without contradictions and contestations.[25] Many celebrated writers have termed them as *Na-Asomiya* (neo-Assamese) as a gesture of welcoming them to the fold of Assamese nationality.[26] (We shall have occasions to discuss their integration and contradictions of the process towards the later part of the book.)

Assamese nationality has always shown resistance against attempts to destabilize its foundation. One such process started during the colonial phase with massive immigration from East Bengal. The Assamese society is still confronting those challenges in present times with various forms and contours. A question may perhaps be raised: Is there a post-colonialist discourse in Assam or are we still trapped in the colonial burden, what Professor Udayon Misra terms as the 'burden of history'?[27]

During the colonial period, Assam fought a bigger war than that of the freedom struggle. The struggle that Assamese leadership fought was for protecting its pride and cultural base which had been evolving since the 13th century, that is, with the coming of Sukapha[28] and the launching of Bhakti movement under the leadership of Sankardeva and Madhavdeva. There was a fundamental intrusion to the essence of Assamese nation through the politics of Muslim League and massive immigration mainly from the Mymensingh district of East Bengal. It may be mentioned that the fight was neither against the Muslim population who constituted an integral component of composite Assamese

---

[25] See Misra, *India's North East*, 198–205.

[26] Perhaps for the first time, the term 'Na-Asomiya' or neo-Assamese was used by Agarwala, *Asomiya Dekar Ukti*.

[27] In the preface, the writer writes, 'My interest in the subject of pre-and post-partition politics and Assam has been spurred by the fact that the issues that were central to the regions' society and polity during the 1940s, such as land, immigration, identity and language, continue to occupy major public space ...' (Misra, *Burden of History*)

[28] When the Ahoms arrived in Assam, they described the region as *Mung Dun Sun Kham* (Land of golden treasure).

culture nor against immigration,[29] as the Assamese society is a melange of the migrant population,[30] but it was against a religious and political force that tried to fundamentally alter the character and nature of Assamese society. The fight was against the inclusion of Assam with Pakistan; the fight was against the transformation of Assamese indigenous composite culture to a predominantly Muslim state. It is not that the Assamese society wanted to freeze immigration. In fact, the Line Committee report welcomed the hard-working immigrant population up to a point and appreciated their hard work. It said:

> None of us could fail to be struck with admiration at the magnificent way in which every available inch of land in immigrant areas is made use of and intensively cultivated and we cannot but feel surprised that the Assamese, living in close proximity with immigrant, have not benefited more by their example and learned more up-to-date and economic methods of tilling their land.

> In all our recommendations we have laid stress on preference being given in settlement, under the colonisation scheme or otherwise, of waste land with immigrants to those who are already in the province ... we recommend that until lands have been made available for all those who came into the province before the 1ˢᵗ of January 1938 no settlement should be made with new immigrants and that before they settle lands with immigrants coming after the 1st January 1938 they should refer the matter to Government for orders ....[31]

Thus, immigration up to 1 January 1938 was a welcome phenomenon and any compelling settlement after that day was to be forwarded to the government for an administrative decision. In fact, the very Line Committee report was an effort for regularizing the incessant immigration. However, the Muslim League was not satisfied with the process.

---

[29] There are a lot of controversies regarding the use of the word 'immigration' as many argue that those EBOM were migrants not 'immigrants' as the movement was within the same country. However, we are using the term as was used in the Assam Legislative Council and later on in the Assam Assembly before independence. Besides, we have used the term as was defined by the British in their administrative communication which is clarified towards the last part of the chapter.

[30] To understand the nature of migration to Assam, one may see Kalita, 'Prabajankarir Samasya Aru Asom'. Also see Hussain, *Assam Movement*.

[31] Assam Secretariat, *Line Committee Report*, 11–12.

Its leaders wanted the abolition of the system itself and vouched for total and complete unrestricted immigration so that Assam could become a Muslim-dominated state and thus become a fit case for inclusion into its future Pakistan scheme.

Roughly from 1930 till 1947, the Muslim League phase was one of the most violent and aggressive phases of Assam's politics. The Congress leadership in Assam had to confront them at all levels. The British and the colonial administration were important partners of Muslim League, as the former wanted the Muslim League to take on Congress to check the burgeoning nationalism in the easternmost part of the country.[32] Besides, the British were all in favour of opening up grazing land, wasteland and agricultural land to the immigrants so that they could earn revenue to the maximum extent possible. The opinions of the British officials were clear. The Assamese and the indigenous people must come up to the level of the immigrants or lest they must get merged with the immigrants. Taking part in a debate on the abolition of Line System as proposed by the Muslim League members, Mr Scott—the revenue member—argued that the system could not be continued indefinitely.[33] The immigrants had cut off all connection with the place of their births and must be regarded as people of Assam. The barriers which, for the time being, separated communities of different economic levels were artificially drawn. Either the indigenous people must rise to the level of the immigrants or be submerged. Another European member, Mr L. A. Roffee, was even blunter in his approach. He said that he had sympathy with the indigenous Assamese people who might be swamped, but eventually, the weaker was bound to be at the back foot in favour of the stronger.[34]

Thus the plight of Assamese indigenous people was caught between two devils: one wanting to take over the state with unchecked immigration, in the process, make, the state a Muslim-dominated state, and

---

[32] See Barua, *Comprehensive History of Assam*, 520–79.

[33] In order to regulate the settlement of the immigrants, the Line System was mooted in 1916 and introduced in 1920 in Nagaon. Under the Line System, the specific areas were differentiated as 'immigrant', 'indigenous' and 'mixed' villages.

[34] *Assam Gazette*, Part-VI A, 1937, 1525.

the other aspiring to make Assam's land and forest open for economic exploitation. In this regard, file notations and observations of government officials are noteworthy when they were responding to a petition by the Assamese people in April 1913 against the settlement of immigrants in Nowgong (present-day Nagaon). The Deputy Commissioner noted 'Personally I am not in favour of discouraging immigration from Mymensingh', to which the then Chief Secretary B. C. Allen opined '[The] Chief Commissioner Assam considers that ... it is the policy of administration to encourage immigration'.[35]

As we cited above, the issue was not the opposition to immigration per se. There are many instances when the Assamese leadership vouched for the interest of the immigrants. Rohini Kumar Chaudhury, the revenue minister during Saadulla's period, spoke for the protection of immigrants' rights. It was at his suggestion that a Line Committee was constituted to look into the various issues of the Line System. However, the Assamese, including the tribal leaders, could never reconcile to the aggressive land-grabbing and encroachment process of the immigrants. What are the problems and apprehensions created by the immigrants? According to Mohammad Taher, there are essentially four grounds for opposition: (a) continuous immigration would swamp the indigenous society and culture; (b) it would also deprive the indigenous people of the cultivable and grazing lands; (c) if large-scale immigration is allowed, the future generations of the indigenous would have no land resources to fall back upon; and (d) more immigrants would create further social trouble and tension.[36]

However, the most objectionable part was that the immigration process which began as an economic and revenue issue soon acquired a political dimension. All of a sudden, a vast treasure of Assam, that is, vast swathes of land, was gone. The British not only changed the landscape, but they also changed the fundamentals of the land use pattern. For the first time, people's lives and culture changed

---

[35] State Archive File, 'Emigration of Mymensingh Muhammadans into Nowgong district', Revenue B for June 1913, nos. 135–37.

[36] See Taher, 'Line System of Assam', 144–45.

drastically. With the increasing number of Muslim immigrants, the Muslim League demanded more and more political rights and, from 1940 onwards, Assam became a typical case for the party for inclusion into the Pakistan scheme.

Ambikagiri Raichaudhury and Assamese Nationality

Here it would be worthwhile to look at the politics of Muslim League from the perspective of a scholar, revolutionary poet, former Assam Sahitya Sabha president, freedom fighter and institution builder— Ambikagiri Raichaudhury. He clearly distinguished 'Asomiya swaraj' from 'Bharatiya swaraj' and argued that the *swaraj* for India might not bring *swaraj* for Assam.[37] It was at the insistence of Raichaudhury that in 1926, the Asomiya Sangrakshini Sabha, later known as Asom Jatiya Mahasabha, was established to protect the interest of the Assamese. His idea about India and other smaller nationalities can be grasped from the following passage:

> India is not a country; it is a continent—a totality of many countries. According to their own social systems, customs everyone is a nationality— and as a result of combination of all these nationalities is growing the great Indian Mahajati—therefore India is the Mahadesh of the Indian Mahajati. Though the people of various provinces may be of same ideology yet they have distinct customs, dresses, eating habits, social norms and distinct natures, system of thoughts are different, literature and culture are different. None of them want to disappear.[38]

'He viewed India as not one nation but as a combination of nationalities which aspire to protect their identities within the Indian Mahajati'.[39] Swaraj to India may not bring swaraj for Assam.[40] With the disappearance of 'Assam Association', the Asomiya Sangrakshini Sabha

---

[37] *Chetana*, an Assamese weekly published from Gauhati, Vol. III, No. 2, p. 2. 'Swaraj' generally means self-rule.

[38] Sharma, 'Ambikigiri Raichaudhurir Pratibha', 597.

[39] Baruah, *Social Tensions in Assam: Middle Class Politics*, 59.

[40] *Chetana*, Vol. III, No. 2, p. 2.

(Forum for the Conservation of Assam) was founded in 1926 under the leadership of Raichaudhury. It demanded the vindication of the rights of the children of the soil. The *Deka Asom*, an Assamese weekly and a mouthpiece of the Sangrakshini Sabha, pleaded for the 'protection of indigenous Assamese people against the aggression of outsiders'.[41]

Raichaudhury's ideology had a unique combination of nationalism and regionalism. His eulogization of Bharat is beyond any doubt. However, he had a layered notion of nationhood. He was a fierce protector of Assamese (*Asomiya*) nationality. Through his devotion to Assamese nationality, he tried to reach to the Indian *mahajati* (grand-nation). His understanding of the 'Assamese' and 'Indian' was not mutually exclusive but rather found upon a unique bond of unity between the two. In an interview in the first year of *Deka Asom* in 1935, he said he used the word *jatiyata* to mean the Assamese collective; he understood the Indian essence as *mahajatiyata* and understood the world community as 'maha-manabata'.[42]

Raichaudhury fiercely opposed the partition of Bengal and the merger of Assam with eastern Bengal in 1905. He started a voluntary group known as Seva Sangha which supposedly had developed terrorist leanings in association with Anusilan Samiti of Dacca.[43] He wrote a patriotic drama *Bandini Bharat*, the manuscript of which was confiscated by the police. Raichaudhury was kept under police vigilance for about eight years.[44]

Raichaudhury never allowed religion to distinguish between people, although he accepted Hinduism as given fact of Assamese-ness. In his treatise *Bartaman Bharat Kaar* (Whose India is this?),[45] he argued that both Hindus and Muslims are equal partners of Assam's growth. They are like inhabitants of the same house. However, he urged all

---

[41] *Deka Asom*, Vol. II, No. 2, 1936.

[42] Jatiyata broadly denotes nationality; mahajatiyata broadly denotes grand-nationality and maha-manabata may broadly be understood as global-humanism.

[43] Baruah, *Comprehensive History of Assam*, 520.

[44] Raichaudhury, *Mor Jivan Dhumuhar Echati*, 16–26.

[45] Raichaudhury, 'Bortaman Bharat Kaar'.

the Mymensingh Muslims to get merged with Assamese culture. To quote him:

> Few years back the Bengali Muslims from Mymensingh and other areas have settled in Assam. The Assamese Muslims have the enormous responsibility to get them educated in Assamese language, make them proud Assamese and thus strengthen the base of Assamese nationality.[46]

Raichaudhury advocated strongly for providing education to the illiterate sections of the Muslims. In an editorial titled as 'Hinduraj and Muslim Raj' in *Chetana*, he urged

> [The] issue of Hinduraj and Muslimraj is emanating actively from the Muslim side. Hindus have never uttered such mala-fide intention anywhere. Therefore we urge the Muslim brothers that rather than spending huge sum of money to convert ignorant illiterate people of other religion to Islam, they should instead try to educate the illiterate Muslims. They should try to influence them who are said to be mainly responsible for spreading communal violence and disturbances in the country—this will greatly enhance the collective Indian nationalistic feeling among them.[47]

Ambikagiri Raichaudhury was deeply saddened by the Muslim League's effort to include Assam in Pakistan. He was an aggressive nationalist and built up organizations to resist the onslaught of the Muslim League. He was extremely critical of the settlement of immigrants in various parts of Assam. In fact, to resist the aggressive postures of Muslim League, Raichaudhury constituted the Assam Atma Rakshi Bahini (Assam Self-Defence Unit) on 15 June 1946. The main purpose of the group was to protect the Assamese people from the gung-ho political activities of the Muslim League. The purpose was to confront Muslim League leaders like Maulana Hamid Khan (also known as Maulana Bhasani) who, along with other Muslim League (ML) leaders from Surma Valley, tried to settle and grant the immigrants maximum amount of *myadi* land. For that purpose, it was very essential for the Muslim leaders to oppose the line system—the most effective institutional mechanism to regulate land settlement in Assam.

---

[46] Ibid.

[47] Raichaudhury, 'Hinduraj and Muslim Raj'.

Bhasani was completely against the eviction policy of the Congress government in its last stint before independence, especially from May 1946. At that point, Hamid Khan gave a clarion call to the evicted immigrants to return and recapture land who re-occupied their land and constructed hats overnight.[48]

Thus, the 'invasion plan' of the Muslim League made a long-lasting impact on the minds of the Assamese people. In his essay titled 'An Appeal to the People of India and Constitution of Atma Rakshi Bahini'[49] Ambikagiri Raichaudhury gave details of how the Muslim League through its Direct Action programme indulged in property looting, arson, murders, killing and forcible conversion of Hindu girls in places such as Calcutta, Dhaka and Noakhali. Elaborating the activities of the organization, he said,

> The Muslim league members declared war against the eviction policy of Congress government and had started forcible encroachment of reserved land. Their main aim is to create lawlessness and anarchy and in the process settle such imported people in the rural areas of Assam. They have brought hooligans from neighbouring areas and have started disturbing the peaceful plural character of the state and society.[50]

Ambikagiri Raichaudhury lambasted the immigrants who even dared to procure the *Patbaushi Satra*, which was established by another Mahapurusha Sri Damodardeva (an apostle of Mahapurusha Sankardeva), at a bare minimum auction price. He expressed his relief that ultimately, at the initiative of Sivaram Dutta, the *Satra* was rescued; otherwise, a Masjid would soon have been established in place of the great Vaisnavite establishment of Assam. He lamented the fact that a great liberal tradition which was established by Sankardeva was now being attempted to be made irrelevant at the behest of the Mymensinghia Muslims. What impacted him most was the systematic effort of the Muslim League to occupy vast swathes of land. Once Congress government had decided to evict such encroachers, ML

---

[48] See Assam Archive, Confidential File No C. 247/46, Political, Assam Secretariat.

[49] Sharma, 'Ambikagiri Raichaudhurir Pratibha', 491.

[50] Ibid.

prepared a team, gave them weapons and made them ready for any eventuality. It is argued in the *Political History of Assam*, vol. III,

> In fact, the militant section of the Muslim League was not satisfied with the Civil Disobedience Movement being peaceful. They preferred to achieve their ends through an underground resistance movement. ... [I]t cannot be ascertained whether the underground resistance movement directed from these *killas* through the Muslim national guards was successful. But it is beyond doubt that the eviction policy adopted by the Congress government provoked the Muslims towards extremism.[51]

Ambikagiri Raichaudhury published a map which Muslim League had prepared for the inclusion of Assam through Direct Action into its future Pakistan scheme. The map was published in the first volume of the anthology of Ambikagiri Raichaudhury's writings published by the Publication Board, Government of Assam. However, for some mysterious reasons, in subsequent publications, the map was deleted. Many thought it was not polite to publish such maps in the newly established secular nation of India.

Raichaudhury made it clear that his opposition to the Muslim League is not against any religion; this was not about Hindus versus Muslims. This fight was between nationalism and anti-nationalism. He was equally allergic to those Bengali forces who, in collaboration with the Muslims of East Bengal, attempted to dislodge the Assamese language in the state. Raichaudhury was never against any outsiders. He urged for the assimilation of Marwaris, Hindustanis, Nepalis, Madrasis, Punjabis, Oriyas and Bengalis with the greater Assamese society. In his presidential address of Assam Sahitya Sabha, he stated

> I know Marwaris, Hindustani, Nepali, Punjabis, Oriyas, Biharis based in Assam would never oppose to our liberal proposal. They have been extending all possible help in conducting this *Sahitya Sabha* session. As the president of Assam Sahitya Sabha, I would like to express my gratitude and thanks on behalf of all the Assamese people.[52]

[51] Bhuyan, ed., *Political History of Assam*, 286–87.
[52] Presidential address in Margherita, 11–12 March 1950.

However, he hastened to add that his proposal did not receive a warm reception from the Bengali Hindus who had been persecuted in the newly created East Pakistan. Those displaced Bengalis who were driven out from their homeland were collaborating with the Bengali Muslims in hatching a conspiracy against the Assamese language.[53]

Raichaudhury underscored the fact that Assam is a Hindu-dominant state and would remain so. Despite being a Hindu-dominant state, Assam had no aversion to other religions. To quote him:

> Assam is a Hindu-dominant state, and the Assamese will make Assam a Hindu-centric society. That is why from the moment India was brought under the domination of the Britishers, we have been waging a struggle for the last 30 years against the import of Bengal's Muslim Mymensinghia immigrants through the Sangrakshini Sabha and *Jatiyo Mahasabha*.[54]

He also stressed that Assam had never discriminated against the Muslims and that there had always been a feeling of brotherhood among the Assamese Hindus, Buddhist and Muslims since the days of the Ahoms. 'Assam would never allow Bengal-like animosity between Hindus and Muslims', he said.[55]

In an article published on 15 June 1946 titled *Purani Pomua Bhai Sakal* (The Old Immigrant Brothers), he assured the immigrants who came to Assam and assimilated with the Assamese did not pose a threat to the Assamese nation.

> But our objection is to those outsiders who have come here with arms and are bent to destroy our national existence. Those hooligans thousand in numbers are creating a war-like situation in the rural areas by encroaching land and property at gunpoint. Their agenda is to create lawlessness and anarchy—those undesirable elements are our enemy.[56]

---

[53] Ibid.

[54] The presidential address was delivered on March 1950. When Raichaudhury said that he had been fighting against the Mymensinghia Muslim immigration for the last 30 years, he meant that the struggle was going on from 1920. Sangrakshini Sabha and Jatiyo Mahasabha were established by Raichaudhury for the said purpose.

[55] Ibid.

[56] Sharma, 'Ambikigiri Raichaudhurir Pratibha', 492.

His strong desire to protect the Assamese people from such atrocities of the Muslim League led to the creation of Assam Atma Rakshi Bahini in May 1946. The purpose of this organization was neither to take away the rights of other people nor to create any bloody violence, but to protect one's own right in their own land. He said:

> We have no place to go and hide. Those oppressors are coming from Mymensingh and Noakhali of Bengal. If Assamese people are subjected to such torture where would they go? We have no place except the hill areas. Even there we shall be eliminated. So what is the way out for the Assamese?[57]

He appealed to the Assamese to join his Defence Unit saying

> The only way out for all men and women of Assam is to join the Atma Rakshi Bahini and resist the Muslim League's hooligans with a unified force! All the Assamese Hindus-Muslims-tribals-Buddhists-Christians—please do come; leave behind your weakness—with all energy at our disposal, let us thwart the attack of Muslim League and thus protect our ancestral properties.[58]

He said,

> in the journey of self-defence, if there are occurrences of violence or bloodshed, it would be considered as pure non-violence. The proponent and father of non-violence, Mahatma Gandhi, also seconded such action. In front of aggressive gung-ho violent postures, a passive projection of non-violence is nothing but acts of inhuman-ness and impotency. Such impotency grossly ignores the valour, heroism, energy and prowess of a nation. Such people without power, heroism and valour have no right to exist in this world.[59]

Ambikagiri Raichaudhury's presidential address at Margherita in 1950 on 11 March was a reiteration of what he had been advocating for many decades. He listed more than 15 points on how the Mymensinghia immigrants and Bengali chauvinists had been conspiring against the

[57] Ibid., 492.

[58] Ibid.

[59] Ambikagiri Raichoudhury (An Anthology of His Writings). Deshbashiloi Nibedan: Assam Atmarakhshi Baahini Gathan, in *Deshbashiloi Nibedon: Assam Atma Rakhshi Bahini Gathan*, edited by S. N. Sharma (p. 495). Guwahati: Assam Publication Board.

Assamese. He said that atrocities on Bengali Hindus in East Bengal were acts of barbarism.

> Rarely people could witness such acts of religious fanaticism. We would overthrow all such forces if they are ever present in the Assamese society. But this opposition is not on religious grounds. Pakistan is a foreign country—enemy of India and Assam—be it Hindu or Muslim.

He urged people to be cautious against the triad—the Communist, the Pakistanist and the Bengalist.[60] Not only Ambikagiri, but many other contemporary leaders of Assam raised their voices against such sudden exposure of the Assamese society to the outsiders. Here, the opinion of Nilomoni Phukan, another stalwart, scholar and two-time president of the Assam Sahitya Sabha, is significant. In his presidential address, he claimed,

> [M]ore than hundred ethnic communities such as Matak-Moran, Ahom, Kachari, Koch, Chutia, Miri, Mikir, Naga, Garo, Lusai, Khasi, Brahmin, Kayasta, Kalita, Keot plus religions such as Hindus, Muslims, Christian and Buddhists combine to form an independent Assamese race.[61]

Phukan was highly critical of the merger of Sylhet with Assam. He said that Assam's age-old culture was diametrically opposite from that of Sylhet district. Although a great advocate of Hindu–Muslim unity, he was highly critical of the concept of Pakistan. The Muslims of Assam gave a tough fight with the Mughals and protected Assam by becoming martyrs. To quote him:

> In Assam we find a unique merger of the melodies of *kirtan* and *jikir*.[62] Assam got one-fourth of Macca.[63] Evil forces could hardly come nearer to the powerful renderings of *naam kirtana* and *ajan*. In rural areas, the

[60] Presidential address.

[61] Presidential address, 19th Assam Sahitya Sabha Session, Sibsagar, October 1944.

[62] Kirtan is a devotional poem written by Sankardeva. Zikirs are the Assamese Islamic devotional songs; they generally depict the co-existence of Hindus and Muslims in Assam. They are mostly composed by Ajan Fakir—a Muslim Sufi preacher of 17th century.

[63] Pua Macca in Hajo is said to be one-fourth of Macca.

Muslim used to identify masjid as our naamghar.[64] Islam's *La Ilahi Ill-lalla-muhmmadar-rusulla* resonates with *Ek Devo, Ek Sevo-Ek Bine Nai Kevo*[65] in the four sessions of naamghar. The chanting of *Naamaj* spread out a resounding feeling of *bhai-biradori*.[66] A society which is agog with eternal unity of Hindu-Muslims, how could one think of a separate 'Pakistan' or 'Hindustan'?[67]

He was horrified by the communal utterances of the Mymensinghia Muslims in a peaceful such as Assam. To quote him:

> The entire Assamese nation is dismayed and anguished by a Mymensinghia procession in Barpeta where in front of two prominent Assamese Muslims, so-called Mymensinghia leaders in their speeches had lambasted Assamese people, their tradition, language and culture in inexplicable languages. The saddest part is that as Muslims they had surrendered in front of the Mymensinghia Muslims; and as Assamese Muslims, they could not make them accept Assamese culture. I truly believe the common Mymensinghia Muslims would not adhere and endorse such communal utterances of their leaders who are immersed in the idea of East Pakistan.

Citing the example of Assam Sangrakshini Sabha, Phukan urged that our parameters for accepting someone as 'Assamese' were very liberal. What Assam wanted was the acceptance of its language and culture. The Sangrakshini Sabha would not interfere in anybody's religion. He cited the examples of Ghosh, Dostidar, Rai, Dutta, Agarwala, the Nepalis and the tea garden workers who had truly become Assamese. Citing the family members of Haribilash Agarwala, Nilomoni Phukan argued that they had become forerunners and torchbearers of Assamese culture. The Nepalis from Tezpur in areas like Gomiri and others had been performing bhaona, theatre and other Assamese cultural activities regularly.

---

[64] Naamghar—Vaisnavite prayer Hall as popularised by Mahapurush Sankardeva.

[65] Chanting the supremacy of cowherd Krishna—He is one, supreme and above all—is the essence of Sankardeva's *Eka Soron Naam Dharma*.

[66] A sense of brotherhood.

[67] Presidential speech.

Amalendu Guha on Ambikagiri Raichaudhury: A Critical Analysis

Raichaudhury was an ardent advocate of provincial autonomy. Why he attempted to oppose the Muslim League was precisely because the organization in cohorts with the British colonial interest made frantic attempts to transform the basic fundamental character of Assamese nationality which was so laboriously built by Sankardeva and other icons of the state. Unfortunately, Raichaudhury, Nilomoni Phukan and a few others were very negatively viewed by the Bengali press and scholars. Raichaudhury was particularly castigated as a leader of the anti-Bengali lobby (*bongal kheda neta*).[68] A prominent Marxist scholar from the state, Amalendu Guha, had very critical opinions about Raichaudhury and Nilomoni Phukan when he said:

> Regional chauvinists—many of them Assamese Hindus—in turn, raised the slogan of the Assamese race being in danger. Ambikagiri Raichaudhury floated Asomiya Sangrakshini Sabha (Association for the Conservation of the Assamese) in 1926 to propagate the Assamese cause. Nilomoni Phukan, who had thrice failed to get himself elected to the council since 1923, soon joined his chorus. The Congress tried to steer a middle course because of its all-India character.[69]

Amalendu Guha undeniably is one of the topmost scholars from the state whose pioneering work of *Planter's Raj to Swaraj* shall remain a milestone in the days to come. His intricate and detailed primary research based on original investigation shall remain a pathfinder for future scholars. However, on account of his ideological and party affiliations, Guha failed to be objective in his analysis, particularly regarding the assessment of Assamese nationality.[70] Guha never minced his words to criticize those who wanted to protect the liberal legacy of Assamese society and wanted to control unchecked immigration. He had very unkind words for another Assamese intellectual, Jnananath

---

[68] See Sharma, 'Ambikagiri Raichaudhurir Pratibha', 11.

[69] Guha, *Planter Raj to Swaraj*, 171.

[70] Guha was an active member of the CPI from 1943 to 1965. See *Oitihya aru Itihas* (in Assamese) (Journal Emporium, Guwahati, 2005), p. 367; cited in Nirode Baruah, *Gopinath Bordoloi*, p. 554.

Bora, but on the same account, he failed to adopt a critical approach towards Maulana Bhasani—an utterly blatant and aggressively communalist leader. Guha also criticized C. S. Mullan and dubbed him as an 'irresponsible British civil servant' as he characterized the immigration process as 'invasion', 'attack' and 'conquest' in the 1931 census report, but how different was the phenomenon then as compared to the present. By 2020, what Mullan had predicted seems to be a reality—his analysis was purely based on statistics and on the nature of how the immigrants started occupying lands in Assam. Interestingly, Guha was using the same census report and a similar language when he said

> It was in 1911 that the census commissioner first took note of the ongoing immigration as a *peaceful invasion* of Assam. ... [L]andless immigrants from overpopulated East Bengal—of whom *85% were Muslims*—found land in Assam's water-logged, jungle-infested, riverine belt. *Used to an amphibious mode of living* and industrious, they came by rail, steamers and boats up the Brahmaputra to reclaim these malarial areas. *All they wanted was land.* From their riverine base, they further pressed forward in all directions in search of *more living space*, to areas *held by the autochthones.* It was then an *open clash of interest* began to take place. (italics in original)[71]

Guha characterized the immigration process as follows:

1. *Peaceful invasion* of Assam
2. *Acknowledged that 85 per cent were Muslims* (he used the word—'the land-hungry Muslim immigrants' on page 170)
3. Used to an amphibious mode of living
4. All they wanted was land
5. Looking for living space
6. Moved to areas held by autochthones
7. Then an open clash began to take place

Even if we look at the statistics about how the immigrants occupied land, the statement of C. S. Mullan's analysis would prove to be correct. Perhaps Mullan could have used softer words like those used by Guha, which would have passed the test of today's Marxist lexicography. Besides, C. S. Mullan's prophecy that Sibsagar is the only place

---

[71] Guha, *Planter Raj to Swaraj*, 166. Italics for emphasis by the author.

where the Assamese race would find a home of its own is not perhaps a false statement considering the present predicament of immigration that the state goes through. Although our purpose here is not to vouch for a pure Assamese race which, I believe, would not be applicable in a multi-ethnic, multicultural state like Assam.

In his laboriously researched book, *Gopinath Bordoloi: The Assam Problem and Nehru's Centre*, Nirode K. Barooah provided a critical analysis of Guha's prejudiced views on the Assamese question and nationality. Barooah said

> In other words, Guha has emerged in this book as an ardent opponent of a composite Assamese nationality ... [T]hroughout the book, he has uniformly taken a partisan attitude. ... [B]esides, he is a fervent supporter of the continued influx of the East Bengal immigrants into Assam, defending Saadulla and Abdul Hamid Khan, the promoters of this influx and condemning all others who opposed the uncontrolled influx of immigrants.[72]

Guha's book has been criticized as the Bengali Settler's Association's view of Assam's history. All along, Guha has denounced all efforts that tried to popularize the Assamese language among the Bengalis. When the then governor made an appeal to the Settler's Association later known as the 'Assam Citizens' Association' to adopt and to accept Assamese, Guha became extremely critical of it. Guha criticized the governor for his desperate efforts to be the champion of Assamese nationalism.[73] Guha finds absolutely nothing wrong in the unrestricted influx from Bengal, and, in this regard, any effort for protecting the interest of a smaller nationality on the part of Ambikagiri, Gopinath and Nilomoni Phukan and many others are dubbed by Guha as 'parochial', 'chauvinist', 'not much of educated' and so on.

Many of Guha's analyses and evaluations about Ambikagiri Raichaudhury, Gopinath Bordoloi and the Grouping Scheme were not visibly in the interest of Assam. Every time he refers to Raichaudhury, Guha never forgets to add the adjective 'chauvinistic'. To quote him:

[72] Barooah, *Gopinath Bordoloi*, 499–450.
[73] Ibid., 505.

The divisive League politics of carving out of India a new state of Pakistan that was to include Assam provided an opportunity for the chauvinistic influence of Ambikagiri Raychaudhury to thrive, particularly when the Congress leaders were in jail from 1942. No doubt his patriotism was genuine; but there was also one aspect of life and works that gave rise to controversies and encourage anti-Bengali chauvinism.[74]

In his further reference to Raichaudhury, he states:

His party *Asomiya Sangrakshini Sabha* - renamed as *Assam Jatiya Mahasabha* in 1935—flourished as a platform for articulation of the widely shared 'sons of the soil' sentiment, also functioning as a pressure group within the Assam Congress. Although without much formal education, poor of means and somewhat unconventional in his ways, Raychaudhury was nonetheless a first rate poet.[75]

Guha ridiculed Raichaudhury for his education and constitutional ideas, including his opinions on the Indian federation. Raichaudhury was criticized for his views on dual citizenship and linguistic nationalism. What made Guha criticize Raichaudhury as someone opposed to multiculturalism is a mystery. Raichaudhury was one of the most liberal and accommodative leaders and was always protective about the rights of smaller nationalities. Of course, it was a fact Raichaudhury did not have a good opinion about communism. In fact, in his presidential address to the Sahitya Sabha, he cautioned Assamese and the Indians in general against communist, Bengalist and Pakistanist, which were perhaps the main reasons for Guha to have developed such critical opinions about Raichaudhury. Some other writers too have criticized Guha for his sweeping comments on Ambikagiri. A. K. Baruah argues

Guha repeatedly calls Ambikagiri a chauvinist, often for wrong reasons and does not even mention the humanist ideas apparent in his writings. ... [T]he principles of linguistic federation and dual citizenship should have been interpreted as progressive ... it is interesting to note that in Guha's book there is no attempt at all to analyse the political activities of Ray Chaudhury. The book merely contains some highly prejudiced sweeping statements on him.[76]

[74] Guha, *Planter Raj to Swaraj*, 258.

[75] Ibid., 259.

[76] Baruah, *Social Tensions in Assam*, 51–52.

Guha, on the other hand, found Maulana Bhasani to be 'a new and autonomous leadership [emerging] slowly and silently within [the] community itself in Goalpara, after Maulana Abdul Hamid Khan Bhasani (1886–1976) immigrated there...'.

Guha's account of Hamid Khan is full of hagiographical impulse and admiration for his work. No doubt Maulana Bhasani organized marginalized Muslim peasantry against the Hindu zamindars and money lenders, but very soon, his struggle for the Muslim peasants transformed into a religious-political struggle, and he became the staunchest supporter of Pakistan and demanded the inclusion of Assam into it. He organized a Praja Sanmilan in December 1932 and demanded the abolition of the zamindars; along with it, they also extended support to the communal strategies adopted by the British. Bhasani was a settlement contractor, one who negotiated with the zamindars and arranged for the occupation of the vacant land.[77] His concern for the peasants soon gave way to regressive communal mobilization in the name of Allah. From 1939, Hamid Khan became the vanguard of a radicalized organization called the Muslim League whose main objective was the attainment of Pakistan and the forcible inclusion of Assam into it. In the actions of Maulana of Bhasani, the people of Assam for the first time witnessed such polarizing politics in the name of God:

> Not only do I kick at the law by means of which the houses of the lakhs of people have been burnt down, I declare *Jehad* in the name of *Allah*. It is not possible for the minority Mussalmans of Assam to end this oppression. It is not possible to solve this problem without resorting to *Jehad* for the sake of Allah. ... [T]he whole world is docile before the Mighty and killer of the weak ... the days have come now to get your demands fulfilled by becoming *Swahids* in the path of *Allah*. Everything depends on your unity and organisation. (italics in original)[78]

Guha not only defended Hamid Khan without looking into his aggressive communal politics (we shall refer to it in our subsequent chapters), but he has in fact also attempted to gloss over some of

[77] *The Statesman*, 4 October 1935 and 30 October 1935.

[78] Special branch report on Muslim League, 1940. Also cited in Dev and Lahiri, *Assam Muslims*, 33.

violent activities of Hamid Khan from March 1947 in the name of civil disobedience movement. Not only did he forget to give a glimpse of such violent activities, but he also compared Hamid Khan's movement with Gandhiji's Salt March. To quote him:

> Bhasani, the provincial League president, contemplated a civil disobedience movement and gave a threat of leading a march of one lakh volunteers upon Assam from the borders of Bengal...[H]e selected Dhubri, on the Assam-Bengal border, as the venue for series of simultaneous conferences of such bodies as the Bengal-Assam Mujahidins, the Bengal-Assam National guards ... all to be held on and around 3–4 March 1947. With Gandhiji's historic salt march in mind as a model, he hoped to lead a similar peaceful march from Mankachar against the Line system.[79]

Guha's understanding of Bhasani's civil disobedience could hardly reflect what had happened on the ground. What made the people of Assam awestruck and baffled was the unprecedented scheme of violence and guerrilla tactics of the Muslim League leaders in the name of 'civil defence action'.[80] We have access to more than 40 pages of police and administrative report on how the Muslim League leaders attempted heavy guerrilla attacks at certain places in Assam, especially in the lower Assam regions of Dhubri, bordering Bengal. Actually, the attempt to train the Muslim national guards started way back in 1944—they planned to destroy all culverts, bridges, roads, breaking open jails, seizing military installations including weapon, and so on. For this purpose, various *killas* (forts) were built, of which the Eastern Pakistan *Killa* at Barbandha in Mankachar was most significant.[81] The *killas* were mainly built for guerrilla operations.[82] The militant section of the Muslim League was not satisfied with the peaceful civil

---

[79] Guha, *Planter Raj to Swaraj*, 259.

[80] To know how the Muslim League planned and adopted violent techniques, one may look at Bhuyan, *Political History*.

[81] See Ibid., 286–87. In addition, one may also look at the archival records of Assam Police and administration to know about the nature of violence and mobilisation of the Muslim League. The issue is being discussed in detail in Chapter II of this book.

[82] Bhuyan, *Political History of Assam*, 286–87.

disobedience movement and made elaborate preparation for underground resistance.[83]

It is hard to believe that Guha did not have access to the government files, especially of the police and home departments that documented such activities of the Muslim League in vivid details, but Guha preferred to refer to such civil disobedience action from an article published in *Yugabichitra* in Bengali from Dacca in 1967 and a press report.[84] Based on such reports, the analogy of Hamid Khan's *killa* politics with Gandhiji's civil disobedience would be nothing but a travesty of Gandhian philosophy. As we have said above, it was precisely against such secessionist provocative politics of the Muslim League that Ambikagiri Raichaudhury constituted the Atma Rakshi Bahini.

On another occasion, Guha criticized the Assam Congress for opposing the Grouping plan. To quote him:

> Both the Congress and the League had at one stage accepted the Cabinet Mission Plan and, for a while, a solution of the communal question without partition of the country was in sight. But Assam's determined opposition to its grouping with Bengal provided an opportunity to League to repudiate its earlier acceptance. The Cabinet Mission plan fizzled out, in its wake, Wavell had to quit his office in March 1947.[85]

The dilemma for a smaller state like Assam was that by including a Hindu-dominant state like Assam with Muslim-majority Bengal, the path would be cleared for her future inclusion with Pakistan.[86]

Gandhiji could understand Assam's dilemma, and he came in Assam's support:

> If Assam keeps quiet it is finished. No one can force Assam to do what it does not want to do. It must stand independently as an autonomous unit.

[83] Ibid., 286.

[84] It may be mentioned that Guha was substantially consulting and referring to police and political department files and reports throughout his book.

[85] Guha, *Planter Raj to Swaraj*, 257.

[86] For details, see Barooah, *Gopinath Bordoloi*, 25.

It is autonomous to a large extent today. It must become fully indepen-
dent and autonomous. ... As soon as the time comes for the Constituent
Assembly to go into sections you will say, 'Gentlemen, Assam retires'. For
the independence of India it is the only condition. Each Unit must decide
and act for itself. I am hoping that in this, Assam will lead the way. ... If
Assam takes care of itself, the rest of India will be able to look after itself.
What have you got to do with the Constitution of the Union Government?
You should form your own Constitution. That is enough. You have the basis
of a constitution yourself. (*Transfer of Power: IX*, pp. 403–405)

On some occasions, Guha could not appreciate the anxieties and
apprehensions of a smaller nationality like the composite Assamese
identity. There are hardly any examples in the world where any
nationality would allow systematic swamping of its economy, society
and polity. The Mymensinghia and other EBOM may be a minority
in Assam[87], but based on faith and religion, this is one of the largest
homogeneous groups in the world. What Assam saw in the days to
come was nothing but a brutal manifestation of the growing number
of Muslims based on which the Muslim League dared to include Assam
with Pakistan. At a later stage, Nibaran Bora, another activist of Assam
agitation and scholar, also criticized Guha for his views on Assam:

He (Guha) has cited Indian Nationalism as big nationalism and Assamese
Nationalism as small nationalism. I do not know whether such classifica-
tions are correct or not; it is difficult for us to appreciate as we belong
to the group of war time graduate. What we have understood with our
limited knowledge is that 'Assamese Nationalism' denotes certain feeling,
realisation, belongingness and pride which we have acquired in the last
600 years. It is our asset, our birth right. We do not wish to lose it. Above
all, there is nothing wrong in this feeling. We feel hurt when someone tries
to snatch it and then we become rebels for the want of any other choice.
For such acts of dissent, we are facing harassment which is worse than the
atrocities committed during the time of the Burmese.[88]

---

[87] However, the Muslims as a group is the largest coherent group in Assam, as Hindus,
although in the majority, are divided along the lines of valley, ethnicity, regionality,
caste and language. Thus, majority-minority does not have a binary classification in
Assam.

[88] Bora, 'Introduction'.

'Immigration': The Conceptual Part

The phenomenon of the flow of population for inter-provincial and outer-provincial purposes has been described with an array of terms such as 'immigration', 'influx', 'infiltration' and 'illegal migrants'. The concepts of 'immigrants' and 'illegal migrants' have changed from time to time as these terms are constantly loaded with cultural, political and legal overtones. After the coming of the British, the concept of immigrants was understood as a means to exclude certain groups of people who came from East Bengal. As a result of the unrestricted influx of immigrants, the Assamese people attempted to classify between 'desirable migrants' (also may be dubbed as 'immigrant Assamese') and 'undesirable immigrants'. This was done to tilt the demographic balance in favour of the Assamese people.

After the Non-cooperation movement was halted, the issue of immigration came into the forefront and took a more communalized tone than before. The colonial masters, to divide the groups, tried to appease both of them. As we have stated above, though the British, on the one hand, supported the immigrants' cause both for revenue and to challenge the increasing nationalism, they tried to assuage the Assamese feeling of being reduced gradually on their own land on the other. In 1924, A. F. Thomas, Deputy Commissioner of Nowgong, by his order dated 22 August 1924, termed the people who settled in Assam from Mymensingh and all other districts of Bengal and Surma Valley as 'immigrants' but excluded the tea garden coolies.[89] The order issued by A. G. Patron, Deputy Commissioner, Nowgong, on 4 May 1928, further aggravated the communal sentiments in the state. It stated that not only Nepalis but Marwaris, Nunias, Mech and other stray settlers from provinces other than Bengal would no longer be treated as immigrants, and the order prohibited the Mymensinghias from acquiring land except in those areas reserved for immigrants.[90] A. W. Botham, the Secretary to the Government of Assam, stated that upcountry men, who were generally ex-tea garden coolies,

---

[89] Kar, *Muslims in Assam Politics*, 86.

[90] *Assam Gazette* (1930), 550–56.

were allowed to take up land like the local Assamese, and there was no objection to this.[91] It was observed, when A. W. Botham noted, that the Assamese petitioned to the Government of Assam to allow the upcountry Hindus to settle with the Assamese as a buffer between the Assamese and the Mymensinghias.[92]

Notably, from around 1928, a religious division started taking place between the Assamese, the Marwaris, the tea garden labourers, the Hindustani sepoys and the Nepalese on one side and the Muslim immigrants on the other. The Muslim leaders accused the Brahmaputra and Surma Valley Hindus for expressing their opposition only to the Bengali Muslims cultivators. It was alleged that although the other migrants came to Assam with their customs, usages and traditions and were allowed to set up their business and depots at several parts of western Assam, it was only against the Muslims of East Bengal origin that such distinction was made. It may be mentioned that the apparent distinction that had cropped up was purely because of the aggressive expansion of the Mymensinghia immigrants. The institutional arrangement of the Line System was nothing but the recognition of that growing apprehension and division between the two communities. A colonization scheme was launched with colonization officers engaged specifically to look into the revenue generation and settlement of immigrants in the specific areas. Through the Line System and the colonization scheme, the physical segregation between the indigenous people and the Bengali immigrants and its consequent social ramifications got reflected onto the psychological and social canvas of a distinct race with specific virtues, vices and culture.[93] As Rinku Pegu argues:

> The first step in this reconstruction was to identify the Assamese people as Hindu adherents thereby defining the Assamese nation as primarily a Hindu nation. In support of this assertion the intelligentsia engaged in showcasing the strong ties that Assam shared with the mainland Hindu tradition and culture. The contribution of Assam as the custodian of *Vaishnav* legacy

[91] Kar, *Muslims in Assam Politics*, 9.

[92] Ibid., 86–87.

[93] Pegu, 'The Line System and the Birth of a Public Sphere in Assam', 586–96.

was highlighted through the chain of 'satras' like Auniati, Dakhinpath, Goroimari, Kamalabari that were held and preserved in the island of Majuli, Nowgong and Barpeta.[94]

As stated above, the challenges from the Mymensinghia immigrants led to the formation of a different class of people known as the 'immigrant Assamese'. Immigrant Assamese primarily included the tea garden workers from Bihar, Orissa and the Central Provinces; trading classes like the Marwaris from Rajasthan; graziers from Nepal; and labourers and officials from Madras and the United Provinces. In fact, it is clear from the letters submitted to the Secretary to the Government of Assam, A. W. Botham, that the indigenous people wanted the settlement of immigrant Assamese as a seal and as a cover to the Bengali settlement.[95] Pegu further argues:

> In addition the defining of Assam as a space essentially peopled by Hindus worked to the advantage of the non-Bengali immigrants. For instance in a testimony given to the LSC (Line system committee), a native justifies his support for the Nepalese immigrants on the ground that 'they are mostly Buddhists'—a branch of the Hindu.[96]

However, there was a change in the official definition of immigration. In May 1940, under Saadulla ministry, the Muslim League called for a conference in Shillong to solicit modifications in the government policy about the understanding of what constitutes immigrants and the Line System. The decisions reached in the meeting included one that caused a qualitative change in the definition of the term. Hence, it included everyone—Hindu or Muslim from Bengal, people from rest of India and Nepal—excluding those from the Surma Valley—who entered Assam before 1 January 1938. Nevertheless, the first official definition of the term already got deeply embedded in the mind and psyche of the indigenous people. The 1940 definition could hardly change that impression, since before the consolidation of Hindus

[94] Ibid., 588.

[95] Kar, *Muslims in Assam Politics*, 86–87.

[96] Pegu, 'The Line System and the Birth of a Public Sphere in Assam', 590. Also one may see 'Line System Committee Report', vols. II and III.

and Muslims and the inter-provincial migrants as Indian, the Muslim League started the Pakistan demand which had invariably included Assam as a part of it. Thus, the imagination of Assamese nationality with EBOM and Bengalis as a constituent of it did not fructify in the colonial period and on the eve of Partition.

About the Book

To begin with, we are trying to conceptualize the nature of Assamese nationality—how the process has evolved historically. Despite having a significant percentage of migrants in the Assamese society, why is it against the immigration of EBOM. How has the process of immigration been conceptualized? In an attempt to answer these questions to analyse how Assamese stalwarts reacted to the politics of immigration and the Muslim League in the Legislative Councils and Assembly, this book is bringing the discourse from all sides, including that of the Muslim League.

In this book, we would like to look at the 'politics of history'—what was the nature of politics that was defining Assam from the beginning of the 20th century. We are also trying to look at how those issues in the colonial period have influenced the two present-day burning impasses of the nation—the controversy over the National Register of Citizens (NRC) and the Citizenship Amendment Act, 2019 (CAA-2019). In contrast to some of the contemporary discussions on these two issues, we are arguing that both NRC and CAA are not something that has emerged as a result of the 'Hindutva agenda'—both must be seen as a continuum of a process that had begun in and on the eve of the Partition of India. The tragedy of Partition changed India's liberal-secular tradition to a great extent in the sense that if we look at the debates on citizenship surrounding CAA, the divisions on the religious line were very much palpable, and a commitment to the protection of the persecuted Hindus and the Sikhs was solemnly made by the majority members. That commitment was reiterated at various levels in the post-independence period also as is evident from various debates on the citizenship issue. Nevertheless, the draft outcome of the law was drafted in such a manner that the Nehruvian secular credential was kept intact—the drafting of the Illegal Immigration Expulsion

Act (Assam), 1950, passed by the Indian Parliament is an example of it. However, a glance into the debates of the said Act would reveal that the MPs had no 'secular qualms' in favouring the persecuted religious people in Pakistan and preventing the Muslims from Pakistan from entering into certain regions of India. Even in the Constituent Assembly debates, there was a huge cynicism towards the 'secular state businesses'.[97] Rohini Kumar Chaudhury, a representative from Assam, was another proactive member in this regard, who openly vouched for the Hindus of East Bengal.[98]

At one point, Nehru was very much annoyed at the constant innuendos thrown at him in the name of secularism. He said:

Another word is thrown up a good deal this secular state business. May I beg with all humility those gentlemen who use this word often to consult some dictionary before they use it? It is brought by members in at every conceivable step and every conceivable stage. I just do not understand it. It has a great deal of importance, no doubt, but it is brought in all contexts, as if by saying that we are a secular State we have done something amazingly generous, given something out of our pocket to the rest of the world, something which we ought not to have done, so on and so forth. We have only done something which every country does except a very few misguided and backward countries in the world, let us not refer to that word in the sense that we have done something very mightily.[99]

With the Bharatiya Janata Party (BJP) taking the reins of the country in 2014, the Nehruvian secular nuances have been relegated to the backstage, and there is no denying the fact that citizenship to the six persecuted communities came well in synchronization with the saffron party's Hindutva ideology. CAA-2019 may be termed as a logical conclusion of a process, the origin of which lies in the Partition and post-Partition developments. The avowedly theocratic Islamic character of Pakistan and Bangladesh has not only denied a respectable space to the minorities but also systematically persecuted them in all conceivable areas. In such a scenario, the issue of Hindus and other

---

[97] See Constituent Assembly Debates, *Official Report*, 351–425.

[98] Ibid., 414–17. For details, see the chapters on NRC and CAA of this book.

[99] Ibid., 401.

minority community does not remain a secular issue but an existential one which a Hindutva party like the BJP cannot remain oblivious to. What P. S. Deshmukh, the first agriculture minister in the Nehru cabinet said still remains relevant:

> Is it then wise that we should throw open our citizenship so indiscriminately? I do not side any ground whatsoever that we should do it, unless it is the specious, oft repeated and nauseating principle of 'secularity' of the state. I think we are going too far in this business of secularity. Does it mean that we must wipe out our own people that we must wipe them out in order to prove our secularity, that we must wipe out Hindus and Sikhs under the name of secularity, that we must undermine everything that is sacred and dear to the Indians to prove that we are secular? ... I am sure the popularity of those who take that view will not last long in India.[100]

Therefore, CAA-19 is not a test of Indian secularism: neither is it an attempt to regularize certain grotesque legacies of the Partition nor does it exclude or deny Indian Muslims from any sociopolitical-economic rights. Likewise, NRC cannot be seen as an instrument of discrimination between the Hindus and the Muslims; rather, it was designed to be a protective mechanism for a smaller nationality like the Assamese way back in 1951. NRC does not discriminate EBOM from others; it only excludes illegal immigrants. The Assamese people would not prefer to remain secular if 'Assamese-ness' or 'Indian-ness' is lost. Communities and societies do not live for secularism; secularism lives for society. If secularism means abandoning one's identity and existence, I think the time has come to revisit it. Nevertheless, granting of citizenship cannot be a never-ending process because of a variety of reasons which we shall discuss in the course of the book. Assam can no longer afford any more population be it Hindus or Muslims, as it is staring at demographic changes with one of the largest population ratios in the country.

After the introduction, the book begins with the politics of the Muslim League and how it attempted to politicize the land question for the immigrants. It delves into the role played by the Muslim League and its leaders like Syed Saadulla and Abdul Hamid Khan alias Maulana Bhasani.

---

[100] Ibid., 354–55.

Three chapters are devoted to the citizenship politics in Assam which has roots in the colonial period. More than the legal angle, we are trying to make a content analysis of how the citizenship issue, the issues of persecution, the Hindu–Muslim dimension of citizenship and refugees were discussed and debated in the Constituent Assembly and the Indian Parliament. We believe any discussion on citizenship cannot be decontextualized from the purview of contemporary history—how these issues were debated in the highest forum of India while passing various citizenship laws and amendments. In addition to that, we are also looking at various administrative and executive decisions pertaining to the rehabilitation and resettlement of refugees in north-east in general and Assam in particular. There is a general uneasiness among scholars to talk about the plight and rights of the Bengali Hindus. A sizeable portion of Bengali Hindus have been rehabilitated in Assam in the post-independence period. There was a vibrant debate regarding the undesirable immigration and displaced Hindus and other minorities in the Indian Parliament in the late 1940s and the early part of 1950s. Somehow those discussions and issues of the Bengali Hindus in the context of Assamese identity got buried and only one dimension got over-highlighted which is that there was a huge resistance towards the Bengali Hindu settlement in Assam, but this is only a half-truth, just one side of the whole narrative. The stalwarts and protectorates of Assamese identity forcefully argued for the rights and rehabilitation of the displaced Bengali Hindus both during the Constituent Assembly debates and in the Indian Parliament debates, and all of this was directed towards protecting Assamese and Indian identity. Glossing over those discussions would cause a serious omission of contemporary history.

The monograph tries to address and fill up such important gaps in the study of citizenship and immigration. Besides, whereas there are a substantial number of books about the role of the Muslim League at the pan-India level, very scant attention is paid to the study of the provincial Muslim League in Assam. No serious effort has been made to look at its ideology, functioning and leadership. Although there is a huge scope for further studies, our effort may be considered an ice breaker in terms of understanding the Muslim League and the nature of its activities in Assam.

Finally, the book looks at the correlations of religion, citizenship and identity. It raises certain fundamental questions concerning the increasing number of EBOM in Assam. While EBOM constitutes the base of Assamese nationality as *Na-Asomiya*, the Assamese nationality is not yet prepared to accept the state as a Muslim-dominant nationality. Here, the issue is no longer whether EBOM are foreigners, but whether the protagonists of Assamese nationality are prepared to accept Assam as an immigrant-driven Muslim state.

Bibliography

Agarwala, Ananda Chandra. 'Presidential Speech' (15th Session). Managaldai: Assam Sahitya Sabha. December 1934: 48–56.

Agarwala, Jyoti Prasad. 'Natunar Puja'. In *Jyotiprasad Rachanawali* (pp. 661–663), edited by H. Gohain. Guwahati Assam Prakashan Parishad, 2007.

———. *Asomiya Dekar Ukti* (Utterances by the Assamese Youths).

Assam Secretariat. *Line Committee Report*. Assam: Assam Secretariat, 1938: 11–12.

Barooah, Nirode K. *Gopinath Bordoloi: Indian Constitution and Centre-Assam Relations*. Assam: Publication Board of Assam, 1990.

———. *Gopinath Bordoloi: The Assam Problem and Nehru's Centre*. Guwahati: Bhabani Press, 2010.

Barua Bahadur, Rai K. L. *Early History of Kamarupa*. Shillong: Author, 1933.

Baruah, B. K. *A Cultural History of Assam*. Guwahati: Lawyer's Book Stall, 1969.

Baruah, Apurba Kumar. *Social Tensions in Assam: Middle Class Politics*. Guwahati: Purbanchal Prakash, 1991.

Baruah, S. L. *Comprehensive History of Assam*. New Delhi: Munshiram Manoharlal Publishers, 1995.

Bezbarua, Laxminath. *Sri Sri Sankardev and Madhabdev*. Guwahati: Jyoti Prakshan, 2018.

Bhuyan, A. C., ed. *Political History of Assam*, vol. III. Assam: Government of Assam.

Bhuyan, Surya Kumar. *Presidential Address*. Shillong: Assam Sahitya Sabha, November 1953.

Bora, Nibaran. Introduction. *Swadhin Asom Sambhavne*. Guwahati: P-D, 1987.

Chakrabarty, Dipesh. 'Modernity and Ethnicity in India'. *South Asia* XVII, Special Issue (1994).

Chetana, Vol. III, No. 2. *Ambikagiri Raichaudhury Rachanavali*, edited by S. N. Sharma (p.440). Guwahati: Assam Publication Board, 1986.

Constituent Assembly Debates. *Official Report*, 351–425. New Delhi: Lok Sabha Secretariat, 2003.

Deka Asom, Vol. II, No. 2, 1936.

Deka, Harekrishna. 'The Assamese Mind: Contours of a Landscape'. *India International Quarterly* 32, no. 3/2 (Monsoon–Winter 2005): 189–202.

Dev, Bimal J., and Dilip K. Lahiri. *Assam Muslims: Politics and Cohesion*. New Delhi: Mittal Publication, 1985.

Gohain, Hiren. Preface to *Asomiya Jatiya Jibanat Mahapurushia Parampara* (in Assamese). 1988.

Guha, Amalendu. *Planter Raj to Swaraj*. Delhi: Tulika Books, 2006.

————. *Planter Raj to Swaraj: Freedom Struggle & Electoral Politics in Assam*. New York: Columbia University Press, 2014.

Hussain, Monirul. *Assam Movement: Class, Ideology and Identity*. New Delhi: Konarak, 1990.

Kakati, Banikanta. *Assamese, Its Formation and Development*. Guwahati: LBS Publication, 1962.

Kalita, Ramesh Chandra. 'Prabajankarir Samasya Aru Asom: Anandaram Dhekiyal Phukanar Para Gopinath Bardaloi Loike'. In *Asom Andolan: Pratisruti Aru Phalasruti*, edited by Hiren Gohain and Dilip Borah. Guwahati: Banalata, Panbazar, 2007.

Kar, M. *Muslims in Assam Politics*. Delhi: Vikash Publishing House, 1990.

Mahanta, Nirupoma. *Satra-Sanskritir Aachar-Ritiaru Utsav-Anustan* (In Assamese). Dibrugarh: Newprint, March 2001.

Mahanta, Nani Gopal. *Confronting the State*. New Delhi: SAGE Publications, 2013.

Misra, Udayon. *India's North East*. New Delhi: OUP, 2014.

————. *Burden of History*. New Delhi: OUP, 2017.

Nath, Rajmohan. *The Background of Assamese Culture*. Guwahati: A. K. Nath, 1978.

Neog, Maheswar. *Sankardeva and His Times*. Guwahati: LBS Publications, 1955.

Pegu, Rinku. 'The Line System and the Birth of a Public Sphere in Assam: Immigrant, Alien, and Citizen'. *Proceedings of the Indian History Congress* 65 (2004): 586–96.

Raichaudhury, A. G. 'Bortaman Bharat Kaar'. *Chetana*, 1st year, 4th issue.

————. 'Hinduraj and Muslim Raj'. *Chetana*, 5th year, 10th issue.

————. *Mor Jivan Dhumuhar Echati*. Guwahati: Kausalya Devi Ray Chowdhury, 1973.

Sarma, Satyendra Nath. *The Neo-Vaisnavite Movement and the Satra Institution of Assam*. Guwahati: Gauhati University Press, 1966.

Sarmah, Chandan. *Asomiya Kun* (in Assamese). Guwahati: Span Publications, 2006.

Sharma, S. N. 'Ambikagiri Raichaudhurir Pratibha'. In *Ambikagiri Raichaudhury Rachanawali*, edited by Sharma. Guwahati, 1986.

Taher, Mohmmad. 'Line System of Assam: Implications & Consequences'. In *Aspects of Land Policy in Assam*. Guwahati: Vivekananda Kendra Institute of Culture, 2012.

The Statesman, 4 October 1935 and 30 October 1935. Archival Record, Political File-1938, Government of Assam.

Muslim League

Pipe Dream of Pakistan

The gap between the Assamese and the Muslim immigrants over the issues of Sylhet transfer and the introduction of the Line System widened in the 1920s. The division of land under the Line System into three types—first exclusively for the immigrants, second for the indigenous and the third for the mixed villages—acted as a protective shield for the Assamese at least at the legal and administrative levels. The immigrants found it increasingly difficult to squat in areas other than the ones reserved for the immigrants and other migrants. On the eve of burgeoning nationalism across the country, the British convinced the Muslim leaders that they would be preferred in the new province of Assam ostensibly for economic prosperity. The Muslim League, which was established in Shillong on 28 January 1928, became increasingly proactive in Assam, and its leaders pulled out all the stops to make Assam a Muslim-dominant state in the coming days.[1] Syed Saadulla's government, especially from the second term,[2] at the behest of Muslim League, tried everything to accommodate the political and economic interests of the Muslim immigrants from East Bengal. From the period of the 1930s onwards, what Assam witnessed was a flagrant violation of all democratic means and institutional politics at the behest of immigrant lobby and Muslim League leaders. In the process, the immigration issue, which initially began as an economic or class issue, soon turned into a political one, with brazen demand for inclusion of Assam into the future of Islamic Pakistan.

Whatever administrative and consensual decisions were reached at various legislative and political forums for a multi-cultural state like Assam were negated by the Saadulla ministry at the patronage of the Muslim League. A few examples of non-compliance or blatant defiance of democratic decisions were: (a) the Line System was questioned, belittled and manipulated from the very beginning[3]; (b) the Line Enquiry Committee Report was hardly implemented, first by Bordoloi ministry, and next by the consecutive Saadulla ministries that almost denied its existence; (c) on May 1940, the Line System conference was held, and a commitment was made for the protection of tribal and other backward classes as well as the protection of indigenous people under 1940 agreements and development schemes which were not implemented; (d) the unanimous all-party agreement of 1944 which formed the backbone for the protection of indigenous rights was not implemented; (e) the 'grow more food programme' was implemented for 'grow more Muslims' with a faulty settlement policy which was opposed by top administrators; (f) A. G. Patton's observation and administrative note and S. P. Desai's report were never considered for implementation[4]; (g) the governor's advice and directives for the regulation of land settlement were not implemented; (h) the tripartite agreement of 1944 was diluted in all possible ways in order to satisfy the Muslim League leaders and (i) the land settlement policy of August 1945 was not implemented; rather, it was twisted to suit the Muslim League's political assertions.

When the governor's rule was imposed[5] after the resignation of Rohini Chaudhury in 1941, the entire issue of the land settlement was re-examined and the administration expressed disappointment at the 'considerable increase and influx of land-hungry immigrants attracted by the opening of Development schemes of late Ministry'.[6] The administration decided to discard the present scheme and declared to grant

---

[3] Report of Line System Committee (RLSC) also known as Line Committee Report (LCR), Assam Secretariat, 1938.

[4] A. G. Patton, the Revenue Secretary of Assam Government prepared a lengthy report on Assam's wasteland and immigration policy. Patton identified the pitfalls with the short-term land settlement projects for the immigrants; however, the Saadulla government preferred to ignore his advice.

[5] Governor's rule imposed from 25 December 1941 to 24 August 1942.

[6] Assam Revenue Department File (RD 23/43) Resolution on Land Settlements, 6 March 1942.

land to the immigrants through the colonization scheme. The policy under the governor's rule stated:

1. Non-availability of adequate wastelands for new immigrant settlements.
2. The policy also declared the government's determination to remove all encroachments from the reserves.
3. Eviction of new encroachers was declared with lot of administrative determination. Provision, however, was made for providing new land to the old encroachers.

The directives were issued mainly from the administrative point of view, but the Muslim League leaders instigated the immigrants to make all kinds of appeals to the government, and all excuses were given to the administration to thwart the new mechanism.[7] Although Saadulla had shown sagacity on a number of occasions, he was throttled by the aggressive and radical wing of Muslim League led by Bhasani. Very soon, the reversal of all these new measures took place when Munnawar Ali was made the new Revenue Minister under the new ministry in August 1942.

The continuous violations of various forms of agreement and decisions created a lot of dissatisfaction among the Congress and civil society organizations of the province. Besides, Congress' engagements in the freedom struggle and war-time boycott of legislature provided an opportunity to the Muslim League to carry forward their design. On return to the legislature, the Congressmen brought forward such violations of agreements to notice in the Legislative Assembly debates. A powerful speaker who could forcefully present the violations of consensually agreed-upon decisions was Sarveswar Baruah.[8]

He pleaded that the Assamese were staring at an existential crisis brought about by the land settlement policy of the present government. He argued:

---

[7] Dev and Lahiri, *Assam Muslims: Politics and Cohesion*, 72.

[8] Baruah, *Assembly Debates*, 6 March 1945.

Though the Assamese race including the tribal people are the natural owners of the soil of the Assam valley districts, which they had defended as their hearth and home in the pre-British days successfully against hordes of invaders from Bengal, now they find themselves in a precarious position as their own Government have now allowed the progeny of those invaders to occupy their land, by coming in huge numbers without any check. What little checks and restrictions had been provided by some districts officers in the shape of the so-called Line System have not only been greatly relaxed but have been altogether done away with, with the result of the Development Scheme or rather the manner in which the said scheme was sought to be worked by the Hon'ble Sir Saadulla's last Government. The working of the scheme was so palpably to the detriment of the indigenous population that soon a hue and cry was raised against it. The benefit of the Development Scheme as mainly meant for the immigrants while very scant regard was paid to the interests of the children of the soil.

Citing evidence of the colonization officer of Nowgong, he expressed that out of 12,000 bighas of land earmarked for settlement, only 2,600 bighas had been allotted to the people of the soil, the remaining 9,400 bighas, or more than three-fourths of the total amount, had gone to the immigrants. Such state of things led to the resignation of Rohini Kumar Choudhury from the Cabinet and to the fall of the then Saadulla ministry.

Land Settlement Conference

Baruah regretted that even when giving shape to the actual recommendations of the Land Settlement Conference, an attempt was visible on the part of the government to whittle down some of the safeguards which were provided to protect the interest of the indigenous people, so much so that the party leaders representing them felt perturbed when they received the official report and hastened to send a joint note of protest against certain omissions and modification which affected the interests of the indigenous people adversely.

He said that the line system was about to be abolished without its formal closure by the Muslim League government, as the Premiere and Muslim League leaders had no intention of implementing it. The policies adopted by the Muslim League were completely repugnant to the basic principles of the Line Committee report (LCR).

Baruah alleged that the revenue minister assured his Muslim friends that, within two years, every Muslim immigrant would obtain land for settlement in Assam. And soon after the conference, settlement of lands with immigrants was started post-haste in areas like the Laokhowa Game Reserve and Bhurbandha, Barghuli, Balijuri and Soraguri grazing reserves in the Nowgong district as well as in different tribal areas, particularly in the Mangaldai subdivision. The undue haste was sought to be justified on the handy plea of the 'Grow-More-Food Campaign'.

Government's Steam-Roller Policy: Convert Assam into Pakistan

Sarveswar Baruah's strong contention was that the attitude of government had been nothing else than a steam-roller policy to crush the people of the soil to favour the huge and rapid influx of Muslim immigrants from Bengal to convert Assam into a Pakistan as soon as possible. In their anxiety to accelerate the settlement of immigrants by de-reserving professional grazing reserves, the government had thrown open large areas of these reserves for settlement and driven away large numbers of graziers from them. This not only greatly accelerated the influx to the de-reserved areas but also the reserved parts of professional grazing reserves. The land-hungry newcomers did not stop at that; they soon started to occupy other reserves as well. In this manner, the encroachers were emboldened by the government's conspicuous lack of firmness in enforcing the orders of eviction through the Line Enquiry Committee, whereas all subsequent committees and conferences, both official and non-official, had pleaded for firmness in the matter. The Line Enquiry Committee recommended in the report on page 19 as follows:

> All our recommendations however will come to nothing without firmness of administration, avoidance of unnecessary interference, and an adequate and competent staff to enforce the executive orders which are passed. The more unruly new immigrant very soon gets out of hand if he finds he can disobey orders with impunity and no solution of the problem is possible unless he is firmly kept in order and made to understand that he only breaks rules at his own peril. Officers to be placed in charge of areas where the problem is acute, particularly in Barpeta, should therefore

be specially selected and well backed up, for by no other means can the protection which it is desirable to give to the weaker people—especially the Kacharis—be ensured, until such time as the immigrant has settled down acquired more peaceable habits and qualified himself for the further relaxation and finally a complete abolition of restrictions which must be the ultimate goal at which we should aim.

Revenue Minister's Complicity

Baruah made a serious allegation against the then Revenue Minister Munnawar Ali. Though it was obvious that the district officers had only one effective weapon of control, namely eviction, and that unless they were given a free hand to use this weapon, they would be unable to implement the government-declared policy, the Revenue Minister, for reasons best known to himself, could not accord sanction for such use of this weapon by the district officers. The non-Assamese members and officials of the last Land Settlement Conference in a joint note in vain pleaded:

The entire Government policy is being viewed and will be viewed with suspicion and distrust so long as the Government will not be prepared to bring about order in the matter of all settlement by enforcing their orders by means of evictions.

The protection guaranteed to the Tribal people since the beginning of the present Constitution in this behalf, has been maintained more in their breach than observation. This fact has been no less true of blocks in other areas also.

Government policy of regularization of encroachments has been carried to the extreme end. The safety to the Tribal and the indigenous people is now nil. Unless Government withdraw this policy it is more or less useless to pursue any scheme of ordered settlement. If in the blocks to be created for communities other than the Muslim immigrants, encroachments by the immigrants subsist as before, how can Government expect to carry out an agreed recommendation? Therefore, eviction must be resorted to.

The action of Government hitherto has been responsible in making the immigrants believe that they have only to occupy any land anywhere to get a 'patta', and this has resulted in immigration in such large numbers that not only are there no more land for settlement, but the immigrant leaders have made then situation worse. We feel that the only way of effectively telling these sojourners for land is not to allow them to squat in prohibited areas. Our earnest request to Government therefore is that they give by eviction and otherwise, the clearest indication that there is no more land to settle.[9]

Instead of doing anything of the sort, the revenue minister was reported to be conniving. He was alleged to have encouraged the acts of Muslim immigrants by which all lands, including large plots of *patta* lands (legal registered lands) of indigenous people, in settled areas, had been forcibly occupied. Wastelands reserved for people of the soil had been freely encroached upon, and many local people had been goaded to leave their hearths and homes. In many reserves, hardly any land was left for the grazing of buffaloes and cattle or a peaceful life of the graziers.

While orders for settlement of the de-reserved grazing reserves seem to have been issued with indecent haste, those for allowing the graziers ousted from them to take their cattle to the Laokhowa Game Reserve, as decided in the conference, had not yet been issued to the Forest Department, with the result that the animals taken there by the helpless graziers had been seized and impounded and heavy penalties were imposed.

Sarveswar Baruah held the Revenue Minister responsible for the grim situation. He said that the minister, instead of doing anything to protect the interests of the helpless graziers and indigenous people, had been telling the immigrants, in talks with them, in course of his frequent tours in these areas, that they should not fear anybody, not even the Deputy Commissioners, as the Raj was a Muslim Raj. The minister was also alleged to be directly ordering the officers for according permission for the opening of reserves at his sweet will. He lamented that the government was only for the Muslims and not there to deal with an equitable policy but only to encourage lawlessness and anarchy in society and to bring about feud and bloodshed among various sections of the people.

---

[9] As was placed by Baruah, *Assembly Debates*.

Indigenous People Deprived of Benefits

Baruah made a serious allegation that, in the Land Settlement Conference, the recommendation of the Assamese party leaders in several respects had been either omitted or materially altered in the official report for which they had to submit a joint note pointing out their objections in the matter.[10]

1. The first and foremost of these was the 'five bighas' landless clause which was likely to hit the Assamese families hard, in as much as the percentage of Assamese families owing less than 5 bighas of land was microscopic, if not altogether nil. Moreover, the joint family system was largely in vogue among them.

2. On the basis of this definition of 'landless' families, almost all such Assamese joint families would be debarred from getting lands in spite of their present marginal landholding pattern. To meet this exigency, it was provided in the government resolution for adopting the recommendations of the 1940 conference that especially in the case of the indigenous people, the government did not wish to exclude from the benefit of the scheme those who, though possessing more than the minimum, had not yet made any provision for the their maintenance. However, in the present land conference resolution, they had not made any provision for the Assamese families holding barely more than the minimum of 5 bighas.

3. The next point on which objection was raised was about the proposal to confine the tribal people to a belt in the submontane areas which were infested with malaria and were deficient in water supply. This had been surreptitiously introduced in the government resolution though absent in the report of the proceedings of the conference.

4. There was no means suggested either in the report or in the resolution of working out the 1938 limit, in other words, of finding out the immigrants who came after 1937. Thus, the agreed definition of immigrants before 1 January 1938 had been made irrelevant.

---

[10] For details, see Baruah, *Assam Legislative Assembly Proceedings*, 203–206.

This had practically rendered this clause nugatory and all kinds of immigrants without any restrictions were being settled.

5. No step was being taken to appoint an officer to find out the number of indigenous landless people in the four districts where the scheme was being put into operation. In order to reduce uneconomic holdings, the Congress representatives in the Land Settlement Conference and also in their joint note urged to comb out the surplus population in the densely populated areas for settlement in blocks under the scheme, but this was ignored by the government.

6. Lastly, regarding the Land Advisory Committee, at both the central and district levels, the Revenue Minister acted as if they did not exist. He had issued instructions to the Deputy Commissioners and Sub-Deputy Collectors without letting the members even know what the instructions were, much less giving them any chance of giving advice. Baruah then asked what was then the meaning of the Advisory Committee? Thus, the Land Settlement Conference seemed to be a big hoax for the Congress leaders.

Muslim League Politics and Role of Maulana Bhasani (Hamid Khan) and Saadulla

The indigenous Assamese tribal people were highly disappointed by the growing immigrant-centric politics in the state. What Assam had lost from 1920 onwards was civic governance where the focus of attention was on education, economic planning, industry, land reforms, gender empowerment and the overall growth of innumerable tribes and communities. Suddenly, the notion of land changed; the ecosystem, vast forest and animal and vast eco-resources became 'wastelands' to be used mercilessly for accommodating the immigrants and the British commercial interests. They were no longer viewed as mother nature where the tribes were attached to organically, and where they would cultivate land according to their need rather than greed.[11]

---

[11] About how the land was utilised by the tribals and during the Ahom period, please see Vivekananda Kendra Institute of Culture, *Aspects of Land Policy in Assam: Continuity and.*

While looking into the autonomy issues for the plain tribes in Assam, The Bhupinder Singh Committee referred to the Bodos as a people who moved from place to place:

> They are erratic cultivators of the wilds; though no longer savages or herds-men, but wholly cultivators, they are so little connected with any one spot, that their language contains no words for village. They never cultivate the same land beyond the second year, nor remain in the same neighborhood after the fourth of fifth year. After four or five years, to allow the jungle to grow and the land to resume its former high productiveness, they return, unless forestalled by other and resume the identical fields they tilted before, but never the houses or site of the old settlement.[12]

The people of the region were highly satisfied with an essentially self-sufficient life without having to venture into the nearby areas. During the pre-British period, the land was not a typical commercial proposition. Community ownership and state ownership were the hallmarks of landholding during the Ahom period. However, with the advent of colonial rule and the coming of the immigrants, the land suddenly became a quest for individual ownership. Abdur Rouf of Barpeta complained, in one of his speeches in Assembly:

> They are very particular about providing land to tigers, rhinos, buffaloes and other wild animals to roam about, but they won't give a single bigha of land to a landless immigrant to live upon.

The forest land, water and forest resources were no longer community resources. Not only were the vast natural resources of the state very systematically exploited, but the cultural mosaic of the state was also changed with a huge infusion of immigrants. Census after census, there was a steady increase in the number of Muslims in Assam, and a primarily economic problem was beginning to turn gradually communal in its political articulation. Added to it was the gradual assertion of the Bengali-language speakers and their proportionate claim in the administration. With the increase of numbers, Muslim politics in the province became very powerful. As noted in a book on Muslim politics

---

[12] Bhupinder Singh Committee Report, Chap. III, 2–3. By Order no. 11010/22/89-NE(iv), 25 February 1991, Archive.

in Assam, 'since the inauguration of provincial autonomy under the Act of 1935 political developments in Assam led to the emergence of an immigrant lobby which in course of time became a powerful force under the dynamic leadership of Bhasani'.[13] In November 1939, the Congress coalition government published its opinion on LCR and suggested for a planned settlement and urged its determination to evict unauthorized occupants. The Bordoloi government also declared that for settlement of land to immigrants, preference would be given to those who had migrated before 1 April 1937.

Muslim League Conferences and Idea of Pakistan

The first provincial Muslim League conference held at Ghamari on 18–19 November 1939 mulled over a plethora of issues regarding the settlement of immigrants and the Line System. Bhasani was the main speaker who launched several attacks on the Bordoloi government. Anti-Congress rhetoric was the main theme of his speech. He also attacked the British for their imperialist policies. He called upon the Muslims of Assam to rally around the League and liberates themselves from the 'domination of Hindus'. The immigrant Muslims were exhorted to surrender their political future at the altar of the Muslim League.[14] In his speech, he said that he had lost all his patience on account of the treatment meted out to the lakhs of poor Muslims. He went to the extent of saying that he kicks at those laws and declared *jehad* in the name of Allah. He urged the Muslims to get their demands fulfilled even by becoming *swahid* (martyr) in the path of Allah. In the conference, the Chairman of the Reception Committee, Ghyasuddin Ahmed, stated his reaction to the Government Communique of November in the following manner:

> The result of this Communique will be very terrible and heart-rending. Thousands would be homeless. Bordoloi Government were eager to save the lives of the beasts and birds, but they had shown their heartlessness

---

[13] Dev and Lahiri, *Assam Muslims: Politics and Cohesion*, 26.

[14] Ibid., 126.

towards men created by God. With this pride the Congressmen want to spread out that they are non-communal and friends of the peasants. This is just like the snake becoming the friend of the frog.[15]

The conference attacked the Line System and the decision of the Congress Coalition Ministry and demanded for newly formed Ministry steps 'to save the poor peasants by giving suitable lands after abolishing the detestable Line System'.[16]

One of the notable features of Muslim politics in Assam was the continuous fight for authority and power between Bhasani and Saadulla. Saadulla was the liberal face of Muslim politics and Bhasani was the most communal adornment of Islamic identity. With his long association with Assam's politics and he himself being an indigenous Muslim, Saadulla was somehow not blatant in his approach. He believed in democratic institutional politics and was sensitive about the plural character of the province. However, this does not condone him as a pioneer of Muslim communal politics as we have argued in the second chapter—his problem was that he could never come out of the whirlpool of communal politics, as a result of which Assam lost a great statesman—otherwise, he would have had far surpassed Md Tayebullah and Fakhruddin Ali Ahmed.

Although Bhasani started his initial political work with the Muslim peasants, very soon, especially from the very first Muslim League conference, his statements became even more communal, and he could never look beyond the Islamic immigrants. In his seminal work, *The Bengal Muslims, 1871–1906: A Quest for Identity*, Rafiuddin Ahmed argues that the growth of solidarity in Bengal Muslim society was caused by successful mobilization of rural Muslims by the mullahs. He argues that the average Muslim people of Eastern Bengal had a relatively more identifiable communal and religious identity than their Hindu counterparts. The propagation of religious and communal solidarity is always easier among the Muhammadan society than in the highly stratified diverse Hindu society. The mullahs played

---

[15] Proceedings of the First Day's Sitting of the First Session of the Assam Provincial Muslim League Conference, File No. C-5(10)39, 162 (SB).

[16] Ibid.

an effective role in bringing various Muslim sections together, particularly in rural areas. Ahmed makes a distinction between the two classes of mullahs—one, the fairly well-educated *maulavis* who were, however, rare in the rural areas. The majority of the Muslim priests in the rural areas were semi-literate or illiterate with a bare knowledge of the tenets of Islam, described sometimes as *kath mullahs* (ignorant and bigoted mullahs). Such mullahs derived their 'support from the ignorance and superstition of the poor classes of their co-religionists'.[17] Bhasani was educated only up to the primary level[18]; nevertheless, his utterances and bucolic appeal, as well as his language, did not evince the image of a knowledgeable *pir* or mullah. Hamid Khan spoke the street language of Mymensingh, and his speech was always shrouded with provocative religious sentiments. He was accepted by the rural Muslims both as a *maulana* and as a forceful political leader. His political articulation was an adept and shrewd mixture of land and bigoted religious concoctions.

Bhasani resisted every effort of Saadulla for any consensual decision on the Line System. He considered the 'development scheme' as the safest bureaucratic method for protecting the system. He vilified Saadulla for having forgotten his promise of providing land to a minimum of 0.2 million landless people. Bhasani's politics sometimes hinged on the propagation of violence. In one of his speeches, he uttered that the Muslims had no faith in 'charkha' and non-violence.[19]

'We Want to See Assam as a Muslim Majority Province'

The second provincial Assam Muslim League conference held on 30–31 January 1941 at Habiganj endorsed the Pakistan demand made by the Muslim League. A resolution was passed 'to wholeheartedly support the Pakistan scheme as adopted by the Lahore conference

---

[17] Ahmed, *The Bengal Muslims,* 29.

[18] Nirode Baruah argues that Hamid Khan's education ended at the primary level. Baruah, *Gopinath Bordoloi: The Assam Problem and Nehru's Centre,* 514.

[19] Dev and Lahiri, *Assam Muslims: Politics and Cohesion,* 37.

of the all India Muslim League'. The provincial Muslim League was requested 'to adopt ways and means to give immediate effect to this scheme'. The Chairman of the reception committee declared:

> The Muslim League stands for Pakistan. Our great leader Jinnah wants us to live for it, pray for it, fight if necessary with the last drop of our blood and even die for it as will not be in a position to live elsewhere. It is for us to understand Pakistan in all seriousness and to carry out at any sacrifice. It is the inevitable goal of Indian Muslims in the process of historical evolution.[20]

The conference once again demanded the abolition of the Line System. A more significant aspect of this conference was the observation made by the two stalwarts of the Muslim League, one of them was none other than Sayed Saadulla. Kazimuddin Ahmed, the mover of the resolution, said 'We want to see Assam as a Muslim majority province. The settlement of the immigrants is the best means of doing it'.[21] What was most surprising was the attitude of Saadulla, who nourished the dream of making Assam a Muslim-dominated province and then include in Pakistan, as he said 'If the Muslims be in majority in Assam, then Bengal and Assam can form one Pakistan State and Punjab, the North West Frontier Province, Sind and Baluchistan can form another Pakistan State'.[22]

The third annual conference of the provincial Muslim League was held in Barpeta on 7–8 April. The *pandal* (meeting place or temporary meeting hall) and adjacent areas were decorated with slogans like 'Ministers, give us land or resign', 'We want to live where animals live', Pakistan is our birth right', 'Open out grazing reserves' etc. Maulana Bhasani, the president of the Provincial League expressed:

> The most powerful blood-sucking British government should pack up bag and baggage and quit our country as soon as possible .... We want Pakistan. All evils will disappear when Pakistan will come into existence; Pakistan is our objective, and Pakistan is our demand .... We challenge the

[20] Ibid., 128.

[21] Proceedings of the Second Session of the Assam Provincial Muslim League, Resolution No. 11, File No. C-5(10)(b)41, 23 (SB).

[22] Ibid.

Government that we shall stop the Line System by force. We shall carry on a struggle, sacrifice ourselves and get the Line System withdrawn.[23]

Bhasani's emphatic declaration was: 'We shall have to shed our blood and become *shahids* on the path of Allah for the sake of Pakistan ....'

In his presidential speech, Choudhury Khaliquzzaman expressed his satisfaction at the relaxation of the Line System in the interest of the immigrants. Saadulla sounded tentative in his address as he admitted his susceptibility and recognized that the immigrant members were 'the backbone of the Ministry'. Citing his age and long association with politics, he even offered to resign in the light of criticism by the Muslim League leaders. He, however, reiterated the government's determination to abolish the Line System except in the tribal areas. The conference urged the government to immediately withdraw 'the pernicious line system' and reaffirmed its faith in Pakistan as its 'political objective and goal' and also desired 'Bengal and Assam to be constituted as the sovereign state of Eastern Pakistan'.[24]

With such aggressive postures of the Muslim League, Assam was in a deep crisis. The province was witnessing multiple challenges at various levels: (a) the demography of the province was being vastly altered; (b) its land forest reserves and professional grazing grounds had been opened to immigrants; (c) the institutional and administrative protections for the indigenous Assamese people provided by various legislative and administrative policies had been nullified at the empirical level at the behest of the Muslim League government; and (d) with the change of demography and geographical proximity with East Bengal, the province now made herself an attractive plan for its inclusion in Pakistan.

At the national level also, a divisive politics was gaining ground. Congress was gradually identified as 'Hindu Congress', and the Muslim League was increasingly becoming aggressive about its demand for Pakistan.

[23] Address of Abdul Hamid Khan, File No. C-5(10)(b)44, 62.
[24] Ibid.

Saadulla's Question to Assamese Leaders

One of the pioneer scholars in the field of Muslim politics, M. Kar supported the assertions of Saadulla by saying that

> since 1940, all decisions of Saadulla cabinets on this complicated problem (land settlements, opening of grazing, immigration) were interspered [sic] with a plethora of 'ifs' and 'buts' and vauge [sic] restrictions and apparent relaxations which, under the prevailing, political circumstances, admitted of political interpretations ... the correctness of these interpretations however, can't perhaps be guaranteed, and even if they were correct, the Hindu leaders of Assam no less cooperated.[25]

He cited a long presentation by Saadulla in the Assam Assembly and justified Saadulla's accusation on the Congress leaders.[26]

If we analyse Saadulla's speech, there were essentially four components on which he was attacking Assamese-indigenous leadership, based on which scholars like M. Kar endorsed Saadulla's viewpoints. Saadulla's first point was regarding the thin majority of Muslims in Bengal and the possibility of emigration to Assam:

> Now let me remove a few misconceptions as regards this question of eviction. It has been stated by various friends opposite that it is a planned immigration. My hon. friends, the Minister-in-charge, also has some misconceptions for in his Budget speech he makes an appeal to the Bengal Government to dissuade these people to come to Assam. Now, every student of politics knows that Muslims are in majority in Bengal only about 56 per cent. And you think that the Muslims are so foolish as to jeopardise their meagre majority by a planned drive to send Muslim people to Assam?[27]

To this accusation, Kar says, '[N]one appeared to have counter-acted this argument ...'. In one occasion, he said, '[T]hese were complaints which the Hindus never answered....'[28] It is really unfortunate that Kar could not understand or did not bother to look into the dynamics of

---

[25] Kar, *Muslim Politics in Assam*, 77.

[26] For Saadulla's speech, see *Assam Gazette*, Part VIA A, 18 March 1946, 179.

[27] *Assam Gazette*, part VI A, 1946, 176–79.

[28] Kar, *Muslim Politics in Assam*, 80.

demographic change in the province of Assam. To cite Kar's statistics: 'Taking the census figure of 1941 which were challenged by the Hindus, and adding this number, the Muslims would have a population strength of 40,96,568 against 45,40,497 Hindus, 28,24,586 tribals and 67,184 Christians in a total of 109,30,388'.[29] If one goes by this logic, in which the tribals were not considered as Hindus in 1941, the Hindus had a slender majority of 443,929 persons only. Saadulla argued that the Muslims in Bengal were majority only by 56 per cent, and they were not so foolish to lose their majority by sending Muslims to Assam. Here, it would be helpful if we look at the population of Muslims in Bengal during 1941.

The Muslim population in Bengal was 33,005,434 (three crores thirty lakhs five thousand four hundred thirty-four) in 1941.[30] Pointedly, even if a considerable chunk of them migrated to Assam, they would not have become a minority there, but they would undoubtedly have surpassed the Hindu population of Assam. To munch some numbers, movement of less than 0.25 per cent of the Muslim population of Bengal was sufficient to make Assam a Hindu-minority state and Muslims the most dominant group in 1941. Added to that, Saadulla himself acknowledged in his speech that Muslims had a higher population growth compared with the Hindus—plus the marriageable age of the Muslim girls was much lower than that of the Hindu girls. Hence, the fear and apprehension of Assam becoming a Muslim-dominant state was real than imaginary—whether it was artificially induced or by the natural flow of immigration. This is clear from two factors—one was the rate of immigration in three decades and the other was that the rate of population increase among the immigrant Muslims, which was so high that it would not perhaps have taken more than a decade or so to counterbalance the Hindu population. To quote Saadulla:

There is this misconception in the minds of many, in spite of the fact that the Hon. Finance Minister has been charitable enough to admit that immigration has been going on for long 20 years. The insinuation has

---

[29] Ibid., 78.

[30] Pakistan Geotagging. *Muslim Population of India.*

been that since the passing of the Pakistan Resolution in December 1940, at Lahore, we have started bringing in these people. I will quote from the census figures. The Muslim Population in the Assam valley in the 1911 census was very nearly three and half lacs. Then in 1931 this has increased to 9,53,299 that is in 20 years, the increase in the Muslim population has been 200 per cent. This increase is partially due to the normal increase in the decade and it is admitted from the Census Report that the Muslim are more virile and whereas the average increase of the Province is 13 per cent, Muslim increase in same decade goes up to 23 per cent.[31]

Saadulla's second point was that no one could have planned the Muslim immigration between January 1946 and March 1946, as the bulk of the migration had already taken place before the Pakistan Resolution of December 1940. He said 'How can you say that there has been influx in order to convert this Province into a Muslim majority Province according to the Lahore Resolution of 1940? Absurdity cannot go further than this'.

Saadulla himself and Muslim League leaders, on some occasions in various forums, candidly expressed about their desire to make Assam a Muslim-dominant province. As we have argued above, Kazimuddin Ahmed, the mover of the resolution in the second provincial Muslim League conference, said, 'We want to see Assam as a Muslim majority province. The settlement of the immigrants is the best means of doing it'.[32] Saadulla, who had nourished the dream of making Assam a Muslim-dominated province and then include in Pakistan, said 'If the Muslims be in majority in Assam, then Bengal and Assam can form one Pakistan State and Punjab, the North West Frontier Province, Sind and Baluchistan can form another Pakistan State'.[33]

Saadulla was a firm believer of the merger of Assam with Bengal. In his Assembly address on the question of grouping and election of members to Constituent Assembly (CA) on 16 July 1946, Saadulla firmly argued for the inclusion of Assam in Bengal and thus forming

---

[31] Kar, *Muslim Politics in Assam*, 80.

[32] Proceedings of the Second Session of the Assam Provincial Muslim League, Resolution No.11, File No. C-5(10)(b)41, 23 (SB).

[33] Ibid.

a part of Pakistan. To quote from one of his earlier letters dated 20 July 1925, Saadulla said

> Recently, the Gauhati Anjuman sought my opinion in this question and I understand that the Jorhat Anjuman has already submitted a representation to Government over the same matter. The view point of these Anjumansis was that 'Sylhet should not be transferred. But if the transfer is effected, then the Assam Valley should also be included in Bengal'. While leading the Assam Valley Muhammadan deputation before the late Mr. Montagu and Lord Chelmsford, at the time of the enquiry for Reforms, I said that Sylhet ought not go over Bengal, but if in defence to popular opinion, Sylhet is transferred, then the Assam districts are kept intact and the privileges obtained in Assam be continued in Bengal.

Of course, he wanted to do a favour—he also vouched for the preservation of the Assamese nationality, culture and language in that revamped Bengal. Hence, Saadulla already had a theoretical vision of the Assam–Bengal merger as to how the merger would happen.

It would be wrong to say that the apprehensions about Assam's inclusion in proposed Pakistan and Assam becoming a Muslim-dominant state were expressed only by the indigenous Assamese people. The officials of the British administration were equally concerned and were determined to ensure the protection of the Assamese indigenous areas, particularly those of the Kacharis and Lalungs, as it was felt that 'the play of natural forces would be driving the Assamese from their lands'.[34] The revenue member W. L. Scott justified some form of protection in the Assam Legislative Council in the following manner:'... their economic and racial advantage are such that without some control they are very likely to drive away the indigenous inhabitants completely off the map'.[35]

The former Governor Robert H. Reid, in a paper to the Royal Society of Arts, said 'On general grounds, these immigrants deserve to be welcomed, for they are good cultivators ... this gives satisfaction to the Muslims but not to the Hindu community. For the

---

[34] *Assam Gazette*, Part VI, No. 18, 1916, 1528.

[35] *Assam Gazette*, Part VI, No. 18, 1916, 1529.

more Mohammedans you have in Assam, the stronger is the case of Pakistan'.[36]

Saadulla's third point of contention was on the settlement of tea-garden labourers. Saadulla stated:

We should consider this matter very dispassionately without bringing in any question of sentiment or community. If you consider from the point of view of community, I cannot but say that whereas there is absolutely no opposition from the people of Assam-indigenous people of Assam, both Hindus and Muslims against the Colonisation of Assam by the 'labour' people who have come from Central India to the Tea Estates, immigration of 95 per cent Muslim and 5 per cent *Namasudra* from East Bengali has made them to howl and protest. Anyone who has gone through the Census figures knows fully well that there are ten lakhs of labour forces coming from outside the province serving in our tea gardens and there is a standing position in our Assam Land Revenue Manual that preference should be given in certain Government waste lands for settlement with these discharged labour forces...we have only got six lakhs of immigrants, yet the cries against them are rending the skies while not even a sigh escapes from our Congress party against those 18 lakhs of tea-garden labourers.

It hardly requires any reiteration that the imperial interest in increasing their commercial revenue encouraged tea-garden and other labourers from central and southern parts of India to come to Assam. As we have argued in the first chapter, because of unchecked Muslim immigration, a sense of religious and Assamese nationality solidarity took place among the Assamese and that was how they came to consider the immigrants from other parts of India as 'Assamese immigrants'.[37] It is clear from the letters submitted to the secretary of Government of Assam, A. W. Botham that the indigenous people wanted the settlement of immigrant Assamese as seal and cover to the Bengali Muslim settlement.[38]

---

[36] Dev and Lahiri, *Assam Muslims: Politics and Cohesion*, 44.

[37] Immigrant Assamese primarily included: tea garden workers from Bihar, Orissa and Central Provinces; trading class like the Marwaris from Rajasthan; graziers from Nepal; labourer and officials from Madras, United Provinces, etc.

[38] Kar, *Muslim Politics in Assam*, 86–87.

Ramesh Chandra Kalita, a prominent Assamese writer, in one of his articles, dealt with a scenario in which the Assamese leadership, on the eve of the Pandu Congress Session, was drawn to accord approval to a proposal by the Congress leader Rajendra Prasad.[39] Eighty-five per cent of immigrants who immigrated into Assam were Muslims, and hence, an environment of communal conflict was brewing. There was a possibility of Hindus being a minority from the viewpoint of population composition in Assam. In order to retain the majority of Hindus, Dr Rajendra Prasad, who later became the first president of India, introduced a scheme to let the Hindus of Bihar immigrate into Assam which drew a positive response from the Assamese middle class. His autobiography provides information on how he introduced a scheme of immigration of Hindus from Bihar to check Muslim immigration from Mymensingh and East Bengal. In his autobiography, he writes

> In my tour of Assam I found large tracts of uncultivated land in Nowgong district. There were no signs of human habitation for miles around, except a few huts here and there. There was no shortage of water and the land was covered with green foliage. There was no sign of the land ever having been ploughed. I was told that there was plenty of such land in the province and, according to the law of the land, anyone who brought the land under the plough and settled there became owner.

In contrast, the adjoining Mymensingh district of Bengal (now in East Pakistan) was a thickly populated area. Many Muslim families migrated from Mymensingh to Nowgong and settled on the land, and when they began cultivation, they became its owners. As more and more unused land came under the plough, the ratio of the Muslim population began to rise.

> When I heard of all this, I had an idea. Chapra is one of the most densely populated districts of Bihar and its people generally have to go out of the province in search of work every year. Thousands of them go to Assam and work as labourers and after earning some money return to their homes. They never thought of settling down in Assam. I saw Biharis and men from Chapra almost everywhere in Assam. I thought that if instead of just going to Assam to earn something and returning to Chapra, they permanently

---

[39] Kalita, 'Prabajankarir Samasya Aru Asom'.

settled down on the land there, not only would their future be assured but also the pressure on land would be reduced in Chapra.[40]

Kalita concludes in his article that

> Dr. Rajendra Prasad favoured the immigration from Bihar to Assam mainly for two reasons; firstly, to lessen population pressure in Bihar and secondly, to continue Hindu majority in Assam through such immigration. His description is based on his experience on his tour to Assam prior to the Pandu session of Indian National Congress in 1926. The president and secretary of the reception committee of the Pandu session were Tarunram Phookan and Nabin Chandra Bordoloi respectively. Among the Assamese who rendered support to the discussion and the scheme announced by Dr. Rajendra Prasad, probably they were also among them.[41]

Unfortunately, the leftist scholarship and those who were driven by their parochial linguistic considerations refused to understand the insecurities of a smaller nationality like the Assamese indigenous people. These considerations of identity crisis were duly reflected in the Assam Assembly debates in 1946.

Congress leader Beliram Das said that Mr Jinnah's demand for the inclusion of Assam in the Eastern Zone of his proposed Pakistan had been to a great extent responsible for the complication of the land settlement problem of Assam. He accused that

> In the three vitally affected districts in the Assam Valley, viz Kamrup, Darrang and Nowgong, Pakistan officers, officially known as the Colonisation Officers, were appointed by the previous Government under the guise of the Colonisation Scheme, who have actually been Promoting the cause of Pakistan only'.[42]

He stated that under the guise of Grow More Food Campaign, valuable lands including professional grazing reserves and game sanctuaries, which were absolutely necessary for the very existence of the Assamese people, had been thrown open for settlement with the immigrants.

---

[40] Prasad, *Autobiography*, 259–60.

[41] Kalita, 'Prabajankarir Samasya Aru Asom' (Translation by the author).

[42] Das, *Assembly Debates*.

From 1939, the onrush of the immigrants had been so great that the very existence of the Assamese people as a race got threatened. Beliram Das argued that what the great Moghuls could not achieve with their vast armies and resources in the past had been achieved by the outgoing League Ministry within the span of a few years. Assam's land settlement problem was nothing but an attempt by the League Ministers to convert Assam into a Muslim-majority province with a motive, pure and simple, to include her in the Eastern Zone of Pakistan, as envisaged by Mr Jinnah by bringing in men from Bengal, particularly in the Assam valley districts.

'Expedition of the Bengalee Muslims— the Holy Servants of Allah': Maulavi Abdur Rouf

Beliram Das contended that the sudden onrush of immigrants into Assam was an actual invasion of the province under the political design of the Muslim League. He referred to the speeches by the members of the League party who expressed that the immigration had no connection with their demand for the inclusion of Assam in the Eastern Zone of Pakistan. In this connection, Beliram Das referred to a speech of Maulavi Abdur Rouf, leader of the immigrant Muslims, in course of his address as the chairman of the Reception Committee of the League meeting presided over by Chaudhury Khaliquzzaman, held at Barpeta on 7–8 March 1944. He said:

> The same fresh blood which runs through their veins even to-day again took the rudder to tow their boats against the Current of the ever flowing Jomuna, to make their way for a new conquest of Assam. Being deprived of their arms shields and swords by the mercy of the British Rulers, they with a cane shield bamboo stick, spears and plough came and effected their landing either in chars or in the jungles adjacent to the rivers. The soul of martyrs and devotees of past, are witnessing this new expedition of the Bengalee Muslims - the Holy servants of Allah, from above with yawning eagerness and thankfulness too with increased vitality in the life of the community and with the help of numerous new reinforcements, the figure in the sub-division of Barpeta alone could be raised up to 65000.

Another leader, who later on became the Chief Minister of Assam and the Governor of Punjab, Mahendra Mohan Choudhury, considered that the acts of encroachments and trespasses in the Professional Grazing Reserves were nothing short of a planned invasion.[43] He deplored

> Mr Rouf, as my hon. friend Beliram Das has rightly stated on the floor of this House yesterday, in his address as the Chairman of the Reception Committee of the Barpeta Session of the Assam Muslim League did most emphatically declare in presence of Muhammad, the then Premier of Assam that the Mussalmans in the 17th and 18th Centuries conquered Assam with gun and cannons and in this 20th Century they will conquer Assam with ploughs and lathis. What does then this mean except a planned invasion on the part of the Muslim League under the garb of 'solution of landless problem' and 'grow-more-food' etc.[44]

Interestingly, Muslim League members, including Saadulla, could not refute such accusations by Beliram Das and Mahendra Mohan Choudhury in the Assembly. It was quite clear that the Muslim League leaders opted for two diametrically opposite policies. In the State Assembly, the issue of immigration and land settlement was projected as an issue of hungry 'landless peasants' who were forced to emigrate from Bengal due to famine. They refuted every possible accusation that there was a link between the demand of Pakistan and immigration. On the other hand, when it came to the issue of political mobilization and propagation of Pakistan and Islam, they would remind the people how Islam defeated Assam and how they would again take over Assam through plough and population. Similar utterances were made in various Muslim League conferences where the leaders, including Saadulla, espoused the cause of two separate nations.

Issue of Eviction

The eviction was a very critical issue for the British administration as well as for the indigenous Assamese people. The Congress coalition

---

[43] Choudhury, *Assembly Debates*.

[44] Ibid.

government[45], before its resignation, published a notification.[46] On the land settlement issue, the government said that their policy was of systematic, planned settlement in the interest of the cultivators, peasants and interests of the indigenous people. The Congress government said that in areas like the village grazing grounds and professional graziers' reserve, the settlement was forbidden to all persons—immigrants or non-immigrants. It was firmly resolved that all such occupations would be evicted.[47] The government notification said that it would strictly abide by the Line committee's suggestion that anybody who came before 1 January 1938 would be given settlement. The government notification said

> Elsewhere where the whole village or a larger compact area is predominantly peopled by backward or tribal classes such village or area may be constituted as prohibited areas. Within the prohibited areas so constituted immigrant cultivators shall not be allowed land either by settlement or by transfer of annual *patta*, and any immigrants so taking up land or by squatting shall be evicted.[48]

However, these resolutions were hardly taken into consideration by the Saadulla government. Here, the stand of the Communist Party of India (CPI) was interesting. The party urged the Saadulla government to abolish the Line System and urged to give land to the Bengali Muslim immigrants.[49] About the CPI party stand, the newspaper *Asamiya* reported that they had pleaded the Muslim League government to ignore the notification issued by last Bordoloi government which set the land settlement date as the 1 January 1938. CPI declared the Congress initiative as 'unjust' and 'oppressive', and that it should be extended till December 1944.[50]

[45] From 19 September 1938–16 November 1939.

[46] *The Assam Gazette* Extraordinary, no. 33, 4 November 1939—'Resolution on the Line System Committee Report'.

[47] Ibid., point 2.

[48] Ibid., point 4.

[49] Bhuyan and Barpujari, *Political History of Assam*, 263–64.

[50] *Asamiya*, 4 August 1945.

Would Assam Remain a Hindu-dominated State?

The most critical question for the indigenous Assamese people was: Would Assam be in a position to maintain its Hindu domination given the systematic Muslim immigration from the East Bengal districts? This question remained central for Assam from the days of the Muslim League until the attainment of independence in 1947. The demand for Pakistan and the inclusion of Assam in the proposed scheme of the grouping and inclusion of Assam into section C were nothing but the consolidation of Assam's fear that the state would soon become a Muslim-dominated state, and the stage would be the set for its inclusion into Pakistan. The *Political History of Assam* commented in the following manner:

> As the influx of immigrants was gradually titling the population ratio, a legitimate fear nagged the indigenous Hindus of Assam that they would in due course be swamped and Assam would be converted into a Muslim majority province. Subsequent actions of Saadulla also contributed to further confirm their apprehensions.[51]

One systematic planning of the Muslim League government in Assam was to segregate the tribals from the Hindu classification domain. In 1941, the Saadulla government took the initiative that the population should be classified based on the community. Saadulla said this in the Assembly:

> The original intention was to classify the population by religion as well as by communities. But funds were not found to be adequate for the double classification by the government who ordered only classification by communities.[52]

Such a decision evoked strong criticism from various quarters of the Assamese civil society and led to a debate in newspapers as well as in the Assembly. Under Gopinath Bordoloi, the Congress criticized the government for manipulating the census operations and the census data. Siddhi Nath Sharma brought an adjournment motion

---

[51] Bhuyan et al., *Political History of Assam*, 266.

[52] Saadulla, *Assam Legislative Assembly*.

to discuss the census operations.[53] Bordoloi demanded independent verification by impartial bodies. The *Assam Tribune* perhaps played the most important in mobilizing public opinion against the census manipulation. The newspaper pleaded that 'the Hindus of Assam should unite and take adequate measures to counteract the "sinister move of Saadulla government"'.[54] Prominent personalities like Veer Savarkar[55] in the Assam provincial Hindu Mahasabha meeting strongly urged the people of Assam not to allow Assam to be converted into Pakistan. Ambikagiri Raichaudhury urged the indigenous tribal people of Assam to reconsider before jumping into the Muslim League and the British colonial trap. He said that any action that might weaken the collective Assamese identity must not be done by anyone. He reminded how Assamese nationality had been evolving in which the tribals constituted an inalienable part of the greater Assamese identity. He urged them not to support community-based enumeration process. He urged that such divisive tendencies would prolong colonial domination and subjugate Assamese as a nationality.[56] The dilemma of Assamese nationality is expressed by a young Assamese scholar in the following manner:

> The overarching concern was the decrease in the population of the Hindus. The concern towards the tribals arose from the fear of growing immigration from east Bengal and census data showing 'alarming' increases in the population of Muslims. The only way visible to the middle class leadership to maintain a demographic balance was to conflate the figures of Hindus by adding to it the numbers for the plains tribe's populations.[57]

Various editorials in newspapers opined that there was nothing wrong in calculating the tribal population but doing so solely based on community bereft of religion projected a distorted impression of reality. The sole purpose of Saadulla government's attempt to reclassify the

---

[53] Sharma, *Assam Legislative Assembly*.

[54] *Assam Tribune*, 22 August 1941, as cited in Bhuyan and Barpujari, *Political History of Assam*, 267.

[55] President of All India Hindu Mahasabha.

[56] *Teenidiniya Asamiya*, Guwahati, 21 January 1941.

[57] Pathak, 'Tribal Politics in the Assam: 1933–1947', 61–69.

population was to show Assam as a Muslim-dominant state which would eventually facilitate for Assam's inclusion in proposed Pakistan.

Grouping and Section C: Another Nail in the Coffin

From March 1946 onwards, the Cabinet Mission (officially called the British Cabinet Delegation), comprising of Lord Pethick-Lawrence, the secretary of state for India, Stafford Cripps and A. V. Alexander initiated a series of discussions with various leaders and organizations. When he was interviewed, Gopinath Bordoloi focussed on provincial autonomy and argued that provinces be constituted on a linguistic and cultural basis. He argued how Assam had been maintaining a separate identity and pleaded the committee for its continuity in its full form with a provincial status. For maintaining Assam's autonomous status, he pleaded for the separation of Sylhet, and he dubbed the demand for inclusion of Assam with Pakistan as preposterous.[58] As the leader of the Muslim League, Saadulla made the last-ditch effort in front of the commission to consider Assam as a Muslim-dominated state. Saadulla tried to 'impress upon the delegation that it was the Muslims who actually constituted the majority of the population in the province but for the partial classification of many tribals as Hindus in the census operations ... [H]e suggested that the whole province might be attached to Bengal'.[59] On 16 May 1946, the Cabinet Mission declared its statement, the most important features of which were that it recommend for the unity of India, a three-tier constitution—the centre, groups and provinces and an interim government with the support of the major political parties till the constitution was complete.

Meanwhile, the Congress and the Muslim League failed to arrive at any consensus about the transfer of imperial power in their discussion on March–June 1946. On 16 May 1946, the British Cabinet Mission declared itself in favour of a three-tier federal government by entrusting defence, foreign affairs and communication with the centre, with

[58] Bhuyan and Barpujari, *Political History of Assam*, 338–39.

[59] Ibid., 339.

all residuary powers to be relegated to the existing provinces further grouped into three zones till the preparation of the constitution was complete.[60] The Cabinet proposal stressed on keeping the unity of India intact.

Allotment of seats was made proportional to the population, roughly one representative in one million. The population was divided into three major communities—general, Muslims and Sikhs—which were to have equal representation. The representatives would be divided into three sections: A, B and C. Bengal and Assam were included in section C.[61] Each section was to decide its own provincial constitution and group matters. Gopinath Bordoloi, the premier of Assam, who was in New Delhi at the time of announcing of the British Cabinet Mission Plan, saw in the grouping part of the plan a mischievous design that would place Assam at the mercy of the Muslim-majority Bengal for all time to come. Secondly, with the Muslim League's continuous effort to club Bengal and Assam into their future scheme of Pakistan, the grouping would pave the way for Assam's inclusion. Consequently, the Assam Congress opposed the plan of including Assam with Bengal in Group C. What was Assam's main objection to the whole scheme? According to Nirode Kumar Barooah,

> The problem with Assam was that since this Hindu-majority province would be together with the Muslim-predominated Bengal in one section. The acceptance of the Section would automatically mean opting for the group and getting thereby submerged in Bengal. In fact there can be no doubt that the grouping provision was especially made to be an essential feature of the Cabinet Mission plan to satisfy the Muslim League.[62]

The resolution of the working committee of Assam Pradesh Congress Committee (APCC) opposed the scheme on the following points[63]:

[60] Guha, *Planter Raj to Swaraj*, 251–52.

[61] Bhuyan and Barpujari, *Political History of Assam*, 344.

[62] Barooah, *Gopinath Bordoloi: Indian Constitution and Center-Assam Relations*, 25.

[63] Siddhi Nath Sharma, General Secretary, APCC. Resolution adopted by the Assam Provincial Congress Working Committee held on 26 May 1946 on the Recommendation of the Cabinet Mission. Assam Archive, Congress File, 1946.

1. 'The official interpretation, given during the last few days on the recommendations of the Cabinet Mission confirms the first apprehension of the Committee that the grouping of provinces is compulsory and freedom of opting out is illusory. Such a compulsory grouping is not only opposed to all principles of democracy and self determination but also negatives the very principles of provincial autonomy'. It particularly threatens to undermine the language, culture and existence of Assam apart from converting the political majority into minority and deprives her of the full enjoyment of her economic resources.

2. The Committee further views that the proposal to split the Constituent Assembly into three sections for the purpose of making the groups final authority for framing constitutions for respective provinces deprives the Constituent Assembly of its sovereignty which Congress has been striving all these years.

3. The Committee regrets that proposal to restrict the election of Muslim representatives to the Constituent Assembly only to the Muslim members of the Provincial Assembly is yet another device on the part of the British authority to show that Congress does not represent the Muslims of India. The Congress has all these years fought against such attempts by the Muslim League and the British Government.

4. That the Committee cannot help protesting, in strongest terms, against the attempt of giving in effect representation and right of election of members to the Constituent Assembly to Europeans in Assam and Bengal, in contravention of the principle of Cabinet Mission's own recommendation of representation of one in a million.

The APCC committee referred to the resolution of the working committee regarding the injustice done to Assam as pointed out by Congress President's letter, dated 12 May 1946, to the Cabinet Mission and resolution adopted by the working committee of AICC on 24 May 1946 in this regard. The committee strongly urged the Working Committee of AICC not to enter into any agreement which transgresses the fundamental principles of the Congress and threatens to undermine the cultural, political and economic existence of the province.

The committee further considered it to be its duty to bring to the notice of the Central Working Committee that there was a strong widespread resentment against the proposed grouping of Assam with Bengal that the people of Assam under no circumstances would tolerate the proposed arrangement. AICC requested the Working Committee not to accept any arrangement under which Assam was being placed in Group C but to insist on an arrangement in accordance with the views expressed by the Congress President in his letter dated 12 May 1946 to Lord Pethick Lawrence that Assam should be left to herself to frame her own constitution as a distant unit of Indian Union. A delegation of APCC comprising of Md. Tayebullah, Omeo Kr. Das, Bijoy Ch. Bhagwati, Hareswar Goswami, Fakhruddin Ali Ahmed, Nilomoni Phukan, Harendranth Barua, Kamakhya Prasad Tripathy and Pushpalata Das was constituted to place Assam's stand in front of the Congress Working Committee. The Congress central leadership, particularly Jawaharlal Nehru, Maulana Abul Kalam Azad and Sardar Patel were initially sympathetic to the cause of Assam. Azad and Nehru, however, continued to hold the view that Assam's stand was helping the Muslim League and acting as an obstruction to freedom. Nehru was reported to have told a three-member delegation from Bengal, which asked him why Assam was being let down after being given such high hopes by him, that 'Assam could not hold up the progress of the rest of India and support to Assam would mean refusal to accept the British Prime Minister's statement of December 6 and letting loose forces of chaos and civil wars' (*Transfer of Power: IX, 510*).[64]

Meanwhile, the Assam Assembly passed a resolution in July 1946 opposing the grouping system in the following manner:

> Whereas the Assembly after very careful consideration of the statement made by the British Cabinet Delegation and His Excellency the Viceroy on the 16th May 1946 is of the opinion that the Province of Assam has an undoubted claim to have the Constitution framed and settled by own representatives elected to the Constituent Assembly and that it would be detrimental to the interest of Assam to form any Sections of Groups

---

[64] How Congress leadership belittled Assam's apprehensions and concerns, please see Mahanta, *Confronting the State: ULFA's Quest for Sovereignty*, 17–19.

with any other Province of British India for the purpose of setting the Constitution for the Province.[65]

The resolution directed the Assam representatives that '[T]hey shall take part in the meetings of the Constituent Assembly for the purpose of framing the Union Constitution and in all matters relating to the Union Constitution'. It was at this critical hour that Gandhiji extended his much-needed help to the cause of Assam, and ultimately, the issue got marginalized with the announcement of Mountbatten plan.

> If Assam keeps quiet it is finished. No one can force Assam to do what it does not want to do. It must stand independently as an autonomous unit. It is autonomous to a large extent today. It must become fully independent and autonomous .... As soon as the time comes for the Constituent Assembly to go into sections you will say, 'Gentlemen, Assam retires'. For the independence of India it is the only condition. Each Unit must decide and act for itself. I am hoping that in this, Assam will lead the way .... If Assam takes care of itself the rest of India will be able to look after itself. What have you got to do with the Constitution of the Union Government? You should form your own Constitution. That is enough. You have the basis of a constitution yourself. (*Transfer of Power: IX, 403–405*)

Bordoloi's Contribution to Assam: Bordoloi and the Partition of India

It would not be an exaggeration at all to say that on the eve of independence, Assam's rescue from grouping and section, and subsequently from the Muslim League's sinister design, was primarily due to role played by Gopinath Bordoloi. In order to exclude Assam from the grouping scheme, Bordoloi launched multiple strategies. As we have seen above, first, he started a process of persuasion and consultation with the members of the Cabinet Mission and later on with Mountbatten. He forcefully demonstrated Assam's uniqueness and argued that Assam's destiny could never be equated with Bengal. Second, Bordoloi and his colleagues initiated a process of appeal, dialogue and persuasion with the all-India Congress leaders who were not very sympathetic to the cause of Assam. APCC submitted a series of

---

[65] Assam Legislative Assembly Proceedings, 16 July 1946, 173–74.

memorandums to Central Working committee (CWC) opposing the grouping of Assam with Bengal. The Assam Congress urged to CWC

> If the working committee don't stand up to safeguard them from against the operations of the sinister proposals then Assam and her people will be compelled to think that the working committee in their anxiety to think of larger provinces have given this small province a go by. It will not be a surprise if many in Assam will consider it to be great betrayal'.[66]

Unfortunately, at an all-India level, Bordoloi could secure very little support, except two Bengali leaders, namely Saratchandra Bose—a CWC member—and Shyama Prasad Mukerjee—a Jan Sangh leader—there were no takers of Assam's cause. CWC was keen to grab power in terms of the new proposal which the committee believed would serve two purposes—first, it would pave the way to attainment of full independence and second, at the same time, it would retain the unity of India. Maulana Abul Kalam Azad, the prime negotiator of the Congress with the Cabinet Mission, considered the Plan as 'a glorious event in the history of the freedom movement'.[67] Third, Bordoloi and his group took the issue to the civil society of Assam. The Assamese newspaper *Asamiya* and the English newspaper *Assam Tribune* perhaps played the most proactive role in generating people's opinion against the grouping scheme. The paper argued that the grouping plan had pushed the Pakistan plan and a sword was being planted on Assam to become a Muslim-dominated state.[68] Regularly, the Assamese newspaper used to narrate a story in a box from the ancient and medieval history of Assam—how Assamese generals and soldiers used to repulse the mighty Turbak and the Mughals.[69] The newspaper used to provide in detail the unfettering role and indomitable spirit of Gopinath Bordoloi. Ambikagiri Raichaudhury, the General Secretary of Assam Jatiya Mahasabha, announced his decision to go for fast-unto-death if Assam was forcefully included in the grouping scheme.

[66] Memorandum submitted by APCC to CWC, Delhi, 19 May 1946, APCC Papers, NMML, New Delhi.

[67] Kakati, 'Gopinath Bardoloi and the Grouping Scheme', 252–56.

[68] *Asamiya*, 25 May 1946.

[69] See *Asamiya*, various issues from 8 April till 25 June 1946.

The Assam Jatiya Mahasabha mobilized people in various places to fight against the grouping and the Muslim League. Even CPI advocated for linguistic and cultural homogeneity and the inarguable right to self-determination. Fourth, the most critical component in Congress and Bordoloi's fight against the grouping scheme was the critical role played by Mahatma Gandhi. However, his first meeting with Gandhiji was not successful, as Gandhiji did not commit anything. A prominent journalist of Assam, Satis Chandra Kakati argues

> In sheer desperation he met Gandhiji at New Delhi's Bhangi Colony and explained to the Mahatma that the proposed dumping of Assam with Bengal under the Grouping scheme created an area over which the Muslims would be the de facto rulers. … It seemed to Bardoloi immoral and unjust to place a Hindu majority province like Assam with Muslim majority province of Bengal. Notwithstanding Bardoloi's request for Gandhiji's help to save Assam from the Grouping octopus, the latter did not appear to support the Assam leader.[70]

However, Bordoloi did not lose hope and sent two emissaries, Mahendra Mohan Choudhury and Bijoy Chandra Bhagawati, to meet with the Mahatma on 15 December 1946 in Srirampur of Bengal, now in Bangladesh, where he was on a peace mission amidst communal disturbances. Gandhiji told the two emissaries: 'My mind is made up. Assam must not lose its soul. It must uphold it against the whole world. Else I shall say that Assam had only manikins and no men. It is an impertinent question that Bengal should dominate Assam in any way'.[71] It was Gandhiji's support to Assam that had practically changed the discourse, and ultimately, Assam's position was vindicated.

Bordoloi's fifth strategy to fight against the grouping was a resolution from the Assam Assembly. Although the move was resisted by the Muslim League and the European members, it was finally approved.

> Whereas the Assembly after very careful consideration of the statement made by the British Cabinet Delegation and His Excellency the Viceroy on the 16th May 1946 last is of the opinion that the Province of Assam

---

[70] Kakati, 'Gopinath Bardoloi and the Grouping Scheme', 256.

[71] Bhuyan and Barpujari, *Political History of Assam*, 380–81.

has an undoubted claim to have the Constitution framed and settled by own representatives elected to the Constituent Assembly and that it would be detrimental to the interest of Assam to form any Sections of Groups with any other Province of British India for the purpose of setting the Constitution for the Province.[72]

The resolution directed the Assam representatives that 'they shall take part in the meetings of the Constituent Assembly for the purpose of framing the Union Constitution and in all matters relating to the Union Constitution'. It was said that the representatives would not participate in any meetings of the group or section of provinces to settle the constitution for the province of Assam.

There were, however, critics and detractors of Bordoloi in India who believed that he was responsible for the partition of India, as he stubbornly stood against the British Cabinet Mission Plan, finally leading to its rejection.[73] In his book *India Wins Freedom*, Abul Kalam Azad, who was a great protagonist of the Cabinet Plan, did not directly blame Bordoloi but observed that 'Gopinath Bardoloi, Chief Minister of Assam, however persisted in the opposition and submitted a Memorandum to the Congress Working Committee opposing the grouping of Assam with Bengal'. There are sections of writers who believed that perhaps Nehru's position was not well understood by many leaders in Assam and indicated a misplaced interpretation of grouping by Congress leaders in Assam.[74]

Assam Governor's Apprehension That Assam Would Become Muslim Majority

The then Governor of Assam, Andrew Clow, confirmed Gopinath Bordoloi's fears that if Assam were to be lumped with Bengal in Group C, this small province would be left at the mercy of the Bengalis. The Viceroy, Mountbatten, had called for a note from the Assam Governor on the validity of Bordoloi's apprehension. In a confidential note to

---

[72] Assam Legislative Assembly Session, 16 July 1946.

[73] Kakati, 'Gopinath Bardoloi and the Grouping Scheme', 259.

[74] For details, see Barua, 'Nehru, Cabinet Mission and Assam', 263–70.

the Viceroy on 20 April 1947, Andrew Clow informed the latter that in Assam, there were 3.4 million Muslims and 2.6 million tribals and Christians (1941 Census) and said in the note:

> The caste Hindus are apprehensive and not without cause that a Constitution framed for Assam in Group C would place them in a weaker position than they hold at present and perhaps an even weaker position than they deserve, and would have a poor chance at getting success at the next election. ... [T]here is substance in the plea that it is unfair to Assam that its constitution should be framed by a body in which 5 out of 6 members are Bengali. Bardoloi's claim that Assam should not have the Constitution framed by Bengal has consequently had some appeal. But I believe that what he fears is that Assam would get a Constitution framed by the Muslims of Bengal and Assam with the aid of the Scheduled caste men of Bengal.[75]

Thus, there is no doubt that Gopinath Bardoloi had acted in that critical stage of history with exemplary foresight that virtually saved Assam from being included into Bengal.

It will be worthwhile to mention here that, at this critical stage of Assam's destiny, some of the Congress stalwarts like Tayebullah and Fakhruddin Ali Ahmed acted differently from the rest of the Congressmen. When CWC was about to accept the Cabinet Mission plan, Gandhiji's stand and Assam's total opposition came in between. To quote Tayebullah: 'On Assam now depended the whole issue. In the pivotal position, Assam's responsibility was grave and immense. The fate of cabinet mission plan was in the balance'. However, Tayebullah the crusader of Assam's cause and the president of APCC, voted in favour of Congress Cabinet Mission resolution moved by Nehru. Interestingly, Fakhruddin Ali Ahmed remained absent. Tayebullah was the only Assamese who voted for the Cabinet Mission resolution.[76] Annoyed with Tayebullah's role at a critical moment, Bhubaneswar Barua, the district Congress President of Guwahati, refused to meet

---

[75] Sir Andre Clow in his communiqué from 24 December 1946 to 3 May 1947 as cited in Kakati, 'Gopinath Bardoloi and the Grouping Scheme'.

[76] Barooah, *Gopinath Bordoloi: Indian Constitution and Center-Assam Relations*, 494.

him or talk for many days.[77] Interestingly, representatives from Assam like Baidyanath Mukherjee and N. Nichols Roy openly expressed their dissatisfaction with the Congress resolution.[78] They said even amended resolution had not removed Assam's fear and apprehension. A prominent Christian tribal leader of the state, Nichols Roy said

> We know what the policy of the Muslim league is in Assam. Even now the Muslim League in Bengal wants to send thousands upon thousands of immigrants to Assam and take possession of the land of Assam. That is feared by everyone. The people of the Hills are afraid of immigration and say that they will fight it to the last. The people of the plains don't want to be swamped. They don't want Assam, which is a non-Muslim majority province now, to be turned into a Muslim majority province. ... Once we go into the section, we are committed to a wrong principle, we are acceding to the unjust demand of the League.[79]

'We Want Pakistan. We Are Different'

The Congress fought state Assembly election held in February 1946 primarily on the issues of the immediate transfer of power and the protection of Assam's identity in the light of the aggressive Muslim League politics. The Muslim League, on the other hand, fought exclusively on the Pakistan issue. It hardly requires any reiteration that voting took place exclusively on religious lines. In tune with the Congress' stated policy on land protection and resolutions taken at various multiparty conferences, district officials were instructed to start evictions in earnest. Hamid Khan immediately came to the rescue of the immigrants and started to mobilize about 0.1 million volunteers to protect the interest of the evicted immigrants. The Muslim League's mouthpiece *The Assam Herald* started a campaign with the purpose of 'encouraging the encroachers to re-build their houses as soon as evicted'. The Muslim League guards offered resistance in various places to thwart

---

[77] Ibid., 494.

[78] Tayebullah's voting in the crucial AICC resolution was baffling for the Congress people in Assam. He released a press statement that AICC resolution would not affect Assam's interest, which was hardly accepted by anyone. For details, see Bhuyan and Barpujari, *Political History of Assam*, 384–87.

[79] Ibid., 384–85.

the government's attempt to evict unauthorized encroachers. However, the eviction went on in May at various places in Mangaldai and Barpeta despite the resistance. According to government records, the Muslim League constituted a committee to start agitation against the government policy.[80] The position of newspapers also differed as per their political support. The Muslim-supported press described the government's action as 'barbarity' and 'excesses of the Hindu Government'.[81] The *Assam Tribune*, on the other hand, stood by the 'rightful move of the Government to evict the unauthorised encroachers to have the land for future expansion of the indigenous people'.[82]

It was Abdul Matin Chaudhury, a close aide of Jinnah, who had increasingly drawn Jinnah's attention to Assam. Muhammad Ali Jinnah wrote a letter to Chaudhury on 25 March 1945:

I have been impressing upon the Musalmans for the last six years, day in and day out, that the only remedy of most of their troubles lies in their own hands. If the Muslims are organised, consolidated and stand unitedly, I have no doubt that not only such things will not happen, but we will realize all our aspirations. ... You are quite right that in Assam Muslims were dead. ... But while I have said all this I do not want you to despair or become despondent. Our cause is honest and righteous. We may have to go through the sufferings and sacrifices and so organize ourselves. Out of ashes the true followers of Islam will rise with the noble spirit of Islam in Assam that will sweep away the traitors, hirelings and quislings amongst us. Face your opponents with power and organisation which will be irresistible.[83]

Meanwhile, Jinnah's visit to Assam in March/April 1946 galvanized the immigrant's Muslim population of the state. His visit was used to whip up enthusiasm among the Leaguers of Assam so that agitational programme could be undertaken against the policy of eviction of the Congress ministry. Bhasani made appeals to the people for

[80] The committee of action was headed by Bhasani. Other members were (a) Saadulla, (b) Abdul Kasem, (c) Md Saleh, (d) Abdul Bari Chaudhury, (e) Moinul Haq Chaudhury and (f) Badrul Hussain. Archive file-Conf B, File no. C240/46, Political, Assam Sectt.

[81] Dev and Lahiri, *Assam Muslims: Politics and Cohesion*, 141.

[82] *Assam Tribune*, 19 May 1946 as cited in ibid., 141.

[83] Pirzada, *Quaid-e-Azam Jinnah's Correspondence*, 20.

indiscriminate encroachment of professional grazing reserves and wastelands. In a public meeting held in Shillong on 4 March 1946, Jinnah declared:

> We are determined to get Pakistan and Assam is one of the Provinces that we claim in the Pakistan Zone. We want Pakistan. Our history, our heroes, our episodes, our language, our culture, our architecture, our social laws, our jurisprudence, our calendar and our entire social structures are different from those of Hindus. It will be a disaster if we are forced to remain in Akhand Hindustan.[84]

In that meeting, the welcome address said that 'the 40 lakhs Muslims of Assam are peppered to rise up as one under the banner of Pakistan, with blood if need be'.[85] At the end of his Assam tour, the provincial Muslim League met in Gauhati where the sensational 'Spread out Resolution' was passed unanimously with the aid and advice of Jinnah.[86] It stated: 'The landless and evicted persons be advised to spread out and cultivate all surplus cultivable Government wasteland to produce food crop, to save themselves and thousands of others from miseries of the famine, starvation and death'. Jinnah also made a remark that 'if the government does not immediately revise its policy and abandon this persecution, a situation will be created which will not be conducive to the well-being of the people of Assam'.[87]

Hamid Khan Alias Maulana Bhasani's Role: 'Muslims Constitute a Nation'

With the launching of civil disobedience and direct action day,[88] Bhasani's role had become more militant and aggressive. Bhasani, an

---

[84] Report of the proceeding of a public meeting held at the Polo Ground, Shillong on 4 March 1946, in connection with the visit of Jinnah, file No. C-5 (13) (a) 46, 15 (SB).

[85] Ibid., 17.

[86] *Assam Herald*, 13 April 1946.

[87] *Star of India*, 4 May 1946, as cited in Bhuyan and Barpujari, *Political History of Assam*, 279.

[88] Direct action day was observed on 16 August 1946 in different parts of Assam, more specifically in the immigrant-dominated areas.

Islamic ideologue, made frantic attempts to prepare the immigrant Muslims in the state for a sustained fight for their Islamic homeland.

In many meetings, he gave extremely provocative speeches. On 19 October 1944, at about 7:30 pm, a public meeting was held in the Karimganj Town Hall by the local Muslim League in connection with his visit, Bhasani urged:

> We the Muslims who ruled India for more than 700 years, lost independence 200 years ago. We are now sleeping. We have not only lost our intelligence and courage but also have forgotten our social and religious culture. What a severe oppression is going on upon us. If we wish to save ourselves, we the 10,000,000 (ten millions) of Muslims should be united and get ready to sacrifice our lives for the freedom of our country. Ten millions of Muslims should give a slogan that we want to be freed from the shackle of slavery. If necessary, we should sacrifice our lives in the midst of the waves of blood. We shall make the blood flow. Without bloodshed there is no means of obtaining freedom.[89]

Bhasani, on the eve of the direct action day, appealed to the Muslims of Assam to remain vigilant: 'Let do or die be the motto of our life; Let us be prepared for any suffering or sacrifice; Let us be prepared give up our lives if necessary to reach the goal of Pakistan'.[90] In a leaflet entitled 'Achieve Pakistan or Perish', it was declared the Muslims constitute a nation and not a minority and Pakistan was declared to be the 'only demand'. In support of the stand, Bhasani declared[91]:

> Pakistan is our only demand,
> History justifies it,
> Numbers confirm it,
> Justice claims it,
> Destiny demands it,
> Posterity awaits it,
> Plebiscite verdicts it.

[89] Report in connection with 'Direct Action Day' announced by Muslim League, File no. 15, 19, 46, 1946 (Pol.). For this speech, the DC and SP ordered the arrest of Bhasani, which was denied by the Muslim League government.

[90] *Star of India*, 5 August 1946, as cited in Dev and Lahiri, *Assam Muslims: Politics and Cohesion*, 86.

[91] Ibid., 86. The leaflet was named as 'Achieve Pakistan or Perish'; issued by Bhasani, 16 August 1946.

Bhasani encouraged the immigrants to defy all government and administrative obstacles on their way, regardless of the consequences and settle down in the available wasteland areas. He said it was their natural and inherent right, and nobody could snatch their inherent rights to settle. In many cases, he succeeded, and by 6 June 1946, about 160 persons reoccupied their holdings and reconstructed their hovels overnight.[92] The secretary of provincial Muslim League, Mahmud Ali, openly threatened the government that if they did not stop these evictions, immigrants would resort to violent activities and would openly violate the laws framed by the Congress government.[93]

Bhasani and Pakistan Killa

Meanwhile, Bhasani moved to Mankachar where Abdul Kashem, an MLA, had formed East Pakistan Killa, just on the edge of the border ostensibly to provide training to 0.1 million Muslim League workers for the achievement of Pakistan. Muslim immigrants in the Assam valley were encouraged by Abdul Majid Khan and others to resist eviction, and there had been an increased influx into the immigrant areas. Half-hearted attempts were made in the past to evict immigrants Muslims from these areas, but the government this time was resolute to address matter seriously.

The *Assam Tribune*, in a leading article headed 'Eviction Policy', had suggested that if the police were not sufficient, the army may be requested to assist. Meanwhile, there were mixed signals from the Surma Valley. It was stated that if these evictions were started in the Assam valley, the Muslims of the Surma Valley would unquestionably start to cause trouble in the valley. The Hindus of the Surma Valley were frightened and received threatening calls. The leader of the Hindu Mahasabha in Habibganj called a meeting at which it was decided that the Hindus would endeavour, where they were in a majority, to send parties to assist Hindus in places where they were in the minority.[94]

---

[92] Conf. B. File No. C. 247/46, Political, Assam Sectt-political.

[93] *Assam Herald*, 13 April 1946.

[94] Home Department (Mr Porter), D.I.B.U.O.No.SA./688 dt. 12.11.46, Secret Intelligence Bureau, Govt. of India Home Dept., Extract from Fortnightly Report No./46 on the

The communal situation had shown definite signs of improvement through a setback occurred during the visit of Major Khursud Anwar of the All India Muslim National Guard. His speeches were the most inflammatory. He urged the Muslims to raise a national guard capable of making any sacrifice for Pakistan and oppose the Assam government's evictions. He alleged that 70,000 Muslims had been slaughtered in Bihar and said that serious disturbance would continue in India. Muslims should therefore be so armed as to be ready to kill 10 Hindus each in self-defence.[95] Such inflammatory speeches had greatly enlivened the pent-up feelings of immigrant Muslims.

Displacement of the Hindus in Mankachar

The continuous appeal of the Muslim League leaders for a more aggressive stance of Muslim populace yielded favourable results. Many mid-level and ground-level leaders of the Muslim League then had three objectives: (a) Resist government eviction efforts and rehabilitate the immigrants, (b) encourage more immigrants from neighbouring districts to Assam, and (c) To make the last-ditch effort for the realization of the goal of Pakistan. Documents seized by police and intelligence branch abundantly clear up the design and intentions of utilizing guerrilla tactics. To achieve their goals, some *killas* or forts were established. The Assam border at Mankachar became the hub of such activities.[96] Mr Kasem Ali, a Muslim League MLA, was the chief architect of mass mobilization, and he defied operation of an order under Section 144 CrPC. His actions caused great panic, and the entire Hindu population of the town fled to the Garo hills. Gradually, the provincial Muslim League branches at the subdivision level became haywire and self-functional. The immigrants in the Barpeta subdivision attacked police parties on two occasions. Police had to open fire on Friday, 21 March. Nine immigrants were killed, and nine others were wounded.[97] On

political situation in Assam, for the second half of October 1946.

[95] Ibid.

[96] Home Department (Pr Porter) DIBUO No. 3/CA/47-A Dated 11.1.1947, Dy. No 2165/47-Poll(I) Dt. 17.3.47.

[97] D.I.B.U.O. No. 91/DG/47 Dt- 24.03.47.

5 March 1947, Muslims from both provinces of Assam and Bengal numbering more than 20,000 attended a meeting in Mankachar, following the instruction issued by Abdul Hamid Khan, president of the Assam Muslim League. According to reports, all of the team carried *lathis* (cane sticks) '5 cubits long'. Due to continuous intimidation and threatening, on March 10, the whole Hindu population of Mankachar town evacuated to the Garo hills.[98] A series of meetings were held both in Dhubri on 2, 3 and 5 March 1947 and at Barbanda (Purba Pakistan Killa) under the Rowmari police station (PS) (Bengal) near Mankachar Bazar. Muslim National Guards leaders from Bengal and Assam largely attended all those meetings.[99] Fiery speeches were delivered by Maulana Abdul Hamid Khan and Maulvi Abdul Kasim, appealing for the enrolment of large numbers of national guards and raising funds for their training. At another meeting at Barbanda (Pakistan Killa), 'invasion of Assam' was fixed on 10 March (anti-eviction day) when it was announced that the Muslim League flag would be planted on every government building in Mankachar and that Pakistan would be established in Goalpara within a day and Assam within a week.[100] It would be interesting to see how the central government agencies recorded the activities of the Muslim League at Mankachar and Dhubri.

> Meanwhile, at Mankachar the excitement was rising, and the entire Hindu Population had evacuated, mostly into the Garo hills. The Deputy Commissioner, Garo Hills, who happened to pass through Mankachar also reported to the Deputy Commissioner, Goalpara, about the tense situation. About this time, Maulana Abdul Hamid Khan who was at Barbanda (Pakistan Keela) received a telegram from the Muslim Council of action at Nowgong with an imperative demand for his presence. And he, therefore, announced that he was leaving on the 8th to surrender and called upon his follower to carry out their duty as he had instructed. Following morning, very large crowds of *Bhatias* armed with *lathis* gathered on the chur opposite

---

[98] Ibid.

[99] It may be mentioned that the training of Muslim National Guards started in 1944 at the Muslim League meeting at Shiekhaghat, Sylhet (1 October). Arshad Ali was appointed as the Commander-in-Chief of all Assam Muslim League National Guards. In 1946, Badrul Hussain of Kulaura was appointed as *salar-i-suba* or the provincial organiser. See various SB/political files. Conf. B. File No-C. 240/46; 119/46, etc.

[100] HD Dy 2695/47- Poll (I) dt. 03.04.47, Intelligences Bureau, Home Department.

Dhuburi town and other bands at Bhasanichar just outside the town and announced their intention of marching into Dhuburi and rescuing the Maulana form Dhuburi jail. With some difficulty, they were assured that the Maulana had not been arrested and was not confined in the jail, when the crowed on the south bank dispersed.[101]

The security forces of Assam had the toughest time tackling the unruly Muslim League members and around 40,000 people had assembled for the Assam invasion plan on 10 March. Meanwhile, a huge contingent of Assam Rifles with officials and troops from Garo Hills had arrived, and a consensus was arrived for a procession without resorting to violence and arson. Had there not been adequate military preparedness, there would have been many causalities. The action by the Muslim League created ripples in the state and national levels. Rohini Kumar Choudhury raised certain questions for an adequate answer from the Defence Secretary of India in the Assembly.[102] He informed that large numbers of armed people calling themselves 'Muslim national guards' had already penetrated certain parts of Assam such as Barpeta, Lakhimpur and Mangaldai, and that there was a clash between the armed police and these people in the course of which a few members of the armed police were injured. He asked the defence department whether the government was aware that about 25,000 armed Muslim national guards had gathered in the border of Assam and Bengal in the Mymensingh district and that about 2,000 armed Muslim national guards had gathered in the Assam–Tipperah border. He also informed that in Bengal, near a place called Mankachar in the district of Garo Hills, a large number of armed Muslim national guards were kept ready for a showdown. The defence secretary informed the House that the GOC in Eastern Command was fully aware of the situation and could be trusted to make necessary arrangements according to the forces at his disposal.

Maulvi Abdul Kasim, the main architect of the Pakistan Killa scheme in the Dhubri/Mankachar area, wrote an explosive letter to Saadulla:

---

[101] Conf. Home department File no. 119/46 (poll) I.

[102] Home Deptt File no. 119/46-poll-(I)—answer for 7 April 1947.

I, in pursuance of a resolution of the joint committee at Bahadurabad, started this *Killa* in the name of Allah. .... I'm in a position, Allah willing, to send at least ten thousand persons to court arrest from this *Killa* to Barpeta or Mangaldoi at fixed places to occupy wasteland ... I'm very much in favour of guerrilla fight especially in Garo Hills *elaka* and attacks may be made at different border places of Bengal. I'm soon going to that side to ask them to be prepared .... (italics in original)[103]

Role of Saadulla

The Muslim League agitation in connection with the anti-eviction campaign continued to grow, and the situation was now nearing the breaking point. The League, however, was waiting for the league communication from the All-India Council of action to approve the civil disobedience campaign, which was already decided upon by the Assam Muslim League.

Saadulla was not a radical Muslim League activist like Maulana Hamid Khan. He thought that the league might have made a mistake and considered that the proper line for the party to take was to come to a compromise on the question of evictions and then to conduct a campaign against the ministry on the floor of the Assembly. Saadulla made many efforts to come to such a compromise with the government. His latest offer was that those evicted persons who should have been given land under the 1945 agreement should now be given land, but instead of giving them 30 bighas, 15 bighas should be given and the land thus saved should be given to other evicted families for whom land, under the agreement, had to be provided. If the government would agree to this, the league would then call off the civil disobedience movement and as a party would make no further demands for land for immigrants.[104]

The communal situation in Assam had further deteriorated with the firing in the Barpeta subdivision. Meanwhile, the Muslim League officially announced the civil disobedience movement which it had

[103] Intercepted Letter by Abdul Kasim to Saadulla, 24 March 1947, Home Deptt file no-119/47-poll-(I).

[104] D.I.B.U.O. No. 91/DG/47, dated 23.4.1947.

been threatening for quite some time, although both Premier Bordoloi and league leader Saadulla tried to avoid it. Constant discussions were taking place ever since the Assam Assembly met and the League walked out. It seems generally to be accepted that the decision to launch a civil disobedience movement was made much against the wishes of Saadulla, and the Assam valley Muslims and the Hindu press had gone so far as to suggest that there was a serious split in the party ranks. It was announced that the movement would be non-violent and be directed against evictions of immigrants and the new maintenance of public order act.

There was reason to believe that the movements and other forms of agitations were being worked out by outsiders. A series of secret meetings were held to determine the lines of direct action. Maulana Abdul Hamid Khan was reported to have paid a special visit to Tengail (Mymensingh) to give immigration a fillip and to establish further help to Assam. Meanwhile, Bhasani instructed all the MLAs to defy Section 144 CrPC and decided to launch a civil disobedience movement without authorization from top-ranking Muslim League leaders. Bhasani inaugurated the movement on 10 March in Darrang in consonance with the 'Assam Day' appeal. The civil disobedience movement was observed in various places of Assam valley, and 'Assam Day' was observed with frequent processions, generating considerable tension and clashes at several places. Bordoloi sent SOS to Delhi for immediate help with security forces and the army. The Home Minister was deeply concerned about the Assam situation and remarked: 'There is a definite attempt to on the part of the League both in Assam and in Bengal to compel the government of Assam by force to yield to the League's unlawful demand on the question of eviction of trespassers from the government reserves ...'[105]

Bordoloi's Counter to Muslim League's Propaganda

Meanwhile, Gopinath Bordoloi set in motion a nationwide campaign about the legality and desirability of his eviction policy. He urged

---

[105] Patel to Baldev Singh, 20 March 1947, 11, referred in Dev and Lahiri, *Assam Muslims: Politics and Cohesion*, 98.

that Assam would welcome any closure on the land question that was consistent with the government's policy of economic and planned settlement of lands, provided the encroachers leave the land and allow the government to pursue their policy unhampered by unruly action.[106] He specifically addressed to the General Secretary of the Assam Muslim Association of Calcutta. This organization had recently adopted a resolution, criticizing the Assam government's eviction policy. A copy of the resolution was forwarded to Bordoloi. He said that the resolution was based on a complete misunderstanding of the situation. He pleaded:

> I desire to point out that the government is not pursuing any new policy about only putting into effect the resolution determined by the last Muslim League Ministry. Hence the preposterous claim for allowing Muslim immigrants in grazing reserves which destroy the wellbeing of cattle-keepers and on grounds kept for planning settlement cannot but be an unjust demand for illegal occupation. We deeply regret that this disorder should be encouraged by Muslim League propaganda. I should also inform you that some of the immigrants already settled down here are occupying hundreds *Bighas* of lands individually in unauthorized places employing a large number of imported landless immigrants as their labourers, holding out the hope that they will be given lands at somewhere. The result of these unlawful encroachments on lands, reserved by government for grazing for the Common benefit of all has been to drive away from all reserves innocent graziers and people of the soil from their lawful occupation.[107]

Bordoloi further argued that in many places, these forcible occupations had been accompanied by regular violence on men and cattle. Such a situation could never be allowed to prevail by any responsible government. If these unlawful persons removed themselves from their unlawful possession and left the government without any obstruction to carry out a peaceful and planned settlement of lands, there would have been no question of eviction, and the use of force by the government to preserve law and order would have been unnecessary.

---

[106] *Hindustan Times*, November 15, 1946, 'No Unlawful Settlement of Land in Assam'.
[107] Ibid.

Lawful Settlement to Prevail

In his writings in the paper, Bordoloi was resolute in saying that lawful and legal settlement should prevail in the place of illegal aggression. If the Muslim League people hoped for a peaceful solution of the problem, they would surely have allowed the government to do so and use their influence to carry forward the settlement peacefully. Instead, hundreds of immigrants were being sent from Bengal to Assam every day, making an already complicated situation more complex. The government, therefore, had no option but take the steps to preserve peace and tranquillity of land. He stated:

> I should like to tell you that my government is not Fascist as you have alleged but always wants to be guided as it has been guided by an earnest desire to do things in consultation and in agreement by counsels of reasons and persuasion. It is only when these fall that they may have no occasion to take recourse to the use of minimum force that is necessary to maintain law and order'.[108]

Many other national papers had highlighted the predicament faced by a small province like Assam. The *Statesman*, in one of its segments, narrated Assam's experience in detail.[109] The paper said

> Assuming serious proportions on account of the large influx of immigrants during the 1942–45 periods the position is causing the Government much anxiety .... Besides encroaching on grazing reserves which are protected lands fresh hordes of immigrants are reported to have committed various other acts of lawlessness creating tension among the indigenous population. According to reports at provincial HQ, about 300 immigrants armed with *lathis* and other weapons attacked professionals' graziers on 9 November at a place in Gauhati subdivision. Seven men were injured. Five buffaloes were killed and several others maimed. The attackers looted property of the grazers and also took away a number of buffaloes. Four men were arrested. Attempts were also made recently at a number of villagers in Mangaldai subdivision to terrorize the permanent inhabitants ....

---

[108] Ibid.

[109] *The Statesman,* 'Influx of Immigrants Becoming Serious'.

The paper estimated the number of immigrants to be more than a million, concentrated mostly in Kamrup, Darrang, Nowgong and Sibsagar districts forcibly occupying grazing reserves wastelands and lands owned by the indigenous people. The paper revealed that the majority of those people were recent encroachers, and in many cases, the houses they lived in were skeletons of sheds designed to show possession rather than serve as dwellings.[110]

It should be mentioned here that the Muslim immigrants alone were not the target of administrative action concerning eviction which was given a communal colour for political purposes by the League. Out of a total of 2,886 encroachers involved in the first round of evictions from 9 selected reserves, as many as 293 persons were non-Muslims apart from 672 protected encroachers. Many such non-Muslim encroachers were also notified in subsequent evictions.[111] Various organizations and parties also endorsed the Congress stand on the eviction. The Assam Provincial Jamiat-ul-Ulema extended full support on 19 November 1946. The All Assam Cachari Association followed suit. The Congress Socialist Party similarly decided to stand by the government.[112]

Bibliography

Ahmed, Rafiuddin. *The Bengal Muslims, 1871–1906: A Quest for Identity*. Delhi: Oxford University Press, 1981.

Asamiya, 25 May 1946.

——, 4 August 1945.

Asamiya, various issues from 8 April till 25 June 1946.

[110] Some of the illegal occupants were described as follows: In the Barpeta subdivision, there were 4,000 immigrants families who settled in Pakabetbari, Theka, Koimari, Mandia, Gobindapur, Fulara, Menisimla and Khela reserves; in Mangaldai subdivision, 989 families were scattered in Bagpuri, Kharparik, Hatipari and Missamari reserves; and in Gauhati subdivision, over 600 families were occupying reserves in Bhanganmari, Pukripar, Malbari and Mekali. In addition, another 1,100 families were there in the Gedarimari area.

[111] *Assam Tribune*, 16 December 1946; *Hindustan Standard*, 17 December 1946; *Star of India* (Calcutta), 18 December 1946.

[112] For details, see *Morning News*, 24 November 1946; *Assam Tribune*, 20 November 1946; *Assam Tribune*, 22 November 1946; and *Assam Tribune*, 23 November 1946.

Assam Herald, 13 April 1946.

———, 13 April 1946.

Assam Tribune, 16 December 1946.

———, 19 May 1946.

———, 20 November 1946.

———, 22 November 1946.

———, 23 November 1946.

Barooah, Nirode K. *Gopinath Bordoloi: Indian Constitution and Center-Assam Relations*. Assam: Publication Board of Assam, 1990.

Baruah, Sarveswar. *Assam Legislative Assembly Proceedings*. Vol. 1, No. 4, 6 March 1945.

———. *Assembly Debates*, 6 March 1945.

Barua, Bhaben. 'Nehru, Cabinet Mission and Assam'. In *Nationalist Upsurge in Assam*, edited by Arun Bhuyan, 261–70. Guwahati: Government of Assam, 2000.

Baruah, Nirode. *Gopinath Bordoloi: The Assam Problem and Nehru's Centre*. Guwahati: Bhabani Press, 2010.

Bhuyan, A. C., and S. K. Barpujari (eds.). *Political History of Assam*, vol. III. Guwahati: Government of Assam, 1980.

Choudhury, Mahendra Mohan. *Assembly Debates*. 16 March 1946.

Das, Beliram. *Assembly Debates*. 15 March 1946.

Dev, Bimal J., and Dilip Kumar Lahiri. *Assam Muslims: Politics and Cohesion*. Delhi: Mittal Publications, 1985.

Guha, Amalendu. *Planter Raj to Swaraj: Freedom Struggle & Electoral Politics in Assam*. New York: Columbia University Press, 2014.

Hindustan Standard, 17 December 1946.

Hindustan Times, 15 November 1946.

———, November 15, 1946. 'No Unlawful Settlement of Land in Assam: Bardoloi's Reply to Critics of Eviction Policy'. Home Department file no 119/46-poll(i).

Kar, M. *Muslims in Assam Politics*. Delhi: Vikash Publishing House, 1990.

Mahanta, Nani Gopal. *Confronting the State: ULFA's Quest for Sovereignty*. New Delhi: SAGE Publications, 2013.

Morning News, 24 November 1946.

Kakati, Satis C. 'Gopinath Bardoloi and the Grouping Scheme'. In *Nationalist Upsurge in Assam*, edited by Arun Bhuyan. Guwahati: Government of Assam, 2000.

Kalita, Ramesh C. 'Prabajankarir Samasya Aru Asom: Anandaram Dhekiyal Phukanar Para Gopinath Bardaloi Loike'. In *Asom Andolan: Pratisruti Aru Phalasruti*, edited by Hiren Gohain and Dilip Bora. Guwahati: Banalata Publications, 2001.

Pakistan Geotagging. *Muslim Population of India: According to the Censuses of 1941 and 2001*. 28 December 2014. http://pakgeotagging.blogspot.com/2014/12/muslim-population-of-india-according-to.html (accessed 20 May 2020).

Pathak, Suryasikha. 'Tribal Politics in the Assam: 1933–1947'. *Economic & Political Weekly* 45 (6–12 March 2010): 61–69.

Pirzada, Syed Sharifuddin. (ed.). *Quaid-e-Azam Jinnah's Correspondence*. New Delhi: Metropolitan Book Company, 1981.

Prasad, Rajendra. *Autobiography*. Bombay: Asia Publishing House, 1957.

Saadulla, Syed. *Assam Legislative Assembly*. 1 December 1941.

Sharma, Siddhi Nath. *Assam Legislative Assembly*. 4 December 1941.

Star of India (Calcutta), 18 December 1946.

Star of India, 5 August 1946. In *Assam Muslims: Politics and Cohesion*, edited by Bimal J. Dev and Dilip Kumar Lahiri. New Delhi: Mittal Publications, 1985.

Teenidiniya Asamiya, Guwahati, 21 January 1941.

The Statesman, 'Influx of Immigrants Becoming Serious'. 27 November 1946.

Vivekananda Kendra Institute of Culture. *Aspects of Land Policy in Assam: Continuity and Change*. Guwahati: VKIC, 2016.

NRC

Quagmire of Competing Claims

As India moved from pre-independence to post-independence phase, Assam's politics could hardly divorce itself from the continuity of colonial history. Questions of land, immigration and citizenship continued to remain as the central variables of Assamese identity. The previous chapters of this book have clearly shown how unchecked immigration from East Bengal was attempted to use to bring a structural change into the composition of Assamese nationality to the extent of annexing the whole province to East Pakistan. The Muslim League had already claimed Assam as the Muslim-dominant state in the Muslim League annual sessions. Assam did not want continuity of similar influx of population in the post-independence period; at the same time, Assam could not behove itself from bearing the burden of partition, that is, the Hindu Bengalis who came to various parts of India, including Assam, as displaced or refugee people. However, the entire process of immigration and refugees was a conundrum of complex dynamics. A certain section of refugees was granted citizenship status by various citizenship laws in the subsequent period. To deal with the continued immigration and to keep a check on the immigrants, the Indian state, along with other paraphernalia, adopted a new mechanism called the National Register of Citizens (NRC).

What is National Register of Citizens?

The National Register of Citizens is a register that contains the names of Indian citizens, and originally, this was prepared only for Assam in 1951 by including those names which appeared in the census of 1951. The Assam-specific NRC was updated only recently under the direct supervision of the Supreme Court under the Citizenship Act of 1955 and Citizenship Rules, 2003. The updating process started in 2015 and over 1.9 million applicants failed to make it to the final NRC list released in 2019.

This chapter tries to look at the issue of citizenship in India in general and Assam in particular, from a historical perspective. To do so, first, it is important to understand how the notion of citizenship is understood in the state-formation and nation-building process. Second, from a conceptual framework, it is imperative to look at the constitutional level concerning how the notion of citizenship is conceptualized and how the issue was debated in the Constituent Assembly. Third, it is also equally important to see how the issue of granting citizenship to certain categories of people was discussed and debated in the parliament, and how a legal framework was developed at the institutional level. The rationale or idea underlying the executive decisions for implementing and granting citizenship rights to certain groups of people and not to the entire bunch of people also needs scrutiny.

Conceptual Framework on Citizenship: Marshall, Roger Brubaker and Subrata Mitra

Essentially, there are three ways of looking at the notion of citizenship in the context of immigration and identity. The first one may be called as the notion of 'national citizenship', the second one 'post-national citizenship' and the third perspective is 'multi-cultural citizenship'.[1]

According to Angus Stewart, national citizenship is state-centred; it involves the identification of citizenship with the elaboration of a distinctive, formal and legal status. It is also inherently related to the emergence of nation-states and their diverse lineages.[2] The most notable contributor in the field of national citizenship discourse is Roger

[1] Joppke, *Citizenship and Immigration*, 23–29.

[2] Stewart, 'Two Conceptions of Citizenship', 63–78.

Brubaker. His book *Citizenship and Nationhood in France and Germany* (1992) is considered to be a ground-breaking work in this regard.[3]

Brubaker brings forward the following aspects for the first time into the study of citizenship: (a) the formal delimitation of the citizenry; (b) the establishment of civil equality, entailing shared rights and shared obligations; (c) the institutionalization of political rights; the legal rationalization and ideological accentuation of the distinction between citizens and foreigners; (d) the articulation of the doctrine of national sovereignty and the link between citizenship and nationhood.[4]

Another scholar who made a seminal contribution to the field of citizenship is T. H. Marshall. He defines citizenship as a status bestowed on those who are full members of the community. Those who possess citizenship enjoy equal status concerning the rights and duties, although there are no universal principles that determine what those rights and duties shall be. Under Marshall's analysis, citizenship contains civil, political and social rights.

> Citizenship is a status bestowed on those who are full members of the community. All who possess the status are equal with respect to the rights and duties with which the status is endowed. There is no universal principle that determines what those rights and duties shall be, but societies in which citizenship is a developing institution create an image of an ideal citizenship against which achievement can be measured and towards which aspiration can be directed.[5]

Marshall's other important characteristics of citizenship are:

1. Citizenship entails a particular kind of social bond involving a direct sense of community membership.
2. Such membership is based on loyalty to a civilization which is a common possession.

---

[3] Brubaker, *Citizenship and Nationhood in France and Germany*.

[4] Ibid., 35.

[5] Marshall, 'Citizenship and Social Class', 87.

3. It is a loyalty of free men endowed with rights and protected by a common law. Its growth is stimulated both by the struggle to win those rights and by their enjoyment when won.

To quote him:

> [A] direct sense of community membership based on loyalty to a civilisation which is a common possession. It is a loyalty of free men endowed with rights and protected by a common law. Its growth is stimulated both by the struggle to win those rights and by their enjoyment when won.[6]

Although Marshall's analysis has immense significance in the study of citizenship, his notion of citizenship is not much helpful in the context of present challenges of immigration and state control. Christian Joppke argues:

> Marshall's concept of citizenship, with its internal focus on rights and inclusion, is an unhelpful point of entry to the topic of this book— immigration and its implications for citizenship because, from the vantage point of immigration, the world is at first divided into sharply bounded citizenries, each protected on the outside by a state and its intrinsically exclusive immigration and citizenship policies. With respect to immigration, citizenship functions above all as a device of external exclusion, and one that is far more robust and immune to the charge of 'discrimination' than the intra-societal exclusions addressed by Marshall and most post-war students of citizenship.[7]

In contrast, Brubaker makes two important contributions to the study of citizenship—first, contrary to the traditional understanding of the state as a corporate and territorial organization, the modern state is presented as a membership organization with the centrality of citizenship as a unitary membership category. This is an effective way of linking to the process of nations and nationalism.[8] Brubaker's second contribution is the idea that the politics of citizenship should

---

[6] Ibid., 96.

[7] Joppke, *Citizenship and Immigration*, 23–24.

[8] Joppke, 'Citizenship and Nationhood in France and Germany', 168–78.

be conceived as a politics of identity, not a politics of interest. Joppke further argues:

> Borrowing Max Weber's concept of social closure, Brubaker conceives of citizenship as an 'international filing system, a mechanism for allocating persons to states'. In the context of sociology, this was doubly innovative, as it entailed a new, post-Marshallian vista on citizenship, but also, more generally, a new vista on the state.[9]

We are leaving out other forms of citizenship discourse as enunciated by post-national citizenship scholars and multicultural membership scholars,[10] mainly because our purpose here is not to provide a theoretical debate on the contemporary citizenship discourse but to contextualize a conceptual framework in the context of our study of citizenship as it unfolds in India in general and Assam in particular. We believe that so far as citizenship issue is concerned, the Indian Constitution and the legal institutional framework provide a unique fusion of accommodation of various approaches, and it would be wrong to dub it as exclusively statist, post-nationalist or multiculturalist. Theoretical discourses on citizenship in the global–national context are not very helpful in understanding the citizenship dilemma in smaller states like Assam where the entire edifice of identity is based on citizen–immigrant distinction. Scholars who have been writing on immigration in the region have expressed reservations that current theoretical literature is not sufficient to understand the citizenship context of Assam.[11]

Nonetheless, some interpretations could provide a broad framework for analysis. Here, it would be pertinent to look at the citizenship debate as enunciated by Subrata Mitra in the Indian context.

---

[9] Joppke, *Citizenship and Immigration*, 24.

[10] For details of post-national category of citizenship, please see, Soysal, *Limits of Citizenship*; Hammar, *Democracy and the Nation State*. For multicultural citizenship, please see Kymlicka, *Multicultural Citizenship*.

[11] Baruah, 'The Partition's Long Shadow', 593–606; and Sadique, *Paper Citizens: How Illegal Immigrants Acquire Citizenship in Developing Countries*: 31.

Subrata Mitra points out three analytical strands of citizenship in India.[12] The first two strands—evolution and involution—conceptualize citizenship in terms that are indigenous and uniquely accessible to India's society and history. The first approach holds citizenship to be a seamless flow and essential to this is the continuous mythical–historical existence of India, that is, 'Bharat' which is ensured by the first article of the Indian Constitution: 'India that is Bharat shall be Union of States'. The Hindutva notion of citizenship largely draws inspiration from such a notion of citizenship. According to Mitra, the involution approach puts the onus of citizenship on ethnicity and accounts for 'different strands of citizenship in terms of the moral communities that underpin them'. The third approach of 'rational construction' holds the creation of *nagariks* (citizens) as the main task of the state which goes on to devise the legislative method to fulfil this goal. The third approach focuses on ontological depth, the institutional stretch of citizenship, impact of colonial rule and empirical measurement of citizenship in India.

The citizenship issue in Assam or India cannot be seen in isolation in terms of certain esoteric cosmopolitan values without connecting to the context under which the concept has been evolving. The rise of citizenship issue has been greatly influenced by the historical process of immigration into Assam at the behest of the Muslim League, land encroachments, vote-bank politics and marginalization of ethnic and indigenous groups. As Mitra argues

> [T]he citizen has been the interface of the State and society, the fulcrum around which battles for nation-building and nation-wrecking have raged .... [T]he imperative has come from above in the form of juridical empowerment and from below, as a consequence of constitutional empowerment, enfranchisement and entitlement, in the shape of struggle for living space, dignity, livelihood and equality'.[13]

In other words, it can be argued that citizenship issues in Assam are a reflection of concerns over territory and border, ethnic versus

---

[12] For details, see Mitra, 'Citizenship in India: Evolution, Involution & Rational Construction'.

[13] Ibid., 162.

immigrant rights and competition over electoral resources. The question of territoriality and ethnic distinctiveness of the Northeast region in general and Assam, in particular, has considerable significance.

As Mitra argues, three general approaches—evolution, involution and rational construction—underpin the discourse of citizenship of India. Evolutionists see citizenship as an essential part of Indian civilization and heritage which connects India to her past as well as her future, a point which was also highlighted by T. H. Marshall ('a direct sense of community membership based on loyalty to a civilisation which is a common possession'[14]). For this school of thought, Indian citizenship and territory are overlapping categories, which may be compared to the notion of *jus soli* (right of soil) of the European discourse.[15] Involution, that is, ethnic construction of citizenship, resembles the *jus sanguinis* (right of blood), another European line of thinking. Mitra calls the strategy of citizen-making as the rational construction of citizenship based on the principles of the Constitution adopted in 1950.

Making and Unmaking of Citizens: National Register of Citizens and the Dilemma of Assamese Nationality

Ever since the publication of NRC and CAA, Assam has become the epicentre of citizenship debate.[16] The first draft of NRC in Assam has identified 28,983,677 as valid citizens of India in Assam and a total number of 4,007,707 applicants could not make it to the first draft. The excluded people's number came down to over 1.9 million in the final list of the NRC—a Supreme Court-monitored exercise that took about five years to complete. National and global media sharply reacted about the exclusion of over 4 million names of residents from the draft NRC. The process has been decried as another act of communalization of citizenship issue at the behest of RSS and BJP.

---

[16] The year 2019 is a very significant year from the point of citizenship discourse. The year witnessed the publication of the final draft of the National Register of Citizens (NRC) in Assam on 31 August, and on 10 December 2019 Citizenship Amendment Act (CAA-2019) was passed in the parliament.

Not only Assam, but the entire country got agitated over NRC and CAA—the main accusation being that both of them have become BJP's main Hindutva plan to polarize the nation. The debate over NRC has been mired by a lopsided disposition and subjective understanding, without looking into the objective situation that brought out such a registration exercise way back in 1951. Most of the commentaries are based on a profound ignorance about the state and its pre- and post-colonial history. Some of the ill-informed arguments against NRC are: (a) The Assamese people are intolerant and communal. (b) NRC, BJP and RSS are synonyms. (c) Is India creating its own 'Rohingya' in Assam? (d) The NRC process is anti-Bengali and anti-Muslim. (e) The entire exercise is xenophobic and dangerously nativist.[17] In other words, Assam becomes another pawn in the latest debate between secularism and communalism. A majority of these writings have focussed only on the Hindu–Muslim and Bengali–Assamese linguistic dimensions of the current debate on NRC. However, the issue cannot be seen from the binary prisms of religious and linguistic dimensions. It has a strong history based on which the Assamese composite identity has been framed.

The massive demographic change due to the unchecked inflow of immigrants to Assam posed a serious challenge to the distinctive ethnic-indigenous character of the Assamese people. Certain procedural lapses of exclusion of genuine citizenry notwithstanding, the final NRC list is not discriminatory on any primordial considerations, be it religious or linguistic. At a time when the otherwise conflict-ridden heterogeneous civil society like Assam has shown great maturity in addressing the issue, the outside politicians and illustrators are still groaning why the prophetic doomsday of civil war has not arrived in the state.

---

[17] A few of such critical interpretations are Mohan, 'NRC: No Clarity on What Awaits the 40 Lakh People Excluded from Assam's Citizen Register', www.huffingtonpost.in (accessed 15 August 2018); Dutta, 'The National Register of Citizens and the Politics of Exclusion and Hate', www.thecitizens.in (accessed 15 August 2018); Bal, 'East India Creating its own Rohingya', www.nytimes.com (accessed 15 August 2018); Bhagat, 'Being Human in Assam', http://blogs.timesofindia.indiatimes.com (accessed 15 August 2018).

The formulation and implementation of NRC at the behest of the Supreme Court was the culmination of a historical process of demographic change that began in the 1930s, mainly at the initiative of the Muslim League governments in Assam. We believe that the debate about immigration and citizenship is about the debate of nationhood—about what it means, or what it ought to mean to belong to nationhood. The nation-state is understood as a distinctive way of characterizing and evaluating political and social membership. The nation-state is associated with certain attributes—sovereignty, territoriality, population and government. From this perspective, certain groups of people belong to the regime of citizenship and not others.

In contrast to a viewpoint of branding NRC as a tool of Hinduization of a smaller nationality at the behest of BJP and RSS, this chapter tries to look at the historical context under which NRC has been evolving. Who are the actors involved in the process of conceptualization, evolution, articulation and implementation of the NRC? Assam has adopted one of the most flexible accommodative approaches to the issue of inclusive citizenship. The cut-off date of 24 March 1971 for granting citizenship, the inclusion of a huge chunk of foreigners from 1966 to 1971 through a legal and political process and amendment of citizenship laws till 2004 are some of the testimonials of such an accommodative character. This process of accommodation shows how Assam's citizenship discourse is inclusive and not exclusive; no other states in India have legally borne such a huge number of immigrants. The cut-off date for a person to be declared as a foreigner for all other states in India was 19 July 1948, and in case of Assam, it was 24 March 1971. Assam took the burden of accommodating foreigners for additional 23 years, from 1948 to 1971, unlike any other state. Incidentally, Assam witnessed the highest number of refugees and immigrants from across the border in those years.

Immigration and Muslim League

The issue of identity crisis becomes predominant when the basic character of a smaller nationality has been jeopardized by the massive growth of the immigrant population. This is exactly what has happened to Assam for which the demand for the detection of illegal migrants through the NRC becomes more pronounced. If one tries to understand the history of NRC, one has to go back to the history of how the Assamese nationality was gradually dominated by the excessive immigration from East Bengal. We have already dealt with those issues in the previous chapters. I have argued elsewhere that the search for a cohesive Assamese identity went along with the search for a pan-Indian nationalism.[18] The first fight was against the domination of the Bengalis by persuading the British to accept the Assamese language as the state language. Along with pan-Indian nationalism, there was a strong move to assert Assamese distinctiveness or nationality against incessant immigration and the Muslim League's effort to transform Assam into a Muslim-dominated society. The Assam Association, established in 1903, served as the platform for the Assamese middle class to articulate their grievances.[19] The first student organization of the state called Assam Chatra Sanmilan established in 1916 and the Assam Sahitya Sabha established in 1917 acted as the catalysts for the mobilization of a nascent Assamese identity.[20] The Bengalis had overshadowed the Assamese both in numbers and representation in government services, profession and business.[21] In the 1920s, the Assamese middle class became highly apprehensive of the continuous immigration of East Bengal people. The most worrying factor for the middle class was the 'immigrants would in due course, further tilt the provinces' demographic, cultural and political balance in favour of the Bengalis'.[22]

The Muslim population in the Brahmaputra valley was 365,540 in 1911, which rose to 594,981 in 1921, and the demographic balance skewed in favour of the Muslims with the abnormal rise of their proportion from 9 per cent in 1921 to 19 per cent in 1931, and then 3 per cent in 1941. In Barpeta subdivision alone, the proportion of

---

[18] Mahanta, *Confronting the State: ULFA's Quest for Sovereignty*, 5–6.

[19] Dutta, *Landmarks of the Freedom Struggle in Assam*, 45.

[20] Barua, *Mor Sowarani*, 217–18.

[21] The Assamese were 23 per cent, and the Bengalis were 42 per cent as per the census of 1931.

[22] Guha, 'Nationalism: Pan-Indian and Regional in a Historical Perspective', 91.

Muslims shot up from 0.1 per cent in 1911 to 49 per cent in 1941.[23] The number of immigrants in the Kamrup district rose from 44,000 in 1921 to 134,000 in 1931, becoming the highest recorded district in the Brahmaputra valley. In one decade (1921–1931), in a particular mauza (cluster of villages created for revenue collection) of Barpeta subdivision, the population increased by 150 per cent, while the Pub- and Pachim-Chamariya mauzas of Gauhati subdivision registered an increase of 142 and 168 per cent, respectively. According to an official report, five mauzas of Nowgong, namely Laukhowa, Dhing, Bokoni, Lahorighat and Juria recorded an increase varying from 100 per cent to 294 per cent.[24]

Various Muslim League conferences, in clear terms, had referred to their plan to include Assam in the future Pakistan. In fact, the provincial election held in the early part of 1946 was primarily fought on the issue of Pakistan. The Pakistan demand and the possibility of annexing Assam had inspired the Muslim League provincial leaguers. In the session, Saadulla declared:

> The Pakistan Scheme demands that in order to avoid conflict between the Hindus and the Muslims they should live separately and establish separate States. What objection can there be against this proposition? The Congress and the Hindu Mahasabha should not object to the Muslims wanting to live as a separate entity for their own advancement. If the Muslims be in majority in Assam then Bengal and Assam can form one Pakistan State and Punjab, N.W.F.P. and Sind can form Pakistan State. It may be noted that the Lahore resolution of 23 March, 1940 did not clearly define and demarcate the limits of Pakistan provinces and consequently a great debate followed on the interpretation regarding the territorial composition of the dream land of Pakistan and even 'the League hesitated for sometime before making authoritative pronouncements on how it considered the boundaries of Pakistan should run'.[25]

Although Saadulla was not a fanatical propagandist of Pakistan like Maulana Bhasani, he was complicit in the whole plan and he directly or indirectly advocated the cause of Pakistan in Assam on many

---

[23] Report of the line system committee, submitted on 3rd February, 1938, p. 27. Accessed through archival record, Government of Assam.

[24] Ibid., 29.

[25] Dev and Lahiri, *Assam Muslim*, 71.

occasions. In Saadulla's presence, the secretary of Assam Islam Mission said:

> But I sincerely believe that this Islam mission ... can do openly, peacefully and lawfully what others of our Muslim organisations cannot do in a similar way. The Islam mission can turn a minority, in course of a few years, into an overwhelming majority and solve the baffling problem of Assam politics today—I mean notorious Line system.[26]

By 1945, Sayed Saadulla—the Premier of Assam and the most moderate face of the Muslim League and an indigenous Muslim by himself—openly advocated the cause of Pakistan when he said 'Pakistan is nothing but the administration of a country on principles enjoined in the Holy Quoran. There cannot therefore be any Muslims who will not support Pakistan'.[27]

Muslim League Politics: Explosion of Immigrant Population, Land Rights, Islam and Pakistan

What the Muslim League did in Assam was a unique blend of the four strands of communal politics. First, due to various push and pull factors, there was huge immigration (90% of whom were Muslims) resulting in a major demographic change in the province. Previous chapters have already depicted how the population had changed in three decades. On the basis of such growth in the Muslim population, the Muslim League dared to imagine Assam as a part of 'Muslim' Pakistan. Second, with the growing numbers of the hard-working immigrant population, what they wanted was land through allotment, squatting and encroachment. Third, political Islam was the main vehicle for the mobilization of illiterate immigrants who believed in the bigotry mobilization by the religious mullahs like Maulana Bhasani. Fourth, the attainment of Pakistan and the inclusion of Assam was the ultimate political goal for the Muslim League leaders in the state. These factors require further elaboration to understand the context under which

[26] Shillong, 10 March 1940, referred in Kar, *Muslims in Assam Politics*, 312.

[27] *Janashakti*, 31 October 1945, referred in Kar, *Muslims in Assam Politics*, 313.

the demand for NRC as a shield for the indigenous people evolved in Assam immediately after India secured freedom from colonial rule.

As the demand for Pakistan had already surfaced, one of the important ways to project Assam as 'non-Hindu'-dominant state was the census. The way in which census data of 1941 was manipulated, the Hindus would have become a minority by 1951. The comment made by the prominent historian H. K. Borpujari is significant in this respect.

> The Assamese Hindus feared that Assam would be converted into a Muslim immigrant's province. This was confirmed by Saadulla's subsequent instruction to the census superintendent that in the census of 1941 the population should be classified on the basis of community and not religion ... resulting obviously reduction in the number of Hindus.[28]

According to a projection, the result was that Hindus had a very thin majority of only 443,929 persons in 1941.[29] Bearing in mind the rates of immigration and population growth among the immigrants, Assam would have become a Muslim-dominated state in 10 to 15 years.[30]However, the cartographical changes in 1947 had halted the process. The issue of census manipulation was also raised in the Assembly by Beliram Das.

> The propagandists of Eastern Pakistan demand inclusion of Assam in the Eastern zone of Pakistan, inter alia, on the grounds that Assam is within the zone where Muslims are in a majority and that the majority of the non-Muslims in Assam are Tribal people, basing their arguments on wrong figures and mis-statement of facts, supplied to them by that immigrant ridden League Ministry of Assam. In the census of 1941 the tea garden labourers have been shown as Tribals. But according to previous census nearly 14 lakhs of such labourers were shown as Hindus. It is also a well-known fact that the bulk of the Tribal population are Hindus. As such it

---

[28] Barpujari, *North-East India: Problems, Policies*, 37–38.

[29] Kar, *Muslims in Assam Politics*, 78.

[30] For details, see *Assam Tribune*, 10 October 1941. In an editorial on 31 January 1941, the newspaper appealed to the people to thwart the designs of the Muslim League. The Congress under the leadership of Gopinath Bordoloi also demanded the rejection of the 1941 census.

was a folly on the part of the League Ministry to enumerate the labourers as Tribals to reduce the number of Hindu Population.[31]

Land Grabbed by the Immigrants in the Brahmaputra Valley[32]

Table 3.1 depicts how immigrants were settled from 1916 to 1925–1926. It was stated in the Assembly that under the 'grow more food' campaign alone, 160,000 bighas of land were de-reserved for settlement of the immigrants.[33] According to an estimate, till 1945, 622,427 bighas of land were allotted to the immigrants.[34] It was alleged in the Assam Assembly that within a period of five or six years, during the

Table 3.1 Land Grabbed by the Immigrants in the Brahmaputra Valley

Subdivisions or Districts	Total Area Settled with Immigrants During the Last 10 Years (in Acres)	Total Area Settled with Indigenous Inhabitants for the Same Period (in Acres)	Total Area Now Available for Settlement (in Acres)	Remarks
Dhubri	15,382	46,131	46,303	From 1916 –1917 to 1925– 1926
Goalpara	Nil	Nil	Nil	
Barpeta	42,089	68,084	135,877	
Gauhati	12,878	52,012	272,731	
Mangaldai	15,260	160,061	427,580	
Tezpur	5,936	154,944	64,657	
North Lakhimpur	405	16,980	478,470	
Nowgong	79,057	68,904	1,756,333	

Source: Assam Secretariat File Rev. B, September 1928, Nos 1810 to 1860, p. 50.

[31] Das, *Assembly Debate*.

[32] Assam Secretariat File Rev. B, Nos.1810 to 1860, September 1928, 50.

[33] Assembly Debates, 14 March 1946.

[34] Kar, *Muslims in Assam Politics*, 78.

first and second Muslim League governments, the League ministry settled 0.5 million bighas of land with the immigrants.[35]

The indigenous Assamese Congress leaders fought with the Muslim League leaders on the issues of land settlement, immigration and inclusion of Assam in Pakistan. No amount of land could satisfy the immigrants' unsatiated demand for land. Abdur Rahman, a Muslim League representative, argued in the Assembly:

> We have been asked to believe that in pursuance of the demand of the Muslim League to include Assam in the Pakistan Zone immigrants have been invading Assam. To ask this House to believe such a fantastic theory is but an insult to the intelligence of the Members of this august House. Invasion of a country by a set of famine-stricken poor people is against the evidence of world history.[36]

Already the province of Assam was witnessing a huge transformation of demography. As we have shown above, in 1941, the difference with the immigrant Muslims was only 440,000. Another important feature of the Muslim League member was to question the facts and figures of the Congress government. When the government stated in the house that 160,000 bighas of reserved land was de-reserved and settled by only Muslim immigrants pursuant to the grow-more-food campaign, Abdur Rahman challenged the accuracy of these figures.

The main demand of the Muslim League members was opening up of land for the immigrants. They goaded the Congress to do it to show 'real sympathy' to the Muslim people, otherwise, they would be dubbed as narrow 'Hindu *Sabhait*'. To quote Abdul Majid Ziaosh Shams:

> So if you really want to consider the welfare of India as a whole, throw open your waste lands to all people and allow the immigrants to come as they came before and thereby show your real sympathy to Muslims. We know what is your policy. You apprehend that there will be a majority of Muslims here in this Province. It was said that if you scratch the Whigs

---

[35] Assembly Debates, 15 March 1946.

[36] Rahman, *Assembly Debates*; ALAP, *Assam Gazette*.

you get the Tories. So you scratch a congressman you will find him in 90 per cent cases an out-and-out narrow 'Hindu Sabhait'.[37]

Beliram Das of Congress provided a detailed analysis of how Assam provided land to the immigrants. He said that the area of settled lands in Assam was 20.6 million bighas in 1941, and the area per capita was about 2 bighas. The Government of Assam had defined 20 bighas as an economic holding for a family of 5, and as such, several actual indigenous landless people would be of 50 per cent. There had not been any attempt in the past to find out the number of actual landless people of the province by the previous Muslim League government, though they made lavish promises to the Government of Bengal to give lands to the Bengali immigrants brought into Assam. Das argued that within a period of five or six years, the League ministry allocated 0.5 million bighas of land to immigrants. If the process of settlement of lands with the immigrants went on like that, there would be no land left for the natural growth of the indigenous population, and they would be compelled to cultivate as tenants on lands of the immigrants. In the meantime, a new class of immigrant zamindars had sprung up. He pleaded that there was no such thing as surplus land in the reserves in Assam; rather, most of the reserves were deficit in the number of areas.

Apart from immigration and land settlement, two other important facets of Muslim League's politics in Assam were Islam as a tool of political mobilization and the search for an El Dorado, where the Muslims of Assam could strive. Pakistan and the inclusion of Assam in it gradually became an important agenda of the All India Muslim League.[38] How the leaders of the organization propagated the cause of Islam in Assam could be understood from a meeting where Saadulla was present as the chief guest. The meeting was addressed by Maulana Azad Subhani, a prominent Muslim leader of Calcutta, accompanied by Sir Syed Muhammad Saadulla. Both of them arrived at the place of the Muslim League meeting at 4 p.m. on 29 November 1938,

---

[37] Shams, *Assembly Debates*.

[38] In his memorandum on 12 May 1946, Jinnah demanded Punjab, NWFP, Baluchistan, Sind, Bengal and Assam be grouped together.

amidst shouts of 'Muslim League Zindabad', 'Maulana Azad Subhani Zindabad' and 'Allah-hu-Akbar'.[39] After the prayer was held, Sir Muhammad Saadulla introduced Maulana Azad Subhani to the people. The crux of his speech was:

> It should be told to the Congress that in Islam the distinction between religion and politics is as thin as between blood and water. If the Congress says that the religion is not necessary, I cannot congratulate them. The Mussalman community will not allow this kind of propaganda. I want to tell the Congress that there is only one work for religion for the Mussalmans and the same word is applied to politics as well. That sentence is this—'la ilaha illallah muhammadur rasulullah'. This is the last gospel for both politics and religion for the Mussalmans. He can sacrifice everything and give you everything but you cannot take away from him 'La Ilahallallah'. You want to bribe him with your bread and demolish his soul but the Mussalman man will not tolerate that. Even if you give him your bread and place him in paradise, he will not give up 'la ilaha illallah muhammadur rasulullah'. The word independence has not come from God but 'La Ilahallallaha' has come from God and it is name of salvation of soul and immortality. When the choice is between 'La Ilahallallaha' and independence, he will prefer to remain in subjugation than give up 'La Ilahallallaha'. This is the last resort for the Mussalman's 'La Ilahallallaha' and independence go together like body and soul. It is impossible that 'La Ilahallallaha' should exist in the body and that body should be slave. But if we are compelled to remain under subjugation we shall prefer to die with 'La Ilahallallaha'. If we are told today to give up 'La Ilahallallaha' on the promise of giving independence, we prefer to remain as slaves till the Day of Judgment; still, we cannot annihilate our soul.[40]

As we have stated above, the Pakistan demand was not only raised in public rallies and various sessions of the Muslim League, but it was also ardently raised in the house of the Assam Assembly.

> I warn Government against the consequences which may result in near future. I know I have no other remedy open to me than to advice [sic] my people to prepare themselves for welcoming martyr's fate. The remedy of all these evils lies in the achievement of Pakistan and we

[39] Report of the Proceedings of a Public Meeting, held at Shillong, Laban Idgah ground, on the 29 November 1938. Obtained from State Archive.
[40] Ibid.

have a right to have it. These criminals against humanity, worse than the war criminals, can only then be brought to book and they shall be Pakistan Zindabad.[41]

Another Muslim League member, Abdul Majid Ziaoshshams, demanded:

I want Pakistan and I want to explain the principle of our stand, and criticise your standpoint. I have got figure to show, Sir that there are exigencies when land should be thrown out for settlement unstintedly [sic] ... Assam cannot really shut out immigrants coming to Assam and thus raise a mountain of barrier against immigrants.[42]

In his speech, Beliram Das of Congress made it abundantly clear that the sudden onrush of immigrants into Assam was an actual invasion of the province for the political design of the Muslim League. He referred to a speech of Maulavi Abdur Rouf, leader of the immigrant Muslims, in the course of his address as the Chairman of the Reception Committee of the League meeting presided over by Chaudhury Khaliquzzaman, held at Barpeta on 7–8 March 1944. In an aggressive tone, Rouf said that the same fresh blood ran through the Muslim's veins even then for a new conquest of Assam. Being deprived of their arms shields and swords by the mercy of the British rulers, they came with a cane shield bamboo stick, spears and plough and landed either in *chars* or in the jungles adjacent to the rivers to complete their conquest which was left half done.[43]

Questions were raised about why Assam became a hot pursuit for the Muslim League. The majority of the non-Muslims in Assam were tribal people; there was a huge scope for the Muslims to become the largest group in the state using immigration and high birth rate, which no communities could match. Polygamy, *talaq* (easy form of divorce), early marriage of Muslim girls, illiteracy, etc., were the major drivers of the massive growth of Muslim population, and the Muslim League

---

[41] Rahman, *Assembly Debate*.

[42] Ibid.

[43] Das, *Assembly Debate*. No Muslim League members could refute the allegations made by Beliram Das.

found Assam as the next most productive ground for the growth of Islam. Various Muslim organizations had systematically churned the possible areas for expansion of East Pakistan, and they found Assam to be the best ground. It was said 'Eastern Pakistan must have sufficient land for its huge population and Assam will give it scope for expansion'.[44]

Post-independence Period: Immigration, Evolution of National Register of Citizens and Assamese Identity

The influx of Muslim immigrants to Assam continued unabated even after independence. In a letter to the Chief Secretary of Assam, vide letter Memo no. I/C-5(3)(M)48, dated 22 September 1948, it was said:

> Subject: 'Influx of Muslims into Assam, from East Pakistan', the DIG, Assam, portrayed the reality: '… [I]nformation received from districts indicate that many Muslims from East Pakistan (Sylhet, Noakhali, Mymmensingh, Tipperaji, Chittagong) have been daily coming into Assam for settling at Lanka, Hojai, Jamunamukh, Kamrup, Silchar, Hailakandi, Karimganj and other places ….' The letter urged the government to take strict measures, particularly to promulgate Ordinance No. XVII of 1948—the Influx from West Pakistan Control Ordinance. A series of letters were exchanged among various government agencies regarding the 'control of influx of Muslims from East Pakistan'.[45]

Here, an observation made by the DIG of Assam on 25 October 1948 is important:

> As there are various unrecognised routes and there is a long border unprotected by natural barriers, it is difficult to check all influx, as the Muslim

---

[44] A Muslim organisation known as the East Pakistan Renaissance society was formed in Calcutta for popularizing and realizing the idea of Pakistan on 30 August 1942. The society vociferously propagated the inclusion of Assam in Pakistan. It said 'Assam had abundant forest and mineral resources, e.g., Coal, Petroleum etc. and Eastern Pakistan must include Assam in order to be financially and economically strong and … in Assam the majority of the people are Bengali speaking', cited in Kar, *Muslims in Assam Politics*, 306.

[45] Chief Secretary, letter no. C.294/48/4, dated 28 September 1948; Memo No. I/C-5(3)(M)-48/37,SB, Shillong, 25 October. Chief Secretary in his letter urged to keep a strict vigil over the 'Cachar-Sylhet boundary in Muslim areas and the Cachar-Rangpur boundary in the south-west of Dhubri subdivision'.

visitors at once will be sheltered by other Muslims, who are already in occupation of the lands in the province specially on the borders of Pakistan. So abetment, in giving shelter, food and other facilities for settlement should be made penal, to get at those who shelter persons coming for settlement should also be made penal, to get at those who shelter persons coming for settlement stealthily without permits.[46]

Archival records and political department Special Branch (SB) reports suggest that (from April to June 1949) there were systematic efforts to rehabilitate the immigrants from East Pakistan.

Credible information reveals that the Muslims of Assam have got secret instructions from the Muslim League stalwarts of Pakistan that there will be a plebiscite in Assam in 1958. And if the present Muslim can increase the member of their population in the Province then Assam will submerge to East Pakistan. To meet that end in view the Muslims are regularly accommodating the Muslims coming from East-Pakistan to Nowgong District. They give them land and make arrangements for having land in co-operation with the land settlement staff. Recently some waste lands were thrown open to the landless people of the soil but majority of the land has been given to the well-to-do Muslims who in their turn accommodate new comers of their religion.[47]

The number of such illegal migrants has been reported to be 0.5 million (500,000) in a White Paper published by the Government of Assam.[48]

In order to counter the immigration issue during the 1948–1949 period, three important steps were undertaken by the Congress government in both the state and the centre. The first was the introduction of a permit system developed by the officials of the Assam government. The main tenets of the permit system introduced in 1949 were that it was lenient to the displaced persons who were certified as having had to leave East Pakistan on account of civil disturbances or fear of civil disturbances in their home areas. These persons would

[46] SAD-political. Memo No. I/C-5(3)(M)-48/37,SB.

[47] State Archival, Political Department. Ibid.

[48] White Paper on Foreigners, Government of Assam, 2012, 6.

carry certificates in a prescribed format. The proposed permit system discouraged all non-refugees, which meant the Muslims.[49]

The then Nehru government took the next two steps to contain the massive influx of immigrants from across the border: The Immigrants (Expulsion from Assam) Act, 1950, and the preparation of NRC along with the census in the year 1951.

The Immigrants (Expulsion from Assam) Act, 1950, provided power to order the expulsion of certain immigrants.

> If the Central Government is of opinion that any person or class of persons, having been ordinarily resident in any place outside India, has or have, whether before or after the commencement of this Act, come into Assam and that the stay of such person or class of persons in Assam is detrimental to the interests of the general public of India or of any section thereof or of any Scheduled Tribe in Assam, the Central Government may by order— a) direct such person or class of persons to remove himself or themselves from India or Assam within such time and by such route as may be specified in the order; and b) give such further directions in regard to his or their removal from India or Assam as it may consider necessary or expedient; Provided that nothing in this section shall apply to any person who on account of civil disturbances or the fear of such disturbances in any area now forming part of Pakistan has been displaced from or has left his place of residence in such area and who has been subsequently residing in Assam.

The Act was later modified after the creation of new states like Nagaland from Assam; nevertheless, it became an important reference point for addressing the foreigner issue in Assam and elsewhere.[50] The Act made a difference between undesirable immigrants and somewhat desirable immigrants. While being very strict on the Muslim immigrants from East Bengal, the legislation was lenient on the Hindu refugees, and such forcible expulsion was not to be applied to those

---

[49] The permit system was prepared by the then Chief Secretary of Assam, S. P. Desai. The detailed proposal was finalized on 22 June 1949. It said 'Non-refugees would in practice cover all Muslims wishing to enter Assam area' (accessed through SB archive).

[50] B. G Verghese says that the Act was repealed in 1957; however, the Supreme Court in its verdict in IMDT case in 2005 re-invoked the Act along with Foreigners Act and Citizenship Act. Verghese, *India's Northeast Resurgent*, 39.

Hindu refugees who had left Pakistan out of civil disturbance or fear of such disturbances. The genesis of the contentious Citizenship Amendment Bill of 2016 or 2018, or the CAA-2019, has its origin in the 1950 Act. The Illegal Immigration Expulsion Act also recognized the distinctiveness of the tribal people of the region, suggesting that if the stay of 'such persons' became detrimental to the people of India or the Scheduled Tribes of Assam, such immigrants might be expelled.

The Government of India prepared NRC in 1951. R. B. Vaghaiwala, the then Superintendent of Census of India in charge of Assam, Manipur and Tripura, said in Volume XII of Census of India (Part 1A, Introduction, pages xxxiii onwards):

> An important innovation of this census was the preparation of National Register of Citizens in which all important census data was transcribed from the census slips transcribed from the census slips, with the exception of census Questions No. 6 (displaced persons), 8 (bilingualism) and 13 (indigenous persons). The register uses the same symbols and abbreviations and is a copy of the census slips. It is compiled in separate parts, one relating to each village and each ward of a town. It will be maintained as a permanent record and kept up-to-date by collecting information through village official. As it was not possible to hand-short for households slips which relate to individuals, the National Register of Citizens 'giving the details of the individuals arranged by households was utilised for sorting and tabulating certain characteristics of the household like their size, ordinary structure and composition. Thus, the National Register of Citizens will maintain intercensal continuity, will be useful for Electoral and various other administrative purposes and also serve as a suitable frame for socio-economic surveys based on random sampling.

The National Register of Citizens of 1951 has been criticized as an incomplete document and is said to have left out many names. The Census Superintendent, on the other hand, claimed a great level of accuracy in conducting the process.[51] Vaghaiwala said,

> Thus if the errors of judgement of the political officers in Abor Hills and Tirap Frontier Tract, and the error in addition committed by Kamrup district alone are left out of the account, the difference between the provisional and final totals falls to only 336 only, i.e., 0.004%. The microscopic

---

[51] Choudhury, 'NRC of 1951', 261.

difference clearly reveals the care and caution that attended the different stages of census operation in the rest of Assam, from the collection of enumeration slips prepared on the spot to their final stock taking in the tabulation offices .... (p. xxxi)

Although great care was taken for the enumeration of all individuals in NRC, the probability of exclusion could not be ruled out. Besides, the exact figures of NRC 1951 which were kept in the district offices may not have been available in its original form.

However, NRC which was implemented in Assam with the Supreme Courts' directives since 2013 adopted a very flexible approach in establishing citizenship in India. To prove citizenship, along with NRC of 1951, more than 22 documents or linkages were said to be valid under the present NRC as vital information for establishing family and legacy tree from 1951.[52]

---

[52] NRC website says, 'The first requirement is collection of ANY ONE of the following documents of List A issued before midnight of 24th March, 1971 where name of self or ancestor appears (to prove residence in Assam up to midnight of 24th March, 1971). (1) 1951 NRC OR, (2) Electoral Roll(s) up to 24th March 1971 (midnight) OR, (3) Land & Tenancy Records OR (4) Citizenship Certificate OR (5) Permanent Residential Certificate OR (6) Refugee Registration Certificate OR (7) Passport OR (8) LIC OR (9) Any Govt. issued License/Certificate OR (10) Govt. Service/Employment Certificate OR (11) Bank/Post Office Accounts OR (12) Birth Certificate OR (13) Board/University Educational Certificate OR (14) Court Records/Processes. Further, two other documents viz (1) Circle Officer/GP Secretary Certificate in respect of married women migrating after marriage (can be of any year before or after 24th March (midnight) 1971), and (2) Ration Card issued up to the midnight of 24th March, 1971 can be adduced as supporting documents. However, these two documents shall be accepted only if accompanied by any one of the documents listed above. The Second requirement arises if name in any of the documents of List A is not of the applicant himself/herself but that of an ancestor, namely, father or mother or grandfather or grandmother or great grandfather or great grandmother (and so on) of the applicant. In such cases, the applicant shall have to submit documents as in List B below to establish relationship with such ancestor, i.e., father or mother or grandfather or grandmother or great grandfather or great grandmother etc. whose name appears in List A. Such documents shall have to be legally acceptable document which clearly proves such relationship. (1) Birth Certificate OR (2) Land document OR (3) Board/University Certificate OR (4) Bank/LIC/Post Office records OR (5) Circle Officer/GP Secretary Certificate in case of married women OR (6) Electoral Roll OR (7) Ration Card OR (8) Any other legally acceptable document. Points to remember: Providing any one of the documents of List A of ANY PERIOD up to midnight of 24th March, 1971

National Register of Citizens, Citizenship Laws and Civil Society Response

The major statutes governing the NRC updating process in Assam were the Citizenship Act, 1955; the Citizenship (Registration of Citizens and Issue of National Identity Cards) Rules, 2003;[53] and the Ministry of Home Affairs directives.[54] The modalities for the updating process were developed jointly by the Government of Assam and the Government of India in adherence to these statutes.

The Citizenship Act of 1955 is very crucial to understand the exceptions made to Assam after the signing of the Assam Accord. It inserted a new clause of 6A that provided new citizenship laws for Assam. This special inclusion shows how citizenship laws have been made flexible in a state like Assam. Whereas in other states of India, July 1948 is the cut-off date for declaring a person as a foreigner, the following exceptions have been made to accommodate immigrants mainly from Bangladesh in the case of Assam (the amended portion became effective from 7 December 1985). The law says,

> (2) Subject to the provisions of sub-sections (6) and (7), all persons of Indian origin who came before the 1st day of January, 1966 to Assam from the specified territory (including such of those whose names were included in the electoral rolls used for the purposes of the General Election to the House of the People held in 1967) and who have been ordinarily resident in Assam since the dates of their entry into Assam shall be deemed to be citizens of India as from the 1st day of January, 1966.

> (3) Subject to the provisions of sub-sections (6) and (7), every person of Indian origin who—

> (a) Came to Assam on or after the 1st day of January, 1966 but before the 24th day of March, 1971 from the specified territory; and

> (b) Has, since the date of his entry into Assam, been ordinarily resident in Assam; and

shall be enough to prove eligibility for inclusion in updated NRC'. (http://nrcassam. nic.in/admin-documents.html)

[53] As amended by 1. GSR 803 (E) dated 9 November 2009.

[54] (Office of the Registrar General, India), Order No. S.O. 596(E), dated 15 March 2010, published in the Gazette of India, Extra, Part II. No. 504 S.3 (ii), dated 16 March 2010, 1.

(c) Has been detected to be a foreigner;

shall register himself in accordance with the rules made by the Central Government in this behalf under section 18 with such authority (hereafter in this sub-section referred to as the registering authority) as may be specified in such rules and if his name is included in any electoral roll for any Assembly or Parliamentary constituency in force on the date of such detection, his name shall be deleted there from.

Here, the observation of the Supreme Court is very critical in the NRC judgement in 2012. The judgement says

it will be seen that as a part of Assam Accord, a huge number of illegal migrants were made deemed citizens of India. It interesting to note that the parliament has not enacted any laws on refugees from other countries. Refugees' status can be granted and has been granted in India through Executive orders passed by the central government. In any case, section 6A did not merely rest content with granting refugees status to those who were illegal migrants from east Pakistan but went on to grant them benefit of citizenship of India so that all persons who had migrated before 24th March, 1971 respectively were to become citizens of India.[55]

The same Citizenship Act made the provision for NRC with effect from 3 December 2004. The Act (14A) says 'Issue of national identity cards—(1) The central government may compulsorily register every citizen of India and issue national identity card to him. (2) The central government may maintain a National Register of Indian Citizens and for that purpose establish a National Registration Authority'.

The next important legal document for updating NRC was Rule 4A of Citizenship Rules, 2003, and its Schedule which is applicable only in case of Assam. Rule 4A differentiates preparation of NRC in Assam from the rest of the country by replacing house-to-house enumeration with the invitation and receipt of applications from all citizens, for collection of specified particulars relating to each family and individual residing in the state. Further, it provides for ascertaining of citizenship status based on the NRC, 1951, and electoral rolls up to the midnight of the 24 March 1971. It also provides for the inclusion of such

---

[55] Supreme Court's NRC judgement (In the Supreme Court of India, Civil Original Jurisdiction, Writ Petition (Civil) No. 562 of 2012, 15–16.

persons who are original inhabitants of Assam and whose citizenship is beyond doubt in NRC. The manner of preparation of NRC in the state of Assam is specified in the Schedule of the Citizenship Rules, 2003. The Citizenship Rules under 4A says:

> The Central Government shall, for the purpose of the National Register of Indian Citizens in the State of Assam, cause to carry out throughout the State of Assam for preparation of the National Register of Indian Citizens in the State of Assam by inviting applications from all the residents, for collection of specified particulars relating to each family and individual, residing in a local area in the State including the citizenship status based on the National Register of Citizens 1951, and the electoral rolls up to the midnight of the 24th day of March, 1971.

National Register of Citizens, Congress and Immigration Issues: Shift of Gear

Because the Congress ruled from the pre-independence period till about 1970, its stand on the immigration issue was more in favour of the indigenous and local people of both Barak and Brahmaputra valleys. It was under Congress's rule that the most stringent anti-immigration laws were promulgated. Although the All Assam Students' Union (AASU) claims to have raised the demand for NRC in the 1980s, it was, in fact, the Congress party, during 1965–1967, that specifically raised the demand for NRC and other protective mechanisms for the indigenous and local people. However, with the gradual decline of the Congress from 1967 to 1968 and, more specifically, after the liberation war of Bangladesh, its stand on immigration had changed.

In 1950, the firebrand Congress zealot from Assam, Devakanta Barua, defended the case of Assam and compared the state to a leaking boat where he suggested for either to flush out the water or to pluck the hole. Meanwhile, there were communal clashes in Assam in 1950 in the districts of Nowgong, Darrang and Kamrup. Nearly 100,000 illegal migrants had left Assam to the original place of East Bengal, although 161,360 came back by 31 December 1950. Out of them, 37,240 were declared to be new settlers.[56]

---

[56] White Paper, referred above, 2012, 7.

In his report on the census report of 1961, the Registrar General of Census assessed that 220,691 'infiltrants' had entered Assam. Here, the report of the Ministry of Home Affairs[57] is crucial. It says:

> The Central Intelligence Bureau have reported that the infiltration of Pakistani nationals into Assam without travel documents is still going on at a fairly high rate. It has been stated that considering the very large number of such cases and others where the Pakistani nationals after entering India throw away or destroy their passports or allow their passports to expire with a viewing to staying on in this country .... This is posing a serious security problem in Assam. The matter has been carefully considered by the Govt. of India and they have no objection to the issue of deportation orders straightaway against the person who are without travel documents.

According to the White Paper, between 1961 and 1966, a rigorous process of deportation had started, and a total of 178,952 illegal migrants were deported or voluntarily left the country, but an estimated 40,000 'infiltrants' did not leave Assam.

The deportation of illegal migrants had caused a serious uproar in East Pakistan, including a backlash on the Hindus which led to the exodus of 180,000 Hindus to Assam. In the Indo-Pak Home Ministerial Conference on 7–11 April 1964, the Pakistani counterpart argued that the communal disturbances in Assam had led to such backlash in East Pakistan. Pakistan warned that it would drag India to the international forum over the deportation issue in Assam for blatant violation of human rights. The issue was discussed in the Cabinet meetings of GOI on 20 April, 19 September, 27 September and 18 August 1964, and despite such pressures, no relaxation was made on the deportation of the illegal migrants.[58]

It was only from early 1965 that the Congress government decided to go midway on the issue of deportation of Muslim migrants from Assam. A Foreigners Tribunal was constituted on 23 September 1964, and four such tribunals were constituted. A total of 35,080 migrants

---

[57] Dated 22 March, 1961, copy of Express letter no1/7/61-F.III addressed to the Government of Assam. Source: SAD.

[58] White Paper, 8. There was consensus in the Congress ministry in Assam that any stoppage of deportation would seriously affect the internal situation in Assam.

were referred to the tribunals, out of which, 33,193 were found to be Pakistanis and 105 Indians. According to government records, 95 per cent of them were deported. The slowing down of the identification and deportation of the migrants was highly criticized in the Congress Party (AICC) in its executive meeting on 22 April 1965 in New Delhi, where members argued that such influx would make Assam an immigrant state. But despite a tough stand by the party, the Congress government decided to relax the identification process on humanitarian grounds. Revised guidelines for the deportation of the foreigners were issued on 19 June 1964, according to which,

- There will be no harassment of people in the railway station in the name of foreigner identification,
- There will be no total checking of villages or any other clusters,
- Emphasis was put on apprehending the fresh immigrants only,
- Watch posts to be set up in the border.

In the early 1960s, the Government of Assam, under the leadership of Congress Chief Minister Bimala Prasad Chaliha, launched an aggressive campaign to flush out the immigrants who had settled in Assam since January 1951. He even disregarded Prime Minister Nehru's plea to go slow on the issue. 'Prime Minister Jawaharlal Nehru wanted the Assam Chief Minister, Bimala Prasad Chaliha to go easy on deportations and even stop them. Chaliha refused, saying that the problem was so critical that Assam's demography and culture would be permanently changed'.[59] In a press note on 27 July 1965, Chaliha said that he would follow a middle and rational path. The Chaliha government armed itself with the Prevention of Infiltration from Pakistan (PIP) Act, 1964, and pursued the campaign. Accordingly, 180 watch posts with 39 armed personnel each and 7 battalions were sanctioned. The 1964 law raised a special border police force of about 2,000 men, besides 6 passport-checking centres. The Act was more secular in its outlook than the existing law of 1950, which distinguishes between Hindus and Muslims. Hindus were considered refugees while Muslims were considered illegal aliens in the 1950 rule. The 1964 law did not make

---

[59] Hazarika, *Rites of Passage*, 60.

any such distinction. Under the PIP scheme, the proposed attempt for a 'no man's zone' in the border area had to be abandoned, as it would have had involved the displacement of 128,000 people in the border area. Even organizations like Jamiat Ulema-E-Hind supported the move of the government and pleaded for providing identity cards and urged the government not to harass genuine citizens.

Even though the Muslim leaders encouraged the Bengali-speaking Muslim immigrants to declare Assamese as their mother tongue to dodge police detection, Chaliha's campaign against the infiltrators pressed a panic button among them. However, 20 Muslim MLAs in the government threatened him to topple his ministry if he did not stop the deportations. Chaliha had to succumb to the pressure, and the PIP Act was put in cold storage. According to reports, those who were deported earlier gradually returned and again settled in Assam.

Another Attempt for National Register of Citizens in 1965

In 1965, there was another attempt to update the NRC in Assam. The Government of India urged the Government of Assam to expedite the compilation of NRC and to issue identity cards based on that register to Indian inhabitants at least in the selected areas.[60] However, the project was later dropped due to a variety of factors. The shift in the central government's stand became more discernible from 1969. In 1969, it decided that only the following three categories of foreigners were to be summarily deported: (a) Pakistani nationals who held Pakistani passports, (b) re-infiltrants who were once deported and (c) fresh infiltrants, caught at the border. Further, the Superintendents of Police were directed not to detain persons who were checked at railway stations, leading to their missing train connections as a consequence of such checking and detention. If a person was suspected to be a Pakistani, he was to be questioned and followed, or information was sent to where he was heading to so that he could be tracked and future inquiries could be made, but he was not be detained at the

[60] White Paper, 2012, 10–11.

station itself. The Superintendents of Police were further instructed that there should be no wholesale checking of villages and houses. Only when there were specific suspicious circumstances surrounding the cases, which needed to be further investigated, would such a probe be made. The Superintendents of Police were also advised that, as far as possible, the investigation should be done under the supervision of a responsible officer.

The tone and language of the Government of Assam completely changed after 1976. A clear instruction was issued on 17 February 1976 stating that persons coming from the erstwhile Pakistan or East Bengal who settled in Assam before 24 March 1971 should not be deported or expelled. The White Paper says

> On February 17, 1976, Ministry of Home Affairs issued a notification entrusting the Superintendents of Police and the Deputy Commissioners (in charge of police) with powers of Central Government in making orders against Bangladesh nationals under Foreigners' Act, 1946. ... While enclosing the above notification dated February 17, 1976 in respect of Bangladesh nationals, Government of India instructed the State Government that 'persons who (had) come to India from erstwhile East Pakistan/Bangladesh prior to March, 1971 are not to be sent back to Bangladesh'.[61]

The policy shift of GOI can be attributed to India's prominent role in the liberation of Bangladesh. India received a huge number of refugees as a result of the civil war in East Bengal. In 1971, Indira Gandhi made a world tour to convince the world leaders about India's inability to receive such a huge refugee population from East Bengal which ultimately resulted in the intervention of Indian Army in the liberation war of Bangladesh. It became a prestige issue for the newly emerging hegemonic regional power like India to exhibit leniency to the refugees or immigrants on humanitarian grounds. This means that Assam had to pay a heavy price by accommodating the illegal migrants and refugees from erstwhile East Pakistan in order to satisfy the emerging regional power status of India.

---

[61] Ibid., 11.

Demand for National Register of Citizens by Various Political and Non-political Groups in Assam

Following the 1951 NRC, the Congress party first demanded NRC for Assam. The party submitted a series of memorandums to the Government of India, where it demanded certain strict measures to be adopted against the Pakistani infiltrators.[62] The main grievance of the party was that illegal migration posed the greatest security threat to the region. The party also highlighted that some organizations had been carrying out pro-Pakistani activities in some parts of Assam with the help of former Muslim League members. In one of the petitions, the Congress party said

> The large-scale Pakistani infiltrations and their continuance in the State has posed a serious threat to the internal Law and Order situation and grave danger to the security of the State. The unauthorised Pakistani infiltrants must be detected and very expeditiously deported. The number deported so far has been insignificant in proportion to the number estimated by the Government of India. Government of India decided setting up of Tribunals on or Special Officers for scrutinizing the genuineness of the Pakistanis before steps are taken for their deportation and the procedure will take time as inevitable to procedural formalities. A target date should be fixed within which illegal infiltrants are to be deported and all possible and necessary measures should [be] taken for completing the task within the stipulated period. The policy in this regard should be firm and clear.[63]

On 1 April 1964, the Pradesh Congress Committee, in a petition to the government of India, made some suggestions for addressing the immigration in Assam:

1. That a target date not later than March 1965 to complete the deportation of Pakistani infiltrants in Assam be announced and acted accordingly.

---

[62] Some of the petitions were submitted on 9 March 1964, 15 March 1964 and 1 April 1964.

[63] Submitted to Guljari Lal Nanda, Home Minister, GOI, 9 March 1964, Shillong. Personal collection.

2. That the citizen's National Register with house numbers intended for preparation of census of 1951 be made on the basis of tracing out Pakistani nationals and deporting them without delay.

3. That adequate number of tribunals to be appointed immediately to achieve complete deportation of Pakistani nationals within the target date.

4. That a strip of land with such depth as may be needed along the entire East Pakistan border be cleared of habitations and declared a 'prohibited area' to be used for the defence of the country in such a manner as may be warranted by the exigency of the circumstances. The population so displaced should be properly rehabilitated. Border roads should be constructed all along it, and existing ones be expeditiously developed to the full measure with all the bridges to ensure quick movement of our security forces to check further infiltration of Pakistani nationals in future and help in defence measures.

The Assam Agitation (1979–1985), which demanded the detection of foreigners, deportations and deletion of their names from the electoral rolls, was nothing but a continuation of their earlier movements. While launching a 12-day agitation in April/May 1974, the students under AASU had placed a 21-point charter of demands before the central and the state governments. The charter contained, among others, the demand for stopping infiltration of foreigners into Assam and control of excessive and unnatural growth of population in the state.

The Assam Agitation re-energized the demand for NRC. Various organizations started demanding it as the major safety valve for the protection of the Assamese people. AASU; the All Assam Gana Sangram Parishad (AAGSP); the literary body of the state—Assam Sahitya Sabha; the Journalists' Association of Assam; Dibrugarh University Teachers' Union (DUSU); and many others joined hands in demanding the re-invocation of NRC for the protection of Assamese identity.[64]

---

[64] For details, see All Assam Gana Sangram Parishad, *The Foreigners' Problem: An Analysis*; Assam Sahitya Sabha, *Eclipse in the East*; Assam Jagriti, *Indian Citizens vs Foreign Nationals*; Assam Freedom Fighters' Association, *Assam's Struggle for Survival*; Dibrugarh University Teacher's Union (DUSU), *Assam: Historic Fight for*

The basic argument of these petitions was

All foreigners staying within the territory of Assam i.e. India be deported forthwith in accordance with the provisions of the Constitution of India. The list of foreigners to be drawn up for the purpose of deportation be prepared on the basis of the National Register of Citizens of 1951 and the Electoral Rolls of 1952.[65]

The organizations argued for the deportation of foreigners on the basis of constitutional laws. In an appeal to the Prime Minister of India on 2 February 1980, the AASU said 'Indian constitution defines in unambiguous terms who can be a voter. *A foreign national cannot certainly participate in Indian elections.* But the sovereignty of the country has been openly insulted by political parties ...' (emphasis laid by the AASU). The Nehru–Liaquat Pact, which was signed on 8 April 1950, allowed all the foreigners who came to India by 31 December 1950 to remain in India. It suggests that all foreigners entering India after 31 December 1950 cannot legally stay in India without holding any valid document or without acquiring citizenship in India. The primary argument of AASU and the Gana Sangram Parishad was that keeping in view the constitutional position, the year 1951 is the only constitutionally acceptable dateline in the matter of detection, deletion and deportation of the foreigners. AASU had developed the concept of 3Ds (detection, deletion and deportation) way back in 1980 as a formula for resolving the illegal migrants' issue. Since then, it has been insisting on the 3Ds formula against the foreigners. One of the petitions of AAGSP said,

Furthermore, the Government of India prepared a National Register of Citizens in 1951 wherein the names of all persons who had entered before 31st December, 1950 were registered and the National Register of Citizens (NRC) can give the best lead in the matter of detection of foreigners for the purpose of deleting their names from the electoral rolls as well as for the purpose of deportation from India.[66]

Survival. All these organisations had demanded updating the 1951 NRC and comparing the successive rolls since 1952.

[65] Petition 'An Appeal to the Honourable Members of Indian Parliament' by Assam Sahitya Sabha, 7 June 1980.

[66] All Assam Gana Sangram Parishad (AAGSP) Appeal to GOI, 1980.

The leaders had argued that 1951 as the base year was not only legally tenable but was also justified in view of the contemporaneous NRC. Almost all the organizations had invoked one statement given by Jawaharlal Nehru on the floor of the Parliament on 27 June 1962:

> I believe much of this infiltration took place in the first five years after independence when the border was not adequately guarded. Probably it will be difficult now to deal with illegal immigrants who come before 1952. We might, therefore, fix 1952 as the date of our enquiry.

The All Assam Students' Union and AAGSP had put the following agreements that became the main fulcrum of a solution to the vexed foreigner issue of Assam[67]:

1. It is recognised that a solution to the problem of detection, deletion of the names from the electoral rolls and deportation will be found within the framework of the Constitution of India including the citizenship laws and the election laws as existing today based on the dateline, 1951.
2. If the government of India finds that some of those foreigners cannot be deported out of India, these must be distributed for residence among the States and the Union Territories on the proportion of the population having due regard to the average national growth rate of population.

    It is farther agreed that the government shall ensure that such foreigners deported out of Assam shall not be permitted to reside and settle in Assam again.
3. No election shall be held in Assam before the correction of the electoral rolls by completing the deletion of the names of the foreigners.
4. The modalities of the detection, deletion from the electoral rolls and deportation from Assam of the foreigners shall be formulated and finalised jointly by the representatives of the Government of India, Government of Assam, AASU and AAGSP not later than fifteen days from the date of this agreement.

---

[67] All Assam Gana Sangram Parishad, 'The Foreigner's Problem: An Analysis', 30–31.

5. The National Register of Citizens (NRC) should be compiled after detection of foreigners on the basis of the present agreements to maintain a proper record of the citizens of India residing inside the territories of Assam to avoid further complications.
6. It is further agreed to render the NRC up-to-date every five years.
7. The census operations due from July 1980 shall not commence unless implementation of these agreements is completed.

From the very beginning, AASU had reiterated its secular, democratic and inclusive character of the movement:

> We are committed to pursue the cause of the present movement with sense of deep conviction on the principle of non-violence, democracy and secularism ... determination to maintain peace and harmony is written on the face of everybody participating in the movement ... but conspiracy has been on. Political elements patronising the foreign nationals are inflaming communal passions among the innocent people in the name of language and religion. Our firm answer has been a foreigner is a foreigner; a foreigner shall not be judged by the language he speaks or by the religion he follows.[68]

The All Assam Students' Union maintains this stand until today. The Assam Accord of 1985 did not directly talk about NRC, but throughout the period and discussions, the promulgation of NRC came up several times. Even after the Assam Accord was signed, AASU never gave up the issue, and in 1990, it submitted a detailed plan to the Government of India for upgrading NRC.[69] To assuage the people of Assam during the heydays of secret killings to counter ULFA,[70] G. K. Pillai, the then J. S., Ministry of Home Affairs, GOI, raised the issue of NRC and provided a financial grant to the government of Assam and bestowed the responsibility 'to preserve and upgrade NRC at the earliest'.[71] In the 11th round of talks between AASU and GOI on

[68] All Assam Students' Union (AASU), Appeal to the PM of India, 2 February 1980.

[69] All Assam Students' Union (AASU), *Implementation of Assam Accord*, 50.

[70] For details about secret killings in Assam, see Mahanta, *Confronting the State*, Chap. 5.

[71] A decision was arrived at on 17 November 1999 in tripartite talks. For details, see AASU, 'Implementation of Assam Accord', 50.

14 February 2003, the NRC issue was raised by the AASU, however, without much result. On the eve of GOI proposal for Indo-ASEAN car rally in November 2004, AASU threatened to disrupt the process if no action was taken on its demands. Backchannel discussions and negotiations led to the finalization of a tripartite meet between GOI, GOA and AASU on 5 May 2005, where, for the first time, a time frame was agreed on to upgrade the 1951 NRC.

Finally, under pressure from various quarters, the state government took up the process of updating NRC in two pilot projects from 1 June 2010 in Chaygaon and Barpeta constituencies, but the work had to be stopped on 21 July 2010, that is, shortly after the starting of the pilot project, due to controversies surrounding the defective modalities adopted by the government and agitations staged by a group of alleged illegal immigrants. Under these circumstances, an important civil society organization of the state, Assam Public Work (APW), backed by some top individuals in the field of education,[72] filed a writ petition for upgrading the NRC process.[73] In its verdict on 17 December 2014, the Supreme Court provided a detailed timetable for the Central and state governments to perform the task. The present declaration of the draft NRC is a product of a long political, social and legal battle that Assam has witnessed since the dawn of India's independence.

'D' Voters and National Register of Citizens

Legally, there are three categories of actual or doubtful foreigners in Assam: the first category is those who are detected by border police in tandem with local police to be referred to the Foreigners' Tribunals (FTs) for their subsequent verdict; the second category is those who were examined under the Illegal Migration (Determination by Tribunal) Act, 1983; and the third category is the 'doubtful citizens'

---

[72] A few notable names who provided all financial logistical help are Pradip Bhuyan (an IIT engineer); Bonti Bhuyan, proprietor of Faculty High School; Jayanta Barua, owner of a popular Assamese daily and TV channel *Asomiya Pratidin*.

[73] Along with APW, other petitioners in the case were Assam Sanmilita Mahasangha and All Assam Ahom Associations.

inserted by the Election Commission in 1997. Before the repeal of the Illegal Migrants (Determination by Tribunal) Act, by the Supreme Court of India in 2005, the detection and deportation of illegal foreigners were carried out under the IM(DT) Act, 1983; the Foreigners Act, 1946; and the Foreigners Tribunal Order, 1964. After the repeal of the IM(DT) Act, which the Apex Court invalided in the landmark case known as the Sarbananda Sonowal case,[74] all the detection and deportation of illegal foreigners were carried out under the Foreigner's Act, 1946, and the Foreigner's Tribunal Order, 1964.

It may be mentioned that out of more than 4 million names left out of the NRC published in 2018, 0.248 million persons have been kept on hold in the draft register. There are four kinds of people that belong to the 'on hold' category: the doubtful (D) voters, the descendants of D voters, those persons whose references are yet to be decided in the (FTs), and the descendants of those persons whose cases are pending in the FTs. It is to be noted that the 'D' voters and cases pending in FTs are two different categories which are mistakenly referred to as one by many analysts.

Under the provisions of the Foreigner's Order, 1948, the question of whether a person is a foreigner or not, he/she is referred to FTs within the meaning of Foreigner's Act, 1946, for opinion. The tribunal shall have the power of civil court with the power of summoning and enforcing the attendance of any person and examining on oath, requiring the discovery and production of any documents and issuing commissions for the examination of any witness. The number of FTs established has varied from time to time with changing situations and court orders by the High Court and Supreme Court.

One of the main demands of the Assam Agitation was the drastic revision of electoral rolls, as it had contained names of illegal migrants. On 27 November 1978, the Law Minister informed the Rajya Sabha that 'It has come to the notice of the Election Commission from time to time that large scale inclusion of foreign nationals in the electoral

---

[74] As a result of this verdict, the former AASU and AGP leader, now the CM of Assam, Sarbandanda Sonowal was accorded the title of 'Jatiyo Nayak' (national hero) of the state.

rolls, especially in the North-Eastern Region, has been taking place'. The issue of foreign nationals assumed a serious implications when, in September 1979, 'the Chief Election Commissioner of India chose to act against the provision of the Constitution and the Peoples' Representation Act to facilitate retention of names of those very foreigners against whom he himself had warned earlier'.[75] He revised his earlier instructions and directed the Chief Electoral Officer of Assam 'not to omit any name included in the existing electoral rolls on the pretext of want of citizenship and also telling him that the scrutiny of electoral rolls with reference to citizenship will be taken up only after the ensuing general election is over'.[76] Pursuant to the instructions of the Election Commission of India, the Chief Electoral Officer issued the following directions on 22 September 1979:

> As per earlier instructions enumerators may have included names of nationals in the Electoral Registration Card with the remarks F. N. (Foreign Nationals) or they may have entered the letters F. N. against the existing entry in the Electoral Roll itself. In view of the current instructions of the Election Commission such remarks should not find place in the supplement containing deletions which will be published along with the draft Electoral Rolls.

This triggered massive discontent throughout the state, as it diluted the basic demand of AASU and other organizations about having an electoral roll which is free from any foreigners' name. Out of the three Ds that AASU keeps on referring to, one 'D' refers to deletion of foreigners' name from the voters' list. There had been a consistent demand for structural modification of voters' list in Assam. The Election Commission became strict on the issue, and during an intensive revision of electoral roll in Assam in 1997, the letter 'D' was marked against names of those electors who could not prove their Indian citizenship status at the time of verification. The marking suggests that the citizenship status of the person concerned is disputed and doubtful. The Electoral Registration Officer would decide whether reference of such an individual is required to the concerned tribunal to ascertain his/her

---

[75] *Assam Jagriti*, 'Indian Citizens vs Foreign Nationals', 6–7.

[76] Ibid.

status. Such cases are referred to the SP of the concerned district for a subsequent referral to the FTs. The persons marked with D can neither cast vote nor stand in the election.[77] According to the White Paper, a total of 231,657 references were made to the competent authorities.

Final Draft of National Register of Citizens and the Assamese Identity Question

Finally, the final NRC list, which was published on 31 July 2019, dropped about 1,906,657 names. NRC, which was conceived to be the final protection mechanism for the indigenous Assamese people, could hardly meet the expectations. Almost all the stakeholders (except perhaps the minority organizations and political parties like Congress and All Indian United Democratic Front [AIUDF]), including AASU, APW, etc., expressed reservations at the figures. Expectedly, the figure was also rejected by the state BJP. Dr Himanta Biswa Sarma, the state finance minister, arguably the most influential BJP national leader from the eastern part of India, said 'I reiterate that as requested by Central and State governments at least 20% re-verification (bordering districts) and 10% re-verification(remaining districts) should be allowed by Hon'ble Apex court for a correct and fair NRC'.[78]

Abhijit Sarma, the leader of APW who filed a petition regarding NRC said,

> In 2009, we approached the Supreme Court to solve this burning problem of Assam. It accepted our case. In the 2006 voter list, there were 41 lakh extra names. We urged the court to help us delete those names so that Indians can vote for Indians in Assam. Then the apex court suggested that the NRC be updated and the process was on since then ... On July 30, 2018, the final draft was released. On August 24, 2018, we requested the Supreme Court to do a 10% re-verification of all the districts because we suspected that names of various illegal immigrants had been included in

[77] White Paper, 2012, 22.

[78] As expressed in a tweet by Dr Himanta Biswa Sarma on 31 August 2019. The state BJP has accused huge manipulation of legacy data by illegal immigrants.

it. We then filed five petitions at the court till August 1, 2019 seeking re-verification of the names in the final draft.[79]

Dr Samujjal Bhattacharya, advisor to AASU and an undisputed leader of the organization, too, expressed his unhappiness:

> We concede that under the supervision of the Supreme Court, for the first time since the Assam Accord was signed in 1985, a serious effort was made to find illegal immigrants and spell out who is a citizen. But we are unhappy with the number we saw today .... It is not that we were chasing a number. But since the past many years, various governments have been quoting figures of immigrants residing illegally in the state. The number we see today is nowhere near those numbers. But we still have trust in the apex court. So we plan to appeal to the court to give it a re-look.[80]

The Assam Gana Parishad, a state regional political party that came to power based on the Assam Accord, considered the number as 'ridiculously small'. Its president said, 'The people of Assam had hoped for a free and fair NRC but it now seems that the very existence of the Assamese will be further threatened'.[81] The reason behind the huge disappointment with NRC was that the Assamese psyche was built with the impression that there are a minimum of 5 million illegal migrants in the state. This figure was stated in the Indian Parliament on various occasions by various political parties.

The number of 1.9 million hardly met the aspirations of the indigenous tribal and the Assamese people. The impression of 5 million illegal migrants was created by various non-BJP political dispensations at the centre and the state; for example, on 10 April 1992, Chief Minister Hiteswar Saikia gave a figure of 3.3 million in the Assam Assembly. On 6 May 1997, the then Home Minister Indrajit Gupta gave a figure of 4 million foreigners in the Indian Parliament.[82] On 14 July 2004, a Parliament statement by MoS Home, Sriprakash Jaiswal, stated that the total number of Bangladeshi infiltrators in India was

---

[79] Pisharoty, 'Why Is No One in Assam Happy With the Final NRC?'

[80] Ibid.

[81] Ibid.

[82] For details, see Mahanta, *Assam NRC Excludes 19 Lakh.*

12 million, out of which 5 million (40% of total) foreigners lived in Assam as of 31 December 2001. The numbers must have increased after that and certainly not declined. A reality check in Assam would reveal a huge change in the demographic and landholding pattern in the border and other districts of Assam. Starting from the two Muslim-dominated districts, Assam today has 11 EBOM-dominated districts. From 1991 until 2011, the Muslim growth in the state has been 5.79 per cent, while the Hindu population in the same period declined by 5.66 per cent. I have argued elsewhere:

> A further analysis of micro data would reveal that in seven border districts of Assam, from 1991–2011, east Bengal origin Muslims have increased by 62.65% in opposition to the decline of 6.41% of the Hindus. Out of 126 Assembly seats, there are 51 constituencies where Muslims of East Bengal origin play most decisive role. This explains the near extinction of a regional party called AGP (a party born out of Assam movement) that ruled Assam twice. The fear is that Assam would soon become an immigrant driven society. Keeping in mind the trend of population growth among the east Bengal origin Muslims, the fear seems to be reasonable one. The low numbers of exclusion in NRC is also attributed to the 'manipulation of legacy data' as the family tree is not biometric based and there is no mechanism to verify the authenticity of such claim and documents (like panchayat certificate).[83]

The protection of the tribal land and culture in Assam was a promise made by Jawaharlal Nehru and other stalwarts in India's Constituent Assembly through 'panchasheel tribal principles'.[84] Various institutional devices that were set up, including constitutional protections, are now being violated by incessant immigration and land encroachment. One has to understand the dilemma of a smaller nationality like the Assamese whose numbers have been declining at an alarming rate and has the possibility of being declared as a minority in their homeland. Numbers matter in a democracy which is still based on 'first past the post' system.

Therefore, the NRC issue is not to be confused with the Citizenship Amendment Bill (CAB) of 2014, 2016 or the CAA-2019, where

---

[83] Mahanta, *Assam NRC Excludes 19 Lakh.*

[84] For details, see Rath, 'Nehru and Elwin on Tribal Development', 35.

certain religious groups are given favourable treatment for citizenship. NRC reflects the anxiety of smaller nationalities that want to keep their distinctiveness which is recognized by the 6th Schedule of the Constitution and other provisions. However, it must also be stated that a certain group cannot be kept in perpetual exclusion of citizenship. The 3D's formula of AASU may not be the best way to tackle the issue of illegal migration. Three issues perhaps could be of particular importance:

1. The formula of 1966–1971, which was applied in the Assam Accord, may perhaps be used for regularizing citizenship in the case of those left out of NRC by curtailing certain political rights.
2. Providing work permits and assurance of certain rights may be one way to resolve the issue.
3. Guaranteeing constitutional protection on the basis of the 1951 formula to the indigenous people in exchange of granting asylum or citizenship to the illegal migrants could be the third way.

Bibliography

ALAP. *Assam Gazette*, Part-VI-A, No. 2, April 1946.

All Assam Gana Sangram Parishad. *The Foreigners' Problem: An Analysis*. Guwahati: Gauhati University Press, 1980.

All Assam Students' Union (AASU). *Implementation of Assam Accord*. Guwahati: Saraighat Printers, 2012.

Assam Freedom Fighters' Association. *Assam's Struggle for Survival*. Guwahati: Labanya & Puravadesh Press, 1980.

Assam Jagriti. 'Indian Citizens vs Foreign Nationals'. Guwahati: Labanya Press, 1980.

Assam Sahitya Sabha, *Eclipse in the East*. Guwahati: Purvadesh Mudran, 1980.

Assam Tribune, 10 October 1941, p. 1. Archival Source, Government of Assam.

Bal, Hartosh Singh. 'East India Creating Its Own Rohingya'. *The New York Times*, 10 August 2018, www.nytimes.com.

Barpujari, H. K. *North-East India: Problems, Policies, Prospects*. Guwahati: Spectrum, 1998.

Baruah, Sanjib. 'The Partition's Long Shadow: The Ambiguities of Citizenship in Assam, India'. *Citizenship Studies* 13, no. 6 (December 2009): 593–606.

Bhagat, Chetan. 'Being Human in Assam: India Can't Strip the Citizenship of People Who Have Built a Life Here for 47 Years'. *Times of India*, 2018.

https://timesofindia.indiatimes.com/blogs/The-underage-optimist/being-human-in-assam-india-cant-strip-the-citizenship-of-people-who-have-built-a-life-here-for-47-years/.

Brubaker, Rogers. *Citizenship and Nationhood in France and Germany*. Cambridge: Harvard University Press, 1992.

Roychoudhury, Anil. 'Assam National Register of Citizens, 1951'. *Economic and Political Weekly* 16, no. 8: 21, February 1981.

Das, Beliram. Assembly Debate, 15 March 1946.

Dev, B. J., and D. K. Lahiri. *Assam Muslim: Politics and Cohesion*. Delhi: Mittal Publications, 1985.

Dibrugarh University Teacher's Union (DUSU). *Assam: Historic Fight for Survival*. Dibrugarh, 1980.

Dutta, K. N. *Landmarks of the Freedom Struggle in Assam*. Gauhati: Lawyer's Book Stall, 1969.

Dutta, Mohan J. 'The National Register of Citizens and the Politics of Exclusion and Hate'. *The Citizen*, 31 July 2018. www.thecitizens.in.

Gohain Barua, P. *Mor Sowarani*. Guwahati: Scientia Book Shop, 1971.

Guha, Amalendu. 'Nationalism: Pan-Indian and Regional in a Historical Perspective'. In *Nationalist Upsurge in Assam*, edited by Arun Bhuyan. Guwahati: Government of Assam, 2000.

Hammar, T. *Democracy and the Nation State*. Aldershot: Gower Publishing Company, 1990.

Hazarika, Sanjoy. *Rites of Passage*. New Delhi: Penguin Books, 2000.

Joppke, Christian. 'Citizenship and Nationhood in France and Germany'. *European Journal of Sociology* 36, no. 1, Threats and Bluffs in East European Transitions (1995): 168–78.

———. *Citizenship and Immigration*. Cambridge: Polity Press, 2010.

Journalists' Association. *Assam: The Crisis of Identity*. Guwahati: Labanya Press, 1980.

Kar, M. *Muslims in Assam Politics*. Delhi: Vikash Publishing House, 1990.

Kymlicka, Will. *Multicultural Citizenship*. Oxford: Clarendon Press, 1995.

Mahanta, Nani Gopal. *Confronting the State: ULFA's Quest for Sovereignty*. New Delhi: SAGE Publications, 2013.

Mahanta, Nani Gopal. *Assam NRC Excludes 19 Lakh: Is the Number Too High or Too Low?* (2019), https://www.dailyo.in/politics/nrc-in-assam-national-register-of-citizens-nrc-assam-accord/story/1/31984.html.

Marshall, T. H. 'Citizenship and Social Class'. In *Sociology at the Crossroads*, edited by T. H. Marshall, 67–127. London: Heinemann, 1963.

Marshall, T. H., and Thomas Bottomore. *Citizenship and Social Class*. London: Pluto Press, 1950.

Mitra, Subrata K. 'Citizenship in India: Evolution, Involution &Rational Construction'. In *Citizenship and Flow of Ideas in the Era of Globalisation*, edited by Subrata K. Mitra, Vol. IV. Heidelberg Series. Samskriti, 2012.

Mitra, Subrata Kumar. 'Citizenship in India: Evolution, Involution, and Rational Construction'. In *Citizenship as Cultural Flow*, edited by Subrata K. Mitra, 121–48. Berlin: Springer, 2013.

Mohan, Rohini. 'NRC: No Clarity on What Awaits the 40 Lakh People Excluded from Assam's Citizen Register'. *Huffington Post*, 31 July 2018. https://in.news.yahoo.com/nrc-no-clarity-awaits-40-030400670. html?guccounter=1&guce_referrer=aHR0cHM6Ly93d3cuZ29vZ2xlLmNvbS8&guce_referrer_sig=AQAAADHsOSqUmcfNeid5B9OJ8JMhk0WdUU6JbjZyE17lJK6vE5xvsypzLU74uCkVAmhPMqG4H9fPPK9KH6RpEd00lDRyNd0-OAAHJbbpiVZQ4hxk_1-A4QG_s4vKh92CiIg9eACVMpz18pY0UAXup-_07keSfJmvqUFxMBGlh7SzNL7H.

Pisharoty, Sangeeta Barooah. 'Why Is No One in Assam Happy With the Final NRC?' *The Wire*, 31 August 2019. https://thewire.in/politics/why-is-no-one-in-assam-happy-with-the-final-nrc.

Rahman, Abdur. Assembly Debates, 14 March 1946.

Rath, Govinda C. (ed.). 'Nehru and Elwin on Tribal Development: Contrasting Perspectives'. In *Tribal Development in India: The Contemporary Debate*, edited by M. Romesh Singh. New Delhi: SAGE Publications, 2006.

Sadique, Kamal. *Paper Citizens: How Illegal Immigrants Acquire Citizenship in Developing Countries*. New York: Oxford University Press, 2009.

Shams, Abdul Majid Ziaosh. Assembly Debates, 15 March 1946.

Soysal, Yasemin N. *Limits of Citizenship*. Chicago: University of Chicago Press, 1995.

Stewart, Angus. 'Two Conceptions of Citizenship'. *British Journal of Sociology* 46, no. 1 (March 1995): 63–78.

Verghese, B. G. *India's Northeast Resurgent*. New Delhi: Konarak Publishers, 1996.

CAA-2019

Unresolved Legacy of Partition

Communal riots on the eve of India's independence due to the Partition resulted in an influx of refugees and other migrants to Assam from East Pakistan (now Bangladesh). The state government initially reported that migrants between 150,000 and 200,000 had entered the state. The number rose to around 0.5 million in a subsequent estimation.[1] Realizing the apprehensive situation, the Government of India decided to formulate The Immigrants (Expulsion from Assam), Act 1950, which granted it the authority to expel illegal immigrants from Assam, and the powers were vested upon the officer subordinate of the central government or any government official of Meghalaya or Assam, but identifying the immigrants for expulsion quickly turned out to be a huge problem. Therefore, the Ministry of Home Affairs prepared NRC 1951; they prepared registers for documenting information on relevant particulars of each person enumerated during the 1951 Census of Assam. However, identification and detection of 'unwanted immigrants' under I(IE)A were far more complex than it seemed on paper, and their identification became nearly impossible.

Furthermore, the passport regulations were not clearly spelt out between the newly independent states of India and Pakistan; it was only in 1967 that the Government of India ruled out the Passport Act, 1967, and provided proper guidelines. The Foreigner Act, 1946, was another major hindrance in the expulsion of the illegal immigrants, as the Act stated that there were no two separate nations called India and Pakistan. Hence, Pakistani nationals were not to be identified as foreigners, which added up as an advantage to the illegal immigrants

[1] White Paper, Government of Assam, 2012, 6.

from East Pakistan in Assam. The Foreigners Act was amended in 1957 to designate the Pakistani nationals as foreigners.

In 1965, the Government of India and the state governments decided to issue identity cards based on the register of Indian citizens in Assam to protect them from harassment. However, the issuing of the identity cards never happened, and the central government dropped the idea altogether. Again, in January 1965, the Government of Assam submitted a scheme to the Union Home Ministry for providing barbed-wire fencing to cover the vulnerable stretches of Assam–Bangladesh border. Like the identity cards, the central government in 1966 dropped the idea of securing the border with barbed wire after initially agreeing to do it, citing that there was a shortage of items to erect the infrastructure (White Paper on Foreigners' Issue, 2012).

There were a few major laws which were already dealing with the foreigners' issue during the colonial rule as well as in independent India. The first piece of such legislation was the Foreigners Act of 1864, which had provisions to detain foreigners, expel and thereafter ban them from re-entering India.[2] After the Second World War, there was widespread use of the Foreigners Ordinance, 1939, which made it mandatory for all the foreigners visiting India on a long-term basis to register themselves within 14 days of arrival in the country. This Act was later followed by the Foreigners Act, 1946; Foreigners Order, 1948; the Foreigners (Tribunals) Order, 1964; the Immigrants (Expulsion from Assam) Act, 1950; the Citizenship Act, 1955; and the Passport Act of 1967, which are also forerunners of the foreigners' issue in India and are elaborated below.

The Passport (Entry into India) Act, 1920

Implemented by the British in colonial India, this Act did not directly address the influx of illegal immigrants issue, but it was an important law that gave proper guidelines on the need of a passport to enter into India. Under Section 3 of the Act, the central government may make

---

[2] Section 14, of the *Judgement of Sonowal vs. Union of India*, 2005 (Strike Down of the IMTD Act).

rules to require individuals entering India to possess passports and all the accessories that the Indian authorities mandates to have for such visits. Section 3, Clause (3) of the Act provides that any contravention done or suspicion of contravention to any order issued under the authority of India will be punishable with fine and imprisonment for a term, which might get extended to 3 months. The special power of removal of such person from India shall be bestowed upon any officer of the Government of India.

The Foreigners Act, 1946

Enacted before the independence of India, the Interim Government of India was granted certain powers by the Legislative Assembly in the matters of the foreigners' issue in India. The Foreigners Act, 1946, provides the definition of a foreigner as 'a person who is not a citizen of India'.[3] Section 8 of the Act states how an individual is detected as a foreigner, which mainly revolves around the determination of the nationality, and when an individual is recognized as a citizen by law in more than one foreign country, he/she is ascribed with the status of a foreigner in India. Supported by Section 9 of the Foreigners' Act, which states if the nationality of an individual is not clear, the onus of providing whether he/she is a citizen of India falls upon the individual itself. Even if that individual is not a foreigner, the burden to prove his/her citizenship is their own. The Act further gives power to the officials prescribed with such authority by the Indian government to detain such person until deportation back to their origin country is possible. The order of events after a person is recognized as a foreigner are as follows:

- He/she shall or shall not enter India at appointed times and appointed routes by the authority, which will be further recorded at the time of their arrival.
- He/she shall or shall only depart from India at specific times or specific routes which are also to be recorded at the time of their departure.

---

[3] Section 2, Foreigners Act, 1946.

- They will either not be allowed to reside in India or will only be allowed to reside in particular places as directed by the Government of India. All their movements will be recorded, and identity cards would be issued to keep a check on them. In addition to identity cards, the individuals will be prescribed to submit to medical examinations by the authority at any time and place in order to prohibit him/her for association with persons of prescribed or specific description or in engaging in particular activities or to possess prescribed or specific articles. (Section 2, The Foreigners Act, 1946)

This Act is complementary to the Passport Act (Entry into India), 1920; the Immigrants (Expulsion from Assam) Act, 1950; and the Illegal Migrants (Determinations by tribunal) Act 1983 (IMDT Act).

Foreigners Order, 1948

The central government of India made the Foreigners Order 1948 to exercise the powers vested by Section 3 of the Foreigners Act, 1946. This Act primarily lays down the guidelines concerning a foreigner's entry into India along with their movement and departure from India. Section 3 Clause (2) of the Act clearly mentions that a foreigner is barred from entering or leaving India if he/she does not have a valid passport or visa for India, if he/she is a person of unsound mind and is suffering from an infectious disease in the opinion of the appointed medical officer by the Government of India, if he/she is sentenced in a foreign country with some serious offence, or if any specific authority under the central government of India has prohibited his/her order. It also mentions in Section 3 Clause (3) that the civil authorities may attach certain conditions as per the requirement to grant entry to or leave from India.

The Foreigners (Tribunals) Order, 1964

This Act was introduced to exercise the powers bestowed by the Interim Government of India in Section 3 of the Foreigner Act, 1946. Section 2 of the Foreigners (Tribunal) Order, 1964, clearly states that this provision is made to inspect whether a person is or is not a foreigner under the Foreigners Tribunals Act. As per requirement, these tribunals will have several officials appointed by the central government as mentioned in Section 2 Clause (2) of the Act. In Section 4 of this Act, the tribunals are anointed with the powers of the civil court while 'trying suit under the Code of Civil Procedure, 1908'[4]; like the tribunal can summon and enforce the attendance of any suspected person for examination under oath; ask to produce documents regarding his nationality; and issue commissions for the examination of any witness. Under Section 3 Clause 2, the authorities are vested with the powers to regulate and develop its own procedure; in Section 3 Sub-Clause (1A), the person in question of his/her nationality with due respect will be given reasonable opportunity to fight for his/her claim.

The Immigrants (Expulsion from Assam) Act, 1950

The name Immigrants Act (Expulsion from Assam) emphasizes the removal of immigrants from Assam, but the Act extends beyond Assam. Section 2 of the Act says that any individual or a group of individuals who have previously been residing in any place outside India and have entered Assam in or after the commencement of the Act and pose a threat to the general public of India or any other Scheduled Tribe may by order:

> These individuals or group of individuals might be removed from India or Assam within any time and by any route as may be specified in the order.

> Or orders might be given in regard to his or her removal from India or Assam as or when necessary; but nothing in this section will be applied to any person who has come in India or Assam on account of civil disturbances or by the fear of such disturbances in any area now forming part of Pakistan.

Section 3 of the Act mentions that any officer subordinate to the central government of India or Government of Assam and Meghalaya or Nagaland may be awarded the powers and duties to take forward the actions mentioned in Section 2 of the Act. If the individual fails,

---

[4] Section 4 of Foreigners (Tribunal) Order, 1964.

disobeys or abets to the contravention of any order made by the designated authorities under Section 2 of the Act, they will be punishable with imprisonment, which may extend to 3 years, and shall also be accountable to fine.

The Citizenship Act, 1955

There are no fixed provisions relating to the citizenship in India, but it clearly categorizes how one acquires the citizenship of India right from the day of promulgation of the Indian Constitution on 26 January 1950, which is to be regulated by the Parliament.[5] Popularly known as the Citizenship Bill, it was passed by both Houses of Parliament and received the consent of the President of India on 30 December 1955, but in the statute book, it was named as 'The Citizenship Act, 1955' (Page 12, Report of the Joint Committee on the Citizenship [Amendment] Bill, 2016). The Citizenship Act, 1955, came into existence under the powers vested in the Article 11 of the Indian Constitution which states that the Parliament of India has the powers to make provisions to the attainment and execution of citizenship and anything else of similar matter.[6] Major provisions of the Act are broadly divided into three parts:

- **Acquisition of citizenship**: The Act provides individuals with five modes to acquire citizenship: firstly by birth, secondly by descent, thirdly by registration, fourthly by naturalization and, lastly, by incorporation of territory.
- **Termination of citizenship**: Termination can happen either through self-renunciation or by termination or by deprivation. Clause (1) of Section 8 mentions that if any Indian citizen of full age and capacity forwards his/her declaration renouncing his/her Indian citizenship in a prescribed manner, he/she after proper registration 'shall cease to be a citizen of India'.[7] Such declaration will be withheld by the Central Government of India during the

---

[5] Jain, 'Explained: The Nuts and Bolts of Indian Citizenship'.

[6] Part II, Article 11 of *Constitution of India* (accessed 11 February 2020).

[7] Section 8 Clause (1), The Citizenship Act, 1955.

time of war where India is engaged. Termination of citizenship can occur if any citizen of India has voluntarily acquired the citizenship of another country at any time between 26 January 1950 and commencement of this Act, as per Section 9, Clause (1).

- **Supplementary provisions**: The Act also provided with additional provisions for the safety and security of the actual citizens of India, for example, Section 13 asks to provide Certificate of Citizenship to protect the Indian citizens from harassment. Along with National Identity Cards for every recorded Indian citizen under the National Registration Authority, the supplementary provisions also has a provision, as stated in Section 15 Clause (1) and 15(A), that any person who has been wronged by the authority under this Act can make an application to the central government for revision of the status within a period of 30 days.

Several amendments were made to the law after it came into effect in 1955, significantly changing it to suit the needs of the time.[8]

Citizenship Amendment Act, 2019: How Is It Different from Other Citizenship Acts?

The Citizenship Amendment Act, 2019 (CAA-2019) seeks to make three changes to the sections of the Citizenship Act, 1955, in which amendment is proposed. These three changes are mentioned here.

First: Amendment to Clause (b) of sub-Section (1) of Section (2) of the Citizenship Act, 1955.

Existing provisions of the Citizenship Act, 1955: According to Clause (b) of sub-Section (1) of Section 2 of the Citizenship Act, 1955,

---

[8] Some of those amendments, according to the Joint Parliamentary Committee report on CAB-2016 (points 1.10), are: (a) The Citizenship (Amendment) Act, 1957 (65 of 1957); (b) The Repealing and Amending Act, 1960 (58 of 1960); (c) The Citizenship (Amendment) Act, 1985 (65 of 1985); (d) The Delegated Legislation Provisions (Amendment), 1985; (e) The Citizenship (Amendment) Act, 1986 (51 of 1986); (f) The Citizenship (Amendment) Act, 1992 (39 of 1992); (g) The Citizenship (Amendment) Act, 2003 (6 of 2004); (h) The Citizenship (Amendment) Act, 2005 (32 of 2005); and (i) The Citizenship (Amendment) Act, 2015 (1 of 2015).

an 'illegal migrant' means a foreigner who has entered into India—(a) without a valid passport or other travel documents and such other document or authority, as may be prescribed by or under any law on that behalf, or (b) with a valid passport or other travel documents and such other documents or authority, as may be prescribed by or under any law on that behalf, but remains therein beyond the permitted period.

Citizenship Amendment Act, 2019, made the following changes in Section 2: Provided that any person belonging to Hindu, Sikh, Buddhist, Jain, Parsi or Christian community from Afghanistan, Bangladesh or Pakistan, who entered into India on or before the 31st day of December 2014 and who has been exempted by the central government by or under Clause (c) of sub-Section (2) of Section 3 of the Passport (Entry into India) Act, 1920, or from the application of the provisions of the Foreigners Act, 1946, or any rule or order made thereunder, shall not be treated as an illegal migrant for the purposes of this Act.

Second change: Section 7D of the Principal Act, after Clause (d)

Existing provisions of The Citizenship Act, 1955: 7D. Cancellation of registration as overseas citizen of India. The central government may, by order, cancel the registration granted under sub-Section (1) of Section 7A if it is satisfied that—(d) the Overseas Citizen of India, within 5 years after registration under sub-Section (1) of Section 7A, has been sentenced to imprisonment for a term of not less than two years.

Citizenship Amendment Act, 2019 (CAA-2019): In Section 7D of the principal Act, after Clause (d), the following clause shall be inserted, namely: Section 4 Clause (a)—'(d) the Overseas Citizen of India Cardholder has violated any of the provisions of this Act or provisions of any other law for time being in force as may be specified by the Central Government in the notification published in the Official Gazette'.

The Citizenship Amendment Act, 2019, adds the following clauses into the principal Act:

a. Insertion of New Section 6B: (1) The central government or an authority specified by it on its behalf may, subject to such conditions, impose restrictions and manner, as may be prescribed, in an application made on this behalf, grant a certificate of registration or certificate of naturalization to a person referred to in the proviso to Clause (b) of sub-Section (1) of Section 2.

b. Subject to fulfilment of the conditions specified in Section 5 or the qualifications for naturalization under the provisions of the Third Schedule, a person granted the certificate of registration or certificate of naturalization under sub-Section (1) shall be deemed to be a citizen of India from the date of his entry into India.

c. On and from the date of commencement of the Citizenship (Amendment) Act, 2019, any proceeding pending against a person under this section in respect of illegal migration or citizenship shall stand abated on conferment of citizenship to him/her: provided that such person shall not be disqualified for making an application for citizenship under this section on the ground that the proceeding is pending against him/her and the central government or authority specified by it in this behalf shall not reject his/her application on that ground if he/she is otherwise found qualified for the grant of citizenship under this section; provided further that the person who makes the application for citizenship under this section shall not be deprived of his/her rights and privileges to which he/she was entitled on the date of receipt of his/her application on the ground of making such application.

Nothing in this section shall apply to the tribal areas of Assam, Meghalaya, Mizoram or Tripura as included in the Sixth Schedule to the Constitution and the area covered under 'The Inner Line' notified under the Bengal Eastern Frontier Regulation, 1873. In Section 7D after Clause (f), the following proviso shall be inserted, namely 'Provided that no order under this section shall be passed unless the Overseas Citizen of India Cardholder has been given a reasonable opportunity of being heard'.

Third change: In the Third Schedule to the principal Act in Clause (d), the following proviso shall be inserted, namely 'Provided that for the person belonging to Hindu, Sikh, Buddhist, Jain, Parsi or Christian community in Afghanistan, Bangladesh or Pakistan, the aggregate period of residence or service of Government in India as required under this clause shall be read as "not less than five years" in place of "not less than eleven years"'.

Criticism of Citizenship Amendment Act, 2019: Protests in Assam

After the enactment of CAA-2019 in the Indian Parliament, there have been considerable criticism and protests against the Act. Many parts of India, including Delhi, UP, Bihar, West Bengal, Assam and some parts of Northeast India have seen both violent and non-violent protests by civil society organizations. Shaheen Bagh in Delhi has become the epicentre of anti-CAA agitation in North India. Assam has witnessed one of the most intense anti-CAA agitations in which five persons were killed in police firing and two persons died in violent protests by the agitators apart from wanton destruction of properties in various parts of Assam. The question arises as to why Assam, which was so much supportive of the NRC update process, became so dissatisfied with the CAA-2019? What are the main grounds based on which many organizations in Assam have launched the anti-CAA movement? There are essentially eight points behind the protests in Assam against the CAA-19:

1. The Assam Accord of 1985 accepted foreigners till 24 March 1971, but the goalpost now, again, has been changed to 31 December 2014.
2. There is no guarantee that people coming in 2020 or even, later on, would not claim their entry date before December 2014.
3. As per CAA-2019 (as per Clause 6B, sub-Clause 3), even a criminal proceeding would not deter a foreigner from acquiring citizenship.
4. People are also worried about the figure—is it 0.5 million or 1 crore of foreigners? CAA will open up the floodgates for the entry of millions of foreigners into Assam.
5. The other parts of the Northeast region have been given all the benefits and protection. It is Assam which is always left behind;

the Assam Accord was promised as a new way of protection, which is again compromised for the sake of Hindu Bengalis.

6. Assam will be the dumping ground, since the Bengali refugees, after being driven out of the 6th schedule areas, would march into Assam, particularly to the Brahmaputra valley, which is already one of the most populous valleys with a high density of populations than the national level.

7. The CAA-2019 has totally negated the sanctity of the Assam Accord, which was a product of heavy loss of lives and property. During the Assam Movement against the foreigners, 855 martyrs had laid their lives for the cause of Assam. A series of insurgency movements followed, a major issue of which was the encroachment of land and culture at the behest of the immigrants.

8. Even a new NRC could hardly make any intervention as the cut-off date has been practically extended to 31 December 2014. By the extension of foreigners' entry date till December 2014, the NRC's base year from 1951 till 1971 had practically become irrelevant.

The AASU leadership has argued that the issues in Assam have not been about the Hindu–Muslim polarization, but they are about the way it is being projected in other parts of India. The issue in Assam is about identity and protection of the Assamese culture, although a few Muslim immigrant pockets have also come out in the anti-CAA movement ostensibly to protect Assam. The subsequent citizenship laws have also accommodated the descendants of foreigners till 2004. There is a strong sense of hopelessness and insecurity among all sections of the Assamese people.

Citizenship Amendment Act, 2019 (CAA-2019) and Its Critics

There is a distinction between the protests by Assamese elites and criticism by all-India left-liberal scholars. The Assamese people are generally in favour of a strong error-free NRC that was expected to identify about 5–6 million foreigners in the state irrespective of their religious affiliations. The all-India criticism is, however, purely from some abstract universalist principles that decry not only CAA-19 but also NRC in a conterminous manner. Such analysis hardly finds any distinction between NRC and CAA-19. These analyses are based on the typical 'secular-communal' divide. In an article in *Economic and Political Weekly* (*EPW*), it was argued[9]:

1. The Citizenship Amendment Act and the NRC is the culmination of a long project of the Hindu right.
2. If both the CAA and the NRC are read together, then they appear to be discriminatory towards Muslims. These acts mask their underlying discrimination in humanitarian garb.

Referring to an article, it was stated that Nigel Harris, in a discussion on citizenship, has written in the *EPW* that the 'identity card' has been a recurring feature in regimes with authoritarian tendencies. The current project of BJP concerning CAA has a long history, scattered through the years, supporting the fact that the Hindu right had formed the government at the centre.[10]

In a different article on 'Why the Citizenship Amendment Bill Goes Against the Basic Tenets of the Constitution', it was argued that[11] the illegal immigrants who are to be granted the benefit of this legislation are to qualify for citizenship only based on religion, a requirement that goes against one of the basic tenets of the Indian Constitution, that is, secularism. Moreover, the Overseas Citizen of India (OCI) and Persons of Indian Origin (PIO) categories have been merged haphazardly, leaving loopholes in the definition of their position as citizens of India.[12] The second dimension of the article pleads that the most glaring discrepancy in the Bill is that it categorically states that religious minorities from Afghanistan, Pakistan and Bangladesh would no longer be treated as illegal immigrants. It specifically names six

---

[9] See https://www.epw.in/engage/article/marking-territories-illegal-immigrants-citizenship-nrc (accessed 18 December 2019).

[10] Ibid.

[11] Thakur, 'Why the Citizenship Amendment Bill Goes Against the Basic Tenets of the Constitution'.

[12] The article by Apurva Thakur (FN-11) was written in the context of the Citizenship Amendment Bill-2016; however, the argument stands as there were no basic changes.

religions—Hindus, Sikhs, Buddhists, Jains, Parsis and Christians. This kind of religious outlook is antithetical to the concept of secularism espoused in the Constitution. The article further argued that the provision of relaxing the criteria of residency from 11 years to 6 years to gain citizenship by naturalization, for the persons belonging to these religious communities, is on similar orthodox lines.[13] Such a condition makes it tough for persons of other religions, most notably, Islam and Judaism, to enter the fold of Indian citizenship, making it seem like a targeted ousting practice of these religions.

In most of the criticisms, it was stated that CAB/CAA would fail the test of reasonable classification as set out in Article 14 of the Constitution. If the bill was tested on reasonable classification, it would fail, as the classification sought was to differentiate between persons who would be granted relaxation in the domiciliary requirement and those who would not. Further it was argued that since at present the process excludes illegal immigrants only on religious grounds, with no reasonable explanation, assigning a qualification based on religion has no rational nexus to achieve that object unless the object is to project India as a Hindu state. The article deplored that the bill has come at a time when the entire world is plagued by ideas of nationality and ethnicity. Unfortunately, the bill does not attempt to define the terms like abstractions of citizenship, nationality and domiciliation, leaving scope for ambiguity in interpretation.

In another article, 'Marking Territories: Illegal Immigrants, the Citizenship (Amendment) Act and the NRC' in *EPW*, it was argued that:

> *The Citizenship Amendment Act and the NRC is the culmination of a long project of the Hindu right.* As mass protests erupt all over the country over the Citizenship (Amendment) Act (CAA), and the possibility of the National Register of Citizens (NRC) being implemented all over the country looms large, the Bharatiya Janata Party (BJP) continues to push its 'illegal immigrant' narrative to denounce the protests. If both the CAA and the NRC are read together, then they appear to be discriminatory towards Muslims.

---

[13] The CAA-19 reduced it to five years instead of eleven years.

A recent *EPW* editorial has discussed that these acts mask their underlying discrimination in a humanitarian garb. (emphasis in original)[14]

Most of these articles or interpretations have failed to grasp the context under which both NRC and CAA-19 have been enacted. The most abject failure of these commentaries was their inability to distinguish between NRC and CAA. If one makes content analyses of these writings since the beginning of the publication of the draft NRC, one would find a similar pattern of criticism against both NRC and CAA. None of the writers has bothered to investigate the contexts under which NRC was conceptualized. None of them has considered the historical context under which CAA-19 has been enacted. While one may legitimately criticize CAA-19, its content, the last date for entry to India and the flagrant violation of the Assam Accord, among many other things, there were no efforts so far to understand how the notion of citizenship has been understood in Indian parlance. How were the Hindu–Muslim issues of citizenship discussed in the Constituent Assembly? Was there any legislation that could reflect on citizenship dilemma in Assam/India? How was the citizenship issue addressed in the Citizenship Acts of 1955? What are the changes brought in by subsequent amendment to the Act? What are the administrative and executive decisions pertaining to Hindu refugees in Assam and the eastern part of India? Were there any preferences given to the persecuted Hindus in Assam? If so, then why India had to accommodate such refugees into the citizenship regime framework? Finally, why did the issue of CAA-2019 erupt in 2019? These issues perhaps require deeper historical and political–contextual analyses that could help to understand the present citizenship dilemma in India in general and Assam in particular. A mere 'secular–communal' divide analogy runs the risk of whitewashing the context under which the present debate has arisen.

This chapter tries to address the above contentious issues we have highlighted.

---

[14] *EPW Engage*, 'Marking Territories', https://www.epw.in/engage/article/marking-territories-illegal-immigrants-citizenship-nrc (accessed 18 December 2019).

National Register of Citizens and the Concept of 'Documentary Citizenship'

The rejection of NRC by the Assamese indigenous people of the state reflects the dilemma of a smaller nationality in India that desperately tries to maintain its numerical strength in all conceivable ways. The final draft of NRC was rejected because of three factors:

1. The figure as we have argued in the Chapter 3 could not meet the expectation of 5–6 million illegal migrants in Assam.
2. Rather, NRC has regularized all the illegal migrants who had adopted fraudulent means to acquire citizenship.
3. The Bengali Hindus were the greatest victims of the process as many refugee certificates were rejected and those people who came to Assam due to persecution in Bangladesh were not considered.

It is acknowledged at various levels that the illegal migrants use various illegal means to legitimize their citizenship. An important study in this regard may be referred to Kamal Sadique's book *Paper Citizens: How Illegal Immigrants Acquire Citizenship in Developing Countries*.[15] He argues that most of the developing countries are governed by a weak and erratic bureaucracy, which helps illegal immigrants to obtain citizenship papers. He introduces the concept of 'documentary citizenship' to explain how paperwork is more often fraudulently obtained. Referring to Assam, Sadique argues that the scenario in Assam is an outcome of document-centric citizenship.[16] Concerning the immigration of illegal migrants from Bangladesh to India and elsewhere, he writes 'documentary citizenship opens the door not only to the exercise of suffrage by illegal immigrants but also to public office, thus directly challenging the boundaries ... between the immigrants and citizens. The recruitment of illegal immigrants as voters also advantage certain political parties'.[17] Thus, a new set of voters across boundaries have

[15] Sadique, *Paper Citizens*.

[16] Ibid., 139.

[17] Ibid., 140.

emerged, blurring the distinction that the state intends to impose. Thus, a duality comes out: on the one hand, the state wants to adopt a rational–legal framework, as we have highlighted in Chapter 3, leaning on Subrata Mitra and Roger Brubaker's articulations. NRC was precisely such a document-centric exercise that tried to define who a legal citizen of this country is. On the other hand, these very documents have been fabricated to lay claims on citizenship, defeating the objective of NRC. Sadique further argues:

> Documentary citizenship in this manner not only 'enfranchise illegal immigrants', but the political participation of these individuals can alter political outcomes in favour of governments that enable illegal immigrants to acquire proof of citizenship and the ability to vote. In effect, illegal immigrants may vote in order to secure their identity and citizenship status.[18]

India's De Facto Policy Preference to Hindu Refugees: Controversy During Assam Agitation

The Citizenship Amendment Act, 2019, has to be seen in this perspective, as NRC has negated some of the historically enacted laws and practices, particularly regarding the Hindu refugees and displaced persons since the dawn of India's independence. Through a process of 'documentary citizenship', NRC has almost legalized the majority of the illegal Muslim immigrants, whereas the Hindu Bengali refugees who had some form of displacement or evacuee certificates could not get their citizenship. It may be mentioned here that since independence, India's citizenship policy has always granted preferential treatment to the Hindus who were persecuted in erstwhile West and East Pakistan. This becomes clear from the (a) debate in Constituent Assembly over citizenship, (b) debates on the Illegal Immigration Expulsion Act (1950), (c) debates and discussions over Citizenship Amendments Act of 1955 and (d) discussion on the Citizenship Act, 1985–1986.

Here, the opinion of Sanjib Baruah is significant. He argues

---

[18] Ibid., 140–41.

In the context of pan-Indian and international politics of the sub-continent, Assam's illegal immigration problem is embroiled in two highly sensitive questions—a) treatment of India's Muslims minority population and b) what many see as an unavoidable legacy of India's partition in 1947; India's de facto obligation to allow Hindu refugees from Pakistan to settle in India. India's policy on immigration to the north-eastern states is framed by a pan-Indian formulation of the problem. There is an implicit acceptance of the rights of the Hindu political refugees from East Bengal to settle anywhere in India.[19]

However, the Assamese leaders and organizations grudgingly accepted the distinction between the Muslim immigrants and Hindu refugees. Arguments made by the Assamese leaders in Constituent Assembly debates and in the I(IE)A-1950 (also referred to as Illegal Immigration Expulsion Act (1950) in our analysis) debate would amply make it clear that they were in tune with the national policy of preferential treatment to the Bengali Hindu refugees in contrast to the Muslim immigrants, and that attitude of the leaders was shaped by the Assamese people's experience during the colonial period. Besides, the Assam government, in view of massive immigration on the eve of Partition to Assam, formulated a permit system in 1947–1948, that granted preferential treatment to the displaced and persecuted Hindu refugees from East Bengal, which was denied to the other groups of people. It would be wrong to conclude as was done by Professor Baruah that 'yet the construction of the problem of Assamese narratives, which among other things, does not generally distinguish between Hindu and Muslim immigrants'.[20] Our subsequent discussion on the issue would become clear from the fact that despite having many prejudices against the Bengali Hindus, Assam provided policy-level preferences to the Hindu refugees. This was not only the case until 1971, but the process of granting asylum or refugee or displaced status to the Bengali Hindus also continued until about 1978–1979, and in some other parts of the region, it continued until 1985. Indeed, Assamese nationality was always suspicious and sceptical of Bengali Hindu's assertion in Assam's sociocultural mosaic, and this distinction is more

---

[19] Baruah, *India Against Itself*, 15.

[20] Ibid.

acutely asserted by AASU's mobilization during the Assam Movement and in anti-CAA agitation in 2018–2019. But such apprehension did not deter the policymakers and Assamese indigenous political leadership to provide asylum to Bengali Hindus at various points of time.

Even during the Assam Agitation, the Bengali Hindu refugee issue was a burning issue at various official-level talks with AASU and others. The issue was more officially acknowledged by the Janata government, including Morarji Desai, Chandrasekhar, Assam CM Golap Borbora and others. As noted by Chhabra,

> While tendering evidence before the committee on Petitions of the Rajya Sabha on August 30, 1980 with reference to the petition signed by Golap Borbora and 16 other MLAs of the Assam Legislative Assembly praying for the Rajya Sabha's intervention to resolve the crises arising out of the foreign national issues, Golap Borbora acknowledged that the Immigrants (Expulsion Act) Act, 1950 provided protection to refugees who were mostly Hindus from East Pakistan.[21]

In addition to the cut-off date, another issue that confronted the leadership of the Assam Agitation most was the issue of Bengali Hindus' settlement in Assam. In the subsequent discussions, the agitation leaders agreed to accommodate only 240,000 refugees who had entered between 1961 and 1971. The student leaders refused to accept 914,000 Hindu refugees who had come from East Pakistan in the subsequent period; thus, the settlement of such a huge figure of Hindu Bengali refugees in the post-1971 period perhaps had remained unsettled.[22] In the subsequent talks, particularly in those held in Shillong from 21 August 1981, GOI insisted that 'all members of the minority community in East Pakistan who had come from there should be treated as refugees. The Assam leaders were opposed to this'.[23] GOI all along insisted on the point that because of the government's longstanding commitment to the refugees in erstwhile Pakistan and East Bengal, the agitation leaders should not insist on turning out those

---

[21] Chhabra, *Assam Challenge*, 107.

[22] Kumar, *Challenge to India's Unity*, 144.

[23] Ibid., 145.

who had come to seek refuge in the wake of communal disturbances in East Pakistan.[24]

Sanjib Baruah further argues:

> The legal definition of Indian citizenship rejects the idea that Hindus and Muslims are separate nations. Yet in political terms, post-Partition India is not in a position to close its doors to Hindus coming in from East Pakistan/Bangladesh. For whatever the legal position, many in India believe that Hindus have an implicit right of return. The continued migration of Muslims—aside from the Partition-induced migration of Hindus—made the issue even more complicated.[25]

What prompted India to formulate a pro-Hindu citizenship regime that Sanjib Baruah considers to be 'India's de facto obligation to allow Hindu refugees from Pakistan to settle in India'? It is important to look at those historical conditions as to how such a policy regime was enacted. It is equally important to see whether the enactment of CAA-2019 precipitated any objective situation that resembled a crisis for 'Hindu citizenship' on the eve of the Partition, when a large chunk of Hindu citizens were subjected to torture and discrimination in neighbouring countries. What facilitated the enactment of the Citizenship Amendment Act, 2019, which is more blatant and direct in addressing the religious dimension of citizenship than those of the 1950s and 1960s?

Constituent Assembly Debates: Issue of Granting Citizenship to Persecuted Hindus and the Question of Secularism

In the Constituent Assembly debates, certain questions were raised, particularly about citizenship: (a) After having migrated to Pakistan, should those Muslims who want to come, or are coming back to India/Assam, be allowed to come and grant citizenship? (b) If granted, what is the total number of those who are granted such citizenship? (c) What will be the status of the minorities living in Pakistan? (d) If

---

[24] Ibid., 148. Also see Murthy, *Assam: The Difficult Years*.

[25] Baruah, 'The Partition's Long Shadow', 596.

they want to come back, would they be considered for citizenship? (e) Given the enormous influx of Muslim and Hindu immigrants to Assam, how would the situation be tackled in Assam? Would some groups of people be given preferences? and (f) Would secularism be compromised if certain groups are given preferential treatment because of Partition and treatment of minorities in Pakistan?

An argumentative debate took place from 11 August 1949 onwards on the Articles 5 and 6 of the Constitution. A majority of the members who took part in the discussion vouched for restrictive citizenship rights and urged for an accommodative policy for the Hindu and Sikh refugees. Dr P. S. Deshmukh, the Minister of Agriculture, in the first cabinet of Jawaharlal Nehru, pleaded,

> I want to make a provision that every person who is a Hindu or a Sikh and is not a citizen of any other state shall be entitled to be a citizen of India. We have seen the formation and establishment of Pakistan. Why was it established? It was established because the Muslims claimed that they must have a home of their own and a country of their own. Here we are an entire nation with a history of thousands of years and we are going to discard it, in spite of the fact neither the Hindu nor the Sikh has any other place in the wide world to go to. By the mere fact that he is a Hindu or a Sikh he should get Indian citizenship because it is this one circumstance that makes him disliked by others.[26]

He urged that the adoption of secularism in principles must not deter India from holding favourable laws to those Hindus who were discriminated in the neighbouring countries that were not secular like Bharat. To quote Deshmukh:

> But we are a secular state and do not want to recognise the fact that every Hindu or Sikh in any part of the world should have a home of his own. If the Muslims want an exclusive place for themselves called Pakistan why should not Hindus and Sikhs have India as their home?

He persuaded that India was not debarring others from getting citizenship here, but the Hindus and Sikhs had no place to go.

---

[26] Constituent Assembly Debates, *Official Report*, Vol. IX (New Delhi: Lok Sabha Secretariat, 2003), 355–56.

We merely say that we have no other country to look to for acquiring citizenship rights and therefore we the Hindus and the Sikhs so long as we follow the respective religions, should have the right of citizenship in India and should be entitled to retain such citizenship so long as we acquire no other.

He further stated that it would not make 'India a non-secular or sectarian or communal. If anybody says so he is to say the least mistaken'.

Professor Shibban Lal Saksena supported the discussion and said:

the Hindus and Sikhs have no other home but India and I do not see how we can include everyone in his category unless we say it bluntly in this form. We should not be ashamed in saying that every person who is a Hindu or a Sikh by religion and is not a citizen of another state shall be entitled to citizenship of India. That will cover every class whom we want to cover and will be comprehensive. The phrase secular should not frighten us in saying what a fact is and reality must be faced.[27]

Another member, Shri Jaspat Roy Kapoor, provided a detailed analysis of how the Hindus and Sikhs had been discriminated and persecuted in Pakistan and suggested that they must be provided citizenship on their return. To quote him:

It seems to me that it is likely to be felt very seriously and bitterly by those of our brethren who took all the trouble and who underwent all that misery and among by migrating from Pakistan to this dear and sacred land of theirs. All the while that they were on their way to this land, they were thinking of this beloved country of theirs, pining and praying to reach our borders, and immediately on reaching those borders, with a great sense of relief they cried out 'Jai Hind' a cry which touched every one of us.

One of the detailed analyses on citizenship was provided by Pandit Thakur Das Bhargava. He said there should not be any problem for the refugees in becoming an India citizen.

When we are making almost a provincial law I am desirous that not a single person who has come from Pakistan as a refugee should have any trouble in being a citizen of India. I am anxious that no obstacle should

---

[27] Ibid., 379.

be placed in the way of those refugees who have come from Pakistan on account of disturbances and who have left their hearths and homes and come to this country.

His second assertion was that those who were desirous to become citizens of Pakistan on the 15th of August 1947 or who left this country to become citizens of Pakistan with open eyes, and with the song *'Hanske liya Pakistan; Ladke lenge Hindustan'* on their lips, should not be made citizens of India. Those persons have now forfeited their right to become citizens of this country. Commenting on the refugees from Pakistan, he said:

> Sir I submit that so far as these refugees are concerned they were the nationals of India. By the mere fact of partition, they have not ceased to be citizens of India, provided they have come here and want to settle permanently in this country. They have every right to citizenship and any obstacle in their way I regard as unjustified and wrong'.[28]

Situation in Assam: Population Invasion

Drawing the attention of the House to Assam, Thakur Das Bhargava urged that after Partition, as many as 0.3 million Hindu refugees from East Bengal Muslims had migrated to Assam. He said that if a Muslim came to India and swore allegiance to India and loves India, all would have nothing but love for that man. 'But even after the partition for reasons best known to themselves many Mussalmans have come to Assam with a view to make a Muslims majority in that province for election purpose and not to live in Assam as citizens of India'.

He supported those who had come to Assam on account of disturbances in Pakistan or fear of disturbances there certainly must get asylum in India. Supporting the cause of nationalist Muslims, he said

> If any nationalist Mussalmans who is [sic] afraid of the Muslims of East Pakistan or West Pakistan comes to India, he certainly should be welcomed. It is our duty to see that he is protected. We will treat him as our brother and a bona fide national of India. In regard to those others who have not come here on account of disturbances, we should not allow them to become

[28] Ibid., 380–82.

citizens of India …. I would rather insist that man should not come here and become a citizen just to bolster up a Muslim majority in one of the provinces of India.

Therefore, the first condition of migration would be that the person comes here on account of disturbances at homeland. For those who want to stay here on that account, the doors of India would be open, but to those who come with sinister motives of occupying lands and usurping the rightful owners by terrorizing them and becoming a majority in this country, no asylum should be offered in India.

Another member, Shri R. K. Sidhwa, supported the Hindu-Sikh refugee cause and demanded a similar status of refugees and citizenship to the 16,000 Parsis who were stranded in various parts of the world and mostly in Iran.[29] Banarsi Prasad Jhunjhunwala also highlighted the precarious situation in Assam and argued that it was important to know the real intention of the person who had come to India and was residing in Assam. They were going to Assam not because they were inconvenienced in Pakistan, but because they simply intended to remain in Assam and increase their population there. Jhunjhunwala moved a resolution to avoid giving citizenship rights to such persons.[30]

Interest of Hindu-Sikh Refugees and Question of Secularism

Sardar Bhupinder Singh Mann (East Punjab, Sikh) put forward his views in the following manner:

> Sir in the definition of citizenship, which covers fairly extensive ground the view point of Hindu and Sikh refugees, has been met to some extent by the Drafting Committee whom I congratulate on that Account. But as usual, a weak sort of secularism has crept in and unfair partiality has been shown to those who least deserve it. I was saying that the Hindu and Sikh refugees view point has been met to some extent, but not wholly. I do not understand why the 19 July 1948 has been prescribed for the purpose of

---

[29] Ibid., 387–88.

[30] The 11 August 1949, Constituent Assembly of India, Friday, the 12 August 1949, Dr Rajendra Prasad in the Chair.

citizenship. These unfortunate refugees could not have foreseen this date; otherwise they would have invited Pakistan knife earlier so that they might have come here earlier and acquired citizenship rights.[31]

He believed it would be very cruel to shut our borders to those who were victimized after 19 July 1948. They were as many sons of the soil as anyone else. The political mishap was not of their own seeking, and now, it would be very cruel to place these political impediments in their way of coming over to 'Bharat Mata', he stated.

Bhupinder Singh Mann opposed the proposed permit system[32] which, according to him, could not be used for citizenship purpose, especially in granting citizenship to those who had settled in Pakistan and expressed intention to come back, as they found asymmetries in their Islamic Pakistan.

He felt that if at all the permit system was intended to confer benefits of citizenship, then a particular authority specifically constituted for that purpose should have been there and that authority should have realized at the time of giving the permit the implication that this was not simply a permit to enable a person to visit India for trade or commerce but that would entail along with it citizenship rights also. He further argued:

> Meos from Gurgaon, Bharatpur and Alwar not very long time ago, on the instigation of the Muslim League, demanded Meostan and they were involved in very serious rioting against the Hindus—their neighbours at the time of Freedom. Right in 1947 a serious riot was going on by these Meos against their Hindu neighbours. These Meos, under this very lax permit system, are returning and demanding their property.

> This is secularism no doubt, but a very one sided and undesirable type of secularism which goes invariably against and to the prejudice of Sikh and Hindu refugees. I do not want to give rights of citizenship to those who

---

[31] Constituent Assembly Debates, *Official Report*, 393–94.

[32] There were three kinds of permits—temporary, business and settlement. The permit system enabled certain groups of Muslims to come back to India and settle their economic business issues. On the eve of Partition, a limited number of Muslims who went to Pakistan, however, came back requesting to confer back their Indian citizenship. Please see Nehru's views on the permit system in the following pages.

so flagrantly dishonored the integrity of India not so long ago. Yesterday Mr Sidhva gave an argument that this proviso will not only cover Muslims who had gone to Pakistan and will return later on, but also other nationals, e.g. Christians. But may I inform him that there is not a single Christian living in India who has gone over to Pakistan and who will come back later on?

Some other members like Mr Mahboob Ali Baig (Madras, Muslim), on the other hand, pleaded for the return of those who wanted to come back. He said that he was very much surprised to hear that such persons who were coming back may be traitors. He argued that 'The arm of the law should be so strong that it must be able to get at any man who became a traitor'. He said

> What would you do if one of your man becomes a traitor, a Communist and tries to overthrow the Government? So, to say those people coming to India might become traitors and therefore they should not be allowed to come back that is no reason at all.

He argued that with such temperament, the nation would never become strong. That kind of psychology should be shunned, must be got rid of. He added 'Moreover, we are only legislating the present. Parliament may in its discretion, if it thinks it to be necessary, deprive any person of his citizenship and expel him. Parliament is supreme in this matter'.[33]

Nehru on Permit System, Citizenship and 'Nationalist Muslims'

It is interesting to look at the viewpoints of Pandit Jawaharlal Nehru. The government had accepted, practically without demur or enquiry, the great waves of migration from Pakistan to India, as citizens. That continued up to sometime in July 1948. He said that in that year, many wrong people might have come over whom the country might not accept as a citizen if each one of them were examined separately, but it was impossible to examine hundreds of thousands of such cases and the whole lot was therefore accepted.

[33] Ibid., 394–98.

Now, all these rules naturally apply to Hindus, Muslims, Sikhs, Christians or anybody else. Nehru argued that the first year's migration was a migration of Hindus and Sikhs from Pakistan. The others hardly come into the picture. It was possible that later, because of the permit system, some non-Hindus and non-Sikhs came in. How did they come in? How many came in?

Three types of permits were issued to these people. One was a temporary permit for a month or two. The condition of the temporary permit was that an allottee must leave or go back within the permit period. The second type of permit was a continuing permanent one that did not entitle a man to settle here but allowed him to come here repeatedly on business. The third type of permit was given to a person to come here for permanent stay, that is, return to India and settle down here. Nehru pleaded:

> Now, in this case of all these permits a great deal of care has been taken in the past before issuing them. In the case of those permits which are meant for permanent return to India and settling here again a very great deal of care has been taken. The local officials of the place where the man came from and where he wants to go back are addressed; the local government is addressed and it is only when sufficient reason is found by the local officials and the local Government that our high Commissioner in Karachi or Lahore, as the case may be issues that kind of permit ... very roughly it may be 2,000 or 3.000.[34]

Nehru referred to those categories of Muslims who came back from Pakistan after having migrated from India as 'nationalist Muslims'. Who were those 'nationalist Muslims'? Nehru said

> Then there are number of cases of those people whom you might call the Nationalist Muslims, those people who had absolutely no desire to go away but who were simply pushed out by circumstances, who were driven out by circumstances and who having gone to the other side saw that they had no place there at all, because the other side did not like them at all; they considered them as opponents and enemies made their lives miserable for them right through from the beginning they expressed a desire to come back and some of them have come back. My point is that the number of

---

[34] Nehru, Constituent Assembly Debate referred above, 12 August 1949, 398–401.

case involved considering everything, is an insignificant number, a small number'.

Viewpoints by Indigenous Assamese Representatives

In this connection, it would be prudent to understand the viewpoints of indigenous Assamese representatives in the Constituent Assembly. How did the Assamese tribal or the scheduled caste representatives view the Hindu refugee issue, bearing in mind the long-standing acrimonious relationship with the Bengali elites in Assam? What were their views about citizenship? How did they look into the illegal migrant dimension? It may be mentioned that the emigration of Muslims from Pakistan to India was not more than 2,000–3,000, as suggested by Nehru. However, 0.5 million immigrated to Assam alone from 1948 to 1950.

Shri Rohini Kumar Chaudhury from Assam provided unanimous viewpoints representing both the ST and SC members of Assam. Chaudhury made it clear that all the members from Assam would like to present consensual viewpoints of the people of Assam. He said

> The same amendment was also tabled by my honorable friend Mr. Jhunjhunwala, (he spoke on yesterday) and was tabled by me who is supposed to represent the Assamese Hindus, by my honorable friend Mr Basumatari[35] who represent the tribal people in Assam and by my friend Mr Laskar,[36] who represent the Bengal Scheduled Castes of Assam. These are the three different groups of people who have supported. I would therefore once more request the house to consider carefully the actual facts, not merely supposition, not merely theories or wish, as to how certain things ought to be done and to decide for themselves.[37]

Chaudhury urged for citizenship rights for those persons in Assam, particularly those who had come from East Bengal, because they found things impossible for them in East Bengal. He said that everyone who

[35] Dharanidhar Basu-Matari from Assam representing the Scheduled Tribes.

[36] Nibaran Chandra Laskar from Cachar representing Scheduled Castes.

[37] Constituent Assembly Debates, *Official Report*, 413–17.

came from East Bengal was not really actuated by fear or disturbance or living in a place where disturbance had taken place. He urged,

> Has that sense of security, now after a period of two years, been enhanced by the fact that Pakistan has been converted into a theocratic State? ... The fear is latent in the mind of everybody. The moment any Hindu or a person of any minority community raises a protest against any action which is taken there, disturbance would immediately follow, is there any doubt about that? Therefore, Sir, in answer to Pandit Kunzru's criticism, I would say that this condition of fear, of disturbance should not all be insisted in the case of a person coming from Pakistan over to West Bengal or Assam or any other place in India.

He was very categorical in demanding citizenship rights to those people of East Bengal who had gone over to West Bengal or Assam out of fear of disturbance in the future or from a sense of insecurity, and for those people who had come over from Sylhet. Chaudhury pleaded for the denial of those citizenship rights to a certain group of people. He said:

> At the same time, I also have the temerity to say in this House that I would exclude those persons who came only three years ago, who set up the civil disobedience movement, forcibly occupied land which was not meant for them, and forced the benevolent and benign Government to have recourse to the military to keep peace in the province I should be the last person to say, and I hope everyone has honestly acknowledged that, that class or persons should by any means be granted citizenship rights in the province.... I desire to exclude these people because they had not long ago set up the struggle for Pakistan, they had not long before taken an active part in compelling the politicians of India to agree for Partition; they have their own property and are living peacefully on their own property; not only that, they have brought about such a state of things that they have been able to purchase property for mere nothing, property which belongs to the minority who had come out of fear.

He passionately voiced for the exclusion of those persons who surreptitiously introduced themselves into the province and who now had mixed themselves with their own brethren desire to have citizenship rights, not out of any sense of insecurity on their part, in their own provinces, but with a desire to exploit more from Assam.

Position of Minorities in East Bengal

Rohini Kumar Chaudhury made one of the longest presentations on citizenship issues from Assam. He also referred to the minority rights in East Bengal. They could not get any government service. No person of minority community held even a junior post there. On the contrary, in Assam, high positions like the secretary of finance and education were held by minorities. Many business organizations and insurance companies in East Bengal had closed their branches there and came to India; even doctors had been denied patronage. Permits by which the majority of business was done were not given to the members of the minority community in East Bengal. He stated

> Then, what is the reason why the people of that majority community in East Bengal who have all these advantages should come to Assam? The reason is to exploit and get some advantages. Are you going to encourage this? You will be surprised to learn that the Government of Assam have requested the Government of India to give them the authority to issue permits to restrict such entries, but they have been denied.

By citing various sources, especially from the Muslim League in Dhaka, Chaudhury argued that more than 0.3 million Muslims had migrated from East Bengal on account of some economic difficulties. He said 'Now, you imagine, if three lacs is the figure which is given by the Muslim League in East Bengal, what must have been the real figure of people who have been infiltrating like this'. Chaudhury was categorical in saying that such kinds of people were undesirable and would adversely tilt the balance of population in near future.

> If you wish to govern a province properly, you should always try to see that the balance of the population is not so much disturbed and you should see that you do not give citizenship to persons whose presence in that province would be undesirable and prejudicial to the interests of the Dominion of India.

He urged that his viewpoints were supported by all communities in the province of Assam, including Muslims who belong to Assam. He said the 'nationalist Muslims' who have made Assam their home would agree with him. From point of view of security also, Chaudhury urged for the proper protection of Assam; otherwise, the country would expose a vital frontier to the demographic machinations of the neighbouring countries and the province would become a source of great danger. He said that the process had already started in Cachar and the district would become entirely one district of Pakistan if the process was not halted.

N. Gopalaswami Ayyangar, a member of the Drafting Committee of the Constitution, focussed substantially on Assam's problem. He said that there was no doubt that a substantial number of Muslims did go from East Bengal to Assam. Assam Government was in need of a Permit system that would regulate movement of citizens between East Bengal and Assam. The issue was discussed at various levels with the Government of India. However, rather than having a permit system, Ayyangar endorsed a piece of legislation to be tabled in the Lok Sabha that would frame an adequate law for dealing with the situation in Assam. He added

> I think it will be possible to devise some kind of legislation which will enable Assam stem the tide very substantially. I would not like that we should adopt any methods which would complicate the situation in the eastern border of the country. A number of Muslim coming in who are not wanted there but we should not altogether ignore the possibility that conditions being what they are in Assam.

However, he cautioned that the overzealous officials of the Assam government might obstruct the Bengalis who have migrated from East Bengal to Assam and perhaps even from West Bengal to Assam.

Citizenship Debate:
Act, Legislations and Executive Decisions in
Post-independence Period

Discussion on the nature of India's citizenship would remain incomplete if we do not discuss how the Illegal Immigration Expulsion Act (1950) was enacted. While moving the bill, the Minister of Transport and Railways, Shri Gopalaswami, said, 'I beg to move the Bill to provide for the expulsion from Assam of undesirable immigrants be taken into consideration'.[38]

Why I(IE)A-1950 for Assam?

In the state of Assam, particularly after the Partition, the influx of immigrants from outside into the state had been increasing in alarming proportions, which caused apprehensions in the government and among the people of Assam about the disturbance that such a number of people would cause to their economy and polity. The Assam government brought this fact to the notice of the central government in 1948, and since then, the matter has been under examination. Many conferences and discussions were held, some with Pakistan and others between the central government and the state government. Various suggestions were considered, including a permit system. After further discussions with the Government of Assam, it was finally settled that instead of introducing a permit system which would control the entry of outsiders into Assam, the government should have the power to expel such foreign nationals from Assam who had entered that state and whose continued stay was likely to cause disturbance to its economy.

It may be mentioned that before the Bill was introduced, an ordinance was promulgated to deal with the emergent situation.

Aim of the Bill

Regarding the aim of the bill, it was said that if any person who was not ordinarily a resident of Pakistan, or as it would be under an amendment, or any country outside India, came into Assam and his/her continuance in that state was considered to be undesirable, then the central government had the power to direct him/her to remove himself/herself from Assam and to give such other directions as may be necessary in that context. The powers were primarily in the hands

---

[38] Parliamentary Debate (Part II—Proceedings Other than Questions and Answers), Wednesday, 8 February 1950, 313–50.

of the central government, but for ordinary administration, these powers were proposed to be delegated to the Government of Assam. As a matter of fact, under the Ordinance, those powers were delegated not merely to the Government of Assam but to a number of Assam officers by designation.

Before an expulsion order could be issued, the central government should be satisfied that any person who, having been ordinarily resident in any part of Pakistan, had whether before or after the commencement of this Act, come into Assam and that his/her stay in the province of Assam would be detrimental to the interests of India. While introducing the bill, the minister said that the Bill was intended to be used only against those persons whose continuance in Assam would be detrimental to the interests of India. It was not intended to be applied to persons whose stay would not be so detrimental, or who, for instance, on account of disturbances and disorder in Pakistan, had come to take shelter in Assam.

Conspiracy of Muslim League: Assam Government Criticized

Sardar B. S. Mann (Punjab) was very critical on both state and central governments for having allowed the problem to proliferate to such an extent.

He said that it was a very sad commentary on the central government as well as criminal negligence on the part of Assam state that, while they were holding conferences when the fact was brought to their notice, instead of stopping or checking the influx by immediate measures, they let the immigrants not only be doubled but trebled.

> After all it was not on one day, in a month or within a limited period during which this invasion took place. It was a slow process of permeation in India. The Government very well knew that it was the offshoot of a deep-laid conspiracy which had started earlier .... I have got the considered opinion of the Assam Government that during the Muslim League regime it was a conspiracy to convert Assam, which was a Hindu majority province into a Muslim majority province. It was a deep-seated and deep-rooted and well planned conspiracy of the Muslim League when Mr Saadullah was the

Premier of Assam and as a result of this large scale immigration started. During the war it increased.

He urged that it was not a secret plan; it was well known. The central government came to know of it in 1948 and 1949 passed, and now, at the beginning of 1950, an Ordinance was promulgated, and a bill is brought before the House. Sardar BS Mann deplored the situation in Assam, and lamented that the situation reflected an imbecile attitude of the Assam government, and that it had allowed, not a few, or thousands of people, but 0.5 million undesirable immigrants to come over and take forcible possession of the best lands in Assam. Worse was that that they had not only settled in the tribal belts but also in the village grazing lands. He wondered why the Assam government, which had so successfully resisted the claims of Hindu refugees from East Bengal and exhibited such a virulent attitude that it had not permitted Hindu refugees to settle now, had not raised its voice against the undesirable immigrants from East Bengal. He considered it to be a sheer case of negligence and incompetency.

Term 'Immigrant' Must Not Apply to Refugees

Shri R. K. Choudhury from Assam urged the members to provide a clear-cut definition of 'undesirable immigrants'. He said that the minister should make it clear by a clause that the word 'immigrant' in this Bill did not include the refugees who had come to Assam. Otherwise, it would mean that it could apply to both the refugees who had come to Assam for shelter as well as the other persons who had come to Assam for a particular purpose. He said that 'economic' argument was not sufficient. If the Bill was allowed to be enacted as it was, which would suggest that the government was going to expel people because they were disturbing the economy of the province, then the same argument might be applied to the refugees as well because the large influx of refugees to Assam was bound to affect in one way or the other the economy of that province, unless a clear policy was laid down by the government to rehabilitate them as quickly as possible. Thus, he pleaded that in the Bill, the government should make it clear that the term 'immigrant' would not apply to refugees at all. He estimated that for every single refugee who had come to Assam, three times that number had come from East Pakistan who could not by any means be called refugees.

Chaudhury further said there were two factors which prevented bona fide refugees from East Bengal coming to Assam. One was that the East Bengal Hindu refugees were not allowed to come freely by the Pakistan government. They demanded passes and permits and certificates from the Income Tax Department. The other factor was, as perhaps also in West Bengal, that the local people did not welcome the influx of a large number of people coming from outside. For that reason, those Hindu refugees had not been able to absorb themselves into the existing Hindu population of that province.

Design of Non-refugee (Muslim) Immigrants

So far as non-refugee immigrants are concerned, those who had come in for economic reasons or reasons of exploitation, a large number of their own people had already settled in that province as a result of the policy which was pursued before the Partition of India. Who else could be more aware of such immigrants than that of Rohini Chaudhury who was twice the Revenue Minister in the pre-independence period of Assam? He said:

> A large number of such people have already settled there who welcome their brethren to the Province and when they come in, not on account of fear of disturbances, there is an organization to help them. They are received at two stations, one of them Badarpur which is on the border of Assam. They are received properly and located in one or two houses and then distributed over different parts of the Province. Whenever any such people come to Assam they are very much welcomed by their brethren who had come in some years earlier, they are allowed to settle down and they gradually spread out. As against all this, the difficulties of the East Bengal Hindu refugees, which I have stated above, are still there.[39]

[39] Parliamentary Debate, Lok Sabha Secretariat (Part II—Proceedings Other than Questions And Answers), Wednesday, 8 February 1950, 313–50.

Protection Required for Indigenous
Local and Hindu Refugees

Chaudhury was well aware of the problem of land and adequate financial revenue in a backward province like Assam. He had demanded certain measures which would be in the interests of the population of the province of Assam and in the interests of those people who had come in as a result of fear of disturbances.

People, who had come, not out of fear, had already settled themselves there. He said that it would be difficult to uproot them unless some strong measures were taken. In other words, if steps were taken to send them out, there might be some room for the other people whom all provinces in India were bound to accommodate, whether they liked it or not.

Chaudhury was quite candid in saying that many immigrants from Bengal had already settled in Assam in different villages and rural areas. These people were harbouring newcomers from their religion and region.

He demanded an enabling clause in the Bill so that the Government of Assam could act against those 'newcomers—these undesirable people' and take action against these 'harbourers'. He urged for strong measures not only against the undesirable immigrants but also against other immigrants who had come before the Partition but were now harbouring these newcomers actively, to the detriment of the interests of the people of Assam and the detriment of the interests of the bona fide refugees coming to Assam.

Pro-Refugee Stand of Assam Government

There were a lot of criticisms against the Government of Assam for not doing enough for the Bengali Hindus. As we have seen earlier, in some cases, Gopinath Bordoloi had resisted unplanned rehabilitation of the refugees.[40]

---

[40] For details, see Mahanta, *Confronting the State*, 21–22.

The Government of Assam was probably doubtful, in the past, about the generosity of the Government of India in the matter of rehabilitation of refugees in Assam, as Chaudhury added. He said that the doubt had been removed by the recent grant, thanks to the visit of Pandit Thakur Das Bhargava for having extended financial help to Assam.[41] Chaudhury demanded a minimum of ₹10 million to the Assam government for the rehabilitation of refugees in the coming year. This being the position, Chaudhury assured that the Government of Assam would fully cooperate with the desire of the Government of India and set to work loyally and faithfully, and turn out only those people whose presence in the province was not desirable or whose presence may be detrimental to the interests of the people of Assam and India.

Shri Surendranath Buragohain, the Congress MP from Sibsagar, Assam, strongly supported the arguments by Rohini Chaudhury and thanked the government for bringing such a bill for the protection of Assam. He said

> I join with my hon. friend Mr Chaudhuri in thanking the hon. Minister for bringing in this measure. The very fact that, although the House was to meet in a few days, an Ordinance was promulgated shows the desperate urgency for a measure of this kind so far as the situation created in this part of India is concerned.... But I must make it perfectly plain that the measure does not go far enough. I understood the hon. Minister the other day to say in answer to a question that was put by an hon. Member from Punjab that as many as 4&1/2 lakhs of Muslims have crossed the border into Assam after the attainment of Independence. If that is so, how many of these immigrants can be treated as 'undesirables' under the provisions of this Bill? Perhaps 5 per cent or maybe less. What is going to happen with regard to the rest of the 95 per cent? Therefore, I have no hesitation in saying, without any fear of contradiction, that the measure is indeed inadequate.

Thus, Buragohain demanded stronger measures than those provided by the Bill to tackle the 'undesirable immigrants'.

---

[41] See Mahanta, *Confronting the State*, pp. 21–22.; see also Chaudhury's Speech, Parliamentary Debate, Lok Sabha Secretariat (Part II-Proceedings Other than Questions and Answers), Wednesday, 8 February 1950, pp. 313–350.

Buragohain added that Assam would have to further bear the brunt of Bengal famine and that immigration would continue.[42] He said that he would not be surprised if that opportunity was taken up by Pakistan to bolster up a counterblast in Assam against India's case for Kashmir. He advised the Government of India to allow the provincial government to introduce the permit system for better control. Buragohain argued that it was never the intention of the Government of Assam to shut out refugees or displaced persons. He urged that the figure of refugees was not high at all in Assam in comparison to the 'undesirable immigrants'. He referred to Rohini Choudhuri who had already told the House that according to the figures with him, it was 120,000.

Peaceful Invasion Continues

Shri Biswanath Das believed that the presence of 0.5 million people on the soil of India was enough to upset the internal economy of India, not to speak of a small province like Assam, with a population 7.4 million under the then set-up. He asked why the Government of India, under these stringent conditions of food shortage, should allow these immigrants to stay in a country which was not at all theirs and to which they have the least claim? He said,

> [E]ven considered from the point of view of the Muslim population in India, it is a serious setback. Our Muslim friends, thank God most of them who had the League ideology have settled themselves as peaceful citizens by casting their lot with us, to stand by us and live with us. If the unfortunate immigrants come with a different ideology, are we to have a war atmosphere in which different conditions would prevail? A secular state like that of India has got enough dangers, dangers because it cannot deal in the same way in which Pakistan deals with Hindus, Sikhs, Christians and the like—the non-Muslims .... The peaceful penetration of India reduces itself to this, namely, that you have no peace now and certainly you cannot have peace during a war.

---

[42] Because of the Bengal famine of 1943, on account of which, according to the official estimate of the Woodhead Commission, the population that was affected in undivided Bengal was to the tune of 6 million. According to the same official estimate, at least 1.5 million people had died.

Under these circumstances, Das insisted India was losing in both ways. He said that Hindu and Sikh Pakistan nationals were being thrown out of Pakistan mercilessly. India must own them and find rehabilitation for them. He spoke against the tendency for accommodation and living space and ploughing lands for the 'non-nationals' immigrants who did not owe allegiance to the Indian state nor had any sympathy for the local people. He appreciated the Deputy PM Sardar Patel for having explored the alternatives with his Pakistani counterpart for the rehabilitation of Hindus in Pakistan. The proposal for alternative land for the Hindus in Pakistan was turned down by Pakistan. Thus, Pakistan would do nothing for their minorities; on the other hand, India must find accommodations for non-national Pakistani immigrants. This was what he called 'losing both ways'. Das suggested for the forcible expulsion of immigrants from Assam, when he said

> the census of 1951 is coming on and active operations have to begin from 1950, if our past experience holds good. Why not take a detailed and early census of Assam and see that people over and above the 74 lakhs we had in 1941 are ejected mercilessly without any consideration?

Undesirable Immigrants' Security Threat

Shrimati Sucheta Kripalini (Uttar Pradesh) argued that no province in India could accommodate such a huge number of immigrants, as that would create problems of law and order, but the weightiest reason, according to her, was security. The security of Assam was not a question of Assam alone but the whole of India because it was the eastern gateway of India, particularly given the present policy of Pakistan. Citing her own experience in Karachi, Kripalini urged that Pakistan was constantly carrying on propaganda that created an atmosphere of war in that country. Anti-Indian scenes were being enacted where Indian soldiers were shown to be committing brutal atrocities, bayoneting children and things like that which aroused the feelings of the people. She further added that in Karachi, there were a large number of shops selling arms at a much cheaper price. She cautioned the government to maintain vigilance at all time, particularly in a border province like Assam.

She wondered how even before the Partition, people were systematically coming into that province to occupy the land. She said she was surprised to learn that such a big number had penetrated Assam without check. She opined that such an Act should have been enacted much earlier. She pleaded for the enactment of stringent law. She equally emphasized giving shelter to refugees by Assam, which she considered being a moral obligation of India. She said

> [N]ow, where are those people to go? We cannot deny our responsibility towards those people. They were citizens of India. They fought for the freedom of India. But today unfortunately they have been left beyond the limits of India. We know that Pakistan has been following a systematic policy by which Hindus have been gradually pushed out. If Hindus of Eastern Pakistan are pushed out they will have to find shelter somewhere. We cannot close our eyes to that fact. Even if it is difficult for our economy to support it, we have to give shelter to those shelter less people. It is a moral obligation.

Shri A. G. Guha of West Bengal urged that there was a fundamental difference between India and its neighbouring countries. His point of view was,

> Our state is a secular State and we are determined to maintain that character of the State and our whole national idea is based on secular outlook. But our neighbouring State is a State committed to a particular faith and is based on a particular faith. That also would not have mattered much, but the whole population of that state has been fed on a psychology of hatred and that is the danger against which the Bill wants to guard. So from the point of view of national security, from the point of view of good neighbourliness between the two States such a bill is must.

Guha argued that Assam was never a monolingual state and the province could never shut the door for the Hindu refugees.

A Peaceful Invasion Began
but Not with Pakistan

Tracing the origin of the problem of immigration, Sardar B. S. Mann stated:

[T]his peaceful invasion really began not with the creation of Pakistan. I have got here the reports with me of the Assam Government itself, in which out of sheer frustration they have said that 'verily the cup of humiliation for the Assamese is full'. It was a very deep-seated and well-planned conspiracy on the part of the Muslim League Ministry which wanted to convert the Assamese grazing lands into Muslim-inhabited areas. I might point out that in revenue courts even now the eviction orders still stand against those settlers who had come without any permission and occupied lands to the prejudice of local grazers. They had come as an off-shoot of a well-planned conspiracy.

The crux of his argument was that no matter whether the immigrants came after Pakistan came into being or before, they were a part and parcel of that conspiracy, which the Muslim League hatched. That was why he pleaded that the application of the Bill should be from a prior date to the creation of Pakistan—a date from which this 'peaceful but pernicious penetration' began. He also alleged because of such demographic change, some of the highly placed Pakistan officials were whipping up an agitation in Pakistan reviving Pakistan's claim for Assam. It was argued that if serious attention was not given, then Assam's territory would be in the possession of undesirable immigrants. He insisted on a retrospective application of the bill so that undesirable immigrants could be driven out.

Pandit Thakur Das Bhargava supported the viewpoints of Mann and traced the origin of the problem to the Muslim League. It became clear to him when he happened to visit Assam in 1928. He made an emotional appeal by saying:

At that time those who were living in Assam complained to us that an attempt was being made to convert Assam into a Muslim Province. At that time there was no substance in it, because then there was no question of Muslim or Hindu Assam. At present also we do not make any difference between Muslims and Hindus as long as they are nationals of India. We are out to have in our midst Kashmiris who are Muslims and in a majority in that State. But that is not the point at issue. The real point which we should not miss or ignore is that in Assam it was the Muslim League Ministry which allowed these Muslims to go there with the specific purpose of seeing that Assam was converted into a Muslim Province. That is the point.

He termed such 'invasion' of Assam as a 'peaceful penetration'. He made it clear that despite the government's reluctance, these persons came in and took forcible possession of the land. On the question of refugee settlement and problem thereof, he said it was the fault of the Government of India, and the Government of India must share the entire blame. He said that the government's policy was 'a very weak-kneed policy'. He said,

> I cannot understand why twenty ministers are sleeping here when the whole of Assam has been flooded with five lakhs of these people. If there is a cataract in one's eye it is not operated unless it is ripe. Perhaps they want that the cup of poison should be full.

Thus, both the Constituent Assembly debates on citizenship and the debate on Illegal Immigration Expulsion Act pertaining to Assam (1950) provide the ideological basis of the citizenship discourse in India. Discussion on citizenship would remain incomplete if these two aspects of legislative means are not looked into. As Shri A. G. Guha of West Bengal said regarding The immigrants (Expulsion from Assam) Act, 1950 (I(IE) A-1950) '[T]hough in the wording, there is no mention of any particular community, the purpose of the Bill is apparent and known to everybody'. India never had problems with the 'nationalist Muslims'—problems were with those 'undesirable immigrants' who were bent to create a Muslim-dominant Assam, forcing the state to bear the burden of 0.5 million illegal 'undesirable immigrants' alone, whereas the figure was less than 3,000 for entire India. In this context, can Assam and India deny accommodation to those refugees who have been there in the state from 1971 till 2014? Here a few questions raised by a prolific writer in the subject are noteworthy[43]:

> Would the Government be justified in reneging on National commitments and abridging their right to claim citizenship by allowing one set of laws like 'Foreigner Act' 1946 to prevail in disregard of 'Immigrants (Expulsion from Assam) Act', 1950 and the 'Citizenship Act', 1955?

[43] Chhabra, *Assam Challenge*, 104–105.

Was the country prepared to uproot people who several years ago had 'their tryst with destiny' and, subsequently, when compelled to flee to India in the wake of disturbances or threat of such disturbances, made India their home? Were they to be made refugees for a second time? If Bangladesh did not even agree to accept a person who had crossed since 1971, where were the so-called foreigners to be sent under these circumstances? Was it feasible to compel dispersal of when efforts for sending back a few hundred families to Dandakaranya had proved utterly futile?

Bibliography

Baruah, Sanjib. *India Against Itself: Assam and Politics of Nationality*. New Delhi: Oxford University Press, 1999.

Baruah, Sanjib. 'The Partition's Long Shadow: The Ambiguities of Citizenship in Assam, India'. *Citizenship Studies* 13, no. 6 (2009): 593–606.

Chhabra, K. M. L. *Assam Challenge*. Delhi: Konark Publishers, 1992.

Constituent Assembly Debates. *Official Report*, Vol. IX, pp. 355–356. New Delhi: Lok Sabha Secretariat, 2003.

EPW Engage. 'Marking Territories: Illegal Immigrants, the Citizenship (Amendment) Act and the NRC'. 18 December 2019, https://www.epw.in/engage/article/marking-territories-illegal-immigrants-citizenship-nrc.

Jain, Shruti. 'Explained: The Nuts and Bolts of Indian Citizenship'. *The Wire*, 19 December 2019, www.thewire.in.

Kumar, D. P. *Challenge to India's Unity: Assam Student's Agitation*. New Delhi: DK Publishers, 1990.

Mahanta, Nani Gopal. *Confronting the State*. New Delhi: SAGE Publications, 2013.

Murthy, T. S. *Assam: The Difficult Years*. New Delhi: Himalayan Books, 1983.

Sadique, Kamal. *Paper Citizens: How Illegal Immigrants Acquire Citizenship in Developing Countries*. New York: Oxford University Press, 2009.

Thakur, Apurva. 'Why the Citizenship Amendment Bill Goes Against the Basic Tenets of the Constitution'. *Economic & Political Weekly* 53, no. 13 (31 March 2018).

Citizenship Politics and Hindu Refugees

In Chapter 4, I provided a historical account of how the issues of citizenship were discussed in the precincts of the Constituent Assembly (CA). We also tried to argue how the Indian Parliament tried to distinguish between 'desirable refugees' and 'undesirable immigrants' through the Immigrants (Expulsion from Assam) Act, 1950 (IEA-1950). The Act spelt out who are refugees, who are to be treated preferentially and under what circumstances.

The Immigrants (Expulsion from Assam) Act, 1950, is very much applicable even today, which is clear from the observation made by the Supreme Court in the historic IMDT case (also known as Sarbananda Sonowal case) of 2005. The court observed:

> However, on account of Section 4 of the IMDT Act the Immigrants (Expulsion from Assam) Act, 1950 has been superseded and the provisions of the said Act have ceased to apply to the State of Assam. Thus by enacting the IMDT Act the Parliament has divested the Central Government of the power to remove migrants from Bangladesh, whose presence was creating serious law and order problem, which fact had been realized by the Central Government as early as in 1950. The IMDT Act instead of maintaining peace has only revived internal disturbance.

While delivering judgement on the Sarbananda Sonowal case, the Supreme Court, clearly validated the operations of the Immigrants (Expulsion from Assam) Act, 1950 in the following manner:

> To sum up our conclusions, the provisions of the Illegal Migrants (Determination by Tribunals) Act, 1983 are ultra vires the Constitution of India and are accordingly struck down. The Illegal Migrants (Determination by Tribunals) Rules, 1984 are also ultra vires and are struck down. ...

> The Passport (Entry into India) Act, 1920, the Foreigners Act, 1946, the
> Immigrants (Expulsion from Assam) Act, 1950 and the Passport Act, 1967
> shall apply to the State of Assam.

Even for the detection and deportation of foreigners from Assam as
per Assam Accord, the Immigrants (Expulsion from Assam) Act, 1950
(IEA-1950) is legally taken into consideration. To quote the Assam
Government Assam Accord Implementation Department:

> After repeal of the IM(D)T Act by the Hon'ble Supreme Court of India on
> 12-07-2005, the following Acts are used for detection and deportation of
> illegal migrants—(a) The Foreigner's Act, 1946 along with the Foreigner's
> (Tribunal) Order, 1946. (b) The Passport (Entry into India) Act, 1920.
> (c) Passport Act, 1967. (d) The Immigration (Expulsion from Assam) Act,
> 1950. (e) The Citizenship Act, 1955.[1]

A question arises regarding what the Immigrants (Expulsion from
Assam) Act, 1950, tried to achieve:

> Power to order expulsion of certain immigrants—If the Central Government
> is of opinion that any person or class of persons, ... come into Assam and
> that the stay of such person or class of persons in Assam is detrimental to
> the interests of the general public of India or of any section thereof or of
> any Scheduled Tribe in Assam, the Central Government may by order ...
> give such further directions in regard to his or their removal from India or
> Assam as it may consider necessary or expedient, provided that nothing in
> this section shall apply to any person who on account of civil disturbances
> or the fear of such disturbances in any area now forming part of Pakistan
> has been displaced from or has left his place of residence in such area and
> who has been subsequently residing in Assam.[2]

If we pay attention to the debate and discussions that took place in the
formulations of the IEA-1950 in the Parliament,[3] it would become clear
that there was a strong suggestion for the confiscation of properties
of illegal immigrants and their cohorts who created a huge network

---

[1] See https://assamaccord.assam.gov.in/portlets/assam-accord-and-its-clauses#Clause (accessed 10 June 2020).

[2] Clause 2 of The Immigrants (Expulsion from Assam) Act, 1950; Act No. 10 of 1950.

[3] For details, also see the previous chapter, particularly debate and discussion on IEA-1950.

for the expansion of their co-religionists. Many MPs, including those from Assam, even vouched for the retrospective effect of the Act so that those Muslim immigrants who had occupied land and patronized other immigrants to come to Assam could also be brought under the purview of the Act. Pandit Thakur Das Bhargava and other MPs from Assam such as R. K. Chaudhury, Surendra Buragohain, Shri J. N. Hazarika, Shri Devakanta Barooah and others strongly vouched for stronger action against 'undesirable immigrants' as well their religious network which had been silently patronizing their inroads into Assam.

Pandit Thakur Das Bhargava said it was difficult to identify those people from the Mymensingh district and other districts of East Bengal whether they were old inhabitants or new entrants,

> Land is trespassed upon and whenever any question arises, it is very difficult to find out whether these men came five years before or two years before or just one month before because after all the oral evidence can be furnished by his compatriots or caste fellows or relations to the effect that he has owned this land for the last ten years or five years or whatever the period he alleges it to be.

Bhargava pleaded for the confiscation of properties of those who had been harbouring such immigrants. Until such confiscation was not done, the vast network would work in the favour of illegal immigrants.

While supporting such property confiscation, Rohini Chaudhury also urged that there were nearly 1 million new Muslim immigrants[4] in the Province, and with some exception, these were the class of persons who had been sheltering the immigrants who had recently come to the province of Assam. They gave them food and shelter, and they also found occupation for them. He pleaded that in the past, these immigrants have forcibly occupied some places in the grazing reserves.

There was no ordinary land available for settlement in Assam but there were lands in the grazing reserves, and in the past land had been acquired by wrongfully squatting on those grazing reserves. It was only unfortunate that the government was unable to turn them out of their

---

[4] It may be mentioned that in the last Saadulla Ministry of the Muslim League, there was a huge immigration of Muslim peasants from various East Bengal districts.

lands in the past. Chaudhury informed that the immigrants feared nothing; they did not fear the jail. His strong contention was that they were ready to go to jail rather than giving up their land which they acquired either lawfully or unlawfully. Their stake was that they were harbouring these immigrants. If they were made liable to forfeiture of their property, that would have a salutary influence on them.

Surendra Buragohain, another MP from Sibsagar, Assam, endorsed the viewpoints of Chaudhury and argued that there could never be a better person to talk about Muslim immigrants than Rohini Chaudhury as he himself had served twice as the Revenue Minister of Assam during the Muslim League and coalition ruling in the state. Justifying both Chaudhury and Bhargava, he said,

> The other day I was telling that the position in the border districts is very serious. My information is that out of half a million that have crossed the borders after independence, the majority have gone into the border districts and this has disturbed the population position there and already the Muslim population is much above 50 percent. That is why I warned the house that this position may well be bolstered up by Pakistan as a counter blast against our case in Kashmir.

Shri Devakanta Barua, who later became the Congress president during the internal emergency in Indira Gandhi period, extended full support to Bhargava, Rohini Chaudhury and other MPs from Assam. He urged that although confiscation clause might look drastic, it would look rather innocent in the eyes of the immigrants who were not known for their lawful habits. Barooah accused the Congress government of adopting a very tentative policy. He said that somehow, the government, whether represented by Shri Gopalaswami Ayenger or others, continued to have appeasement psychology. He asked what the use of the half-hearted policies was. He acknowledged that their government had miserably failed in every field, and it affected the relationship with the Government of Pakistan. He gave a figure of 4,000 Muslims waiting at Banaras and wanting to be absorbed. He asked the government

> Has anybody from India gone to Pakistan and been absorbed there? We know the whole question of Assam. Many of us who have taken considerable interest in the problems of those years know what happened. In those

days we were helpless but today with our own Republican Government we are not going to talk of moral, philosophical or ethical principles on a matter on which hinge the security of India.

Proposed Permit System in Assam

It may be mentioned that at the instruction of Gopinath Bordoloi, the then Chief Secretary of Assam prepared a permit system. The purpose of the permit system was to provide permission for a certain group of people to come from East Bengal to Assam under certain situations. The permit system was lenient to the displaced persons who were certified by the competent authority as having had to leave East Pakistan on account of civil disturbances or for fear of civil disturbances in their home areas. (These persons would carry certificates in the prescribed form.) For these rules, persons of East Bengal who were in Assam were divided into two classes, namely:

1. 'Settlers', meaning persons who had settled permanently and had land and house of their own in Assam.
2. 'Sojourners', meaning all those who were not Settlers.

When the permit rules came into force, they made provisions for the following classes of persons wishing to come to Assam: (a) Non-Muslims—displaced persons mainly, if they were driven out by civil disturbances, or fear of such disturbance, certificates would be enough. If, on the other hand, they wished to come on account of other persons, including due to the Partition of India, they must apply for the appropriate permit. (b) Muslims—Settlers in India. They would apply for a temporary visit permit. On the issue of Muslim settlers, the permit system was very clear: 'We propose that till the refugee problem is satisfactorily solved non-refugee will not be encouraged or permitted to come to Assam. Non-refugees would in practice cover all Muslims wishing to enter Assam area'. There were three classes of permits, namely:

1. Permit for return.
2. Permit for a temporary visit.

3. Permit for settlement.

The settlers or permanent residents of Assam who found themselves in East Pakistan, when these rules came into force, were entitled to apply for a permit to return. Their applications would be in the prescribed form and must mention the particulars that could be verified Sojourners and others who wished to visit Assam should apply under temporary visit permits.[5]

Refugee-cum-Displaced Persons' Settlement in Assam: Old and New Refugees

Who Is a Displaced Person?

The Census of India 1951, Vol. XII, Assam, Manipur and Tripura, Part II-A refers to a displaced person as,

> Any person who has entered India having left or being compelled to leave his or her home in Western Pakistan on or after the 1st March, 1947 or his/her home in Eastern Pakistan on or after the 15th October, 1956 on account of civil disturbances or on account of the setting up of the two Dominions of India and Pakistan.[6]

The Department of Economics and Statistics, Government of Assam, had undertaken a statistical survey of displaced persons from East Pakistan in Assam in 1955–1956. Under the survey, a 'displaced person', a 'refugee' or a 'migrant' from East Pakistan meant a person who was ordinarily a resident in the territories now comprised in East Pakistan but who, on account of civil disturbances or the Partition of India, had migrated:

1. In the case of persons migrated from the districts of Noakhali or the districts of Comilla now forming part of East Pakistan, on or after the 1 October 1946 and

---

[5] The permit system was prepared by the then Chief Secretary of Assam, S. P. Desai. The detailed proposal was finalised on 22 June 1949 (accessed through archive). U/o no-S894/49/10, Shillong, 22 June 1949.

[6] Census of India 1951, Vol. XII, Assam, Manipur & Tripura, Table D-V, p. 136.

2. In case of persons migrating from any other area in East Pakistan, or after the 1 June 1947 to the territories now included in Assam to take up permanent residence.[7]

The Assam Displaced Persons (Rehabilitation Loans) Act, 1951 (Assam Act, XVI of 1951) was enacted to provide for the grant and recovery of loans to displaced persons for their rehabilitation. Section 2(c) defines displaced persons. The said definition after its amendment by Assam Act, XX of 1957 reads as follows:

Displaced person means (a) a person who, on account of the Partition of India or on account of civil disturbances in area now forming part of India or Pakistan, has been displaced from or compelled to leave the place of residence in such area on or after the prescribed date. The prescribed dates are:

(i) In relation to a person displaced from or compelled to leave his place of residence in the district of Noakhali or the district of Commilla now forming part of East Pakistan means the 1st day of October 1946.

(ii) In relation to a person displaced from or compelled to leave his place of residence in any other area now forming East Pakistan, means the 1st day of June 1947.

(iii) In relation to a person displaced from or compelled to leave his place of residence in any area, now forming part of East Pakistan, means the 1st day of March 1947.

(iv) In relation to a person displaced or compelled to leave his place of residence in any area now forming part of India, means the 1st day of January 1950.

According to the 1951 Convention relating to the status of refugees, a refugee is defined as a person who

owing to a well-founded fear of being persecuted for reasons of race, religion, nationality, membership of a particular social group, or political opinion, is outside the country of his nationality, and is unable to or, owing to such fear, is unwilling to avail himself of the protection of that country.[8]

[7] Government of Assam, *Statistical Survey of Displaced Persons from East Pakistan in Assam 1955–56.*

[8] United Nation High Commissioner for Refugees, *Protecting Refugees: Questions & Answers.*

Needless to say that most of the refugees into Assam from East Pakistan were Bengali Hindus – the persecuted religious minority in Islamic Pakistan ruled by modern and politicised armed forces. The partition made their position extremely vulnerable. ...[T]heir existence with dignity, both actual and perceptional, propelled their movement across the border.[9]

Various mechanisms were considered for identifying the Hindu refugees in the state.[10] To obtain any rehabilitation benefits from the state, the migrant would have to produce either of the following documents as evidence of migration from East Pakistan, namely migration certificates, citizenship certificates, and documents proving the option taken in case the migrant was a government servant. If these were unavailable, then the following could also be used as a proof of migration: refugee registration certificate, border slip, border ration slip, a certified copy of National Census Register. In case these were also unavailable, then their status as displaced persons would be determined based on circumstantial evidence.

Those migrants who came during the first phase of migration (1947–1958) were referred to as the 'old migrants'. They were identified as refugees coming out of genuine grievances of political nature and hence, accepted as government liability. Migrants after that phase were known as 'new migrants'.

Modalities for the Rehabilitations of Hindu Refugees

A conference of senior officials and concerned ministers was held in Shillong on 8–9 May 1950 where the modalities for the rehabilitation of refugees were finalized.[11] In the presence of various administrative heads, a detailed mechanism of refugee settlement process was

[9] Hussain, 'Refugees in the Face of Emerging Ethnicity in North-East India', 123–29.

[10] Some of these were discussed in the Ministry of Rehabilitation, Annual Report, 1955–56; also discussed in the Conference of the Rehabilitation Ministers from the Eastern States held at Darjeeling, 20–22 October 1955, 86–87.

[11] Members present were Minister, Relief and Rehabilitation; Minister, Revenue, Chief Secretary, Assam; Comptroller, Assam; Deputy Commissioners of Nowgong, Darrang, Kamrup, Khasi and Jaintia Hills, Garo Hills, Goalpara; and Relief and Rehabilitation

finalized in Assam under the leadership of the Revenue Minister Bishnu Ram Medhi. The minister informed the conference of officers that the question of permanent rehabilitation of new refugees on land did not come in before 31 December 1950, as, under the Indo-Pakistan Agreement, Muslim migrants who came back to Assam before that date had to be restored with the immoveable property evacuated by them. All that was to be done was that new refugees were to be placed on the land vacated by Muslim migrants temporarily till 31 December 1950 to grow jute and/or food crops. Even if some of the Muslim migrants returned before that date, new refugees in temporary possession of lands were not to be disturbed till the end of the year.

In every case of a claim for restoration of land by Muslim migrants, an enquiry was to be made whether the claimant had a valid title to the land. No claim for lands under annual *patta* was to be entertained if the Muslim migrants had settled in Assam after 1938. Additionally, no tenancy rights were to be recognized in lands covered by the annual *patta*. Under the Agreement, trustee committees for vacated lands would come into existence after 31 December 1950, and the question of exchange of land would be taken into consideration. Only after the settlement of these questions could the question of permanent rehabilitation of new refugees on land be taken up in Assam. Medhi referred to the Indian Tea Association's scheme to settle new refugees on surplus wasteland in tea-garden grants in Assam and explained the Revenue Department's policy in that regard.[12] All Deputy Commissioners and Sub-divisional Officers were to prepare a list of all available surplus wastelands in tea-grants in their jurisdiction, requisition them without loss of time and allot them for the cultivation of food crops to people in the following order of priority:

1. Indigenous landless cultivators, flood-affected people and people with uneconomic holdings.

Commissioner, Shillong, 8–9 May 1950 (Source: Political Department, File No. C.198/51, 1951; H.N. Relief and Rehabilitation).

[12] This was expressed in their Circular Letters Nos. RRQ. 56/49/58 of 2 February 1950, and No.RT.44/49/13 of 4 May 1950.

2. Tea-garden labourers who wanted a subsidiary occupation as an additional source of income.

To avoid a clash with the local people and consequent breaches of the peace, the question of settling new refugees on tea-garden lands be taken up only after the above categories of landless people needed to be given the land required by them. The Relief and Rehabilitation Commissioner pointed out that the first Revenue Department Circular on the requisition of surplus tea-grant land for indigenous landless people was issued as early as November 1949 and suggested that a date should be fixed before which all such landless people should apply for and receive lands so that any land available after that date could be allotted to new refugees.

The conference also decided to provide similar benefits to the new refugees who were still pouring into the state. The Relief and Rehabilitation Commissioner referred to Government of India's new directives according to which 'new' refugees who were likely not to return to East Pakistan were to be permanently rehabilitated in India on the same lines as 'old' refugees.[13] New refugees could be divided into three categories:

1. those staying in camps and registered there;
2. those registered in camps but had left camps for other destinations; and
3. those who did not go to any camp but had been staying with friends, etc.

Though a large majority of new refugees were stated to consist of agriculturists, the question of their permanent rehabilitation on land had to wait because of the Revenue Department's policy explained above. It was decided that the Deputy Commissioners should conduct a rapid survey of non-agriculturist, new refugees of all categories in the districts whose rehabilitation, which was independent of the land question, could be taken in hand immediately. Sufficient notice should

---

[13] Government of India's letter No. RRH/CRG/18/50, dated 20 April 1950, Political Department, File No. C.198/51, 1951.

be given, however, to enable all such refugees to register themselves at the Deputy Commissioner's office. In the conference, certain 'border camps' were identified for effective management in the districts of Goalpara, Garo Hills, and Khasi and Jaintia Hills.[14] In the border camps, all new refugees who came had to be admitted, their names and other relevant information were entered in a register, and they were to be given registration cards at the time of departure to settlement areas.

The meet decided to provide free passage to:

1. new refugees desirous of rehabilitation in Assam from place of entry to reception camp and from reception camp to place of rehabilitation;
2. new refugees desirous of returning to Pakistan, to their homes in East Bengal; and
3. Muslim migrants desirous of leaving Assam, up to the Pakistan border. The Government of India and the provincial government gathered minute details about how to engage the refugees and minimum facilities to be provided.[15]

It was decided that new refugees should be given gratuitous relief in camps normally for 2 weeks only; the intention was that within that period, they should be moved to the rehabilitation centre where they might be given gratuitous relief for a period of another 2 weeks. Where an able-bodied male refugee refused to perform the work assigned to him, he should be deprived of gratuitous relief, but the women, children and disabled men, if any, of his family might continue to receive such relief. In the case of unattached women and children and unemployable men and members of their families, the government should bear the expenditure on their maintenance till they or members of their family were in a position to earn. For this purpose, efforts should be made to train up one or more members of such family in productive work and work centres should be opened wherever

---

[14] Those camps were located in the following manner. In Goalpara, Mankachar, South Salmara; in Dhubri, Rupsi and Chhatrasal; in Garo Hills, Mahendraganj, Dalu, Angratoli and Baghmara; in Khasi and Jaintia hills, Dawki, Shella and Bholaganj.

[15] Vide No. RRH/CRG/18/50, dated 17 April 1950; File No. C.197/51, 1951.

possible. In case it is not possible to find work for all able-bodied men in a camp, gratuitous relief could be continued to be given to all women, children and disabled men in the family, but the available work should be distributed so as to give employment in turn to as many able-bodied men as possible in the camp. In various sessions, the Deputy Commissioners had provided details about how the refugees, local people and other Muslims were allotted land. The Deputy Commissioner of Goalpara stated that in his district, about 0.15–0.2 million bighas of land, including tribal and 'char' areas, were abandoned by the Muslim migrants; on this area, about 70,000–80,000 bighas had been already temporarily allotted (according to orders of Minister of Revenue dated 6 April 1950) to deserving local persons and committees who had put about 13,000 new refugees on to the cultivation of jute and food crops. Parts of the vacated lands have been occupied by local landless persons and some by the returning Muslim displaced persons.

Rehabilitation of 'Muslim Displaced Persons'

In Darrang, 15,273 bighas of land was vacated by Muslims, of which about 300 bighas was temporarily allotted to 41 refugee families. The rest was mostly requisitioned and allotted to landless local people from flood-affected areas on the banks of the Brahmaputra.

In the Barpeta subdivision of Kamrup District, 129,972 bighas (including tribal blocks) were evacuated by Muslims. Of this, about 3,700 bighas were temporarily allotted in Baghbar mouza to 183 refugee families for cultivation. About 47,400 bighas of vacant land in Barpeta subdivision was settled with local landless people. In Gauhati subdivision, 42,953 bighas was vacated by the Muslims. Refugees temporarily settled in 225 bighas, and local landless people settled in about 42,000 bighas of land.

The Deputy Commissioner, Kamrup, stated that the Revenue Department had authorized him to allot land to refugees only from the Baghbar mauza. In Titapani mouza, about 46,000 bighas and in Jania mouza, about 15,000 bighas of land were available for temporary allotment to refugees. The Deputy Commissioners of Goalpara and Kamrup stated that in their experience, new refugees did not like to settle in low-lying land allotted to them, as these were in flood-prone areas. It was decided that the Deputy Commissioners should collect information regarding the kinds of land preferred by refugees and others through their revenue officers' statistics and keep the government posted of such information. The char and other areas which neither the refugees nor the local people wanted had to be settled with displaced Muslims who were accustomed to living in flooded areas. To tackle the refugee issues, the conference had created vast paraphernalia of the Relief and Rehabilitation Department with the creation of many administrative posts and assistants in the capital as well as in the districts.

The Assam Minority Commission was constituted on 4 June 1950 with Minister, Relief and Rehabilitation, as the Chairman and Moulvi Syed Muhmmad Saadulla (MLA) and Raja Ajit Narayan Deb (MLA) as members, and the Secretary of Relief and Rehabilitation Department as the Secretary of the commission. The commission held its first meeting on 11 June 1950 where its Rules of Procedure were adopted. The meeting asked for certain facilities to enable the members to tour in the districts.

Various scholars who were concerned with growing communalism in Assam have referred to the number of Muslims who had left Assam during disturbances in 1950, but hardly is it mentioned that not only all the displaced Muslim returned and had taken their properties but also, as per record, more Muslim immigrants came to Assam, claiming to be affected and displaced Muslims on the eve of Partition. Professor Monirul Hussain argues

> Assam experienced communal riots in the wake of partition of India in 1947 causing displacement of more than hundred thousand Muslims living in lower Assam (Table 1). Distinguished Asamiya parliamentarian Hem Barua admitted '53,000 Muslim families were displaced'. One can imagine the actual number of affected people by multiplying 53,000 with an average of five to seven members in a family. All these displaced people involuntarily migrated to East Pakistan in the wake of the riots. However, following the Nehru-Liaquat Ali Pact of 1950 involving India and Pakistan,

which assured them safe return as well as rehabilitation, many returned home about two years later.[16]

In support of his argument, Professor Hussain provided a figure of 0.1 million 'displaced Muslims' and remarked 'obviously, communalism was the major factor, together with the colonial and the incipient post-colonial Indian state, in the first major internal displacement of a religious minority in post-colonial Assam'. However, Professor Hussain never provided the figure that came back and claimed properties, which would perhaps negate his theoretical premise which he developed based on data. Not only did all the displaced Muslims came back, but 42,537 additional illegal Muslim immigrants also entered Assam on the pretext of emigration due to disturbances on the eve of Partition, as Table 5.1 would make it clear.

Since the beginning of 1951, the figures of migration between Assam and East Pakistan, as reported by the District Officers are presented in Table 5.1.[17] Table 5.2 provides a detailed arrival of refugees in Assam from 1946 till 1951.

In fact, for some time, the immigration of illegal immigration went on, and according to the White Paper published by the Government of

Table 5.1 *Figures of migration between Assam and East Pakistan*

Category (Entering and Leaving Assam)	Total Numbers	Date (from August 1947 up to September 1950)
Hindu refugees entering Assam	393,926	30 September 1950
Hindu refugees returning to Pakistan	22,963	30 September 1950
Muslim displaced persons leaving Assam	119,093	30 September 1950
Muslim displaced persons returning to their homes in Assam	161,630	30 September 1950

Source: Political department, File no-C.198/51; HN Relief and Rehabilitation.

[16] Hussain, 'State, Identity Movements and Internal Displacement in the North-East, 4519–23.

[17] Political Department, File No. C.198/51, 1951; H. N. Relief and Rehabilitation.

Table 5.2 *Arrival of Partition Migrants/Displaced Persons/Refugees in Assam (Year by Year)*

From East Bengal	----------	1946	6,860
From East Pakistan	----------	1947	42,346
	----------	1948	41,740
	----------	1950	144,512
(January and February)	----------	1951	3,479
		Total =	272,075
From West Pakistan	----------		647
District of origin not known	----------		1,733
		Grand total =	274,455

Source: Census of India 1951, Vol. XII, Assam, Manipur, Tripura Part IA-A Report, CH.VIII—Displaced Persons.

Assam in 2012, 0.5 million illegal migrants entered Assam from 1947 to 1950. About 22,000 families of displaced Muslims had returned to their homes in the Goalpara district by the end of October 1950 (930 persons out of 17,500 families were restored partially or fully, and the rest 10,600 families were given rehabilitation loans in addition to gratuitous relief which was given to all displaced people). Up to the end of October 1950, ₹1,473,000 had been spent in Goalpara district alone on loan, and another ₹250,000 on gratuitous relief to displaced Muslims.

In the Kamrup district, about 9,100 families of Muslims were displaced, of whom almost all had returned to their homes by the end of October 1950. Of these, about 5,300 families had been restored to their lands, partially or fully, and about 4,760 families were given the first instalment of rehabilitation loans. About ₹215,000 was spent on this in Kamrup district. A consolidated amount showing these details up to 31 October 1950 is presented in Table 5.3.[18]

This includes both migrants and the displaced Muslims who did not actually leave Assam. A similar rehabilitation of Muslims was also

[18] These are statistics of two districts only—rehabilitation of affected Muslims was also carried in other districts.

Table 5.3 *Rehabilitation of Affected Muslims in Goalpara and Kamrup (Similar Exercise Was Also Undertaken in Many Districts)*

	Nature of Relief	*Goalpara Dist.*	*Kamrup Dist.*	*Total*
1	Number of Muslims displaced from the district	27,000 families	9,100 families	36,100 families
2	Number of those who have returned	22,000 families	9,000 families	31,000 families
3	Number of those to whom lands have been restored, fully or partially	17,500 families	5,300 families	22,800 families
4	Number of those in receipt of rehabilitation loans	10,587 families	4,766 families	15,353 families
5	Amount spent on gratuitous relief and free transport of displaced Muslims	₹250,000	₹1,900	₹251,900
6	Amount issued as rehabilitation loans to displaced Muslims	₹1,473,000	₹213,700	₹1,686,700

Source: Political department, File no. C.198/51; HN Relief and Rehabilitation.

ensured in other districts like Nowgong and Darrang. It has been found that, along with the returning migrants, a huge number of other Muslims had also entered Assam from East Bengal. A study of the detailed rehabilitation plan (which we could not provide due to constraint of space) would reveal that as a result of the Nehru–Liaquat Pact of 1950, Pakistan could ensure the protection of life, liberty and property of all Muslims in Assam and other places of India, but India could not ensure a similar protection of Hindus and other minorities in West as well as East Pakistan. As a secular-democratic country, India was committed to protecting its minority people, their life, liberty, property and other rights, but the pure theocratic Islamic character of Pakistan and Nehru's profound ambivalence in ensuring minority rights in Pakistan made a tiny state like Assam a double victim—as the inflow of Hindu refugees, as well as immigration of illegal Muslim migrants, continued unabated. Assam had no way out but to accept them as this is what is called 'secularism'—otherwise Assamese had the risk being dubbed as 'communal'!

Citizenship Act 1955 and Hindu Refugee Issue

When the first Citizenship Act of 1955 was formulated and debated in the Parliament, the citizenship issue concerning the Hindu and other minorities from Pakistan figured prominently. A specific provision was included in the Citizenship Act for providing acquisition of citizenship by registration. The relevant provision, that is, Section 5 of the Citizenship Act, 1955, is reproduced below:

5. Citizenship by registration—(1) Subject to the provisions of this Section and such conditions and restrictions as may be prescribed, the prescribed authority may, on application made in this behalf, register as a citizen of India any person who is not already such citizen by virtue of the Constitution or by virtue of any of the other. Provisions of this Act say: (a) persons of Indian origin who are ordinarily resident in India and have been so for six months immediately before making an application for registration; (b) persons of Indian origin who are ordinarily resident in any country or place outside undivided India; (c) women who are, or have been, married to citizens of India; (d) minor children of persons who are citizens of India; and (e) persons of full age and capacity who are citizens of a country specified in the First Schedule.

Provided that in prescribing the conditions and restrictions subject to which persons of any such country may be registered as citizens of India under this Clause, the Central Government shall have due regard to the conditions subject to which citizens of India may, by law or practice of that country, become citizens of that country by registration.

Explanation—For the purposes of this sub-section, a person shall be deemed to be of Indian origin, if he, or either of his parents, or any of his grandparents, was born in undivided India.

(2) No person being of full age shall be registered as a citizen of India under sub-section (1) until he has taken the oath of allegiance in the form specified in the Second Schedule.

(3) No person who has renounced, or has been deprived of, his Indian citizenship, or whose Indian citizenship has terminated, under this Act shall be registered as a citizen of India under sub-section (1) except by order of the Central Government.

(4) The Central Government may, if satisfied that there are special circumstances justifying such registration, cause any minor to be registered as a citizen of India.

(5) A person registered under this section shall be a citizen of India by registration as from the date on which he is so registered; and a person registered under the provisions of Cl. 1. (b) (ii) of Art. 6 or Art. 8 of the Constitution shall be deemed to be a citizen of India by registration as from the commencement of the Constitution or the date on which he was so registered, whichever may be later.

Debates and Discussions in Parliament on Citizenship Status to Hindu Refugees

A series of debates and discussions took place in the Indian Parliament on the recognition and inclusion of refugees in the proposed Citizenship Act. During the debates in the Rajya Sabha, the then Deputy Minister in the Ministry of Home Affairs clarified that sub-Section (5)(1) was intended to cover refugees from Pakistan.[19] Members cutting across party lines and ideological persuasions were highly concerned about the plight of the refugees and urged the government that they must not face any hardships for no fault of their own. Many members wanted assurance that such persons who became unwanted citizens of Pakistan would, whenever needed, be given refuge in India and not denied citizenship.[20] Some members raised objections to the provision of registration procedure; they urged that there should be automatic conferment of Indian citizenship on the refugees and no registration should be required.

Pandit Thakur Das Bhargava was against any financial obligation on the part of the refugees.[21] He wondered whether the government expected that the 3 million Bengalis who had come in the past 4 or 5 years would make applications to the authorities and file affidavits. Each one of them would have to spend ₹5–10 for making affidavits and putting the stamps and going to courts. He criticized the government

[19] Rajya Sabha Debates, Col. 2368 to 2370, 13 December 1955.

[20] Chhabra, *Assam Challenge*, 60. Also see Rajya Sabha debates from 7–20 December 1955. In fact, the remaining Hindus in Pakistan were declared as 'potential Refugees', who may request for rehabilitation and citizenship in India due to their condition in Pakistan.

[21] Rajya Sabha Debates, Vol. II (Discussion on Citizenship to Refugees), 7–20 December 1955.

which had assured the safe stay of the minorities in Pakistan. He commented

> I remember Pandit Nehru saying that other methods would be employed to see that those persons were properly treated in Pakistan or returned to their homes. What happened? Those methods have never been employed. Those districts have not been ceded. The thirty or forty lakhs of Hindus who still remain there are potential refugees ... East Bengal Hindus are our kith and kin, the flesh of our flesh, the bone of our bone. I do not want to make any difference between those who are coming and those who have come in the year 1948. They are as much the citizens of our country as those Bengalis who have come during 1948. I am referring to those that have come after this date and to the potential sons of India who are remaining there and who are going to come during the coming years ....

On immigration of Muslims from Pakistan, he pleaded that there was no comparison between refugees from East Bengal and Punjab and those people who did not belong to India or opted for Pakistani citizenship. He referred to Clause 5 and asked why they should be placed on the same footing.

Shri T. S. A. Chettiar (MP from Tripura) endorsed the viewpoints made by Pandit Thakur Das Bhargava. He lamented that the Hindu population in East Bengal would gradually dwindle, and eventually, the remaining would be converted to Muslims. He said originally, there were about 12.6 million Hindus in East Bengal. A few years later, it came down to only 9 million. What happened to the rest? He said,

> I have been told that our Ministry is convinced that sooner or later, most of the Hindus will have to convert themselves into Muslims or cross the borders and come to India. What is going to happen to these 90 lakhs of Hindus who are there? If they are coming where is the space that you are going to provide for them? The hon. Member pleaded that when they come they must be received, and the refugee problem must be tackled.

He predicted that the Hindus in East Pakistan were not secure and, sooner or later, they would be compelled to come back to India. He further argued that similar treatment must not be given to Muslims who were residing in Pakistan and looking for opportunities. He further stressed

We are a secular State. In agree. In our own State, there is not even a minute difference between a Hindu and a Muslim in the matter of appointments, conduct of institutions, etc. This has been laid down in the Constitution. This applies only to Indian citizens and not Muslims and others who live outside the borders of India ... reports are also current that many Muslims who had been disillusioned by going to Pakistan are coming back to India. ... While we can have no objection to admit Hindu refugees from Pakistan—I am glad the House also had agreed—I would like to say that the Muslims who had crossed over from India to Pakistan need not be taken back; they need not be given the same facility which we are bound to give the Hindu refugees from East Bengal.[22]

The citizenship provisions must not treat at par, he argued.

Responding to the debate on the refugee issue and citizenship, the Deputy Minister of Home Affairs, Shri B. N. Datar responded by saying:

Shri Bhargava suggested that so far as the refugees from West Pakistan or East Pakistan are concerned, they ought to be recognised as Indian citizens as such without going through the process of registration, I would sympathise with him, I would point out to him that even in the Constitution itself, in Article 6 (b) (ii) a provision has been made for the purpose of registration. That itself has been carried further on and I would assure him that there is no particular difficulty in getting oneself registered. I am not prepared to accept his very wide statement that very many people are remaining unregistered or unrecognised as Indian citizens under the Constitution. There may be some people here and there. But, you will find that even now it would be open to any refugee who has come to India even recently to get himself registered under clause 5 (1)(a) which says:

'persons of Indian origin who are ordinarily resident in India and have been so resident for one year immediately before making an application for registration'

That would show that if 1-3-1956 is to be taken as the crucial date, all those persons of Indian origin who have come back to India before 1-3-1955 for permanent residence here, for getting rights of Indian citizenship.[23]

---

[22] Ibid.

[23] B. N. Dattar, Deputy Home Minister, Rajya Sabha Debates, Vol. II, 7–20 December 1955.

The only thing that was required was that they had to apply and get themselves duly registered. That need not be considered as a great hardship because the government could set up effective machinery for that purpose.

Shri S. Barman opposed the sub-clause (a) which required that the East Bengal migrants be ordinary residents in India for 1 year. He said that originally, that was only 6 months in the case of the Constitution under Article 6. He argued that once the government had accepted a migrant from East Bengal, how could they then make a distinction between migrants from East Bengal and other persons? He said

> [O]nce these migrants from East Bengal—who were once our own kith and kin and enjoyed the same liberties and citizenship—come over to India with a migration certificate and are registered, they are treated differently from those who had been citizens here before and others are not subject to this sub-clause (2)(b) of clause 10 … I should say that it is derogatory for a migrant from East Bengal to come and accept citizenship in India under this clause.

Shri S. V. L. Narasimham (Guntur) endorsed the views by Pandit Thakur Das Bhargava and Shri Barman that persons who had migrated from Pakistan should be treated on an altogether different line from the rest of the categories mentioned in clause 5 (1). He reminded the members of parliament not to forget some historical facts. He said:

> Did we not make assurance to those brethren of ours who unfortunately had to be left behind in the area which is called Pakistan that their stay in Pakistan and their interest certainly shall be watched carefully and diligently by us in what is known as India and in case their position in that area will be threatened and they come back to India, we shall welcome them as brothers with the same spirit of relationship that we used to maintain prior to partition? If we are prepared to submit them to a process of registration with all these conditions and at the same time threatening them with deportation also under certain circumstances, may I ask whether it will not amount to a repudiation of the solemn assurance that had been made on behalf of India by her leaders, to those unfortunates who are displaced persons?

In fact, one member, J. V. K. Vallabharao pleaded for more liberal terms to be granted to the refugees for acquiring citizenship. He thought that the refugees should be treated as persons who were entitled to citizenship by descent rather than by registration. He said that it was difficult for everyone to go through the ordeal of registration as many of them were not educated.

Four Waves of Hindu Refugees to Assam

Four waves of refugee influx are visible in the case of Northeast India in general and Assam in particular. The first wave of refugees was up to 1958. The second wave was from 1964 to 1971 (March), the third wave was from 1971 (April) until about 1979, and the fourth wave was from 1979 onwards until 1988–1989.

According to data made available to Lok Sabha, 487,000 out of 4,117,000 refugees were registered in Assam up to 31 March 1958. For details, see Table 5.4. The bulk of these refugees were registered in West Bengal and some had gone to other states such as Tripura, Uttar Pradesh, Madhya Pradesh and Andaman and the Nicobar Islands.

Table 5.4 *Distribution of Displaced Persons from East Pakistan*

State	Number of Displaced Persons		
	Rural	Urban	Total
Andaman and Nicobar Islands	8,700		87,00
Assam	333,000	154,000	487,000
Bihar	16,000	50,000	66,000
Madhya Pradesh	11,700		11,700
Manipur	1,000	1,000	2,000
Orissa	10,000	2,000	12,000
Uttar Pradesh	11,000	1,000	12,000
West Bengal	1,572,600	1,570,000	3,142,600
Tripura	236,000	138,000	374,000
Rajasthan	1,000		1,000
Total	2,201,000	1,916,000	4,117,000

Source: Estimate supplied to Lok Sabha, 10 March 1959.

Distribution of Displaced Persons
from East Pakistan[24]

It may be mentioned that no precise data are available on refugee influx as many persons had been crossing over to India even without documents. They got easily mixed up due to linguistic and ethnic similarities despite restrictions imposed by the Government of India and Assam from time to time. Census could be an important mechanism to suggest how Assam's population had been changing as a result of the influx of refugee population and illegal immigrants of Bengali Muslims from former East Bengal.

The second wave of Hindu refugee influx to Assam started in January 1964. Various relief camps and relief and rehabilitation programmes were undertaken to accommodate the refugees.

Relief Camps in the States (Estimate Supplied to the Third Lok Sabha on 20 February 1964)

The arrival of refugee, however, continued until March 1971. Of the 1,113,958 migrants coming from East Pakistan from January 1964 to March 1971, 214,318 came to Assam, 756,690 to West Bengal and 143,021 to Tripura.[25]

Citizenship Issue to Refugees and
Stand of Government of India

The question arises as to how the issue of citizenship to the Bengali Hindu refugees was addressed in the case of Assam. Here we may mention a secret letter No. 4/366/63-IC of 16 June 1965 from the Union Home Ministry to the Chief Secretary, Assam. The letter says:

> Subject: Conferment of Indian citizenship on migrants from East Pakistan Policy and procedure in regard to.

[24] Estimate supplied to Lok Sabha, 10 March 1959.
[25] Chhabra, *Assam Challenge*, 63.

As State governments are aware, the question of registration as Indian citizens of members of the minority communities who have recently migrated from East Pakistan has been under consideration. The matter has been examined in the light of the views expressed by the State governments. It has been decided that such of the migrants (when they have come with or without migration certificates or travel documents) as have severed their ties and connections with Pakistan and have settled in service, trade or profession in India, may be registered as Indian citizens under section fl 5(1) (A) of the Citizenship Act 1955 provided they fulfil conditions laid down in section 9 of the Indian Citizenship Rules 1956. It is requested that necessary instructions may be issued to the registering authorities concerned and the number of migrants registered during each month intimated to this Ministry by the 15th of the succeeding month ....

In its letter no. 11/180/72/TX of 30 September 1972, the Union Home Ministry laid down comprehensive guidelines regarding the repatriation of various categories of refugees explaining that 'according to the understanding between the government of India and Bangladesh the refugees who came to India before March 25 '71, whether Bengalis or non-Bengalis would not be sent back to Bangladesh'.[26] In another secret Union Home Ministry letter of 4 October 1972, the Union Home Ministry explained that among the post-March 1971 entrants too, only the Bengalis were to be repatriated. The state government was told to ignore the non-Bengalis, particularly the Bihari Muslims, whose repatriation would have communal implications, as it was explained in the letter. The letter goes on to say:

At the same time we cannot compromise on our basic stand those all Bangladeshi nationals, whether Bengalis or non-Bengalis, who entered India after 15.12.71, without valid travel documents or have continued to stay after their expiry, must be returned to that country. However, if it feels that repatriation of any group is likely to lead to any political controversy or agitation, you may consult us before actually undertaking any repatriation.

Another letter, F.9/7/60-I, dated 21 July 1960, was issued by the Union government to the Assam government. According to the extract of the letter, a distinction had to be made based on those who were security risks and those who were not, while dealing with Pakistanis staying

[26] Murty, *Assam, the Difficult Years*, 80.

in India for a long time without a travel document. As we have argued in the chapter on NRC and citizenship, a clear instruction was issued on 17 February 1976 stating that persons who came from erstwhile Pakistan or East Bengal and settled in Assam before 25 March 1971 should not be deported or expelled. The White Paper says,

> On February 17, 1976 Ministry of Home Affairs issued a notification entrusting the Superintendents of Police and the Deputy Commissioners (in charge of Police) with powers of Central Government in making orders against Bangladesh nationals under Foreigners' Act, 1946. ... While enclosing the above notification dated February 17, 1976 in respect of Bangladesh nationals, Government of India instructed the State Government that 'persons who (had) come to India from erstwhile East Pakistan/Bangladesh prior to March 1971 are not to be sent back to Bangladesh.[27]

Liberation War of East Bengal and Refugee Crisis

The liberation struggle by the East Bengal people against the oppressive rule of West Pakistan led to a civil war-like situation in East Pakistan. Assam, along with other states such as West Bengal and Tripura, became a victim of Pakistan's diabolical plan. In the security and economic sectors, Assam faced multi-pronged challenges. M. M. Choudhury, Chief Minister of Assam, gave a sketch of the situation in the Assam Assembly on 25 October 1971. He stated in the State Assembly:

> On top of this, due to the militant and aggressive attitude of Pakistan in relation to India during recent weeks, a situation is fast developing which at any time may assume the most serious proportions so far as the Country's security and integrity are concerned. Our State has been the target of very serious attempts at large scale sabotage especially in respect of vital communication links. In particular the Cachar border has been the scene of Pakistani sabotage operations during recent times causing serious concern.

Sabotage activities, in a planned and calculated manner, started from about the middle of August 1971, and since then, there have been as

---

[27] White Paper; ibid., 11.

many as 28 attempts to disrupt vital communication links, thereby creating panic and demoralization. The rail line between Badarpur and Dharmanagar in Tripura was a scene of such sabotage activity apparently under a plan to completely disrupt the slender communication links between Assam and Tripura, which had also a long border with East Bengal.

The sabotage attempts, as the CM informed the house, were aimed at preventing movement of essential supplies and security personnel, to create panic and cut off normal life. In one case, due to sabotage in a passenger train, one person lost his life and 15 others were injured.

It appears that besides planting high explosives to destroy railway tracks and blow up wagons and compartments, even anti-tank mines of considerable size and weight were systematically used. Some of the explosives used were of special types, the operational mechanism of which called for special examination by expert agencies.

In the Garo Hills, the border of which Pakistan had paid special attention to, two persons lost their lives after unwittingly walking over an area where mines were planted by Pakistani saboteurs. About seven bridges and culverts in the border were also destroyed in sabotage activities with high explosives and mines. While giving an account of Pakistan's effort to destabilize the region, CM Chaudhury said that in the early hours of 24 October, there was a serious attempt at disrupting the train communication between Assam and the rest of the country at a place between Jorani and Srirampur railway stations in the Goalpara district, near the Sankosh bridge bordering the Jalpaiguri district. In that sabotage attempt, the rail joint was removed and the line displaced, leading to the cancellation of train services. Referring to the Pakistani attack, MM Chaudhury, the CM of Assam, stated:

There has been consistent firing from the Pakistani side on important targets and border outposts and once even on Karimganj town in the Cachar-Garo Hills sectors during recent weeks. In that connection I would like to draw attention of the House to two serious cases of actual Pakistani intrusion into our territory at Sutarkandi in Cachar and Dalu in the Garo Hills by the end of May last when there had been several casualities on our side. Firing across the border appears to have been intensified during the last few days. Heavy shelling started in the Dalu area in the early morning of

20.10.71 which continued for a long time. On 19th October, Putni T.E. in Patharkandi P.S. of Cachar was the target of shelling from the Pakistani army, as a result of which four workers received injuries. Many families had to leave the garden for shelter in safer places.

However, the Indian security forces succeeded in capturing sizeable quantities of arms and ammunition. Reports indicated that about 50 vehicles, including some belonging to the Pakistani troops and the Pakistan Police, were captured. The state CM emphasized that the need of the hour was to maintain the absolute peaceful condition in the region intact in order to help the security forces to perform their duties effectively and ensure the security of the region.[28]

The CM also provided a detailed account of refugee's entry to the state. They were given shelter in evacuee camps within Assam and Meghalaya. This could be said to be the third wave of refugee influx to the state. By 25 October 1971, the state government had accommodated 736,384 evacuees in various camps, including 539,847 in camps in Meghalaya. Nearly 144,562 evacuees had been staying outside the camps with their kith and kin after registration. All the evacuees were required to be registered with detailed particulars under the Foreigners Act to avoid any difficulty in identifying them for convenient return to their homes in due course.[29]

Along with those evacuees, about 12,287 persons who had earlier been deported from the state as illegal Pakistani infiltrators also entered Assam as evacuees. Given their past antecedents, those evacuees were placed in a few special camps, and they had not been allowed to mix up with the general body of evacuees. Special care was taken so that Pakistani agents and saboteurs could not take advantage of the situation. The state was undergoing a great economic recession at that time and, as suggested by the CM in the Assembly, agricultural production was at its lowest and the settlement of refugees had severely strained

[28] CM Secretariat Department, Influx of Refugees from East Bengal, File No. CMS6/71, State Archives of Assam.

[29] There is no proper account of how many of them had actually gone back. Various reports as will be highlighted would show the number of refugees going back to newly born Bangladesh was very less.

the state exchequer. Maintaining such a large number of evacuees in camps near the border with difficult communication facilities in many cases had posed stupendous problems due to which arrangements for the supply of essential commodities, medical and other services were insufficient. The problem of malnutrition and a lack of adequate child welfare work for a large number of children and old and infirm persons in the evacuee camps caused a serious concern.

Influx of Refugees from April 1971 Until September 1971

The CM had informed the house that the influx of refugees into Assam and Meghalaya from the beginning of April 1971 was estimated at nearly 410,000 up to 16 June 1971. Out of these, about 328,135 were admitted in camps, and the rest were either staying with relatives or awaiting admission into the camps. In Meghalaya, about 223,000 refugees were staying in camps.

However, the number provided by CM was a conservative figure as the number of refugees in Assam was continually on the rise on account of daily entry on a considerable scale and was likely to continue, judging from reports of developments in East Bengal. On top of that, the refugees took Meghalaya as transit route on their way to Assam. On the other hand, the people of that state were anxious at the tide of refugees without any signs of abatement. The communal incident of Badarpur and the other incidents involving linguistic groups in the Brahmaputra Valley indicated that various provocateurs were actively engaged in creating seeds of discord throughout the state and taking advantage of the people.

In the context of the situation prevailing in the state, Mahendra Mohan Chaudhury opposed the proposal to establish large refugee camps at Ledo and Sarbhog and argued that it would impose a well-nigh insupportable burden on the state government. The state government was not against setting up new camps, but it urged to shift the existing refugees to other states, not bordering East Bengal. CM emphatically opposed the suggestion to bring fresh refugees from Tripura to Assam. He pleaded that as a last resort, if the situation

Table 5.5 *Rehabilitation Camps in India*

State	Number of Camps	Number of Refugees	Number of Refugees on Their Own	Total
West Bengal	492	4,849,786	2,386,130	7,235,916
Tripura	276	834,098	547,151	1,381,249
Meghalaya	17	591,520	76,466	667,986
Assam	28	255,642	91,913	347,555
Bihar	8	36,732		36,732
Madhya Pradesh	3	219,218		219,218
Uttar Pradesh	1	10,619		10,619
Total	825	6,797,615	3,101,660	9,899,275

Source: Government of India, Ministry of External Affairs, Bangladesh Documents, 1972

demanded, camps be set up in Assam for refugees shifted from Tripura; however, it should be clearly understood that those would be only transit camps for refugees to halt for a few days en route to other states. Table 5.5 provides an idea regarding the nature and numbers of rehabilitation camps in India. By the end of 1971, Assam received a total number of 819,751 non-Muslim refugees in Assam—a fact which is blissfully neglected by the protagonists of 'Assamese nationalists' (for details, see Table 5.6)'.

Special Branch report on the number of refugees in Assam by the end of 1971 due to civil war in East Pakistan.[30]

Administrative Guideline for Repatriation and Management of Evacuees

In an express letter from J. C. Agarwal, the Joint Secretary to the Government of India, to all state governments and Union Territory administrations, the following instructions were issued pertaining to

[30] Ref: Order Issue under the Foreigner Act 1946 Reg. Influx from E. Bengal, File No. PLB 127/71, Home Political.

Table 5.6 *Total Number of Camps in Assam*

Bengali Muslim	10,1458
Non-Bengali Muslim	183
Non-Muslim	673,942
Total	775,583
Total number outside the camps	
Bengali Muslim	15,110
Non-Bengali Muslim	17
Non-Muslim	145,809
Total	160,936
Total number of evacuees	
Bengali Muslim	116,568
Non-Bengali Muslim	200
Non-Muslim	819,751
Total refugees including Muslim immigrants	936,519

the registration of displaced persons from East Bengal.[31] To facilitate proper arrangements for the relief of the persons displayed from East Bengal as a result of what happening in that area, it was considered necessary to register them. They were to be kept under the Foreigner Act, 1946. The entire order was published in a Gazette Extraordinary on 5 May 1971. Through the letter, GOI advised the state governments to be extremely careful in handling the refugees. It was stated in the letter that the displaced persons were in great distress and desperately in need of relief. The letter communicated

> Displaced persons are in great distress and are in need of relief. Order will have to be given effect to with full sympathy and understanding and sharing that no feeling of harassment is created. Assistance of suitable individuals among the displaced persons maybe unlisted in ascertaining the required particulars and filling the declaration forms.

[31] No. 11013/5/71-f.i, Government of India, Ministry of Home Affairs, FILE NO. PLB 127/71, New Delhi, 5 May 1971.

Permission to stay was restricted to the following group of people: (a) those staying in camps provided by the government to places in which day camps are located, and (b) in the case of those staying with friends and relatives. Movement from one place to another was rarely permitted unless there were exceptional reasons in any particular cases. In case of persons who were suspected of subversive activities, fomenting communal troubles, etc., orders may be made placing for the restrictions on their movement and/or requiring them to report to the police station. In suitable cases, they might be also required to enter into a bond, with or without security, for the due observance of the restriction imposed on them and the conditions under which they had been permitted to stay in India. Such orders might, however, be made only where they were necessary bearing in mind that no harassment should be caused to the persons who had been in this place from their homeland and were in severe distress. Powers to make such orders were available under Section 3 of the Foreigners Act 1946. Permission to stay was initially given for 3 months at a time. Importance was given for the due observance of the restrictions imposed on them and the conditions under which they had been permitted to stay in India. Search orders were issued only in necessary cases, bearing in mind that no harassment be caused to the persons who had been displaced from their homeland and were in severe distress.

In another communiqué, the evacuees were directed to register and obtain the necessary permit during their stay. It said

> Due to the present political unrest in East Bengal, a large number of people have left that country to seek shelter in the adjoining area of the Indian Union because of the emergent nature of the Exodus; the Refugees are not in possession of any travel document normally required of a person visiting a foreign country. To give temporary permission for their presence in this country, Government of India has promulgated an order under the Foreigners Act 1946, calling upon all refugees to obtain a permit to stay in this country.[32]

---

[32] Directorate of Information and Public Relations. Government of Assam, Press Note no. 35, Shillong, 15 May 1971.

Accordingly, all persons who had entered India were asked to get themselves registered by 31 May 1971 and subsequent incomers should do so within 24 hours after entry into India. The understanding between India and Bangladesh was that only those who were forced to leave Bangladesh and take refuge in India after 25 March 1971 would be returned to Bangladesh for resettlement. It was, accordingly, part of the understanding that the refugees who came to India before 25 March would not be sent back to Bangladesh. There could, however, be individual instances of other persons who had come to India before 25 March 1971 from territories now comprising Bangladesh and who would not return or who were prevented from doing so for any reason.

Such individual cases would be taken up with the Government of Bangladesh separately and, for that purpose, detailed particulars in respect of such persons would be furnished to the Ministries of Home Affairs and External Affairs. The Government of India released another letter on the management of refugees.[33]

Persons who had come to India from territories now comprising Bangladesh after 25 March 1971 and before the Liberation of Bangladesh, that is, 16 December 1971, may comprise the following:

1. Bengali refugees still living in camps or staying with their friends and relatives;
2. non-Bengalis, such as the so-called Bihari Muslims, and
3. Bengalis as well as non-Bengalis apprehended on suspicion and under internment/detention or involved in criminal cases.

Those who came to India after 16 December 1971 would fall into the following broad categories:

1. those who came to India without valid documents or having come to India with valid documents and continued to stay after the expiry of such documents and

---

[33] In a secret/immediate letter by Government of India to all State Governments and Union Territories administration, New Delhi, dated 30 September 1972. Subject: Action to be taken in respect of persons who had come to India from Bangladesh.

2. those who may have been apprehended on suspicion and may be either under internment/detention or involved in criminal cases.

The letter stated that all these categories of persons had to be repatriated to Bangladesh. It was, however, decided that while non-Bengalis who came to India during the period from 25 March 1971 to 16 December 1971 and were in separate camps or staying with friends and relations or under internment/detention custody, might ultimately be required to return to Bangladesh, the communiqué said that they were not be immediately deported.

Pending repatriation the letter mentioned three important steps: (a) present arrangements for their stay in India may continue, (b) those who were in camp may continue to be kept in such camps and (c) those staying with friends and relatives might be permitted to continue to do so. The order suggested that the movement of evacuees may be suitably regulated under the provisions of the Foreigners Act.[34] The Bengalis or non-Bengalis who came to India after 16 December 1971, whether with or without valid travel documents, should all be required to return to Bangladesh, the latter on the expiry of the duration for which date travel documents are valid.

In respect of persons under internment/detention as well as those involved in criminal cases, it would be necessary to distinguish between those involved in petty or technical offences and those regarding whom evidence was available after involvement in serious offences such as espionage or sabotage. All those against whom there is no evidence of such involvement in serious offences would have had to be repatriated to Bangladesh in convenient batches if they were under internment/detention.

There were a large number of suspected Razakars militiamen[35] among the persons in custody. It was agreed in principle that the Razakars would be repatriated to Bangladesh by the Government of Bangladesh which desired that they might be sent in small packages as

[34] Ibid.

[35] Razakars were a private Islamic militia organised by Qasim Razvi, a Hyderabadi politician.

and when indicated by the government. Instructions for the release of the first batch of 80 Razakars had already been sent to the Government of West Bengal. Instructions regarding the repatriation of the remaining militiamen were sent to the concerned state governments in due course.

Thus, officially, the refugees were registered, and they were made to understand that their stay was temporary and was contingent upon the improvement of the situation, and once it bounced back to normalcy, they were bound to return. However, the question arises whether those who were there in camps or with relatives and friends actually left or had GOI planned for their repatriation? The numbers of such returnees were extremely low, and there were no authentic government data to show how many of them had actually left. On the other hand, Government of Assam (GOA) issued several orders for the refugees to stay with relatives, friends and among communities.

Government of Assam Report on Refugees

Although the initial estimate of the Government of Assam about the refugees was about 0.9 million, the number kept adding up as the flow of incomers continued. The military operations by the Pakistan Army and the war for liberation resulted in about 1.2 million Bangladeshi nationals crossing over to Assam for shelter. Out of them, about 1.1 million stayed in the refugee camps in Meghalaya and Assam, and 0.1 million (mostly Hindus) stayed with their relations and friends outside the camps.[36]

According to the report, after the war, many of refugee camps were made to go back to Bangladesh. However, a sizeable number of those who were outside the camps managed to stay on conducting petty businesses such as tea stalls, grocery shops or as tenants on land. Due to India's cordial and friendly relations with Bangladesh in 1972 and 1973, the situation at the border remained very fluid, and there was a relaxed check on traffic between Assam and Bangladesh.

---

[36] PLB 376/79; Political Department, Assam Secretariat.

The report referred to another wave of refugee influx to Assam in 1974, which may be cited as the fourth wave of refugees to the state (including the influx in 1975 due to army coup). In 1974, due to acute economic distress caused by floods and a severe shortage of food, a large number of Bangladesh nationals tried to enter Assam. This huge influx of Hindus could be attributed to a sense of panic and insecurity. Similarly, in August 1975, the report asserted that a large number of people tried to enter into Assam from Bangladesh due to Army coup and murder of Sheikh Mujibur Rahman. A large number of such infiltrators were detected and sent back to Bangladesh. Various political department data confirm that the process of crossover of both Hindus as refugees and Muslims as illegal migrants to the border continued.

Due to the political stability in Bangladesh, the influx had reduced, but the communal tension created by some political parties (e.g., Muslim Leaguers and pro-Pakistani elements) during the presidential election had again created panic among the minorities. The influx of Burmese Muslims to Bangladesh and consequent pushing out of some non-Muslims from the Chittagong Hill Tract District increased the influx.

The issue of Bengali Hindu refugees was discussed in-depth during the Assam Agitation, and the total figure of refugees cited was about 1.3 million.

> In 1971 Bangladesh came into being out of erstwhile East Pakistan. In its wake, more than 13 lacs (1.3 million) of Bangladeshis officially entered Assam and Meghalaya and stayed in refugee camps – as official records reveal. The number of those who have directly gone to their ubiquitous kinsmen is also very high and one does not know how many of them have gone back. In 1974 and 1975 the influx of Bangladeshis started afresh and its genesis is found in the acute food shortage in Bangladesh in 1974 followed by the political turmoil in 1975 and the consequent assassination of Sheikh Mujibur Rahman.[37]

---

[37] All Assam Journalists' Association, *Assam: The Crisis of Identity*, 7–8.

Nalini Kanta Barkatkati further argued

> [T]he matter did not end there—this exodus became a continuous process. The Bangladesh liberation war brought a mass exodus of the Hindu population and they were sheltered in Assam and Meghalaya and fed by opening evacuee camps even by levying extra indirect tax until Bangladesh was formed and the world recognized it. Thereafter, these camps were abolished and the evacuees ordered to go back to their own country. But several lakhs of them also stayed on, barring the few who managed to get themselves registered as citizens of India in Assam and West Bengal.[38]

Citizenship Amendment Act, 2019, Constitutionality and Question of Hindu Refugees

Professor Anupama Roy from JNU is a pioneer in citizenship study in India.[39] She has made the following main arguments regarding the then Citizenship Bill and the NRC.[40] She argues:

1. The law of citizenship in India, I argue, must not be seen as embedded in a continuum of chronological time, as unfolding in a sequential time frame in which each amendment in the law, effectively put in place a new one.

2. The Citizenship (Amendment) Act, 2003, may be seen as a hinge point, from which two mutually contradictory tendencies emerged, in the form of the NRC and the CAB. These tendencies had their roots in the category of illegal migrants, which was inserted by the 2003 amendment restricting citizenship by birth.

3. More specifically, the CAB has ruptured the political consensus on the NRC in the North East, especially in Assam. The two citizenship tendencies that emerged out of the 2003 hinge point were of hyphenated citizenship associated with the NRC, which made citizenship contingent on conditions of descent specific to each

---

[38] Barkakati, 'Foreigners vis-à-vis Assam, 35.

[39] Two of her remarkable books in the field are—Roy, *Mapping Citizenship in India* and Roy, *Citizenship in India*.

[40] Roy, 'The Citizenship (Amendment) Bill, 2016 and the Aporia of Citizenship. For details, also see Roy, *Mapping Citizenship in India*, particularly her chapter on 'Blood and Belonging', 135–58.

state, and a national citizenship associated with the CAB which made religion a principle of distinguishability in the creation of bounded citizenship.

4. Indeed, while religious persecution is a justifiable grounds for extending state protection, it is not clear why it should be selective in its identification of those who can be considered persecuted on religious grounds. It is also not clear why a change in law must be carried out to insert a principle in the Citizenship Act which goes against the Constitution, when administrative measures at the local level can be strengthened to address such concerns in consonance with the 2015 executive order. The manner in which 'displaced persons' were absorbed into the fold of citizenship in the 1950s in the absence of statutory provisions on citizenship, is an example of how it can be done.

It would be wrong to say that CAB has made religion as a principle of 'distinguishability in the creation of bounded citizenship'. If 'gender' or 'caste', 'class' or 'ethnicity' could be categories for positive discrimination, there is no reason why 'religion' could not be a category or class for making a historical wrong right. The identified religious groups were picked up because as a class and (and that constitutes the 'intelligible differentia') as a category, these groups were persecuted in those countries which happened to be theocratic Islamic countries. Had those countries been secular with protection for minority rights, in that case, such classification based on 'religion' would have been wrong.

Now the following question arises: (a) Is the act of persecution an objective truth or not? (b) It is argued that CAA-19 violated constitutional and secular principles of the country. If this is so, it is important to ask how these questions of persecutions and citizenship were addressed in CA, in Parliament like Lok Sabha and Rajya Sabha. (c) How did the Congress party and other political parties that had been opposing CAB and CAA-19 look at the issue of persecution of Hindus and others, previously? (d) If citizenship is granted to the six communities, why have the 'Muslims' as a category been excluded, and if, for example, the 'Muslim immigrants' are allowed to come in legally or legalize their stay, what will be its impact in the body polity of Assam? (for details, see Chapter 6). (e) Professor Roy justifies state action in case of persecution but believes that there was no need for incorporating it in the law, which could have been done through 'executive order' in the way 'displaced people' were absorbed in the 1950s. The question arises as to whether it is a feasible suggestion because there has been a huge human rights' violation of the refugees who have been languishing in various camps without enjoying citizenship rights in various states of the eastern region. In other words, what is the plight of these 'stateless' people? Should we continue with uncertainties and dualities and leave their plight to the bureaucratic machinations?

Any discussion on 'citizenship' cannot be divorced from context and history. Our previous chapters, including the present one, are nothing but vivid reflections on how the citizenship issue was discussed in various legislative forums and how these decisions were arrived at since the dawn of Independence.

The Left Pleading

Interestingly, on various occasions, it is the political parties, mainly CPI, CPM and Congress, that fought for the forcible stay of the Hindu and Muslim immigrants in Assam. It may be mentioned that Left parties like CPI and CPM were the staunchest supporters of the Hindu refugees when the issue was comprehensively debated in the Parliament on the eve of the Assam Agitation. Apart from their ideological stand on the plight of minorities in East Pakistan, the Left parties drew their political support from the Bengali-dominated areas of East India. For a long time, the Left parties had undisputed domination in West Bengal and Tripura and certain pockets in Assam.[41] Interestingly, when a legal provision was made in 2019 for granting citizenship to the persecuted people, the same political parties were fighting against the process. It is important to look at how these political parties have fiercely protected them for their stay in Assam.

---

[41] Chhabra, *Assam Challenge*, 104–105.

Here, the report of the CM Secretariat is noteworthy.[42] In its report on the activity of any individual/group of any individual/organization in support of the retention of infiltrators in Assam, it was said that

[i]nformation received from various sources during the week indicate that C.P.I. and R.S.P. leaders of Golokganj area in Goalpara district are organizing volunteers from Halakura, Agomoni and Laldoba area under Golokganj P.S. with a view to put obstruction on Police personnel in the process of detection and deportation of Bangladesh nationals. They even planned to assault Police on way while escorting Bangladeshi (B.D.) nationals from Golokganj P.P.C.P. to B.S.F. Camp for push back. The names of prominent leaders are given below:

1. Sri Jogen Rai, C.P.I. of Halakura,

2. Abdul Rahman, C.P.I. of Sindurai,

3. Majobar Rahman, tailor of Agomoni,

4. Raghu Nandan Bepari, Revolutionary Socialist Party (RSP) of Kalduba,

5. Sudhir Rai, R.S.P. of Kalduba.

The report said that on 1 March 1979, a secret meeting was organized by the leaders of Muslims of Serfanguri under Goalpara district in the house of Md. Abdul Rahman with Md. Rabi Hazi of Oxiguri in the chair, as well as (a) Abdul Khaleque Maulabi, (b) Anwar Hussain, teacher of Hasrabar L. P. School and (c) Md. Abdul Karim, as the prominent participants. The meeting expressed grave concern in the process of detection and deportation of Bangladeshi nationals and decided to send a deputation to Gauhati under Abdul Karim to meet the ministers in this connection. The meeting also decided to collect ₹5 from each family to meet the expenditures of the delegators. It was reported that the villagers of Serfanguri were contemplating to resist and assault the police when they would go and search for Bangladeshi nationals. On 5 March 1979, a public meeting was organized jointly by CPM, RSP and CPI and Congress I at Mahamaya Maydan in the Gauripur Town of Goalpara district with Shri Kalipada

---

[42] Obtained in State Archive, File No. CMS.5/79, ROY/29/3/79. Subject: Weekly Intelligence Reports, On Infiltration of Bangladesh Nationals.

Das Gupta as the chair. The meeting vehemently criticized the police and the Janata Government of Assam for the alleged harassment of Bengalis and deportation of Indian nationals. The meeting urged upon the government to set up tribunals for determining the status of the persons charged as infiltrants so that unnecessary harassment to Indian nationals could be stopped. The meeting also decided to force a district-level ad-hoc committee in this respect. It is learnt that in the last part of February 1979, some CPM workers, including Shri Bipin Daimari, Shri Bali Charan Singh and Santosh Guha, advised the Bengali Hindu and Muslim people of Basugaon, Kokrajhar and Salakati of the Goalpara district to keep their papers ready to prove their nationality. On 6 March 1979, the members of the Asom Khetiok Santha and the United Students' Federation (USF). of Barpeta started a demonstration in front of the office of the SDO, Barpeta, shouting slogans condemning police action in respect of alleged deportation of Indian nationals on the plea of deporting Bangladesh nationals. On 7 March 1979, the Hojai Branch of CPM took out a procession under the leadership of Shri Ashok Paul Choudhury at Hojai and submitted a memorandum to the O/C, Hojai P. S., and B. D. O. Hojai, demanding stoppage of alleged deportation of Indian nationals in the name of Bangladeshi nationals.

Needless to say, all these demonstrations and agitations were carried out ostensibly to protect the genuine Indians; however, in connivance with civil society groups, the political parties facilitated all possible help for their illegal brethren to stay in Assam to act as their vote bank and supporters.[43]

Persecution of Bengali Hindus: Objective Truth or Myth

Persecution of Hindus in Pakistan and former Eastern Pakistan—now Bangladesh—is more of a historical reality than imagination. Jogendra Nath Mandal's resignation letter to Liaquat Ali Khan from the position

---

[43] A detailed enquiry on how political parties vouched for the refugees/foreigners to stay in Assam is included as 'annexure' at the end of this chapter.

of the first Minister for Law and Labour, Government of Pakistan, was a telling experience of the treatment of the minorities in East Pakistan.[44] In his resignation letter, he said:

> It is with a heavy heart and a sense of utter frustration at the failure of my lifelong mission to uplift the backward Hindu masses of East Bengal that I feel compelled to tender resignation of my membership of your cabinet. It is proper that I should set forth in detail the reasons which have prompted me to take this decision at this important juncture of the Indo-Pakistani subcontinent.

As the SC leader of East Bengal, Jogendra Nath Mandal was included in the Cabinet of the Muslim League Ministry in April 1946. The 16th day of August of 1946 was observed in Calcutta as 'The Direct Action Day' by the Muslim League which resulted in a holocaust. He said

> I cannot but gratefully acknowledge the fact that I was saved from the wrath of infuriated Hindu mobs by my Caste Hindu neighbours. The Calcutta carnage was followed by the 'Noakhali Riot' in October 1946. There, Hindus including Scheduled Castes were killed and hundreds were converted to Islam. Hindu women were raped and abducted. Members of my community also suffered loss of life and property.

Mandal was included as a cabinet minister in the new ministry. Mandal requested Khwaja Nazimuddin who formed a provisional Cabinet for East Bengal to take two Scheduled Caste Ministers in the East Bengal Cabinet. However, several meetings with the top-level leaders went in vain. He alleged:

> [M]y outspokenness, vigilance and sincere efforts to safeguard the interests of the minorities of Pakistan, in general, and of the Scheduled Caste, in particular, were considered a matter on annoyance to the East Bengal Government and few League leaders. Undaunted, I took my firm stand to safeguard the interests of the minorities of Pakistan.

Referring to the anti-Hindu policy pursued by the Pakistani government, he said,

---

[44] Mandal, *Resignation Letter to Liaquat Ali Khan*.

> You will recollect that from time to time I brought the grievances of the Scheduled Castes to your notice. ... I brought to your notice incidents of barbarous atrocities perpetrated by the police on frivolous grounds. I did not hesitate to bring to your notice the anti-Hindu policy pursued by the East Bengal Government especially the police administration and a section of Muslim League leaders.

In his letter, Mandal referred to five reasons why the Hindus were persecuted in various places in Dacca. He said there was apprehension regarding the launching of a movement for the reunion of East and West Bengal, both by Hindu and Muslim leaders. It made the East Bengal Ministry and the Muslim League nervous. They wanted to prevent such a move at any cost. They believed that any large-scale communal riot in East Bengal was sure to produce reactions in West Bengal where Muslims might be killed. They concluded that the result of such riots in both East and West Bengal would prevent any movement for the reunion of Bengals. Besides, Mandal further cited that feeling of animosity between the Bengali Muslims and non-Bengali Muslims in East Bengal was gaining ground. This could only be prevented by creating hatred between Hindus and Muslims of East Bengal. The language question was also added to it. He said that the Muslim League wanted to divert the Muslim masses from the impending economic breakdown by some sort of Jihad against the Hindus. In his resignation letter, Mandal further said that he was deeply saddened by the killing of more than 10,000 thousand Hindus. In a heart-wrenching description, he said,

> During my nine days' stay at Dacca, I visited most of the riot-affected areas of the city and suburbs. I visited Mirpur also under P.S. Tejgaon. The news of the killing of hundreds of innocent Hindus in trains, on railway lines between Dacca and Narayanganj, and Dacca and Chittagong gave me the rudest shock. On the second day of Dacca riot, I met the Chief Minister of East Bengal and requested him to issue immediate instructions to the District authorities to take all precautionary measures to prevent spreading of the riot in district towns and rural areas. On the 20th February 1950, I reached Barisal town and was astounded to know of the happenings in Barisal. In the District town, a number of Hindu houses were burnt and a large number of Hindus killed. I visited almost all riot-affected areas in the District. I was simply puzzled to find the havoc wrought by the Muslim rioters even at places like Kasipur, Madhabpasha and Lakutia which were

within a radius of six miles from the District town and were connected with motorable roads. At the Madhabpasha Zamindar's house, about 200 people were killed and 40 injured. A place, called Muladi, witnessed a dreadful hell. At Muladi Bandar alone, the number killed would total more than three hundred, as was reported to me by the local Muslims including some officers. I visited Muladi village also, where I found skeletons of dead bodies at some places. I found dogs and vultures eating corpses on the river-side. I got the information there that after the whole-scale killing of all adult males, all the young girls were distributed among the ringleaders of the miscreants. ... All Hindu shops of Babuganj Bazar were looted and then burnt and a large number of Hindus were killed. From detailed information received, the conservative estimate of casualties was placed at 2,500 killed in the District of Barisal alone. Total casualties of Dacca and East Bengal riot were estimated to be in the neighbourhood of 10,000 killed. The lamentation of women and children who had lost their all including near and dear ones melted my heart. I only asked myself 'What was coming to Pakistan in the name of Islam?

Referring to West Pakistan, especially Sind and West Punjab, he stated that a large number of SCs were converted to Islam. The condition of the small number of Hindus that were still living in Sind and Karachi, the capital of Pakistan, was simply deplorable. He said,

I have got a list of 363 Hindu temples and *gurdwaras* of Karachi and Sind (which is by no means an exhaustive list) which are still in possession of Muslims. Some of the temples have been converted into cobbler's shops, slaughterhouses and hotels. None of the Hindus has got back. Possession of their landed properties was taken away from them without any notice and distributed amongst refugees and local Muslims.

He mentioned that declarations were being repeatedly made by the Muslim League leaders that Pakistan was and shall always be an Islamic State. Islam is being offered as the sovereign remedy for all earthly evils.

In that grand setting of the Shariat Muslims alone are rulers while Hindus and other minorities are *zimmies*[45] who are entitled to protection at price, and you know more than anybody else Mr Prime Minister, what that price is. After anxious and prolonged struggle I have come to the conclusion that

---

[45] A *zimmi* is a non-Muslim in an Islamic state who pays the capitation tax called *jizyah* and obtains protection.

Pakistan is no place for Hindus to live in and that their future is darkened by the ominous shadow of conversion or liquidation.[46]

A Suppressed Chapter in History

The woes and agonies of the Hindus did not end in the 1950s and 1960s. A more sinister phase began with the liberation struggle of 1971 and continued until recent times. In his book, *A Suppressed Chapter in History: The Exodus of Hindus from East Pakistan and Bangladesh*, Tathagata Roy has provided an elaborate narrative on how Bengali Hindus were suppressed in Bangladesh. He argues:

> For the Hindus there were relatively good times, like the first five years of the republic, average times like the period of Awami League rule in the late nineties up to September 2001, and the brief rule, in 1991, of temporary President, Mr. Justice Shahabuddin Ahmed. There were bad times like the period of Ziaur Rahman's, or his widow Khaleda Zia's rule, or Ershad's rule around the time when he declared Islam to be the state religion. And there were horrible, abysmal, worse-than-Pakistani times like the period when there was a Writ Petition filed in the Calcutta High Court against the Qur'an, when the disputed structure in Ayodhya, often referred to as the Babri Mosque of Ayodhya, India, was demolished by Hindus, and after Khaleda's Bangladesh National Party (BNP)-led coalition came to power in October 2001.[47]

Roy cites four factors behind the persecution of the Hindus in Bangladesh, particularly in the rural areas, which almost cover the entire country except for a few areas such as Dacca, Chittagong and Khulna.

First, Roy argues that Muslims were intolerant towards the infidels (which he elaborates in Chapter 12). He argues that the rural masses, mostly illiterate, were under the influence of the village *mollahs*, and there was no reason for the *mollahs* (local village-level Muslim religious ladders) to love the Hindus. He says the distinction between the

---

[46] The resignation letter was sent by J. N. Mandal on 8 October 1950. The resignation letter is long—more than 18 pages.

[47] Roy, *A Suppressed Chapter in History*, 316.

rural–urban is getting blurred, and they attacked the Hindus during the post-Babri days.

Second, according to Roy, the appeal of Bengali Hindu women was irresistible to the Muslim males.[48] He says 'Many Muslim men are prepared to go to extraordinary lengths to possess a Hindu woman, and that does not make Hindu men particularly dear to them'.

The third factor, he states, is the economic motive, couched in a religious package. Rural Hindus still had considerable property, and a large part of the fundamentalist Muslim rural populace saw no reason why Hindus should be allowed to possess so many properties since the bulk of Bengali Muslims were poor peasants, and they had an unsatiated demand for land.

Fourth, the popular perception among the average Muslim was that every Hindu was an Indian agent, an India sympathizer, and

> every Hindu is thus the obvious 'fall guy' in real or imagined Indian acts against the interests of Bangladesh, such as robbing the country of water (causing a drought) or sending too much water (causing a flood) by operation of the Farakka Barrage.[49]

However, Roy finds a distinction between the previous form of state persecution and its later manifestation. Unlike during the 'Pakistani era, there was, until 2001, no overt state sponsorship of the persecution, and in most cases very little covert sponsorship either'. He said there was no mass exodus of Hindus but what was present was animosity or indifference towards Hindus at the individual level of police officers and other public servants.

The plight of Hindu Bengalis has been depicted in a very detailed manner by Taslima Nasrin in her novels *Lajja* and *Phera*. As Roy explores,

> [S]he cites as many as 145 instances of persecution of Hindus in present-day Bangladesh, taking care to mention the precise location where the act

---

[48] Roy made a detailed analysis in Chapter 4.

[49] Roy, *A Suppressed Chapter in History*, 317.

was perpetrated, in terms of Zilla, Upazilla and Gram (respectively district, sub-district and village). These are mostly instances of small-scale, localised persecution, quite apart from the type of countrywide atrocities that took place in October 1990 and again in December 1992.[50]

Apart from her, many other progressive Muslim scholars and journalists have taken up the cause of the Hindus in Bangladesh. Some of them are Salam Azad, Shahriyar Kabir, Humayun Azad, Zillur Rahman Siddiqui, Muntassir Mamoon, Abdul Gaffar Choudhury and Noorul Ullah.

Francois Gautier, a French journalist residing in India, correspondent of the Paris newspaper *Figaro*, and A. J. Kamra together with Koenraad Elst, have elaborated the deplorable condition of the Hindus in Bangladesh. According to Gautier,

It would be nice to say that the Hindus in Bangladesh are prospering but it is the reverse which has happened. There were 28% Hindus in 1941, 10.5% in 1991, and less than 9% today. Pogroms, burning of temples (specially after Ayodhya) have all ensured that the Hindus flee Bangladesh.[51]

Koenraad Elst has also considered Bangladesh as 'concentration camp for Hindus'. Jamaat-e-Islami, a fundamentalist Islamic political party and their student wing Islamic Chhatra Shibir and Nizam-e-Islami, Islami Oikyo Jote were considered to be among the main tormentors against the Hindus in Bangladesh and have no qualms in expressing their animosity.[52] The year 1990 had witnessed the destruction of many Hindu properties and temples in the Dacca city itself. Some of them included the famous Dhakeswari temple which was burnt down. The raiders burnt the main temple, Najmandir, Shiva temple, as well as the guest house. At Gaudiya Math too, they destroyed the main temple, Natmandir and the guest house.[53]

[50] Roy analysing *Lajja*, 326.

[51] Cited in Roy, *A Suppressed Chapter in History*, 318–19.

[52] Ibid., 319.

[53] Ibid., 327. Some other temples include the Madhva Gaudiya Math, the Jaykali temple, the Ram–Sita temple and the Banagram temple.

Congress' Views on Persecution of Minorities in Pakistan and Bangladesh Period

Interestingly enough, the party that propagated the cause of the refugees most strongly was the Congress party. From the discussions on citizenship at CA and consecutive sessions of parliament, it is clear that it was the only party that had come out strongly in their defence. When Assam was flooded with 'undesirable immigrants', it was Congress party that introduced I(IE)A-1950 in the parliament. In the Assam Assembly, Chief Minister Bimala Prasad Chaliha made a scathing attack on Pakistan for its shabby treatment of the minorities.[54]

It is highly regrettable that the Government of Pakistan have never appreciated our genuine feelings and efforts for safeguarding the interest of the minorities in this country. The paternal role which they seek to assume over the minorities in India is not only presumptuous but is also extremely ridiculous. On the contrary, what consideration has been weighing with Pakistan in squeezing out the minorities from their country? Apart from the large numbers of refugees who migrated to India from Pakistan earlier, the influx of nearly 1,80,000 refugees belonging to the different religious groups from East Pakistan to Assam during the period from January, 1964 to January, 1965 is a clear evidence of the oppressive treatment meted out to the minority communities in Pakistan. So far as the minorities in the State of Assam are concerned, I can boldly say that they are quite happy and secure. If the Government of Pakistan continues to indulge in mischievous propaganda with a view to undermining the secular policy of the Government of India while deliberately concealing their lapses in providing securities to the minorities, they will be only doing harm to both the countries. I wish the Government of Pakistan could see reasons and refrained from such malicious propaganda.

It is worthwhile to see how Congress had analysed the Hindu refugee question. The party made a very detailed analysis of the Hindu refugee issue in its meeting of the General Secretaries of the Congress (I) to the seventh General Conference of the North-eastern Co-ordination Committee, Guwahati, on 3 July 1992.[55] The report said the movement

---

[54] Statement made by the CM on 27 July 1965, see 'White Paper on Foreigners' by Government of Assam, 2012. 56, Annexure 4.

[55] Kumar, *Illegal Migration from Bangladesh*, 233, Annexure IX.

for autonomy, resisted by the fundamentalists, resulted in the liberation of East Pakistan and the Republic of Bangladesh came into existence. The report said that India's moral and material support to the cause of the revolution was based on the assumption that, in the new political establishment, the remaining minority population would be able to live in dignity and peace. Anticipation was that a secular atmosphere on both sides of the border would ensure sustained economic cooperation, as well as prosperity and growth and, accordingly, prevent migration of people from eastern Bengal to India's eastern region which, between 1947 and 1971, had to absorb, at a terrible cost, history's largest exodus. The religious minorities, who accounted for 29.7 per cent of the population in the area comprising East Pakistan in 1947, were reduced to 14 per cent of the total population in 1974, the influx period being 1947–1971. In the post-liberation phase, Bangladesh became a secular democratic republic. All communal and religion-based parties like Jamaat-e-Islami, Nisan-e-Islam, Pakistan Democratic Party and the Muslim League were banned.

After the assassination of Sheikh Mujib in August 1975, Khondkar Mustaz Ahmed and others tried to lift the ban but without success, and at the social level, however, these parties were busy propagating their cause. Mosques were the focal points in this exercise. The report said,

> It was at this time that the fundamentalists scored their first victory. The unifying Slogan of 'Joy Bangla' of Bengali nationalism was replaced by the slogan, 'Bangladesh Zindabad.' Similarly, the name 'Bangladesh Betar' was replaced by 'Radio Bangladesh.' These were very subtle and sophisticated moves, reminiscent of East-Pakistan days, away from 'Bengali Nationalism' to 'Bangladeshi Nationalism'.

The first action of General Ziaur Rahman as the President on 21 April 1976 was to erase secularism from the Directive Principles of the Constitution. Accordingly, ordinances and rules were passed to provide permission to the fundamentalist parties to function openly and legally. By 1986, almost all fundamentalist political parties gained ground in Bangladesh. In the 1986 elections, the Jamaat got 10 seats while it had won only 6 seats in 1979 under the protective banner of Islamic Democratic League. Between 1979 and 1988, the persistent efforts of the fundamentalists to wean away people from secularism, socialism and democracy in favour of the Islamic ethos continued unabated.

To indoctrinate the youths in the cause of Islam, the Madrasah Education System was reformulated with much sophistication. Today, it is a parallel system, recording a faster rate of growth than that of the secular education system. Science and other modern subjects have been introduced into the Madrasah syllabi so that the Madrasah students can go to technical lines and occupy decision-making positions in society with an Islamic bent of mind. This is a unique phenomenon witnessed in Bangladesh today since the establishment of the Calcutta Madrasah in 1971. In 1972–1973, there were 7,792 secondary schools as against 1,351 Madrasahs. In 1989–1990, there were 9,822 secondary schools and 5,766 Madrasahs. It is clear that the rates of increase in the number of teaching staff and the number of Madrasahs were far higher than those of secondary schools. In June 1988, Islam was declared the state religion of Bangladesh. The fundamentalists, thus, acquired enough legitimacy and ground to continue with their other plans. The report lamented by saying:

> We are thus back to square one. Against this backdrop, it is easily understandable why migration of minorities (i.e., Hindus and 'Buddhists') continues unabated. With the steep fall in the numerical strength of the religious minorities, there is, however, a qualitative change in the causes of migration. Riots and killings have yielded place to other means of oppression. Minorities today find that they are seldom able to protect their faith, property and women. Reports of forced marriages and conversions have been pouring in. With the Muslim population growing at a faster rate, there is a rising pressure on land and minority properties are the obvious targets Even temple lands are not being spared. Certain iniquitous laws in force like the Vested Properties Act and the Enemy Property Act are handy weapons to deprive the minorities of their properties Added to the atmosphere of general insecurity; there is the economic insecurity due to continuous shrinkage of job and other economic opportunities.[56]

The report provided a vivid account of how Hindu temples, houses and institutions were destroyed and desecrated after widespread communal disturbances over Ram Janma Bhoomi–Babri Masjid controversy

[56] Kumar, *Illegal Migration from Bangladesh*, 245–46.

in India. Large-scale destruction and damage were inflicted from 30 October 1990 until 2 November 1990 by the ruling party in Bangladesh.[57] The report referred to another phase of harassment of the Hindus after the 1991 Parliamentary elections by the ruling BNP and its ally, Jamaat-e-Islami, for allegedly voting for the Awami League. This had further heightened the insecurity of the minority community and contributed to their influx to India. Thus, there is a general consensus across political parties regarding giving protection to the persecuted people in Bangladesh.

Professor Anupama Roy's Views

In her criticism, Professor Anupama Roy made an argument that it is not clear why the government 'should be selective in its identification of those who can be considered persecuted on religious grounds'. I think the above interpretation of the minority people in Bangladesh would make it clear why they need protection in the form of some laws. In addition, Professor Roy argues

> It is also not clear why a change in law must be carried out to insert a principle in the Citizenship Act which goes against the Constitution, when administrative measures at the local level can be strengthened to address such concerns in consonance with the 2015 executive order. The manner in which 'displaced persons' were absorbed into the fold of citizenship in the 1950s in the absence of statutory provisions on citizenship, is an example of how it can be done.

If this argument is accepted, it would lead to a huge human rights violation and the denial of justice to a group of people who have been facing all kinds of discrimination and exploitation in the name of unresolved refugee citizenship. It hardly needs any reiteration that the 'displaced people' of the 1950s were regularized through the 'registration clause' in 1955 citizenship laws. It is grossly inadequate to say that these people could be accommodated through executive orders like the one in 2015. The rules that were amended on 7 September 2015 under the Passport Order, 1950, and the Foreigner Order, 1948, stated:

[57] Ibid., 246.

In the Passport (Entry into India) Rules, 1950, in rule 4, in sub-rule (I), after clause (h), the following clause shall be inserted, namely:- (h) persons belonging to minority communities in Bangladesh and Pakistan, namely, Hindus, Sikhs, Buddhists, Jains, Parsis and Christians who were compelled to seek shelter in India due to religious persecution or fear of religious persecution and entered into India on or before the 31st December, 2014 - (i) without valid documents including passport or other travel documents; or (ii) with valid documents including passport or other travel document and the validity of any of such documents has expired: Provided that provision of this clause shall take effect from the date of publication of this notification in the Official Gazette.

However, as it could be observed later on, the executive order of 2015 could not address the problems of refugees. According to the 2015 order, removing 'the illegal migrant' tag was of remote possibility. What is the methodology to get a waiver from being declared as 'illegal migrant'? Ministry of Home Affairs (MHA) says '[P]ersons covered by the notification dated 7/9/2015 will be required to submit an online application form of LTV (long term visa)'. New SOPs in this regard were issued to all the state governments on 8 January 2016.[58] The main ter.ets were as follows:

1. Applications are to be submitted online and Long-term visa (LTV) will be granted after detailed enquiry by the Foreigners Regional Registration officer, security agencies, IB, SB, etc. and recommendation by respective governments.
2. However, in case applicants have incomplete or no supporting documents, their cases will be referred to Foreigners Tribunal.[59]

Thus, the grant of LTV would have been dependent on field verification by Foreigners Registration Regulation officer (FRRO), opinion of the Foreigners Tribunal and security vetting by IB, SB, etc. Thus, the procedure for removing the tag of 'illegal migrant' was not at all easy; rather, it would have created another group of 'stateless people',

---

[58] For details, see JPC Report on CAB-2016, 109–111.

[59] The cases of those persons who have no documents such as Pakistan or Bangladesh passport or any proof that they are minority/bank account, proof of religious persecution will be referred to the Foreigners Tribunal.

as their case would be referred to the Tribunal for decision. In her disposition, the Congress leader and then MP and president of All India Mahila Congress, Sushmita Dev, said in front of the committee,

> Now comes the fatal blow—where documents are found incomplete these will be referred to Foreigners Tribunal for its opinion. And needless to say that anyone who cannot satisfy the Tribunal will be declared a foreigner and in all likelihood 'Stateless'... Therefore to my mind nothing has changed for persons who have no documents. He will be back in the Foreigner's Tribunal; the only difference is that this time he has to prove to be a Bangladeshi national ...[60]

Thus, Sushmita Dev did not oppose the bill per se but wanted more protection for the refugees so that they do not have to perpetuate their status as belonging nowhere. She asserted,

> In other words, the bill of the government appears to give amnesty but will land people in Foreigners Tribunal and eventually in jails unless and until the grant of citizenship is guaranteed and is deemed without leaving any discretion with the government to reject such application or deny citizenship. It must be done with the requirements of showing any documents from the government of any other country.[61]

Thus, the 2015 executive order and subsequent SOPs which Professor Roy would like us to consider for dealing with the refugees are highly inadequate to address the concerns of the refugees. Here, we would also like to refer to the Seventieth Report, Estimates Committee (1988–1989), (eighth Lok Sabha); Ministry of Home Affairs (Rehabilitation Division), entitled 'Rehabilitation of Migrants from East Bengal', presented to the Lok Sabha on 12 April 1989.

Unwritten Woes of East Bengal Refugees

The Estimates Committee of the Lok Sabha reprimanded the government for spending a huge amount of money and not even cared once 'to resort to legislation to incur such huge expenditures and carried on

---

[60] For details, see JPC Report on CAB-2016, 106–107.

[61] Ibid., 106.

the activities merely by the issue of executive instructions from time to time'. The committee was not convinced by the government's contention that 'no legislation in this regard was considered necessary as no compensation was to be paid to migrants from East Bengal'. Not only in the financial domain but in other settlement areas also, the committee criticized the government for resorting to 'ad hocism' and not bringing adequate legislative measures into practice. The committee opined that those 'displaced people' who could not register themselves as citizens by registration before 25 March 1971 consequently had to 'live in India as 'stateless people' many of whom have failed to acquire the citizenship for one region or another', and they had been 'denied either employment or thrown out of jobs on the ground of citizenship'. The status of those migrants appeared to the committee to be 'in stark contrast with the displaced persons from West Pakistan' who were then absorbed as citizens.[62]

The committee thus viewed that the resettlement/rehabilitation and migration from former East Pakistan could not be deemed full and complete until and unless the Ministry of Home Affairs (Rehabilitation Division) categorically satisfied the committee and others that all the old and new migrant families claimed to had been settled/rehabilitated in various parts of the country and allotted homestead plots. The government must ensure those migrant families who had been settled in agriculture had actually been allotted agricultural land according to the scales prescribed from time to time, and full ownership rights had been conferred to the migrants from agricultural lands to homestead plots allotted to them.[63]

The committee was disappointed to note that within less than 2 years of the opening of the camps in Tripura for about 49,000 refugees which started migrating in April 1986, as many as 3,083 migrants had been reported missing from the five camps in the state by the end of

---

[62] Estimates Committee (1988–1989), (eighth Lok Sabha); Ministry of Home Affairs (Rehabilitation Division), entitled 'Rehabilitation of Migrants from East Bengal', presented to Lok Sabha on 12 April 1989; Introduction, point 5.

[63] Ibid., point 7.

1987.[64] That could have happened due to several reasons, including getting assimilated with the Bengali-speaking people of the state. Apart from missing persons, the number of deaths were also quite high. The Ministry had stated that as on 25 July 1988, 2,984 refugees, including children, died since their migration in various camps due to diseases/ epidemics and unnatural causes like starvation. According to the state government, the deaths, as ascertained by a team of medical experts, were due to various diseases such as diarrhoea, respiratory tract infection, bronchopneumonia and worm infection. 'Further, habits of the tribal refugees such as using local water resources from rivulets instead of using tubewells provided in the camps and non-utilisation of dug-well latrines by the children have contributed to unenvironmental pollution and contaminated sanitation'.[65]

The committee report is a telling document regarding the pathetic plight of refugees residing in various parts of India. Citing All India Organisation of Migrants, the Parliamentary Estimate Committee indicated how the refugee families were treated.[66] Besides, the committee cited many 'still uncertain' settlements in Garo Hills, Cachar, Nowgong, Goalpara in Assam and Meghalaya: 'Land problem of migrants still persisting' in Khoidum Lamjoa and Lahupat areas of Manipur, position of migrants 'still not satisfactory' in the Ralma Serma Valley Scheme of Rehabilitation (Tripura), migrant 'colonisers still not settled' in Kagaz Nagar near Hyderabad (Telangana), position of migrants 'still unsatisfactory' in the Rehabilitation Centres at Adilabad-Isagaon area (former Andhra Pradesh) and 'sub-human conditions

---

[64] Ibid., point 13.

[65] Point 5.4, Chapter 5 of Estimates Committee (1988–89) (eighth Lok Sabha); Ministry of Home Affairs (Rehabilitation Division).

[66] (a) 365 families being deprived of land allotment in Dakaachat colony and Netaji Subhash Nagar colony at Nauresha in Pilibhit Distt. (UP), (b) 630 families under threat of cancellation of land allotment in Vijaya Nagar Gram Sabha in Dineshpur in Nainital Distt. (UP), (c) land not transferred by Forest Department to 416 families in Chandiya Hazra Bengali Colony in Pilibhit Distt. (UP), (d) 'Still unsettled' and unemployed migrants families in Rehabilitation Centres at Rampur, Bareilly, Bijnor, Kbera, Kanpur (Dehat) and Hrdoi (UP) and (e) 2,500 migrants in the outskirts of Jamshedpur (Bihar) 'staying there as trespassers and stateless people over a period of 23 years'.

with no prospect of their rehabilitation' of about 0.1 million migrants staying in Jhugi-Jhopri areas in different parts of Delhi.[67]

Whether to Grant Citizenship to the Refugees of Post-1971 Period

The committee also dealt with the issue of whether it was the right time to reconsider the earlier decision not to grant citizenship to the persons who had migrated to India from East Bengal after 25 March 1971. The Home Secretary replied:

> After 1971 the situation changes in the sense that a new country comes into being. Now this is a new situation. There is no reason for accepting this kind of migrants as such. The law provides how citizenship can be acquired. All that happened in 1987 was that the law had been made more stringent in so far as residential qualification is concerned. There were specific directions that people; who came after March, 1971 cannot be treated as ordinary residents of the area (in India). They are expected to co-turn to their native places as the situation improves. If such refugees make applications, the applications should be rejected. And the presumption is that those who came after 1971, we are not accepting them as migrants.[68]

The opinion of the Home Secretary was clear; however, he, too, insisted that they were expected to co-turn to their native places as the situation improves—whether the situation improved, would they find their properties back in Bangladesh were some difficult questions to answer.

The committee, however, had a different suggestion to make to the government:

> The Committee note that while most of the families who migrated to India from former East Pakistan between March-December, 1971 have been repatriated to Bangladesh, some of these migrants could not be repatriated due to one reason or the other and stayed on in India. The Committee suggest that the Government should examine the feasibility of liberalising the legal

---

[67] Point 4.6, Chapter 1 of Estimates Committee (1988–89), (eighth Lok Sabha); Ministry of Home Affairs (Rehabilitation Division).

[68] Ibid., point 1.21.

requirements for these families to acquire citizenship of India taking into consideration the individual compulsion due to which they could not be repatriated to Bangladesh in 1971–72.

It may be mentioned that in its 107th report on the 'Citizenship Amendment Bill-2003', presented to the Rajya Sabha on 12 December 2003, the committee members expressed the view that the commitment made by the national leaders at the time of partition was to facilitate the entry of Hindus from Pakistan to India to save them from religious persecution as Pakistan had proclaimed herself to be a theocratic Islamic nation. This commitment, they felt, depended on circumstances; however, it was not an unending or open-ended one. Given the growing population, poverty and unemployment, it would be difficult to sustain such a process forever. At the same time, the committee appealed to the government not to forget those commitments made during the time of Partition, and that the committee distinctively made a distinction between such refugees and those coming out of economic reasons.

> At the same time those Members were of the view that the Government should not completely forget the commitment of our national leaders at the time of partition and it should keep into account the plight of those displaced persons who were uprooted from their homes due to failure of their sovereign governments to protect them in the wake of certain developments.
>
> Insofar as the migration of people from neighbouring countries to India due to economic reasons, Members were of the view that such migrants should be sternly dealt with as per the law of the land.[69]

The committee stuck to the existing law and suggested that the post-1971 foreigners would be sent back to their homelands. At the same time, the committee also hastened to add that so far as consideration of refugees was concerned 'in that context it was clarified that each case or a group of cases would be considered on merit'.[70] It may be

---

[69] 107th Report on the 'Citizenship Amendment Bill-2003', presented to Rajya Sabha on 12 December 2003; Points 6 and 6.1.

[70] Ibid., point 6.1 of the report.

mentioned that the Government of India's executive order allows citizenship to Bangladeshi refugees in India in certain other conditions. In this regard, we may refer to a Government of India letter to the Chief Secretaries of the state, titled as 'Grant of Indian Citizenship to Bangladeshi Men Who Have Married to Indian Women under Section 5(1)(c) of the Citizenship Act, 1955'. The letter, along with other clauses, made it clear that requests from the minority communities of Bangladeshi Hindus and Sikhs may be considered sympathetically after thorough checks from a security angle.[71]

APPENDIX

Supplementary historical data about how Leftist political parties and other organizations prevented the due process of law in the exodus of illegal immigrants and refugees.

Report Submitted by Various Security Forces

Secret information received indicates that on 3 January 1979, a public meeting was held by the CPM, Silchar branch with Sri Dwijendra Sengupta in the chair. The speakers criticized the police and the government for allegedly harassing Indian citizens in the name of Bangladesh nationals. It was further learnt that CPM leaders, namely Nitish Das, Dipak Bhattacharjee, Biresh Misra and Nurul Huda (all CPM MLA) had been holding secret meetings in areas predominantly inhabited by Hindus and advised them not to help the Police in the detection of Hindu Bangladesh nationals. They had been asked to plant some genuine Indian nationals and pose themselves as Bangladesh nationals before police so that they would not be pushed back. Then they would go scope to make an issue out of it and blame the police and the government for harassing the Indian nationals, and thereby, they would succeed in thwarting police action in the detection of the Bangladesh nationals. It was further learnt that the above CPM leaders had been doing this obviously intending to increase the number of

---

[71] No. 26011/3/89-I.C.I, Government of India, New Delhi, 8 November 1989.

voters/supporters of their party so that in the coming elections, they can annex more seats in the Assembly.

Source: Memo No. DIG (B) C.57/78/, dated 24 July 1978.

PART II. Any Activity of Any Individual/ Group of Individual/Organization in Support of Infiltration in Assam

1. Information received indicates that on 12 February 1979, at 16.00 hours, a public meeting was held at the Golokganj Pragati Sangha premises with Sri Lok Nath Rai in the Chair. Shri Upen Bhattacharjee, a teacher, Sishu Pathsala, Dhubri, Dilip Chakravarty, Editor of Gana Sabak Dhubri, Paresh Baruah, Secy. R. S. P., Fazal Hoque of Dhubri and Radhaballav Saha Roy of Golokganj criticized the police and the Assam government for deporting Bangladesh nationals from Assam in their speeches. The speakers urged the public not to show any document/citizenship certificates, etc. to police stating that the police have no authority to check such documents. They instigated the public to *gherao* and assault the police officers who would go for enquiry and detection of Bangladesh nationals. They ever went to the extent of urging people to check the citizenship certificates of police officials engaged in detection work. After the meeting was over at 18.00 hours, Upen Bhattacharjee, Paresh Baruah, Dilip Chakravarty, Fazal Hoque, and Loknath Ray were forwarded in custody vide South Salmara PS case No. 12 (12) 79 U/S 380 IPC and a Non FIR case U/S 6 (a) IPP Act.

2. Information received indicates that on evening of 7 January 1979, a group of leading Bengali people of Bongaigaon town was held in the house of Sri Purna Ghose, Bhanu Choudhury, Rakhal Dasgupta, Asis Biswas, Sudhir Ghose and Thakur Das of Bongaigaon. The meeting condemned the action of the border task force for detecting and pushing back Bangladesh refugees from Bongaigaon. They criticized the police and the government for alleged harassment of Bengali Hindus in Bongaigaon town. The meeting deliberately decided to collect subscription from among the Bengali people or Bongaigaon town and its suburb to

give protection to Bangladesh nationals who are residing in the area by filling cases against their deportation to Bangladesh and to raise the issue before the Central and State governments to stop such illegal deportation. They had already collected a sum of ₹6,000 and decided to safeguard the Hindu Bengali infiltrants by acquiring Indian Citizenship Certificate from West Bengal and Assam.

Source: Memo No. DIG (B)C/57/79/, Guwahati, dated 5 March 1979.

3. Reports emanating from various sources during the week under review indicate that 20 Hindu families and 2 Muslim families consisting of 115 members of Bangladesh nationals who were pushed back to Bangladesh on 21–22 January 1979 through Golokganj PPCP again re-infiltrated India on 23 January 1979 morning through Balabhut border of Coochbehar district (West Bengal) and came to Tufanganj on foot in several groups. On seeing them, some local leaders including CPM MLA took those Bangladesh nationals to a godown near a bridge of Tufanganj for temporary settlement. Local CPM MLA, SDO Tufanganj and Deputy Commissioner, Coochbehar met them on 24 January 1979 when those Bangladesh nationals allegedly reported that Assam police forcibly pushed them back to Bangladesh. Reportedly, Deputy Commissioner, Coochbehar, SDO Tufanganj, CPM MLA instructed them to go to their respective residence assuring that the matter would be discussed with the Government of Assam to stop such deportation.

4. This refers to Golokganj PS Case No. 30 (1) 79 U/S 397 IPC and investigation is continuing. Secret information received indicates that Secretary Tamid Ul-Ulema-E-Hind, Nowgong visited Hojai on 20 January 1979 and held a meeting in the house of Anjur Ali of Hojai Town and discussed about the detection and deportation of Bangladesh nationals, especially Muslims. He advised the members that if any Muslim Bangladesh national is detected by police, he should be proved by any means as Indian national.

5. It is learnt that CPM took a procession (150/200) at Juria of Nowgong district on 27 January 1979 against alleged atrocities on Indian Citizens by certain police officials and converged at a

meeting at Juria bazaar where revolutions demanding a probe into the alleged atrocities and even dismissal of the police officials concerned were adopted. Further details are awaited.

6. This refers to Gauhati PS Case No. 19 (2) 79 U/S 14 F. Act. Again a batch of 14 (fourteen) Muslims of Burmese origin were detected on 21 January 1979 at Gauhati Railway Station by Inspector (B), Gauhati Railway Zone and they have since been sent to Golokganj PCP for their push back to Bangladesh. On interrogation, they stated that they hailed from Chittagong, Sylhet district and crossed over the border of Chandinagar under Katigora PS in Cachar district Strict vigilance was being maintained to check re-infiltration.

7. It is learnt that a public meeting was held at Barpeta Road near Municipal office with Sri Gyanendra Nath as president and most of the Bengali-speaking CPM supporters attended the meeting where six resolutions were reported to have been taken in the light of alleged detection and deportation of Bangladesh nationals. CPM/MLA Sri Hemendra Das of Sorbhog constituency was also present in the meeting. He criticized the government for alleged harassment by police on Indian nationals in the name of deportation and demanded to punish the guilty officers. MLA Hemendra Das was involved in several cases of mobilization of Bengali Hindus and Muslims against the Government. Apparently, it was voting interest that prompted MLA to take side with the refugees and infiltrators.

   Source: Memo no. DIG(B)C/S7/79, dated 3 March 1979.

8. Information has been received to the effect that Sri Romesh Ch. Sohoria, MLA (Independent) has been interfering with the police in Kalaigaon and Tongla area in the matter of detection and deportation of Bangladesh nationals. He has issued many certificates to B/D nationals certifying them to be Indian citizens. His activities there have greatly hampered the work of detection and expulsion of Bangladesh nationals.

   Source: KB: 9/2/79, MEMO NO. DIG (B)C. 57/78/, dated 8 January 1978.

9. Reports emanating from various sources during the week under review indicate that on 22 February 1979, under the leadership of Sunil Dhar and Pradyut Bose, CPM leaders took out a procession

from the office of the CPM, Lumding and paraded the main streets of Lumding shouting slogans criticizing the action of the police in deporting Bangladesh nationals from Assam. Later they submitted a memorandum to O/C, Lumding PS in this respect. Further, the CPM members and supporters ransacked the police station and rebuked the police personnel.

10. It has been learnt that Sri Sontosh Kr. Gulia, Secretary of Krishak Sobha CPI (M) visited different places mainly Bengali-inhabited areas under Kokrajhar Sub-Division on 1 February 1979. During his visit, he expressed before some people that Bangladesh nationals have been driven from Assam and some Bengalies (Indian nationals) are being driven out in the name of Bangladesh nationals. He urged the people of Kokrajhar area to resist such drive.

11. Another piece of information has been received to the effect that on 18 February 1979, a meeting was held at Sastrapara LP School under PS jointly organized by CPM and CPML leaders. The meeting adopted a resolution in respect of detection and deportation of Bangladesh nationals, mainly the Bengali Hindus of Paneri PS. The meeting urged them to offer resistance to police instead of assisting them in the matters of foreign nationals. The names of the leaders are:
   1. Subhas Sarkar of Satrapara (CPM)
   2. Khitish Sarkar (CPM) of Ruphat, Tangla
   3. Akhil Mitra (CPM) of Bar Tangla
   4. Nagen Rai (CPML) of -do-

Source: Memo No. DIG(B)C/57/79/, Guwahati, dated 15 March 1979.

Bibliography

All Assam Journalists' Association. *Assam: The Crisis of Identity*. Guwahati: Labanya Press, 1980.

Barkakati, Nalini Kanta. 'Foreigners vis-à-vis Assam'. *The Foreigners Problem*. Assam: Gana Sangram Parishad, 1982.

Chhabra, K. M. L. *Assam Challenge*. Delhi: Konark Publishers, 1992.

Government of Assam. *Statistical Survey of Displaced Persons from East Pakistan in Assam 1955–56*. Shillong: Department of Economics and Statistics, 1958.

Hussain, Monirul. 'Refugees in the Face of Emerging Ethnicity in North-East India: An Overview'. *Studies in Humanities and Social Sciences* II, no. 1 (1995): 123–29.

————. 'State, Identity Movements and Internal Displacement in the North-East'. *Economic & Political Weekly* 35, no. 51 (16–22 December 2000): 4519–23.

Kumar, B. B. (ed.). *Illegal Migration from Bangladesh*. New Delhi: Concept Publishing Company, 2006.

Mandal, Jogendra Nath. *Resignation Letter to Liaquat Ali Khan*, 9 October 1950. New Delhi: Dr Syama Prasad Mookerjee Research Foundation, 2019.

Murty, T. S. *Assam, the Difficult Years: A Study of Political Developments in 1979–83*. New Delhi: Himalayan Books, 1983.

Roy, Tathagata. *A Suppressed Chapter in History: The Exodus of Hindus from East Pakistan and Bangladesh*. New Delhi: Bookwell Publications, 2007.

Roy, Anupama. *Mapping Citizenship in India*. New Delhi: OUP, 2010.

————. *Citizenship in India* (Oxford India Short Introductions). New Delhi: OUP, 2016.

————. 'The Citizenship (Amendment) Bill, 2016 and the Aporia of Citizenship'. In *Economic & Political Weekly* 54, no. 49 (14 December 2019): 28–34.

United Nation High Commissioner for Refugees. *Protecting Refugees: Questions & Answers*. Geneva: UNHCR, 2002.

Hindu–Muslim Question

With multiple ethnic and linguistic groups, Assam was never a mono-lingual state, although Assamese was the dominant language in the region primarily as a means of communication. Traditionally, Assam, for all practical purposes, was understood to be Brahmaputra valley or Assam valley, which was described by historians as Assam Proper. Assam's journey with heterogeneous linguistic and religious compositions began in 1874 when Assam Proper was annexed with other hills and plains areas of the Surma Valley.

A new province of Assam emerged with four mutually incompatible elements: first, the hill districts with diverse languages; second, the five Assamese-speaking districts of the Brahmaputra valley which has traditionally been known as an Assam Proper; third, Goalpara of Brahmaputra valley with a mixture of Assamese and Bengali culture; and fourth, Sylhet and Cachar—the two Bengali-speaking districts of the Surma valley.

Such amalgamation of diverse elements had created fissures and contradictions in Assam's politics, particularly since the Assamese ruling middle class felt highly threatened from the politics of the heavily populous Surma valley. However, as Sanjib Baruah argues, not all Bengali Hindus can be viewed as immigrants:

> Of course not all Bengali Hindus in these positions can be seen as immigrants into the Assam colonial rulers had created. Given the way the British defined the territory of Assam, Bengalis from Sylhet were local residents and were simply moving from one part of the province to another.[1]

---

[1] Baruah, *India Against Itself*, 59.

Besides, from 1905 to 1912, when the provinces of Assam and Eastern Bengal were combined into a single province with Dacca as the capital of Assam, intra-provincial migration had become broader in scope.[2]

The Assamese elites viewed the threat from Bengali Hindus and Bengali Muslims through two different lenses. The threat from the Bengali Muslims was linguistic (which later on receded during and after Independence), political, religious and cultural, whereas from the Bengali Hindus, the threat was essentially linguistic and administrative. On many occasions, the Bengali Hindus sided with the Assamese leadership to thwart the jingoistic, communal ambition of the Muslim League.[3]

East Bengal-origin Muslims in Post-Independence Period

A question arises about how EBOM[4] are involved the Assamese nationality formation process. How has the Muslim politics been sprouting in the post-Independence period? How is it different from colonial politics? How has Muslim politics in Assam transformed to the tune of

---

[2] Ibid.

[3] In all important issues that confronted Assamese identity like Sylhet transfer, voting on Line System, land settlement, Grouping and Pakistan issue, the Bengali Hindus' stand always favoured the Assamese cause. In a lead reporting, the vanguard of Assamese nationalism, *Asamiya*, said in a highlighted box that 'previously Assamese used to call the invaders as "Bongals". However, "Bongal" and "Bengali" are two different words. The Assamese have no animosity towards the Bengalis of Assam or elsewhere. But whoever voices against Assam, whether they were from inside or outside—all of them are "Bongals". ... Sylhet's Basanta Kr Das, Voidyanath Mukherjee etc have been advocating for Assam's cause—they are true brothers of Assam although they speak Bengali ...' (*Dainik Asamiya* (22nd *Jeth*), 14 June 1946). Nonetheless, certain sections were there for aggressive Bengali nationalism in Assam as was highlighted by Nirode Baruah and Ambikagiri Raichaudhury. However, the Bengali Hindu's support on all critical issues could hardly be ignored.

[4] They are also known with various monikers such as 'Na-Asomiya', 'Abhibhasi Musalman', or the 'Chorua' or 'Pomua', 'Mymensinghia', 'Miya Musalmaan', 'Bhatia', etc. Udayon Misra uses terms like 'immigrant neo-Assamese', 'immigrant Muslims', 'Bengali-immigrant Muslims', 'neo-Assamese Muslims', 'immigrants', 'Bengali-speaking Muslims' etc.; see Misra, *India's North-East*, 197–200. The term 'Miya Musalman' is also used by Sanjib Baruah, See Aggrawala, 'Call Me by My Name'.

broader Assamese identity? How far could the Muslim identity merge with the Assamese identity? Has such assimilation or integration process been causing any contradiction? Do the Muslims in Assam have a global Islamic network? What are the challenges of EBOM politics in Assam today? How can the gap between Assamese nationality and EBOM politics be bridged?

The Muslim population in Assam is not a homogeneous group; it has its variations. Muslims in Assam may be divided into four broad caste-like groups as far as the social divisions are concerned. They are Syed, Goriya, Sheikh and Moriya. The caste-like groups are as follows: Uzani, Bhatiya, Charua, Dathiya and Baramasi or Sandar.

Immediately after India's independence, the Muslim League lost its edge and gave way to the Congress party for their part to lead the Indian Muslims in the nation. Up until Partition, the Muslim identity was largely based on their Islamic identity that ruled India till the coming of the British. However, in the post-Independence period in India, the Muslim community gradually identified themselves as a religious 'minority' with constitutional rights and privileges. In the pre-Partition days, the Muslims spoke more as Muslims than as a minority community. However, in the post-Independence period, constitutional safeguards and other socio-legal and religious facilities to the Muslims in India made them one of the most well-protected minority communities in the world, while Hindus, Sikhs and other minorities in Pakistan could barely access any such facilities. Rather, they faced mayhem of all kinds and discriminations from the very beginning thereby forcing them to flee to India in the subsequent period.

Immediately after Independence, Congress and other non-Congress parties such as CPI, CPM, RCPI, SUCI, and PSP represented the Muslim-dominated constituencies of Assam, although the Congress remained the most preferred party from 1951 to 1985. Until about 1975–1976, the Muslims in Assam did not have many differences with the Congress. However, in a meeting at Gauhati held in February 1975 under the leadership of the then Parliamentary Affairs Minister, Syed Ahmed Ali, and Moinul Haque Choudhury, some burning issues of the Muslims were raised. They talked about the 'problem faced by 40 lakh Muslim population of Assam' and complained of 'obstacles' to Muslim participation 'in all spheres and branches' of life. They demanded better representation in employment, representation in public bodies, nationalized banks, cooperatives, public undertakings, universities and Islamic education. On 8 May 1977, a section of educated Muslims gathered at Haji Musafir Khana, Islampur and formed the Eastern India Muslim Association (EIMA). The meeting was presided over by Mr Amjad Ali, advocate; ex-Vice President, Assam Provincial Muslim League; and ex-MP and attended by delegates from all over Assam. In the 1978 election, a front to be known as Progressive Democratic Front (PDF) was constituted, comprising EIMA, Kamata Rajya Parishad, Janata Congress, Yuva Linguistic Minority Committee and the Citizens Democratic Front. The Front's Legislature Party was led by Premadhar Bora of the Janata Congress with Sirajul Haque of EIMA as the Chief Whip. In a House of 126 members, there were 28 Muslims and 98 non-Muslims. EIMA was formally dissolved and merged in the Indian Union Muslim League in October 1977 to re-emerge as the Eastern Zonal Muslim League.[5] Another effort for mobilizing the Muslims of Barak was made by Abdul Muhim Majumder in 1992 when he formed a new political group known as Muslim Forum. Because of his clash of interest with Congress, Majumder—the architect of IMDT Act and a shrewd politician—constituted another Muslim party called United People's Party of Assam (UPPA) and became a constituent partner of the second term of Prafulla Kumar Mahanta's AGP government. It may be mentioned that UPPA was a party that was essentially constituted to mobilize the Muslims of the state; the executive president of UPPA was Capt. Robin Bordoloi—the eldest son of Gopinath Bordoloi. Other important office bearers of the party were Gulam Akbar, Abdul Ajij, Mun Chaudhury, Ishak Dewan and others. Most of the members later joined the Congress.

The United Minority Front (UMF) and All Indian United Democratic Front Phase of Muslim Politics

The Assam Agitation led by AASU from 1979 to 1985 against the 'outsiders', which later turned into 'foreigners', especially illegal

---

[5] Kar, *Muslims in Assam Politics*, 363–64.

migrants from Bangladesh, is considered as one of the largest mass-based movements in the post-Independence period of India. Although the agitation was against illegal migrants from Bangladesh, during the agitation, a bulk number of genuine citizens belonging to the Bengali Muslim and Bengali Hindu communities living in Assam were affected. In some cases, citizenship rights were questioned; they were harassed by the activists of the organizations who led the movement. Besides, the leaders of the movements pressurized the government to serve hearing notices to a large number of citizens to prove their Indian citizenship which also affected a high number of genuine citizens of India belonging to the said communities. Nevertheless, as a result of the Assam Movement, various heinous incidents like the Nellie Massacre of 1983 took place.[6] Finally, at the end of a long agitation, on 15 August 1985, an accord, known as the Assam Accord, was signed to protect the socio-economic, cultural and political rights and interests of the indigenous Assamese people of Assam. The main signatories of the accord were the representatives of AASU, AAGSP, Government of India and Government of Assam.

The leaders of AASU formed AGP, while a section of influential leaders belonging to the minority communities (both Bengali Hindu and Muslim) formed UMF by challenging the signing of the Assam Accord. They alleged that the clauses in the accord were discriminatory because the victims of the Assam Movement were the Bengali Hindus and Muslims, and no representative from those communities was invited to take part in the signing of the accord.

As an immediate reaction of the signing of the accord, the minorities residing in Assam for generations expressed the fear that it would lead to discord instead of bringing permanent peace to Assam. They feared that the accord would result in massive eviction under the provisions of the agreement. To prevent such a circumstance, several existing minority-based organizations came together under an umbrella with an action plan to seek an alternative to Congress. Organizations

[6] For details, see Kimura, *The Nellie Massacre of 1983*; also see 'A Field Report on Nellie: Interview with Makiko Kimura' in *Nibedon-Swajan Cinta* (in Assamese); Kakoti, *Assam Agitation and Assam's Muslim Politics*, 163–68.

like Jamiat Ulema-E-Hind, Citizen's Rights Preservation Committee (CRPC), and All Assam Minority Forum began to execute their plan of action in different phases. First, with the initiative of Abul Fazal Golam Osmani, a well-known barrister, a coordination committee of the minority organizations was formed, with Emran Shah as the convener. Second, the coordination committee explained and showed their standpoint in their published pamphlet entitled 'The Memorandum of Settlement and The Minorities' in September 1995.

The second phase of the minority politics can be traced to 2005 when the IM(DT) Act of 1983 was nullified by the Supreme Court of India in 2005. The annulment of the law again led to the growth of fear psychosis among the Muslims in Assam, who believed that it would lead to undue harassment and humiliation of Muslims in the name of detection and deportation of Bangladeshi in Assam. The Muslim community also felt that the government had failed to address the cause of the Muslims and failed to protect their interests. It was in this backdrop that another minority-based political party named AIUDF emerged[7] in 2005 under the leadership of a businessman and an influential religious leader, Maulana Badruddin Ajmal.

Jamiat in Politics of Assam

Jamiat Ulema-E-Hind, one of the leading Islamic organizations in India, was established in 1919. The people involved in its formation were Abdul Mohasin Sajjad, Qazi Hussain Ahmed, Ahmed Sayeed Dehlvi and Abdul Bari Firangi Mehli who were also scholars of Islamic ideals. Jamiat shows its loyalty to the Constitution, and it argues for a mutual contract between Muslim and non-Muslims to establish India as a secular state.

Since its inception, Jamiat had vehemently opposed the idea of partition of Hindustan and Pakistan. Members of Jamiat also participated in the Non-Cooperation Movement during the Indian freedom struggle. Though Jamiat was established in the pre-Independence period,

---

[7] Interview with Hafiz Rashid Ahmed Choudhury, Sr. Advocate Gauhati High Court and a prominent former UMF leader, dated 2 April 2015.

it still exists in its full vigour as a religious organization. Fractional conflicts split the organization into two groups in 2008, one led by Maulana Arshad Madani and the other by Maulana Mehmood Madani.

Although Jamiat is a socio-religious organization, it has been observed that its activities go beyond their avowed goals and it is actively engaged in political activities. In the recent past, it has been observed that Jamiat has become very active during the time of elections. Members of this party exert strong influence at the time of elections by taking advantage of religion and religious emotions of the illiterate Muslims, and they have a strong support base in the Muslim belts and blocks.

In many cases, Jamiat's role has been ambiguous; for instance, when the government passed the IM(DT) Act in 1983, it strongly opposed the Act by alleging that the Act would sharply obstruct the minorities. As a response to the Act, minority-based political party, UMF, was created in 1985. Interestingly, Jamiat made a complete U-turn when the Supreme Court repealed the IM(DT) Act and stated that the repealing of the Act would hamper the minority in the name of foreigners. The repeal of IM(DT) Act led to the creation of AIUDF in 2005 by the state president of Assam Jamiat, Maulana Badruddin Ajmal. Apart from the stated objectives of the party, Ajmal's political aspirations, which he had been nourishing since 1985, were a major driver behind the establishment of a minority-based political outfit.

Changing Contours of Jamiat in the Politics of Assam

As mentioned earlier, Jamiat has had a strong presence in the politics of Assam. They had strongly and openly supported Congress before the creation of UMF in 1985, but it withdrew its support when UMF was created. In the 1985 election, UMF, which was funded by Maulana Badruddin Ajmal, got 17 seats. All the seats were in the minority belts of Brahmaputra valley. Although Jamiat contributed to achieving that, the enactment of the IM(DT) Act, 1983, and the signing of the Assam Accord overwhelmingly benefited UMF. Again, in the 1991 Assembly election, when the presence of UMF became insignificant and almost all the leaders returned to Congress, the members of Jamiat extended their support to Congress. But the most interesting and curious point is Jamiat's support to AGP in the Assembly election of 1996. There were three important reasons behind this: (a) there was every possibility of AGP forming the government, (b) the father-in-law of Badruddin Ajmal had a good relation with AGP (who also happened to be a candidate) and (c) the opportunistic role and the personal gain of the Jamiat leaders. These reasons can be substantiated by the fact that Jamiat supported Jayashree Mahanta of AGP in Nagaon in 1996, since the father-in-law of Maulana Badruddin Ajmal had a good relationship with AGP. The same Jamiat, however, supported the Samajwadi Party in Dhubri because the candidate was Mehmud Madani, the son of Arshad Madani (the President of Jamiat National Executive Council).

However, in the 2001 Assembly election, Jamiat supported Congress on two conditions: (a) Congress would nominate 10 minority candidates in the name of 'Jamiat Quota' and (b) Congress would nominate Maulana Badruddin Ajmal in the 2003 Rajya Sabha election. Although Congress gave the nomination 10 ten minority candidates in the Assembly election of 2001, it did not nominate Maulana Badruddin Ajmal in the 2003 Rajya Sabha election. This act was construed as a betrayal, with Jamiat alleging that Congress cheated Jamiat and failed to keep its promises, which the party gave at the time of the 2001 Assembly election. With the relationship between the two organizations nearly tarnished, the political ambitions of Maulana Badruddin Ajmal were not fulfilled in 2003. Meanwhile, in 2005, one significant development took place in Assam when the Supreme Court revoked the IM(DT) Act, on the grounds that the Act was unconstitutional and undemocratic. Hence, the repeal of the law and the Congress failing to nominate Maulana Badruddin Ajmal to Rajya Sabha provided ample arsenals to Badruddin to constitute a new minority party in Assam.[8]

---

[8] There were some other factors responsible for the growth of AIUDF. The formation of AIUDF is also associated with two important causes. First was the arrest of the important Muslim leader Mukti Khairul Islam of Arire Sariah by a police sub-inspector, and the second was the inept handling of the BTAD communal clashes by CM Tarun Gogoi. The arrest of Mukti Khairul Islam was the turning point of clashes between Congress and State Jamiat. And during the tenure of Tarun Gogoi, gross human rights violation took place in the BTAD areas but Gogoi failed to take effective measures to

With enough political fodder to feed on, the presence of AIUDF in the politics of Assam gradually became stronger. Badruddin Ajmal politicized the insecurity of EBOMs to his advantage, and AIUDF's seats increased from one in 2009 to three in Lok Sabha election of 2014. The growing disenchantment of the immigrant Muslims against the Congress also helped Ajmal to consolidate his party's influence among them.[9] An important leader and intellectual from the Muslim community, Hafiz Ahmed believed that communal politics in Assam was launched at the behest of Jamiat and UMF.[10] Their main plank was forging the interests of Bengali Hindus and Bengali Muslims, which would ultimately lead them to form the government in Assam. In the Assembly election of 2006, AIUDF got 10 seats. Like UMF, the support base of AIUDF is also mainly in the EBOM minority belts of the Brahmaputra valley. Hafiz Ahmed further argued that both the parties capitalized on the insecurity and had taken advantage of their socio-economic backwardness of the community.[11] He said 'In reality, they have done nothing. Rather the presence of Jamiat, UMF and now AIUDF polarised the votes on communal line'.[12]

Subsequently, Jamiat was used by various political-cum-religious leaders to meet the narrow political interests of Congress and AIUDF. When the state Jamiat faction got trapped in the pockets of Badruddin

address the issues of displacement, killing and arson. However, all these were only facilitating factors. The repeal of IM(DT) Act was the most immediate cause for the formation of AIUDF.

[9] In an interview on 8 June 2014 at Guwahati, Mozibar Rahman, an ex-MLA from Dhing and an important Muslim leader of the state, said that although Maulana Ajmal said that the party was created to fight for the cause of minority, it was his utter hypocrisy. The main reason to create the party was to fulfil his political aspirations. With both its national and state leaders Jamiat openly supported AIUDF in 2006 election. In this election, Jamiat also had shown its hypocrisy regarding the issue of IM(DT) Act, 1983. Jamiat opposed the enactment of the act during the Assembly election in 1985 and supported UMF in that election. The same Jamiat in the 2006 Assembly election opposed the repealing of the Act and created a political party under the leadership of state president of the Jamiat.

[10] Interview with Hafiz Ahmed, President, Char Chapori Sahitya Parishad, dated 6 June 2014.

[11] Ibid.

[12] Ibid.

Ajmal, Congress then attempted to create their own Jamiat. Rakibul Hussain, the topmost powerful Muslim leader of Congress, whose father was a Muslim League leader in Nagaon and a strong advocate of Pakistan, tried to divide the group so that Congress also got benefits from Jamiat. He had succeeded in creating the divide; the Arshad Madani faction is now closely associated with Congress and the Mehmud Madani faction is aligned with Badruddin Ajmal.

Many Muslim scholars and leaders are extremely critical of Jamiat and Maulana Badruddin Ajmal for their ultra-communal approach and attempt to keep certain sections of Muslim immigrants perennially backward. In an article titled 'Nation-breaking Politics by Badauddin in the Name of Jamiat', Mufti Nur Mahhmad argued 'The main objective for the formation of AIUDF by Badaruddin was his narrow personal political aspiration which he could not fulfil by putting pressure on Congress. When his ambitions were thwarted by Tarun Gogoi, Badaruddin started mobilising the illiterate-underdeveloped Muslim community in the name of religion and thus created a communal polarisation on emotive issues'.[13]

His main observations may be put in the following manner:

1. Such brand of politics would greatly affect the traditional peaceful bond between the Hindus and Muslims in Assam.
2. By dint of his industrial and business power, Badaruddin started a new brand of money politics in Assam, especially among the Muslim people.
3. In order to realize his narrow political gains, he used two important religious organizations—Jamiat and Tanjimmul Madarasia Komiya.[14]

Badaruddin Ajmal holds the presidentship of the two most important of religious Muslim organizations in Assam: the Tanjim Board and the Jamiat Ulema-E-Hind (Assam chapter). The former controls about 800

---

[13] Ahmed, 'Nation-breaking Politics by Badaruddin in the Name of Jamiat'.

[14] These are the private madrasas of Assam, and the Badaruddin Ajmal is the chief of about 800 private madrasas in Assam (to be illustrated later on).

private madrasas in Assam, mostly located among the Mymensinghia Muslims in lower Assam. The government has no control over the functioning of these madrasas. The syllabus, teachers and funding, all are controlled by the Tanjim Board. As has been suggested by Abdul Aziz (a former AAMSU–AGP leader) in an interview to the author, all of Badruddin's modern scientific sociocultural health and educational activities are confined among the Sylheti Muslims (Muslims migrated from the Sylhet district of Bangladesh), particularly in the Hojai district of Assam.[15] What he spreads among the lower Assam illiterate poverty-stricken immigrant Mymensinghia (Muslims migrated from the Sylhet district of Bangladesh) is traditional Wahabi and Salafi-based education and thought process. A majority of these private madrasas are located in the lower Assam Mymensinghia Muslim-dominated areas.

Apart from his religious role as the leader of Jamiat, he is the president of AIUDF. Thus, Badaruddin is a unique fusion of communal politics where religious and political roles are intertwined into one person. Badaruddin plays this dual role of political and religious headship in complete contravention with the constitution of the Jamiat Ulema-E-Hind, which says the office bearer of the Jamiat cannot hold parallel political positions in any political party.[16] It was because of his dual role that Ajmal was removed from the position of the president of Assam Jamiat by the president of all India Jamiat Ulema-E-Hind, Syed Arshad Madani, which ultimately led to the division of Assam Jamiat into two factions.[17]

From the above discussion, it can be suggested that AIUDF is not a democratic secular political party; rather, it is a faith-based religion-centric political organization.[18] The party can hardly be divided from

---

[15] Abdul Aziz was the former founder-leader of All Assam Minority Students Union (AAMSU—the most important minority students' union in Assam); later on, he joined AGP and then Congress. Hojai is the epicentre of Ajmal's socio-economic and educational activities. All his major hospitals, universities, colleges, etc. are located in Hojai.

[16] Ahmed, 'Nation-breaking Politics by Badaruddin in the Name of Jamiat'.

[17] Ibid.

[18] It may be mentioned that the party fields a few non-Muslim candidates and party posts in order to look avowedly secular, but the party is highly centralised and almost all important decisions are taken by Ajmal and his brothers.

religious organizations like Jamiat; rather, its sustenance is dependent on support received from Jamiat. Issues of human development and gender justice hardly find a place on their agenda. They hardly talk of livelihood security of the people and take advantage of their poverty. With various religious activities, this type of organization consolidates the voters. Their support base is very strong among the illiterate womenfolk compared to the menfolk. The voters in the rural *char* areas believe that Badaruddin Ajmal's political credential comes later; first, he is a Maulana with mystic healing powers, which makes him extremely sought after in political rallies where people assemble with a bottle of water to be purified by the Maulana's touch. Since he is a faith leader, with an honorific title *hujoor*, Badaruddin is expected to touch the bottles of water of the Muslim populace with his 'healing hands', which could be later on used during distress. Interestingly, in *char chapori* areas, Muslim voters, particularly women, give salience to the authoritative voices of the husband and religious leaders in exercising their voting rights. In a PhD research on political participation and voting behaviour of women in the char areas of Assam, a young scholar has expressed that 42 per cent women voters in those areas vote as per their husband's wishes and 36 per cent vote as per the directives laid by the religious leaders and Mullahs.[19]

Jamiat Avowedly Apolitical but Political Considerations Galore

Maulana Mehmood Madani, the General Secretary of Jamiat Ulema-E-Hind, said,

> We have no connection with any political party and we are purely a religious organization. Some people for their own benefits are floating organizations having similar names with our organization. These organizations are working for some political parties for their own benefits .... Some people are creating confusion among people and projecting themselves as representatives of Jamiat. But the fact is that we are completely apolitical.[20]

[19] For details, see Rizvi, *Political Participation and Voting Behaviour*, 142.

[20] Greater Kashmir. *Jamiat-e-Ulema-e-Hind Clarifies*. http://m.greaterkashmir.com/news/kashmir/jamiat-e-ulema-e-hind-clarifies-have-no-connection-with-politics/181807.html (accessed 2 April 2017).

The Jamiat's basic objective has been to defend Muslim personal law and it opposes 'any attempt by the state to change or interfere with it through either specific law or through the enactment of a uniform civil code'.[21] Although Mehmood Madani denies any link with any political party, for the cause of Muslim welfare, the organization can support any political party from outside.[22]

The Jamiat Ulema-E-Hind's political support to various parties can be illustrated in the following manner:

Jamiat's political role in Assam became more prominent after the Assam Accord was signed. The Assam Agitation created a huge fear psychosis among the immigrant Muslims that they would face serious consequences in the days to come, including deportation and deletion of their names from the electoral list. The fear psychosis further enhanced by the Muslim organizations and political parties formed thereafter. Since 1985, Jamiat has been playing various roles in the formation of government in Assam. Particularly in 1991, 1996 and 2001 State Assembly elections, Jamiat's role was crucial in the formation of governments. Few features are decipherable in Jamiat's role, which are mentioned below (please see Table 6.1).

Table 6.1 *Jamiat's Political Support to Political Parties*

Year or Period	Jamiat's Support to Political Parties
Pre-Independence to 1985	Largely Congress
1985–1991	UMF
1991–1995	Congress
1996–2001	Largely AGP (plus Samajwadi Party)
2001–2005	Congress
2006 onwards	AIUDF

Source: Prepared by the author.

---

[21] Brass, *Politics in India Since Independence*, 236.

[22] Nath, 'Communal Politics in Assam', 92.

First, in many occasions, the Jamiat played an architectural role in ensuring the Muslim immigrant's (EBOM) overwhelming vote for the Congress. In two occasions this role played by Jamita had helped Congress to gain power in 1991 and 2001.[23]

Second, the victory of Congress in 2006 and 2011 makes it amply clear that Congress can survive beyond Jamiat's support. In fact, in these two elections, Jamiat opposed Congress and sided with AIUDF. BPF and the indigenous Assamese stood behind Congress helping the party to form the government. Tarun Gogoi's utterances of 'who is Badaruddin' helped him to find huge acceptance among the indigenous Assamese and tribal people.

Third, simultaneously, when Jamiat did not support Congress but succeeded in providing an alternative, the immigrant Muslims opted for that alternative. Their relevance was never lost into oblivion.[24] The Assembly elections of 1985, 2006 and 2011 would prove that. This consolidation of Muslim votes helped the Jamiat to provide effective opposition.

Fourth, it is clear that the core support base of Jamiat is among the immigrant Muslims; Jamiat has to stick either to Congress or any other immigrant Muslim-based political party (like UMF or AIUDF) for their survival. If they go beyond their traditional support base, the voters may be sufficiently confused; for example, in 1996, there was confusion regarding Jamiat's support, and finally, the former has ended up supporting AGP and Samajwadi Party. The voters, however, opted more for Congress, and although the AGP-led coalition won the election, Congress had improved upon its performance among the immigrant Muslim-dominated areas.

Fifth, Jamiat had entered a most critical phase after the election of 2016. Despite its overwhelming support to AIUDF, it lost many seats either to Congress or BJP. The Jamiat supreme and the AIUDF president, Badaruddin Ajmal, himself lost the battle in the South Salmara seat, which is considered to be the safest bastion for the Jamiat politics,

---

[23] Nath, 'Communal Politics in Assam'.
[24] Ibid.

to the Congress candidate. Jamiat was the most important platform for the rise of minority politics in Assam, particularly the rise of UMF. However, Jamiat's opportunistic role in 1996 took it away from UMF. UMF severed its relationship with Jamiat Ulema-E-Hind on the eve of Assembly and Parliamentary elections in Assam in 1996 along with severing the relationship with UPPA (United Peoples' Party of Assam). In this connection, it is worthwhile to mention here that the United Peoples' Party of Assam, under the Chairmanship of Abdul Muhib Mazumder, took birth in the mid-1990 on the eve of the election in Assam. Since the emergence of UPPA as a regional party (although the party had no grassroots organization) in the state politics of Assam, it became very close with the Jamiat Ulema-E-Hind. UPPA, along with Jamiat Ulema-E-Hind, severed the relationship with UMF on the eve of the election in Assam in 1996 as both of them had supported AGP. Abdul Muhim Majumder became a cabinet minister in the AGP ministry. It may be added here that along with Jamiat Ulema-E-Hind, a few other faith-based Islamic organizations have also played a critical role in both the valleys of Assam.[25]

Dilemma of Assamese Nationality and Identity Issues over Land and Population Explosion of East Bengal Origin Muslims

The numerical preponderance of Assamese indigenous people has remained the most central question of Assamese identity. The Assamese nationality in the colonial phase remained dominant through a process of stakeholdership and building alliances with various nationalities. Being taken over by the burgeoning Muslim population, it remained and would remain a recurring theme of Assamese

[25] There are various other socio-religious Islamic groups in Assam those which directly or indirectly play a big role in Islamic society. These include Ahle Sunnat, Emarat-e-Sharariah, Nadwaut Tameer and Tablighi Jamaat. These are not directly political, but they certainly mobilize people in the name of Islam and Allah. All these organizations have a strong support base among the Muslims in Assam. It would be worthwhile to mention here that in the Brahmaputra valley, Jamiat has a strong support base, whereas in Barak valley, Ahle Sunnat and Emarat-e-Sharariah and Nadwaut Tameer have strong support bases. Tablighi Jamaat, an Islamic pure faith-based organization, works silently in various parts of Assam.

nationality in the days to come. I have argued elsewhere that during the period of 1940s, there was a strong secessionist and separatist feeling among the section of Assamese elites because of continuous immigration and marginalization of Assamese nationality:

> In this chapter we shall attempt to see how the identity of Assamese nationality has been formed and how certain historical-political factors have been nourishing the idea of separateness although in a nebulous form which have acquired new connotations and dimensions in the periods of 1980s & 90s. ... Nevertheless, the secessionist urges existed in the minds of a section of Assamese elite albeit in a rudimentary form. Most of the time it remained dormant but in some occasions it came into surface.[26]

Despite the strong secessionist feeling to protect the distinctiveness of Assamese nationality, it did not develop into a systematic sustained struggle because of the fear of being taken over by the Muslim population. Udayan Misra argues in the following manner:

> One of the major reasons for the low profile kept by the separatist forces was the fear of Muslim domination and the need to stay with the rest of India. These forces knew only too well that given the demographic pattern of the province and its past experience with the Saadullah ministries, a *Swadhin Asom* would be even more vulnerable to the machinations of Muslim of East Bengal. The hill leaders too were aware of the need to stay with India in order to avert a Muslim take-over. ... The fear of Pakistan and the demographic challenge posed by immigration actually contributed largely towards neutralizing the demand for a *Swadhin Asom*. Those who were advocating the cause of a sovereign Assam knew only too well that they had neither the organization nor the strength of purpose to follow up their demand.[27]

The vulnerabilities of Assamese indigenous population and their numerical strength became burning issues in the recent elections of Assam. It looks like the concerns of colonial politics have been limping back to Assam. The protection of land and maintenance of Assamese indigenous way of life and culture were the most dominant quests during the colonial period. There is a huge apprehension that if the

---

[26] Mahanta, *Confronting the State*, 3–5. The first chapter deals with these issues.

[27] Misra, *Periphery Strikes Back*, 95.

trail goes on in this manner, the Assamese will be reduced to a minority by 2030–2040. By and large, the Muslims of Assam have responded in the following manner regarding the issues of contestation between the Assamese nationality and EBOM:

First is the democratic political articulation and mobilization of the community by UMF, AIUDF and Jamiat, as we have presented above in this chapter.

The second response of the elites or the leaders of the Muslim community was to deny the very existence of foreigners or population increase of Muslim population or provide justification to the population growth in the name of socio-economic underdevelopment. Issues of land encroachment by the immigrants were simply branded as harassment of genuine citizens by the Hindutva forces.

Third, in recent times, there has been an attempt by a section of the community of the immigrant population to brand the Assamese as intolerant, xenophobic and bigotry by appealing to the global and national human rights and leftist groups. 'Chalo Paltai' and Miya poetry are some of the examples of such assertions.

The fourth response is a process of covert and overt radicalization which has been engulfing mostly the rural and char-based Muslims of the state.

Assimilation, Accommodation and Contestation: Assam Agitation as Cornerstone

However, such responses notwithstanding, it may be mentioned that the majority of the masses, particularly young educated EBOMs, are in the process of assimilation and absorption with the larger Assamese nationality. Many of them do not want to be associated with covert and overt forms of radicalization process and want to project a modern, secular and sensitive image of EBOM to the collective psyche of the Assamese nationality. There is no denying the fact that the Assamese language could remain as the dominant language in the state for about six decades due to a sizeable section of the community return-ing Assamese as their official language rather than Bengali. This is a notable contribution of EBOM as most of the other communities in the state, including the ethnic groups of the state, have the propensity to declare their mother tongue as their first language. Many scholars and intelligentsia of Assam have acknowledged that the role of EBOM earned them names such as 'Na-Asomiya' or Neo-Assamese.[28] Besides, the contribution of the community, particularly in the agricultural sector, has remained enormous.[29] EBOMs have provided the major chunk of labour economy in the state. Without them, the construction sector, the agricultural chain and other labour-centric professions would remain unthinkable. It will be no exaggeration to suggest that during the time of Eid and elections, most of the cities in the state remain clueless as they lock, stock and barrel march to their respective places in lower Assam.

Regarding the assimilation process of EBOM, two important Muslim scholars of Assam, Professor Abu Nasser Ahmed and Professor Adil-ul-Yasin raised certain questions about the Muslims identity in Assam:

> The Muslims of Assam, being confronted with the identity crisis, are putting to themselves a few but extremely important questions having far-reaching implications. Unlike the Muslims of northern India, the Muslims of Assam have been trying to resolve their identity problem by actively participating in the state politics. Yet they often have to find an answer to disturbing questions: Who are they? Are those Muslims born and brought up in Assam and whose forefathers came to Assam in the thirteenth century, whose mother-tongue is Assamese, whose cultural foundation has been shaped by the folk-tradition of Assam, really Assamese or Muslims or both? Are the immigrant Muslims who too have accepted Assamese as their mother-tongue and recorded thus in 1971, whose children are taking education in Assamese-medium schools in their respective areas, whose new generation has produced a good number of Assamese poets, writers and intellectuals, really Assamese, Bengali or Muslims? Where do they stand? Shall they declare themselves as Assamese and consider themselves, as a part of the mainstream Assamese but not recorded recognition by the mainstream?[30]

---

[28] Gohain, *Assam: A Burning Question*, 25.

[29] Choudhury, *Asomot Bangladeshi*, 33–38.

[30] Ahmed and Adil-ul-Yasin, 'Problems of Identity, Assimilation and Nation-Building', 148; quoted in Misra, *India's North East*, 198.

Most of the Assamese Muslim scholars blame the Assam Agitation as responsible for widening the gap between the Assamese and EBOM.[31] Certainly, in the post-Independence period, till the beginning of Assam Agitation in 1979, there was a process of assimilation and accommodation of EBOM into the Assamese cultural mosaic. However, the Assam Movement and the growing illegal migration issue widened the wedge between EBOM and the Assamese. Although the Assam Agitation made no distinction between foreign Bengali Hindus and Muslims, yet cultural homogeneity of the Bengali Hindus with the Assamese did not create a huge acrimonious relationship the way it developed between the EBOM and the Assamese. Instead of narrowing down, the gulf widened slowly as almost all the Muslim scholars or EBOM leaders, rather than appreciating the identity crisis of a smaller nationality, denied its very existence and decried the whole agitation as RSS-Hindutva-centric and chauvinistic. With the support of Bengali leaders and journalists, in search of a 'socialist-secular' El Dorado, the Leftist scholarship took Assam as the platform of the potential communal cauldron at the behest of RSS and other Hindutva forces. While one could hardly deny the influence of rightist forces in the Assam Agitation, however, to reduce it to an RSS-Hindutva-guided agitation was nothing but an abysmal failure to understand the dynamics of Assam's identity politics. Also, the failure of the leaders to take along all the communities, including the Assamese Muslims and progressive section of EBOM, certainly left a question mark on the part of the agitation leaders.

However, it would be completely wrong to say that during the Assam Agitation, it was only the Muslims who were the targets. In many violent clashes, Assamese Hindus, tribals and people of other communities like those of the tea-gardens and the Nepalis also died. In places like Dhomdhoma, Musalpur and Udalguri, many Assamese and

---

[31] Misra, *India's North East*, 197–200. Also see Hussain, *The Assam Movement*. Mannan, *Infiltration: Genesis of Assam Movement*. According to Professor Mannan, two police officers and RSS had changed the course of the Assam Movement against the outsiders and the EBOM. The two police officers were Hiranya Kumar Bhattacharjee and Premkanta Mahanta.

indigenous people died as a result of violent clashes.[32] The year 1983 was the bloodiest among all. On 12 February in Somoria in Boko, nine Assamese people were hacked to death by the immigrants.[33] Besides, during the Assam Agitation under AASU–AAGSP, 860 persons died and were declared as martyrs in their fight against the foreigners, of which, 24 persons were Muslims.[34]The Assamese Muslims hardly differentiated their interests from the Assamese Hindus. Those incidents in which EBOMs were killed were unfortunate incidents triggered by many local and land factors. The most tragic and unfortunate incident of Nellie in 1983 was triggered by a long-drawn conflict of land. As former *New York Times* reporter and writer, Sanjay Hazarika, has argued:

> We are surely aware of the agitation of eighties, which resulted in the ethnic, linguistic and religious blood bath of 1983. As a reporter of the New York Times, I had the rather unfortunate task of covering this tragedy. In one area alone, which is Nellie, 1753 people were killed just because they happened to be Muslims. Some of them were new settlers but many of them were old ones and they were killed by their neighbours, by a fairly, well organised group which had been planning it for weeks. But again, the core issue there was land. The immigrants there, who were almost one hundred per cent Muslims, had basically taken over land belonging to the Tiwa tribals illegally by getting a 'chappa' (or thumb) impression on pieces of papers and when they wanted the land back, the agitation and the elections of 1983 proved to be a good opportunity to settle scores.[35]

A celebrated scholar, litterateur, poet and former DGP of Assam, Harekrishna Deka, also held similar views by saying that the issue of land is central to the immigrant–Assamese conflict in Assam, particularly in the context of Nellie. Deka argued:

---

[32] Some of the places where such incidents took place were Bijni, Boihamari, Goreswar, Jamugurihat, Khoirabari, Sotea, etc. In all those places, Assamese Hindus and tribals died in large numbers. To see how Assamese Hindus, Assamese Muslims and other communities were affected, see Sarmah, *Asom Andolanar Asompurna Itihaas*, 652–82.

[33] Ibid., 677.

[34] For the martyrs' list published by the Government of Assam, see Mahanta, *Asomiya Jatiyatabadar Itihass*, 180–96.

[35] Hazarika, 'Illegal Migration from Bangladesh', 29.

Behind the massacre of Nellie in 1983, the conflict of interest between the native tribal people and the migrant Muslim community over land cannot be brushed aside as an insignificant cause, it is rather a main cause. Though resistance to 1983 Assembly Election by the Assam Movement supporters and support to the election by some minority organizations triggered immediate tensions between the locals and the migrants, animosity between the two communities had been growing over a long period of time as the migrants went on squatting on village reserve lands undisturbed, which was encouraged politically by vested interests and conveniently ignored by the government officials concerned either under pressure or due to corruption. The native tribal community must have felt that by tradition they had the right over the land for the community's shared use, even though this perception of the indigenous people had no legal backing as the domain right remained with the State Government. Not only they felt sense of deprivation when the land got occupied by a migrant community culturally quite different, but also the encroachment on an area which had earlier vast open land interfered with their daily movement and cattle grazing. The undercurrent of tension was brewing for a long time before it flared up over an immediate emotional issue.[36]

Misrepresentation of Assam Agitation and Identity Question

As we have mentioned above, one of the chief techniques of Muslim leaders and writers was to deny the very existence of the immigration problem and the challenges it posed to the Assamese nationality. We shall cite here a few examples of how Assam's illegal migration issue was projected as a 'Muslim annihilation' project by Muslim journalists, Jamiat Ulema-E-Hind and other Muslim scholars.

In a report on 'Bangladeshi Problem of Assam: Myth and Reality' prepared by journalist Zamser Ali and sponsored by Jamiat Ulema-E-Hind, the following observations were made about the Assam Movement:

In post-Independence period Muslims of the State were targeted as anti-national Pakistani or Pakistani infiltrators and they were deported from Assam in large scale without any trail.... The issue became more complicated during the period between 1963–1969 A.D., when about

---

[36] Deka, 'Infiltration of Bangladeshi Nationals into India', 44.

6,00,000 Muslims were deported under the discriminatory P.I.P. (Pakistani Infiltrations Prevention) Scheme. ... In the last quarter of 20th century it created a social havoc in the state due to anti-foreigners Assam Movement (1979–1985) under All Assam Students' Union (AASU).[37] ... In all these cases only Muslims were targeted and murdered. They were murdered only because of their religious identity. Though the RSS-VHP forces were behind these sorts of attack, no one is ready to assume it as a communal attack. Because, the Muslims who were killed are assumed as illegal Bangladeshis and land grabers.[38] ...But the chauvinist forces of the Movement primarily attacked upon Muslims and CPI (M) workers in large scale. During Assam Movement, BJP leaders like Atal Bihari Vajpayee, L. K. Advani and right-wing intellectuals like Arun Shoorie frequently visited Assam and worked like Guru of Assam Agitators. All RSS-VHP workers took active part in the agitation and diverted it into Anti-Muslim and anti-Communist. ... But all these Communal propaganda was the part of long run issues faced by the Muslims of Assam.[39]

A majority of these smearing campaigns were based on fallacious arguments and gross fabrication of facts and figures.

Another protagonist of illegal migration in the state, Dr S. U. Ahmed of Nagaon College remarked:

At this time AASU and AAGSP unitedly more [sic] intensified their agitation to detect and deport so called foreigners ... at the beginning, the agitation was against the 'Bahiragatas' (outsiders) which might include Bengali Muslims, Bengali Hindus, Nepalis, Marwaris, Sikhs, Biharis and others. But after coming to close understanding with the RSS, the agitation turned against the foreigners which directly or indirectly meant Muslims ... the views of the Muslims intellectuals were that this agitation was a move for the extermination of Muslims from the state.[40]

The writer went to the extent of saying that 'from non-official sources, it was said that more than ten thousand Muslims were killed by arm agitators and their supporters'.[41] Dr Ahmed further stated '[the] AGP

---

[37] Ali, *Bangladeshi Problem of Assam*, 7.

[38] Ibid., 9.

[39] Ibid., 36.

[40] Ahmed, *Muslims in Assam*, 69.

[41] Ibid., 73.

was formed for the greater interest of the Assamese Hindus. They supported the agitation and promised to implement the Assam Accord which was basically against Muslims'.[42]

Except for a few progressive Assamese Muslims, all other Muslim scholars and organizations could never understand the agonies of a smaller community of being reduced to a minority in their own state; rather, they made a serious allegation that

> Attack and insulting on Muslims are day to day happening in Assam. All ethnic, chauvinist and communal forces are united in their anti-Muslim attitude in the name of Bangladeshi. Parts of Media, some social, religious and even some Government Institution are playing biased role in the inhuman atrocities upon Muslims. They are all united in whatever they are doing all are justified. They are doing all these for the safeguard of Indigenous people of the state. But, the Government is remaining as silent spectator.[43]

The most alarming fact was that, apart from grossly exaggerating the threat and insecurity perception which all communities in the state had to undergo due to state and group atrocities, the writers gave figures which were neither substantiated by independent sources nor verifiable at all; for example, the Jamiat-sponsored report written by an 'objective' journalist Zamser Ali said that 0.6 million Muslims were deported from Assam in the period from 1963 to 1969, but he never bothered to cite any sources. In the absence of objectivity and neutrality, this kind of statement might lead to a situation of great misunderstanding and mistrust among communities.[44]

Again, Dr S. U. Ahmed made a serious allegation that 10,000 Muslims were brutally murdered by armed agitators, but he never bothered to cite any sources except non-official sources, which he even did not mention.[45] Allegations of such nature should be objectively verified and presented; otherwise, these writings become the reference points for the cosmopolitan citizens to determine the nature

[42] Ibid., 74.

[43] Ali, *Bangladeshi Problem of Assam*, 51.

[44] Ibid., 7.

[45] Ahmed, *Muslims in Assam*, 73.

of democracy in Assam. Being a senior academician from a college, this was a minimum expectation from the academic community. The agenda behind such a write-up did not matter. At least in methodology, it needed to be objective and scientific.

Another instance of such bias or misinformation (howsoever unintended) was being propagated by Dr Abdul Mannan, a passionate defender of immigrant rights, former Associate Professor of Statistics, Gauhati University, who also wrote a book titled *Genesis of Assam Agitation*. Amid CAA-2019, Dr Mannan was interviewed by Citizens for Justice and Peace (CJP), a self-declared human rights movement for upholding and defending the rights of the minorities, among others.[46] Dr Mannan said that there were three strands in which Muslim immigrants were targeted in Assam. At first, he said that an Act was passed by Gopinath Bordoloi in Assam Assembly in 1950, which was known as the 'Expulsion of Illegal Migrants' Act. He said that 0.25 million EBOMs were expelled from Assam under the said Act. The second wave of Acts against the Muslims, according to Dr Mannan, started in 1962 when 'again another bill was passed in 1962 under the stewardship of CM Bimala Prasad Chaliha that was PIP scheme. On the strength of the Act approximately 5 to 6 lakh Muslims [were] expelled from Assam'. The third phase against the Muslims 'began from 1979—till today it continues'.

There are certain gross factual as well as interpretative errors in the analysis of Dr Mannan. An Associate Professor of Statistics may not have certain knowledge about history and politics; however, to interpret those events without verification is unacceptable, as such interpretations would project a wrong image about the state of affairs in the state. It is rather ironical that as a retired Associate Professor of Statistics at Gauhati University, he should have maintained the basic ethos of statistical accuracy. First of all, regarding his first point, the

---

[46] See https://cjp.org.in/a-brief-history-of-the-insider-vs-outsider-debate-in-assam (accessed 8 August 2020). The interview was conducted on 18 March 2019. The programme headline stated: 'Prof. Abdul Mannan takes us through the genesis and evolution of the insider vs outsider divide in Assam. He also explains how the animosity that for born out of a fear of change in the ethnic demography of the region gradually also ended up taking a communal hue'.

Act was not passed in the Assam Assembly; it was passed by the Indian Parliament and promulgated by the Government of India.[47] A total number of 0.5 million Muslim immigrants came to Assam (excluding the refugees) from 1947 till 1950.[48] All those displaced Muslims who went to East Pakistan came back with the proper settlement of their properties.[49] In fact, the number of people who returned return was more than the displaced people. 'The agreement (The Nehru-Liaquat agreement) facilitated the return of almost all the displaced persons. By 31st December 1950, there was a net influx of 161,360 people into Assam who had entered Assam through recognised routes of travel'.[50] Thus, Dr Mannan's figure of 0.25 million EBOM's expulsion from Assam is not based on verifiable facts. Besides, he never bothered to mention the numbers who had returned.

Second, as stated by Dr Mannan, the PIP scheme was more of an initiative of central government to be implemented by the provincial government. In 1962, the project 'Prevention of Infiltration into India of Pakistani Nationals' (PIP) was approved by the Ministry of Home Affairs, GOI.[51] According to him, 'on the strength of the Act approximately 5 to 6 lakh Muslim immigrants have been expelled from Assam', but here again, a scholar like Dr Mannan never bothered to cite his source. Such an imaginative figure in critical topics like the expulsion of 'Muslims from Assam is a serious issue, as these figures could become the reference point for other neutral observers. To cite the White Paper report on Foreigners, published by the Congress Government in 2012: 'During the period 1961–1966 approximately 1,78,952 infiltrants were either deported or had voluntarily left the

---

[47] As I have argued in the fourth chapter: 'Realizing the apprehensive situation, the Government of India decided to formulate The Immigrants (Expulsion from Assam), Act 1950, which granted it the authority to expel illegal immigrants from Assam, and the powers were vested upon the Officer Subordinate of Central Government or any Government official of Meghalaya or Assam'.

[48] Government of Assam, 'White Paper on Foreigner's Issue', October 2012. Home and Political Department, 6.

[49] For details, see the eighth chapter of this book.

[50] Government of Assam, 'White Paper on Foreigner's Issue', 6–7.

[51] For details, see White Paper, referred above, 9.

country but an estimated 40,000 infiltrants did not leave India'.[52] This figure is nowhere close to Dr Mannan's figure of 'approximately 5 to 6 lakh people'.

Third, Dr Mannan's assertion that 'outsiders in Assam specially means the Muslims' and 'the third phase of Muslim expulsion began in 1979 and till today it continues' is too much of a simplified and generalized statement. Such statement padlocks him closer to the highly communal views of Jamiat as we have expressed above. It is precisely because of such grotesque interpretation and manipulation of facts that such a wrong image of Assamese people is being projected to the outside world, and when they write the epitaph of Muslims in Assam, they are expected to show a modicum of sensitivity to substantiate their arguments with verifiable facts.

Reclaiming Muslim Identity through 'Miya Poetry' and 'Miyaness'

A similar kind of wrong projection was also made by the recent campaign of 'Miya poetry' to the outside world, which became popular across the nation through a viral video. The terms 'Miya' and 'Miya poetry' have been defined in the video 'I am Miya—Reclaiming Identity through Protest Poetry' in the following manner: (a) Miya poetry is defined as an act of reclaiming one's Muslim identity. (b) The video claims that the term 'Miya' is used as a 'racial slur' in Assam. (c) It is used to define someone as 'Bangladeshi' or 'illegal immigrant'. (d) 'Miya poetry can be considered as a form of a protest against "abuse and recurring communal violence".[53]

Through his poem 'Write Down I am a Miyah', Hafiz Ahmed makes the following claims:

1. Miyas are known to the world through their NRC number.

---

[52] Ibid., 8.

[53] The video is sponsored by Karwan-E-Mohabbat led by Harsh Mander, a civil rights activist. For details, see https://sabrangindia.in/article/i-am-miya-reclaiming-identity-through-protest-poetry (accessed 8 August 2020).

2. The Assamese people are hatemongers—will they carry this hate to the next generation, he asks.
3. The Miyas undertake all the dirty activities—they are always at the service of the Assamese people, yet the Assamese people are always dissatisfied.
4. Miya is a citizen of democratic secular republic of India—but they have no rights; they are branded as 'D' voters.
5. The Miyas are killed, driven out of villages and their paddy green fields are snatched at will by the Assamese.
6. The Miyas are rolled over by bulldozers.
7. The Miyas are killed at any time or any moment by the Assamese people. Bullets can shatter their breast without committing any crime.
8. The Miya people are regularly tortured; their bodies are burnt black.
9. That is why their eyes are reddened with fire.

Hence, the poet cautions the Assamese people—'I have nothing but anger in stock. Keep away! Or Turn to Ashes'. Another poet, Abdul Kalam Azad, says that the Miyas are killed by bullets; the Miya girls are gang-raped! Abdul Rahim, another Miya poet, asks 'How long shall I keep my feeling suppressed? How long shall I be silent? After how many tears will I be considered a human being? How much blood should I lose to get my rights?' Thus, the poets present that the Miya community is suppressed, not treated as human beings, and the Assamese society is a blood-spilling society as the Miyas lose blood regularly.

The manner in which Miya poetry is expressed through the five poems in the propaganda video is the best example of how poetry as a genre could be used as a weapon to instigate one community against another. The Assamese community has been castigated as racial, xenophobic, hatemonger, communalist, gang rapist and killer. If these accusations are considered to be correct, then the entire state should have been in a continuous Hobbesian state of affairs—'Kill whom you can, snatch what you get'. This is nothing but a travesty of truth and is the best example of 'politics of victimhood' in the garb of narrow sectarian communal agenda. As we have empirically shown above, false information and exaggeration of facts remain a vital facet of the recent immigrant discourse, especially from the Assam Movement period, at the behest of the immigrant lobby. As a result of unabated and unhindered immigration from the pre-colonial period onwards, it is precisely the Assamese community which is at the risk of being reduced to a minority in its homeland in about 10 years. Already 51 legislative constituencies have become immigrant-dominated, and, in the process, the political powerplay is shifting towards the immigrant community. Vital cultural institutions like the satras, naamghars and resources like land, forest reserves and grazing grounds, etc., are being occupied by a section of immigrants' community. Assam has borne the burden of foreigners till 25 March 1971, whereas in the case of other states, the cut-off date is July 1948. However, all those issues notwith-standing, the immigrant community is considered as 'Na-Asomiya' and considered as part of the greater Assamese nationality, and, ultimately, the very Assamese community is labelled as intolerant and rapist, as if the hunter is writing the history of the hunted.

'NRC' and 'D-voter' are not something invented by the Assamese society in recent times. These are historical processes mandated by the Supreme Court and other judicial bodies of this country, which apply to all, irrespective of religion and caste, to scrutinize the citizenship status as Assam bears the maximum number of illegal immigrants which no other states ever have had to.[54] Although the Assamese people are branded as rapists by the recent assertion of Miyaness and Miya poetry, government and police statistics would reveal otherwise, and these are some unpalatable truths which could never be avoided. It perhaps requires introspection on the part of the Miya poets as to why the government had to abandon appointment of women Teachers' Eligibility Test (TET) teachers in certain char-chapori areas.[55]

---

[54] Our previous chapters of this book have provided a historical account of this trajectory.

[55] To get a glimpse of such incidents of rape of Assamese girls, see the discussion in the Assam Assembly on 23 March 2018. Also, see https://www.youtube.com/watch?v=xfbHkPG8qzl (accessed 10 August 2020). Interestingly, both the political parties, AIUDF and Congress, were silent on the rape issues.

The Assamese people are not the enemies of the Miya people. Their enemy lies within. Rather than blaming the Assamese community, the new Miya elites should introspect about the factors that are causing a sense of insecurity to the Assamese nationality and holding the Miya community back. The population growth of EBOM is the most serious among them. A progressive section of the Muslim scholars has acknowledged this phenomenon. According to Dr Abdul Mannan, a strong advocate of immigrant rights in Assam,

> One thing is very clear—I want to draw your attention that there is no doubt that the Muslims in this part of the country, their number is disproportionately increasing—there is no doubt about it .... I also feel there is a systematic attack on a particular group because of their religious belief. But at the same time we must also respect this apprehension of the majority community because nobody will like to become a minority to be guided and administered by a group which was minority till other day ... this can be curbed only by some scientific steps.[56]

However, the traditional Islamic religious authority in the rural char-chapori areas hardly allows such efforts on the part of the government to curb population growth and introduction of modern scientific health care. A Padmashree awardee, Dr Illias Ali, was engaged in EBOM-inhabited char-chapori areas of Assam for the propagation of proper health care. In a place in Champur of Darrang district in 2009, a few *matabbars* told Dr Illias Ali:

> They have sent you once again to reduce our numbers. This time you are coming with tablet, needles and other surgical methods. After a few days you will come with rifles and pistols. Therefore we need at least five-six children so that even after killing three-four children at least two will survive.[57]

According to Dr Ali, multiple factors act as the facilitators for the growth of the immigrant Muslim population in Assam. Such population increase is posing as the main obstacle in their growth and development leading to the decline of the quality of lifestyle. Lack of

---

[56] See https://cjp.org.in/a-brief-history-of-the-insider-vs-outsider-debate-in-assam (accessed 8 August 2020).

[57] Ali, *Jonobisfuronor Pom Khedi*, 85.

population planning has led to impoverishment all-around—women folks are working as manual labourers, children are not going to schools, and anti-social, criminal activities and clashes among themselves have been increasing.[58]

> Poverty, illiteracy, religious fanaticism and lack of family planning, etc. are mainly responsible for the growth of EBOM population. Lack of education, child marriage, polygamy, poverty, etc. are making the population issue more complex ... the illiterate *char-chapori* people believe that more children can eradicate their poverty and hence more children is the answer to their poverty. Added to it, religious fanaticism and superstitions are galore—they believe that children are the greatest gifts of Allah and He will also provide food and shelter to them. Human beings have nothing to do—they are just means. Hence they consider birth control exercises as anti-Islamic practices.[59]

Dr Ali further said,

> [C]hild marriage or marriage of the non-adults remain a dangerous practice in *char-chapori* areas. For the immigrant Muslims, girls are forced to get married at the age of 12–14, as if this becomes their main agenda of social reforms. Girls are forced to get married at an early stage and they become mother of two-three children at a very tender age. As a result their health never recovers. Majority of them suffer from malnutrition and anaemia. Their life cycle is also very less. Majority of the women are exploited, subjugated and neglected ... in addition domestic violence, abuses are day-to-day phenomenon of the Muslim immigrant women. Currently, they are also becoming the main source of income for the family. Women daily-wage earners have been disproportionately increasing. In cities like Guwahati and other metros, the immigrant women-labourers with kids at their lap come regularly along with male counterparts to work as daily-wage earners.[60]

Dr Ali further argues that frequent child delivery and hard manual labour make the Miya women look like aged women and they remain unattractive to their husbands. Such husbands take *talaq* (divorce) from the previous wife and get married to a new woman. Many consider getting married to three–four women as a matter of pride. Such

---

[58] Ibid., 87.

[59] Ibid., 87.

[60] Ibid., 89.

a dangerous trend of subjugation of Muslim women in char-chapori areas is now getting manifested in Guwahati also. Dr Ali also made a detailed analysis of how certain *mullahs*, intellectuals, *munshis* and *maulanas* in the immigrant areas propagate ideas like 'family planning is against Islam', 'family planning means sterilisation' and so on.[61]

These are the burning issues that keep EBOM subjugated, which the progressive group like the elites of Miya poetry should take note of if they truly want to emancipate the community from shackles of traditional fanatical ideas. Instead, they have decided to brand the Assamese people as rapists, communal, slaughterers, subjugators, etc.

Having said that, the purpose here is not to pass over a series of mindless violent incidents that affected thousands of EBOM, particularly in the Bodoland Territorial Areas. I had argued in a special article in the *Economic & Political Weekly* (EPW) titled the 'Politics of Space and Violence in Bodoland':

> Quest for peace in the Bodo heartland in Assam seems to be an un-ending chimera. The magnitude of human tragedy is enormous. More than 100 people have been killed so far, 4,85,921 people displaced—primarily in the districts of Kokrajhar, Chirang, Baksa, Dhubri and Bongaigaon in western Assam, mostly belonging to the immigrant Muslims and the indigenous Bodo people—demonstrate that peace in the trouble-torn area is very fragile and shortlived. The Bodoland Territorial Autonomous District (BTAD) area, popularly known as the 'Bodoland', is one of the most violence-ridden areas in post-independence period of India. The area has witnessed a saga of ethnic-hostility, wanton killing, destruction and displacement; more systematically right from the days of first failed Bodo Accord of 1993, though the identity assertion of the autochthon Bodo tribes goes back to the days of the pre-independence period.[62]

However, EBOMs are not the only people who are affected by such mindless ethnic violence. In a multi-ethnic, multicultural state like Assam, an assertion for ethnic land rights and cultural recognition by both violent and non-violent groups led to the killing and displacement of many subnational and religious groups. In a report

[61] Ibid., 90–91.
[62] Mahanta, 'Politics of Space and Violence in Bodoland', 49.

published by the Government of Assam, it was suggested that a total of 14 'linguistic, communal and ethnic conflicts' took place between 1990 and 2013. Out of those, six conflicts involved mostly Muslims and other communities such as Santhals, Rabhas and Bodos. The rest eight conflicts in one way or other involved Adivasis, Nepalis, Bodos, Hmars, Dimasas, Kukis, Zemi-Nagas, Garos, Rabhas, Rengmas, etc.[63] ULFA and many other insurgent groups had killed hundreds of non-Assamese and Assamese people, which are not included in the above list. Militant Bodos perhaps have killed more Bodos more than non-Bodos for territorial power and authority.[64] Thus, Assam remains a theatre for multiple identity politics in which millions of people are affected by almost all walks of life, but all other affected indigenous or non-indigenous groups have not maligned Assam's name as a land of slaughterhouse and rapists.

Assam Agitation and Leftist Interpretation

Even the Left scholars of the state failed to make a correct analysis of the nature and character of the Assam Agitation, which was acknowledged by one of the greatest leftist critics of Assam agitation.[65] Professor Hiren Gohain was perhaps the staunchest critic of the Assam Agitation:

> The Fascists are having a field day as a result. Apart from chauvinist thugs dealing out spasmodic violence, there are systematic campaigns, carefully planned and conducted, against the Muslims in certain areas. As such the Assam movement is neither anti-Islamic nor anti-Muslim. But the fear of 'foreigners' is inextricably linked in the minds of the threatened Hindu gentry with the political challenge from the Muslim immigrants who are bona fide citizens.

---

[63] Barua, 'A Brief Report on Linguistic, Communal and Ethnic Conflicts in Assam', 60–86.

[64] For example, between 2006 and 2009, more than 130 Bodos were killed by the Bodo insurgent groups. See *ABSU Patrika*, 'Bodoland: The Battle Ground. http://www.satp.org/satporgtop/countries/india/states/assam/terrorist_outfit/ndfb

[65] Borkataki, *Nivedan Swajan-Chinta*.

The declining political influence of the Caste-Hindu gentry has goaded it to attempt an alliance with backward Hindu groups based on the RSS ideology. Though the thinking of the RSS is not particularly in favour of the coexistence of distinct national groups within India, it has supported the Assam movement in the hope of communalizing the Assam situation, where large numbers of immigrants are Muslims.[66]

Professor Gohain's main thesis is that the Assam Agitation is a product of Assamese chauvinism which grew at a fast pace, with the connivance and under the active patronage of the ruling classes in Delhi and Shillong. For Professor Gohain, immigration is not an issue. A section of Assamese Hindus has made a frantic attempt to play to the fears and anxieties of the Assamese masses.[67] He further argued that the Assamese Hindu middle class desperately tried to assert its hegemony by whipping up traditional fears for about a year or so before the movement started. Besides, the Assamese press had been hysterical with reports of the huge influx of Bangladesh and their assorted crimes. His decisive analysis about the agitation was:

The real secret behind such mindless ecstasies was whispered in the elegant drawing rooms of the well-to-do Assamese families of towns: if the Muslims and other groups team up and reduce the Assamese Hindu legislators to a minority in the Assembly, how will it be possible for the latter to retain the lion's share of the loot from the state? But the explicit propaganda reiterates the time-honoured all: Assam is in danger. There is a more sophisticated slogan for the vain intellectual: Our cultural identity has been threatened.[68]

For Professor Gohain, the Assam Movement was about allowing the Assamese middle-class Hindus to retain the lion's share of the loot from the state. It is really unfortunate that Professor Gohain could never appreciate the fact that immigration has remained the single most crucial factor for the identity threat of Assamese people since the dawn of colonial politics in Assam. For a smaller heterogeneous composite

---

[66] Gohain, *Assam: A Burning Question*, 20.

[67] Ibid., 25. For Gohain, the reason why Assamese Hindus played and politicised the fear of Assamese masses was for the exclusive enjoyment of financial and other benefits from the state government.

[68] Ibid., 26. Professor Gohain carried forward a similar argument in his EPW writings. Most significant in this regard is perhaps Gohain, 'Cudgel of Chauvinism', 418–20.

Assamese nationality, the immigration and ever-increasing cohesive and homogeneous Muslim population remain the single most important identity threat. The issues of Assamese nationality cannot be seen as an effort of the Hindu middle class to loot state resources by raising the alarm of identity bell. Unlike what Professor Gohain argued from his ideological prism, for Assam, the immigration issue is more of an identity issue rather than a religious issue. Unlike the Hindu–Muslim divide in central Indian states on issues like *gou-satya*, the celebration of festivals, cow vigilante, mandir-masjid, *smashan-kabarsthan*, etc., the primary issue here is about Assamese identity, which is threatened by ever-increasing immigration and the resultant pressure on land. As Sanjib Baruah has argued, such secular pretensions have increased the insecurities of various smaller nationalities. It is precisely the negligence of such a burning identity issue of a smaller nationality that it is getting transformed into a communal divide between two communities—sooner we realize it better it is for all.

There was an interesting debate on the character and nature of Assam Agitation in EPW.[69] Responding to Professor Gohain, Sanjib Baruah had pleaded:

> The problem with Gohain's analysis is that he refuses to take the question of influx into Assam, which rightly or wrongly is the central focus of the present events in Assam, seriously. It is not a question of agreeing or disagreeing with the aims of the Assam movement. But the fact is that immigration into Assam on a scale that has few parallels anywhere in the world, within a relatively short period of time, has hopelessly tangled Assam's nationality question.[70]

Baruah cautioned that negligence of the immigration issue would come at the peril of Assamese nationality. He argued,

> [T]he so called ambiguity in the term 'foreigner' reflects only the historically structured contradictions of mass upsurge—primarily based on one community and oblivious of the demographic changes in Assam—which in highlighting an old issue is having to pretend that the divides of a plural

---

[69] For details, see Ahmed, *Nationality Question in Assam*.
[70] Ibid., 35.

society don't exist. Given the explosiveness of the issue, the movement has posed to raise the issue in secular terms. But such a secular definition in Assam's complex ethnic reality has only succeeded in increasing the insecurity of various communities.[71]

While contesting Professor Guha and Professor Gohain, Gail Omvedt, a celebrated sociologist, argued[72]:

But I am still not convinced. There are some fundamental questions— fundamental from the view of a communist response, not journalistic exposure—that have not been dealt with thoroughly by the writers.

(1) Is the Assamese peoples' agitation fundamentally one of chauvinism or of national self-determination? This is not a question of the progressive or reactionary nature of the leadership but of the fundamental class/national characteristics of the society and the movement. I am puzzled as to how in particular those Marxists who characterize India as a 'multinational country' can so lightly throw around the concept of 'chauvinism'?

(2) If the movement is fundamentally around issues of national self-determination, should the response of communists be to condemn it because the leadership is reactionary or to take part and attempt to provide an alternative leadership?

(3) Is there any objective basis for the fear of the Assamese people that they and their cultural-national identity may be swept by the Bengali influx? If there is, then what kind of assurance that this won't happen has been given - historically and at present - by the communities?

(4) Is the CPI (M) really based only among the Bengalis in Assam? If this is true after 50 years of communist presence in the area, then isn't it understandable that the Assamese people find it hard to understand what communism means?

Immigration Issue and Land Encroachment: Analysis by the Assamese Writers

Along with the Leftist viewpoint, here it will be pertinent to present an analysis of other liberal scholars, how they looked into those issues of Hindu–Muslim, immigration and land encroachment.

---

[71] Baruah, 'Assam Cudgel of Chauvinism or Tangled Nationality Question?', 543–45.

[72] Omvedt, 'Assamese People's Agitation', 580.

As we have shown in the previous chapters, the Assamese people have had great apprehension about the Muslims who under the tutelage of the Muslim League demanded Assam's inclusion into Pakistan. That worry—the drive to make Assam a Muslim-dominated state through immigration—still looms large in the minds of the Assamese people. A senior political scientist of the region, Professor Girin Phukan, argues:

> The Assamese who happen to be the dominant group in the Brahmaputra valley feel that the continuous influx of people from outside the state (particularly, from Bangladesh) has been posing a threat to their distinct sociocultural identity. The movement (1979–85) on the issue of Foreign Nationals was a manifestation of such a feeling. It is believed that of the immigrant communities, particularly the Muslims, constitute one of the important vote banks in the state and thus determine the trend of Assam politics. A section of the Assamese even expresses the apprehension that if the Muslim immigrants become the dominant group in Assam in the years to come, a day may come when they might demand Assam's secession from India. Some suspect that Bangladesh has deliberately been conspiring to send large numbers of people in order to change the communal ratio in the state in the hope of justifying the annexation of Assam by Bangladesh. The Bengali Muslim has already held the balance of political power in Assam. Their political clout is reflected in the state legislature. A directive from the centre in 1975 to detect foreigners and deport them was not implemented by the then Assam Government because the issue provoked the compact bloc of 25 Muslim MLAs and they threatened to withdraw their support from the Ministry.[73]

Professor Phukan further argues that the issue of apprehension towards EBOM is not of recent origin,

> This study shows that the problem of immigration in Assam is not a post-Independence phenomenon, rather it is rooted in the past. Therefore, this problem and its impact on Assam politics could be better understood in the context of its legacy left by the colonial rule.[74]

Baneswar Saikia, a noted writer of Assam and academic par excellence, has many milestones to his credit. He was the torchbearer of Assam

---

[73] Phukan, *Politics of Regionalism in Northeast India*, 34.

[74] Ibid., 41.

College Teachers' Association, a communist leader since his college days and had gone to jails many times on account of his association with communist ideology. Although he was a communist leader, he was very much grounded on Assam's politics. Unlike many of his communist activists and scholars who denied the very existence of immigration and foreigner problem, Baneswar Saikia, on the other hand, was very much perturbed by the immigration problem, particularly the ever-increasing number of Muslims of East Bengal origin.

He argues in 'Problems of Illegal Migrants':

> What is most relevant is the fact that in ten districts of Assam, there is abnormal growth of Muslims. In districts like Nagoan, Morigoan, Darrang, Barpeta the increase of Muslim inhabitants is quite phenomenal—not talk about Hailakandi, Cachar and Karimganj. This has created a panic situation among the non-Muslim population of the state. Now the Muslims has been demanding 40 seats from Congress party in the coming assembly election ... noteworthy to mention that the Muslim immigrants have been occupying the forests reserve and riverine areas and now they have been demanding the legalisation (Miyadi Patta) of their land holding and the Congress government is yielding to those demands.[75]

He also argues that to continue in the ruling, the bourgeois Congress party has been indulging in *Ali-Kuli-Bongali* (the Muslims, the tea-garden communities and the Bengalis) vote bank politics. They have been encouraging a religious fanatical assertion among the Muslims. By aligning with the Jamiat Ulema-E-Hind and other Muslim organizations, the Congress Party has been encouraging a separate political identity among Muslims. Such actions reminded one of the diabolical roles played by the Muslim League during the colonial period. Unfortunately, Muslims have also acted as a separate group detached from the Assamese nationality. The inevitable result is the dominance of 'mullahs' and 'matabbars' among Muslims. What has been most appalling in the preceding few years is the rampant intensification of religious feelings and fanatical assertions. Politics of religion gained preponderance over the politics of livelihood. He further argued that

---

[75] Sabhapandit, *Prottoi Aru Annewesan*, 265–66.

it was violence during the Assam Movement that widened the gap between the Muslims and the majority group.[76]

Baneswar Saikia makes an elaborate analysis of how religious fanaticism has been engulfing Bangladesh since 1975. He further argues:

> Where are the safety and security and livelihood among individuals in Islamic countries? People are ruled by Shariat laws. Radical forces like Jamat-E-Islami and other bigoted political forces dominate Bangladesh. Both Hindus and Muslim are in flight to Assam in search of food and shelter. ... [I]t must be kept in mind that Muhhammmad Ali Zinnah and Muslim League wanted to establish a greater Bengal by including Assam into it. However this did not happen. ... But a section of Muslim radical forces still keep their predatory eyes on Assam.[77]

Islamist Global Network, East Bengal Origin Muslims and Islamic Seminaries

One major concern of the Assamese nationality is that because of the Islamist global network, the Muslims of Assam may switch the pendulum from the 'neo-Assamese identity' to a 'pan-Islamic identity' as it had happened during the colonial period. Sajjad Hussain, a senior academician from Lakhimpur of northern Assam, has been writing on the issues of Muslims of Assam. In one of his writings, he was referring to the role of big powers like the USA in mobilizing the Islamic radical forces which had its resonance in Assam also in the post-Assam Agitation period. He was particularly referring to how the USA period started mobilizing the radical Islamic forces for their interest during the Cold War.

> [S]ome Mullahs at the behest of Ijtema, Jalsa and Tablighi Jamat in Pakistan organised a big Islamic conference where promises were made to salvage sins of Islamic people and rescuing them their next birth by providing a radical and deep seated interpretation of Islam. Interestingly all Sunnis of Pakistan are the followers of the Deobandi school of UP, India. What had taken place in Pakistan also had its resonance in India and such bigotry religious practices also started in India. ... In these exercises organised by

---

[76] Ibid., 266.

[77] Sabhapandit, *Prottoi Aru Annewesan*, 267 (translation by the author).

Tablighi and Ijtema, various engineers, doctors, teachers, etc. actively took part. By talking about emancipation in next birth, they attempted to create a bunch of holy warriors in India. Since then, in our country even in our state (Assam), hitherto unknown Ijtema-Tablighi and world Islamic conferences had started taking place. These activities in Assam started from 1980. Such activities make Muslims fatalist, ritualistic, exhibitionist in their dress and mannerism, detached from reality, made them illiterate and oblivious to modern scientific education.[78]

Following the Assam Agitation, consolidation of a sizeable section of Muslims along with radical organization was observed. What had happened in Assam had its repercussion in Bangladesh also. Tenets of radical Islam were gaining ground in certain pockets of the Bangladeshi society at the initiative of Afghan Mujahideen. At the behest of official patronage of Bangladesh, certain sections of Islamic groups were planning an enlarged version of Islamic Bengal by including Assam into it. It was this force that extended 'death fatwa' to a less famous writer like Taslima Nareen. Later on, in connivance with the Pakistani ISI and Al Qaida, these groups conspired to create disturbances in Assam.[79] Hussain further argued:

Naturally, the immigrant Muslims, accused often as 'foreigners' may get tempted to manipulations of those radical forces. Many of them, according to information, had gone to the other side of the border for arms training. However, the indigenous Muslims are not running after such mirage. Although at the personal level, many Muslims may want to maintain the puritan practice as propagated by these forces, however, they are averse to the idea of taking up arms in the name of mystical Islamic homeland.[80]

The Islamic militant groups were gaining ground in Assam, particularly in collaboration with ULFA during the period of 1990s.[81] In July 2009, in the Assam Assembly, the Congress Minister Rockybul Hussain referred to two militant Islamic groups working in

[78] Hussain, 'Asomor Muslim Rajnitee', 31–32.

[79] Ibid., 32.

[80] Ibid., 33.

[81] For a detailed analysis on how Islamic militant radical forces have had been operating in Assam, see Mahanta, *Confronting the State*, 236–53.

Assam—Harkootul Mujahideen (HuM) and Muslim United Liberation Tigers force (MULTA).[82] According to the senior journalist and writer, Wasbir Hussain:

> Alternatively, the jihadis could decide to lie low and even try to sneak across the border into India. If they decide to cross over into India, their favoured destination would be West Bengal and Assam, two states that share long and porous borders with Bangladesh with rivers criss-crossing these borders. Moreover, in both West Bengal and Assam, Bangladeshi jihadi outfits like JMB has some presence, demonstrated by several arrests by the Indian security agencies in the past few years. The chars or sand bars in the riverine areas in western Assam, along Bangladesh, is ethnically and geographically the ideal hiding place for such elements.[83]

Islamic seminaries like the madrasas play an important role in Assam in mobilizing the Muslim population of the state. The numbers of government madrasas are very few in comparison to private madrasas.[84] However, the majority of madrasas are private and mostly unregistered without having a uniform and recognized curricula. There are about 870 such madrasas, which may be broadly classified as Hafizia, Kharijia or Qawmi also known as Arabi madrasas.[85]

Commenting on the sorry plight of the Madrasas in Assam, Professor Abu Nassar Saied Ahmed said that ill education, mismanagement, bad

---

[82] See http://www.ipcs.org/comm_select.php?articleNo=3814 (accessed 2 August 2020).

[83] Ibid. Hussain provided graphic details on the activities of militants and jihadis in Assam. In answering the question why radicalisation and jihadi activities have been increasing, he argued '[I]n the last few years, some incidents have occurred that indicate that there is an attempt at radicalising a section of the Muslim population in the state, a development that cannot be brushed aside as a minor security matter. … Another reason that many believe is the reason for the increased penetration by jihadi elements into the state is the unabated illegal migration from Bangladesh. This migration through the porous India-Bangladesh border has remained a cause of concern and it is surely abetting the influence of Islamist fundamentalism among a section of the Muslim population'.

[84] According to an estimate, under the Secondary Education Board of Assam (known as SEBA), there are 164 madrasas out of which only 6 are for girls. In the second category under the Directorate of Madarsa Education, there are 706 madrasas, 14 title madrasas, 9 Arabic colleges. Ahmed, *Madrasas in Assam*, 12.

[85] Ibid., 12.

teaching, creation of unemployable products whose only place of accommodation are mosques, come from those run by the Directorate of Madrasas Education Board and most often from the private Hafizia, Kharjia and Arabia Madrasas. Professor Ahmed argues:

> The condition of the third variety (Hafizia, Qawmi, etc.) is all the more deplorable as their strength is not known owing to reluctance of many of them to register under any umbrella organization; what they teach does not come under public scrutiny, as also where from their funds come. They are not accountable to the society at large. Consequently, their *locus standi* as educational institutions is not clear, leaving enormous scope for the public to go by the often raised allegation that these madrasas are the breeding ground of Jihadi elements threatening not only social stability and communal harmony but also the integrity of the country. It is alleged that these private madrasas are carbon copies of those in Sherpur, Kurigram, Jamalpur, Mymansingh district of Bangladesh, which are situated near our international border with that country.

Most of these Islamic seminaries are terribly gender-biased[86]; students are kept away from the outside world, not allowed to read newspapers or listen to the radio or watch TV. Under such hard compartmentalized thought processes, when the students face the outside world, they feel at a loss and are susceptible to manipulation by any Islamic radical organization. In such a scenario, in a sensitive state like Assam, 'where foreign nationals continue to intrude, with agents are allegedly and reportedly active and determined to foment trouble, using Madrasas as a springboard for such activities'.[87]

Thus, the states of affairs of these madrasas are causes of concern for all. The private madrasas lack accountability and transparency, and the authorities refuse to share anything regarding the sources of funding and nature of expenditure. According to Professor Ahmed, '[N]ot a single Madrasa provides any concrete reply ... most of them would

---

[86] As Professor Ahmed argued, 'In the case of the girls Madrasas, they are virtually kept like 'prisoners', as some of the guardians complained. They are allowed to go outside the premises of the Madrasas, only when parents come to take them out', 156.

[87] Ibid., 13.

say 'Allah keeps us going' ... they would not name any individual or organisation offering contributions or donations'.[88]

The most appalling part is the gradual preponderance of Salafi tradition among the Muslim population of Assam. As a leading *maulana* and currently the *muhtamim* of a leading madrasa in Nagaon had said:

> The Salafi influence in madrasas in Assam, as in the case of Darul Uloom Deoband and also in the Baskandi madrasa, is very strong. They are backed by the Saudi based Salafi groups and individuals. Their version of puritan Islam does not represent the vast majority of Muslims, who are the followers of Sufism. The Salafis have been trying to control the Muslim society, and in this way, they are keeping the Muslims backward. They are against any idea of reform in terms of syllabi or courses. We do not think they are doing good to the young Muslims, by telling them that they should study only Islamic theology, and saying that to take up subjects like English, Science, Mathematics and Social Studies or to go for Computer Education is tantamount to deviation from Islam.[89]

Encroachment of Land

Ramesh Chandra Kalita, a perceptive writer of Assam, referred to the land encroachment process in the following manner:

> Assam movement was a very ineffective mass assertion against the 150/200 years of historical evolution .... In democracy numbers play an important role. During the time of Assam Movement in order to strengthen their position in democratic pattern of the state the people who were considered as immigrants or foreigners and the non-residential Bengali Hindu and Muslim and Nepalese of Assam brought people of their respective communities to Assam and after the movement it received serious concern. The then D.I.G. who became a part of the Movement Mr. Hiranya Kumar Bhattacharya says, '...after 1980 i.e. during the time of the movement 25 villages of Marigaon district totally became Hinduless and the non-Muslim population of many villages have started to leave their places. The people who have occupied villages do not belong to Assamese Muslim community.'

> 'Mention can be made of Karanipam *mauza* of Ghaguwa, Kapoujari pam, Malou Ati pam, Barkarani, Sagalikata pam, Dihuti Dimal *mouza* of Uttar

[88] Ahmed, *Madrasas in Assam*, 158.

[89] Ibid., 161.

khola, Bhutnimara, Bhogduba, Basundhari Barjalai, etc. ...It has to be mentioned that during the war of 1965–66 many immigrant Muslims shifted to East Bengal from India. But now they have returned and created tension by demanding their rights over their left over property. In undivided Goalpara district many Rabha and Koch-Rajbangshi families were forced to leave their places in similar circumstances. Srirao has given information of 74 villages. These villages were Hindu villages before 1983. And gradually transformed into immigrant Muslim villages. Statistics of entire Assam may show a more dangerous picture.'[90] ... So Assam Movement has practically no impact in addressing the cause of the Assamese people.[91]

Dr Jayanta Kumar Ray, former Centenary Professor of International Relations, Calcutta University, and former Vice-Chairman, Maulana Azad Institute of Asian Studies, found a pattern in the nature of land encroachment or gradual takeover of land in Assam. According to him, in Assam and some areas of West Bengal,

whenever Muslims form a majority in a specific area, they try to evict Hindus from that or a nearby area and often succeed. For this purpose, infiltrators initially try to resort to thefts, dacoities, murder and molestation of women. But, eventually, they do not hesitate to stage large-scale riots.

According to Professor Ray, for political expediency, the ruling politicians turn a blind eye as they constitute an important component of vote banks and winning short-term political gains. In the process, they remain oblivious of the long-term cultural–economic–political impact.[92]

Pulin Kalita, a young promising journalist of Assam and recipient of a national fellowship on journalism, completed a project on behalf of Panos South Asia on 'Conflict Resolution: A Field Study Report on Juria'.[93]It may be mentioned that Jamunamukh, Juria, Dhing and Rupohi are among a few places in the Nagaon district which, as the very names suggest, have been typical habitation and cultural centres for indigenous people of the state since time immemorial. However,

[90] Bhattacharya, *Sinta-Duhsinta*, 164.

[91] Kalita, 'Prabajankarir Samasya Aru Asom', 34–35.

[92] Ray, 'Migration from (East Bengal/East Pakistan) Bangladesh to India', 36.

[93] For details, see Kalita, *Constitutional Protection of the Assamese*, 203–28.

over around 80 years, the entire demographic pattern had changed leading to the displacement and flight of indigenous people from their ancestral places so much so that these areas have almost become 90 per cent Muslim-dominated.[94] Kalita's project attempted to look at the sociopolitical and demographic changes in the area called Juria. In fact, in that project, the most substantial portion was devoted to the issues of land grabbing and possession by EBOM. He argues that the Muslims create such a situation that the Hindus are forced to leave the place voluntarily or by selling their land and hearth for peanuts. In his project, the writer argues that to take the land, EBOM allow their hens and chickens to move around in Hindu-dominated places, which are considered as unholy by the latter. Occupying of the land of the Hindus, throwing bovine flesh and bones, honey trapping Hindu girls with fictitious Hindu names, and bringing co-religionists to the areas for habitations are some of the techniques adopted by EBOM to possess and force Hindu people to sell their land to EBOM. In fact, precisely for these reasons, a police station was established in Juria. Rather than being engaged in fighting with EBOM, the Assamese people preferred to leave their place quietly for other places in Nagaon.[95] Kalita presented four such case studies of villages to show how the local people were overthrown by the immigrant people.[96] In some cases, the immigrants used to pay high prices depending on the value and utility of those places.

Various illustrious writers of Assam have written in detail about how lands are occupied by EBOM in tribal areas. According to the poet and litterateur, Sahitya Akademi award winner and former DGP, Harekrishna Deka, in tribal blocks and belts, there is an area of 12,447,355 bighas or 1,659,647 hectares.

---

[94] Interestingly, these areas and constituencies have become the political epicentre for AIUDF and Congress Party where both the parties contest election with tacit understanding.

[95] Kalita, *Constitutional Protection of the Assamese*, 219–20.

[96] These villages are Salopara, Lalung Gaon, Dagoan Satra (the total families here around the 1930s were 300—now reduced to 45 families) and Simolu Aati Gaon. Ibid., 220–22.

According to report, as per a survey conducted in 1980, 79,594 *bighas* of land in the tribal blocks and belts have already been alienated. A large percentage of illegal settler appears to be Muslim settlers whose citizenship is doubted by the indigenous people on compelling reasons.[97]

One may get a glimpse of how lands are occupied in Assam from what the former DG BSF and a former Assam cadre IPS officer observed in his report on 10 February 1997:

> As Additional S.P. in 1968 in Nowgaon, I did not see a single Bangladeshi village in Jagi Road or in Kaziranga. In 1982, when I was posted as DIGP, Northern Range, Tezpur, five new Bangladeshi Muslim villages had come up near Jagi Road and hundreds of families had built up their huts encroaching into the land of the Kaziranga Game Sanctuary.

He mentioned that, in 1971, the large island of Chawalkhoa comprising 5,000 bighas of land was being cultivated by Assamese villagers from Gorukhut and Sanuna. He further stated:

> In 1982 when I was posted as DIGP, Tezpur, there was a population of more than 10,000 immigrant Muslims on the island. The pleas of the Assamese villagers to the District Administration to evict those people from the island fell on deaf ears. Any honest young IAS, SDO of Mangaldoi Sub-division who tried to do this, found himself transferred. In 1983 when an election was forced on the people of Assam ... the people of the villages living on the banks of the Brahmaputra opposite Chawalkhoa attacked the encroachers on this island, when they found that they had been given voting rights by the Government. It is of interest that Assamese Muslims of Sanuna village attacked the Bengali Muslim encroachers on this island. I am a direct witness to this.[98]

A renowned Vaisnavite and Sankardeva scholar, former professor of Assamese at Dibrugarh University, Dr Kesavananda Dev Goswami, devoted several of his articles to the challenges faced by the satra institutions at those areas, which are situated in the immigrant-prone

---

[97] Deka, 'Infiltration of Bangladesh Nationals into India', 43–44.

[98] As cited in the 'Report on Illegal Migration into Assam' published by the Governor of Assam, 8 November 1998, p. 8. Submitted to the President of India.

areas.[99] Professor Goswami's ancestral Bali Satra, which is located in an interior place of Nagaon, the hotbed of immigration, faced the wrath of immigrant Muslims.[100] He said that satras were mostly created to propagate Sankardeva's religion and culture at places which are away from the domestic indulgences and mass gatherings of hoi polloi. Those satras which were located away from the mainstream areas faced numerous challenges. These institutions became the centre for many anti-social elements. Many precious ornaments, valuable possessions treasured through many centuries as well as artefacts, books, etc., were either stolen or destroyed in the process of forceful possession of those items. Those incidents have often been reported in the newspapers, but these old institutions have rarely received any protection from the state authority. He lamented

> [I]t could be hardly denied in those nefarious activities of theft and burglary people of other religions are involved. Nobody can deny the fact the former religious minority people have turned the local Assamese as the minority in their own places. But if these incidents faced by the local people are told in public forum, they are immediately dubbed as the ultra Hindutva forces. ... [I]n this connection we may refer to the ghastly murder that took place in the Bor Elengi Satra at Uttar Lakhimpur. About seven years back from our own Bali Satra, many silver idols and other important jewels were stolen. ... [I]tems brought to build a museum at Bali Satra were also stolen. Those were reported to the police stations, but with no results. In fact in many cases, police themselves have become the object of attack from the immigrants. When the police officials came for the eviction of the Satra land, the police officials were injured by the encroachers by pelting stones.[101]

Professor Goswami further appealed to the people of Assam to ponder over the intentions of the religious people who are involved in those activities. Goswami found a pattern in those activities.

---

[99] Professor Goswami was conferred with the highest state government of Assam award, the 'Sankardeva Award' by Smti Sonia Gandhi for the year 2007.

[100] It may be mentioned that Bali Satra possessed many historical antiques and relics, of which the most important was the *Chitra Bhagawat* and many other historical items such as handwritten *sachipunthi* (bark manuscript).

[101] Goswami, 'Crisis of Satras of Assam and Appeal for Its Preservation', 163–67. Professor Goswami also blamed the Satrdhikarrs for sale of their lands to the Muslim immigrants.

Many suspect [that] they have been indulging in such activities with purposes. Sometimes people provide example of how even the Muslims have looked after Satras. However we must not forget how the Patekekbari Satra, even after erection of pillars at the land boundary—all were removed and occupied in one single night. Those Satras located in the far flung areas face such challenges.

Professor Goswami cited examples of many such satras which were extremely vulnerable to such challenges in the peripheral areas of Nagaon.[102] Satras and satriya culture represent the essence of Assamese culture, the role of which has already been outlined in the introductory chapter. The only all-India recognized classical dance of Assam is known as the 'satriya dance'. However, as statistics suggest, even today, various satras are located mostly in the immigrant-prone areas. According to a study, a total of 5,548 bighas of land belonging to the satras of Assam has been under illegal occupation and mostly by Muslim immigrants.[103]

Population Explosion of East Bengal Origin Muslims: 'Assam as an Immigrant-Driven Society'

An important question in Assam today is not merely about illegal migration; immigration process has slowed down, but it is about population explosion of homegrown EBOM, which has been acknowledged by many progressive Muslim writers, as we have mentioned above. The population explosion of EBOM is an issue that needs to be addressed. They are highly apprehensive about majoritarian notion of democracy that hardly considers their land, cultural and political rights. According to an estimate made by various scholars, Assam turning into a Muslim-dominant state is a question of time; what matters is when the state

---

[102] Some of these *satras* are Malancha, Roumari, Bali Satra, Raghunath, Somoria, Nikamul, Gonok-kuchi and Thukubil. Ibid., 166.

[103] SATRA Research Committee, *Encroachment of Satra Land*.

Table 6.2 *Satras Land under Occupation*

S. No.	Satra	District	Amount of Land (in Bighas)
1	Ramraay Kuthi	Dhubri	11 (132)
2	Shimalabari	Dhubri	195
3	Barpeta	Barpeta	460
4	Kaljar	Barpeta	136
5	Haripur	Barpeta	48
6	Patbaushi	Barpeta	81
7	Bhabanipur	Barpeta	117
8	Bahari	Barpeta	190
9	Joneea	Barpeta	160
10	Dhupardhal	Barpeta	182
11	Kobaikata	Morigaon	46
12	Patekeebari (Alipukhuree)	Morigaon	77
13	Bordowa	Nagaon	283
14	Balisatra	Nagaon	462
15	Rampur	Nagaon	584
16	ShalguriSatra (Dhing)	Nagaon	4
17	AdiElengy	Lakhimpur	1,900
18	BorElengy	Lakhimpur	105
19	Khatpur (Naoboicha)	Lakhimpur	48
20	Chipahi	Lakhimpur	34
21	Nikamul	Sonitpur	10
22	Bapopara	Goalpara	110
23	Damodar	Goalpara	46
24	Bishnupur	Goalpara	161
25	Chamareeya	Kamrup	50
26	Malancha	Kamrup	48
		Total	**5,548**

Source: SATRA Research Committee, *Encroachment of Satra Land.*

would become so.[104] Also, according to an estimate made by the Jamiat Ulema-E-Hind report, the Muslims in Assam had already attained the fifth generation in 2011, whereas the indigenous Assamese Hindus had attained only third generation in 1997.[105] Dr Abdul Mannan had also confirmed such a projection as a result of which, in about 11 years or so, Assam is likely to become a Muslim-dominant state. Further, it may be mentioned that with 34.24 per cent population (as per the census of 2011), Muslims are already the single most dominant homogeneous group in a multi-ethnic society like Assam. Hence, the very distinction of Hindu majority and Muslim minority based on the religious divide in Assam is more relative than actual. As a category, The Hindus maybe the largest, but the Hindus have more immediate primordial identities such as the Barak-Brahmaputra regional, tea garden-Adivasi, ethnic, Nepali, linguistic, upper and lower Assam identities. Moreover, the distinctions among Muslims whatever get blurred during critical periods such as the election. Besides, the voting turnout of the Muslims (which is more than 90%) is much higher than that of the Hindus. In addition, the Muslims vote as a community—as a group; an analysis of election results in EBOM-dominated areas would make it clear.

Incrementally, the number of Assam's Muslim-dominated districts has been increasing. The best reflection of this phenomenon could be found in the growth of AIUDF, an EBOM-dominated party. Leftist scholars Akhil Ranjan Dutta of Gauhati University have argued:

> The rise of AIUDF is directly linked to the issue of changing character of demographic change in the state. The 2011 census is very important in this regard. As per the census of 2011, total Hindu population stands at 61.47% and Muslim population at 34.22%. At the rural areas Hindus comprise 58.57% and Muslims comprise 36.85%. In 1971, Muslims in Assam comprised of 24.6%. Facts reveal that in 1971 only Dhubri and Hailakandi districts were Muslim majority; in 1991 four districts have

---

[104] For details, see Nath and Nath, 'The Change of Religion and Language Composition in the State of Assam in Northeast India', also see Mahanta, 'Population Winter in Assam'. Also see Sharma, 'Last Phase of Assam Agitation'. According to Sharma, if the voter list is counted as the population of the state—the rate of growth is much faster than the census population. He argues that in this manner Assam will become Muslim-dominated in about 10 years' times.

[105] Ali, *Bangladeshi Problem of Assam*, 25.

turned out to be Muslim dominated—Dhubri, Hailakandi, Goalpara and Barpeta. In 2001 six districts have become Muslim dominated; and in 2011 nine districts have become Muslim dominated. ... In these districts there are dominance of East Bengal origin Muslims. Immigration of Muslim to Assam mainly started in order to meet the British colonial economic interest. On the eve of partition and even in post partition days, the process of immigration more or less continued. The immigration process heightened during Bangladesh liberation war. The issue of unnatural growth of Muslim population in the state was linked to the issue of Immigration of Bangladeshi Muslims to Assam.[106]

It is clear that the Muslims dominate about 51 constituencies in Assam; in a total of 40 constituencies, they constitute about more than 35 per cent of the population. This is a formidable combination as minor alliances with any political party like Congress-I may change the political scenario of Assam permanently.[107] With more than 25 per cent concentration of population, the Muslim voters can make a swing in favour of any candidate considering the fact that the voting percentage of Muslim-dominated seats is highest in the state and they vote en bloc on religious considerations. Anything beyond 35 per cent population is considered to be a dreadful force for any electoral system which is based on first past to the post system.

Muslim-Dominated Seats as per Provision of 2014 Data (Computed from District Offices) (see Table 6.3)

Out of these 51 Muslim-dominated seats, AIUDF had won in 38 constituencies in various parliamentary and legislative assembly elections from 2006 to 2019. Looking at the way the EBOM population has been increasing, the expansion of these constituencies from 38 constituencies to 51 would only be a question of time. These constituencies where AIUDF has won are—(1) Karimganj (North), (2) Karimganj (South), (3) Badarpur, (4) Hailakandi, (5) Katlichera, (6) Algapur, (7) Sonai, (8) Borkhola, (9) Katigora, (10) Mankachar, (11) South Salmara, (12) Dhubri, (13) Gauripur, (14) Golokganj, (15)

---

[106] Dutta, *Possibility: Assam Assembly Election 2016*, 55 (translation by the author).

[107] A party in the Assam Assembly requires 63 seats to be declared as the single largest political party to form the government.

Table 6.3 Muslim-Dominated Seats as per Provision of 2014 Data (Computed from District Offices)

S. No.	Constituency (A)	25–34 (%)	S. No.	Constituency (B)	35–44%	S. No.	Constituency (C)	45 and above (%)
1	Udharbond	28	1	Patharkandi	35	1	Karimganj North	45
2	Lakhipur	28	2	Katlicherra	44	2	Karimganj South	63
3	Gossaigaon	27	3	Barkhola	41	3	Badarpur	55
4	Kokrajhar West	27	4	Katigora	41	4	Hailakandi	50
5	Bhabanipur	27	5	Goalpara East	35	5	Algapur	52
6	Sipajhar	32	6	Sorbhog	36	6	Sonai	57
7	Raha	29	7	Boko	44	7	Salmara South	98
8	Nowgong	32	8	Chaygaon	39	8	Mankachar	89
9	Hojai	30	9	Hajo	40	9	Dhubri	65
10	Lumding	27	10	Barkhetry	44	10	Gauripur	52
11	Naoboicha	30	11	Mangaldoi	43	11	Golakganj	45
			12	Samaguri	41	12	Bilasipara West	74
						13	Bilasipara East	49
						14	Abhayapuri North	51
						15	Abhayapuri South	45
						16	Goalpara West	55

(Continued)

Table 6.3 Continued

S. No.	Constituency (A) 25–3+ (%)	S. No.	Constituency (B) 35–44%	S. No.	Constituency (C) 45 and above (%)
				17	Jaleswar 82
				18	Barpeta 50
				19	Jania 92
				20	Baghbar 95
				21	Sarukhetri 55
				22	Chenga 76
				23	Dalgaon 73
				24	Laharighat 57
				25	Dhing 90
				26	Batadroba 47
				27	Rupohihat 81
				28	Jamunamukh 84

Number of constituencies above 25% (A+B+C)=51

Number of constituencies above 35% (B+C)=40

Number of constituencies above 45% (C)=28

Source: These figures are collected by the author from various district headquarters.

Bilasipara (West), (16) Bilasipara (East), (17) Abhyapuri (North), (18) Abhyapuri (South), (19) Goalpara (East), (20) Goalpara (South), (21) Joleswar, (22) Bhabanipur, (23) Barpeta, (24) Jonia, (25) Baghbar, (26) Sarukhetri, (27) Chenga, (28) Boko, (29) Boko, (30) Mangaldoi, (31) Dolgaon, (32) Roha, (33) Dhing, (34) Botodroba, (35) Rupohi Haat, (36) Jomunamukh, (37) Hojai and (38) Lumding.

In Assam, the dilemma is of two kinds: on the one hand, the sanctity of the Assam Accord which accepts 25 March 1971 as the cut-off date; on the other hand, fast-changing nature of the population in the state, thus justifying the acceptance of CAA-2019 in some form as it might facilitate the balancing of the Hindu population against the burgeoning Muslim population. It may be mentioned that due to Muslim population growth, the regional caste Hindu Assamese regional political party AGP has lost more than 10 seats in the state and never AGP had any chance of regaining those seats due to demographic change. That AGP has substantially reduced its grip in the state is not exclusively due to its lack of performance or deficiency of organizational strength; it is rather due to the huge demographic change that has been occurring in its former base. Some of those seats which AGP had lost permanently are (1) Gauripur, (2) Bilasipara (East), (3) Abhyapuri (South), (4) Goalpara (East), (5) Bhabanipur, (6) Sorukhetri, (7) Boko, (8) Chaygoan, (9) Abhyapuri (North), (10) Algapur, (11) Dhing, (12) Bilasipara (East), (13) Bilasipara (West), (14) Samaguri (15) Gossaigoan, etc. In addition, there are more than 15 seats which are placed almost on 50:50 chances for both AGP/BJP and AIUDF or EOBM candidates of Congress. It is just a question of time that these seats would permanently shift from the Assamese indigenous people to the other parties. Now, these issues may be brushed aside as 'secular-communal' issues; however, people on the ground do not accept such shift of seats as a normal secular issue. They are hugely concerned not only about the change of MLAs from their constituency but also about other sociocultural changes that occur on account of demographic change. It is precisely because of such demographic insecurity that the mantra of 'secularism' is almost getting confined to the discussions in a TV studio or the academic discourses of the Leftists ideologues rather than as an ideological plank for co-existence and mutual respect. Secularism in Assam must be based on mutual respect—of both majority and minority—to each other. In the absence of it, secularism in Assam ends as an 'identity crisis' for the indigenous and the local people. The Assamese nationality could hardly overcome the curse of history when continuous Muslim immigration pushed Assam to the proposed 'Pakistan'. It is based on the 'Muslim' as the single most dominant community of Assam that Assam was demanded to be included with Pakistan in the Muslim League conference held at Delhi in 1943:

> Assam is the land of minorities, where no one community has absolute majority over all others. Caste Hindus, Scheduled Castes, Muslims and Tribals are the four principal groups in the British territories in Assam. The population was 35 lakhs caste Hindus, 6 lakhs scheduled castes, 34 lakh Muslims and 25 lakhs tribals according to the census of 1941. Since then the usual influx of immigrants from Bengal, who are overwhelming Muslims, into Assam has continued. Apart from this, during the Bengal famine of 1942, it is roughly estimated that nearly half a million people, 90 percent of whom were Muslims, had migrated to Assam. It is therefore reasonable to conclude that Muslims form the single largest group of all communities today.[108]

The Muslims already comprise the largest bloc or community today in Assam. Will the process enrich Assamese nationality?

Bibliography

ABSU Patrika. 'Bodoland: The Battle Ground'. Guwahati, 2012. http://www.satp. org/satporgtop/countries/india/states/assam/terrorist_outfit/ndfb.

Aggrawala, 'Call Me by My Name: How Miyas of Assam Are Re-appropriating the Slur'. *Indian Express*, 31 July 2019.

Ahmed, S. U. *Muslims in Assam*. Nagaon: H. Nessa, 1999.

Ahmed, Abu Nasar. (ed.). *Nationality Question in Assam: The EPW 1980–81 Debate*. Guwahati: OKD Institute of Social Change and Development & Akansha Publishing House, 2006.

---

[108] A long proposal was submitted by the Muslim League working committee member, Abdul Matin Chaudhury—a representative from Assam. For details see, Sabhapandit, *From Sayyid Saddullah to Gopinath Bordoloi*, 219.

Ahmed, Abu Nasar. *Madrasas in Assam*. Guwahati & Delhi: Akansha Publishing House, 2015.

Ahmed, Mufti Nur. 'Nation-breaking Politics by Badaruddin in the Name of Jamiat'. *Janambhumi*, 1 February 2017 (translation by the author).

Ahmed, Abu Nasser, and Adil-ul-Yasin. 'Problems of Identity, Assimilation and Nation-Building: A Case Study of the Muslim of Assam'. In *Politics of Identity and Nation-Building in North-East India*, edited by Girin Phukan and N. L. Dutta. Dibrugarh: Dibrugarh University, 1997.

Ali, Zamser. *Bangladeshi Problem of Assam: Myth and Reality*. New Delhi: Jamiat Ulema-E-Hind, 2014.

Ali, Illias. *Jonobisfuronor Pom Khedi* (in Assam). Guwahati: Maleka Foundation, 2015.

Barua, Jishnu. (ed.). *A Brief Report on Linguistic, Communal and Ethnic Conflicts in Assam*. Guwahati: Government of Assam, CM Secretariat, 2014.

Baruah, Sanjib. 'Assam Cudgel of Chauvinism or Tangled Nationality Question?' *Economic & Political Weekly* XV, no. 11 (15 March 1980): 543–45.

———. *India Against Itself: Assam and the Politics of Nationality (Critical Histories)*. Pennsylvania: University of Pennsylvania Press, 1999.

Bhattacharya, Hiranya Kumar. *Sinta-Duhsinta: Ji Koth Nohol Kuwa* (in Assamese) Guwahati, 1993.

Borkataki, Arindam (ed.), *Nivedan Swajan-Chinta* (interview between Pradip Jyoti Mahanta and Dr Hiren Gohain). Nagaon: Kailash Kumar Rajkhowa, Krantikaal Prakashan, 2016.

Brass, Paul. *Politics in India Since Independence*. Cambridge: Cambridge University Press, 2006.

Choudhury, Anil Roy. *Asomot Bangladeshi*. Nagaon: Jagaran Sahitya Prakashan, 2009.

CJP. *A Brief History of the Insider vs Outsider Debate in Assam: In Conversation with Prof. Abdul Mannan*. https://cjp.org.in/a-brief-history-of-the-insider-vs-outsider-debate-in-assam.

Deka, Harekrishna. 'Infiltration of Bangladesh Nationals into India'. In *Illegal Migration from Bangladesh*, edited by B.B. Kumar. Delhi: Concept Publishing Company, 2006.

Dutta, Akhil Ranjan. *Possibility: Assam Assembly Election 2016*. Guwahati: Rainbow Publication, 2016. (in Assamese; translation by the author)

Gohain, Hiren. 'Cudgel of Chauvinism'. *Economic & Political Weekly* XV, no. 8 (23 February 1980): 418–20.

———. *Assam: A Burning Question*. Guwahati: Spectrum, 1985.

Goswami, Kesavananda Dev. 'Crisis of Satras of Assam and Appeal for Its Preservation' (in Assamese). In *Annunad: Srimanta Sankardeva and Assamese Culture*, edited by Ranjit Dev Goswami. Guwahati: Setubandha, 2012.

Government of Assam. *White Paper on Foreigner's Issue*. Home and Political Department, October 2012.

Greater Kashmir. *Jamiat-e-Ulema-e-Hind Clarifies: Have No Connection with Politics*. https://www.greaterkashmir.com/news/kashmir/jamiat-e-ulema-e-hind-clarifies-have-no-connection-with-politics/.

Hazarika, Sanjay. 'Illegal Migration from Bangladesh: Problem and Long-Term Perspective'. In *Illegal Migration from Bangladesh*, edited by B. B. Kumar. New Delhi: Concept Publishing Company, 2006.

Hussain, Monirul. *The Assam Movement: Class, Ideology and Identity*. New Delhi: Manak Publications, 1993.

Hussain, Sajjad. 'Asomor Muslim Rajnitee' (Muslim Politics of Assam). In *Nivedan Swajan-Chinta*, edited by Arindam Borkataki. Nagaon: Kailash Kumar Rajkhowa, Krantikaal Prakashan, 2016a.

Hussain, Wasbir. 'Jihadis from Bangladesh: Eyeing Trans-Border Playing Fields?' 11 July 2016b, http://www.ipcs.org/comm_select.php?articleNo=5077.

Kakoti, Arindom. (ed.). *Assam Agitation and Assam's Muslim Politics*. Nagaon: Krantikal, 2016.

Kalita, Ramesh Chandra. 'Prabajankarir Samasya Aru Asom: Anandaram Dhekiyal Phukanar Para Gopinath Bardaloi Loike'. In *Asom Andolan: Pratisruti Aru Phalasruti*, edited by Hiren Gohain and Dilip Borah. Guwahati: Banalata, Panbazar, 2007.

Kalita, Pulin. *Constitutional Protection of the Assamese* (in Assamese). Guwahati: Jagoron Sahitya Prakash, 2020.

Kar, M. *Muslims in Assam Politics*. New Delhi: Omsons Publications, 1990.

Kimura, Makiko. *The Nellie Massacre of 1983: Agency of Rioters*. New Delhi: SAGE Publications, 2013.

Mahanta, Nani Gopal. 'Politics of Space and Violence in Bodoland'. *Economic & Political Weekly* 48, no. 23 (8 June 2013a): 49–58. (Special Article)

———. *Confronting the State*. New Delhi: SAGE Publications, 2013b.

Mahanta, Manas Kumar. *Asomiya Jatiyatabadar Itihass*. Nagaon: Jagaran Sahitya Prakash, 2017.

Mahanta, Nani Gopal. 'Population Winter in Assam'. (in Assamese: *Jonosankhyak Sitkalin) Amar Asom*, 14 June 2018.

Mannan, Abdul. *Infiltration: Genesis of Assam Movement*. Guwahati: Aaina Prakashan, 2018.

Misra, Udayon. *Periphery Strikes Back*. Shimla: IIAS, 1991.

———. *India's North-East: Identity Movements, State, and Civil Society*. New Delhi: OUP, 2014.

Nath, Manoj Kumar. 'Communal Politics in Assam'. *Economic & Political Weekly* LI, no. 16 (16 April 2016): 88–93.

Nath, Bhupen Kr, and Dilip Nath. 'The Change of Religion and Language Composition in the State of Assam in Northeast India: A Statistical Analysis Since 1951 to 2001'. *International Journal of Scientific and Research Publications* 2, no. 5 (May 2012): 1–6.

Omvedt, Gail. 'Assamese People's Agitation'. *Economic & Political Weekly* XV, no. 12 (22 March 1980): 580.

Phukan, Girin. *Politics of Regionalism in Northeast India*. Guwahati: Spectrum, 1996.

Ray, Jayanta Kumar. 'Migration from (East Bengal/East Pakistan) Bangladesh to India'. In *Illegal Migration from Bangladesh*, edited by B. B. Kumar. New Delhi: Concept Publishing Company, 2006.

Rizvi, Tabassum. 'Political Participation and Voting Behaviour'. PhD Thesis, Department of Political Science, Faculty of Arts, Gauhati University, 2018.

Routray, Bibhu Prasad. *India's Northeast: Islamist Militancy in Assam?* (13 February 2013). http://www.ipcs.org/comm_select.php?articleNo=3814.

Sarmah, Anjan. *Asom Andolanar Asompurna Itihaas*, 652–82. Guwahati: Bhabani Books, 2018.

SATRA Research Committee. *Encroachment of Satra Land: A Field Report*. Guwahati: North East Policy Institute, 2011.

Sabhapandit, Ranjit. *From Sayyid Saddullah to Gopinath Bordoloi*. Guwahati: Assam Publishing Company, 2014.

———. (ed.). *Prottoi Aru Annewesan: Selective Writings of Baneswar Saikia*. Guwahati: Assam Publishing Company, 2017.

Sharma, Rajdip. 'Last Phase of Assam Agitation' (in Assamese: *Asom Andolanor Antim Parjaya*). *Amar Asom* (22 July 2013).

Conclusion

Political Hindutva, CAA-NRC and Ethnic Identity

Assam has always been a favourite destination for migrants, which poses substantial challenges to the Assamese identity process. This book attempts to address questions like how the composite Assamese nationality has been evolving—who are the stakeholders and how did they contribute to the nationality formation process? How has the entry of new stakeholders created contestations and contradictions? How did land, language and culture become the central theme of Assamese identity, and how have they been undermined since the days of colonial politics?

I have argued in the first chapter that the character of Assamese society is defined by a liberal and humanitarian outlook. The Vaisnavite philosophy, as enunciated by Sankardeva, Madhavdeva and his apostles, defined the cultural essence of Assamese nationality. By visiting various holy places of India, Sankardeva drew his philosophical essence from the Vedas, Puranas, Upanishads, Tantras and the Gita. The 'Bharatabarsha' was considered as a *punya bhumi* (holy land), *janma bhumi* (motherland) and *karma bhumi* (land of 'karma' or action). Sukapha, the great Ahom king, and his successors and other provincial kings such as those of Koch kingdom and many others, too, contributed to the Assamese nationality formation process. The Assamese society thus is a unique melange of Aryan and non-Aryan cultures.

For co-existence in a multicultural and multi-religious society, the maintenance of the Assamese version of the Vaisnavite Hindu tradition will be critical in the days to come rather than following the central or South Indian versions of Hinduism. While there is no distinction in the essence of Hindu religion, the local dynamics and local processes do add certain nuanced versions of culture, which are of critical importance for a state like Assam. Even Sankardeva, who drew his inspiration from Vedas and Upanishads, contextualized them within the Assamese society—elements that were essentially Assamese. With the growing Hindutva awareness in the state, there have been attempts to mix the nuanced version of Assamese Vaisnavism with the more ritualistic version of Hinduism. Institutions like *satra*, *naamghar*, *Sankar Sangha* and *Satra Mahasabha* are not merely religious institutions, but they are also sociocultural organizations that have contributed to the composite character of Assamese identity. The *naamghar* and the *satriya bhakti* way of life depict a certain lifestyle that encompasses the entire social system of Assam.

Religion has never been the central marker of Assamese identity, although the centrality of religion becomes critical when *Sanatani-Mahapurusia* culture is challenged. This was more so when the Muslim League attempted to systematically overthrow the Assamese essence during the pre-colonial period. However, even then, the struggle was never depicted as a struggle between the Hindus and the Muslims. As we have argued in the first chapter, nationalist stalwarts like Ambikagiri Raichaudhury were highly critical about the Muslim League and resisted their efforts to encroach the indigenous symbols of Assam like the Patbausi Satra where a mosque was about to be constructed. Raichaudhury decried such effort through his organization called *Atmarakshi Bahini*. However, Raichaudhury made it clear that his opposition to the Muslim League is not against any religion, whether Hinduism or Islam. This fight is between nationalism and anti-nationalism.

The emergence of BJP in Assam in the post-2014 period was preceded by the efforts of the Jan Sangh/BJP and RSS to establish its footprint in Assam's anti-foreigner agitation of 1979. It may be mentioned that the RSS/Hindu Mahasabha had a long presence in Assam since the pre-independence period when an effort was made by the Muslim League to convert Assam into a Muslim-dominated state through census in 1941. Gopinath Bordoloi and the Congress vehemently opposed the efforts of the Muslim League and demanded that it should be verified by an independent body. 'The Assam Tribune editorially commented on 31 January that the Hindus of Assam should unite and take adequate measures to counteract the sinister move'.[1] Veer Savarkar—the President of All India Hindu Mahasabha—played an important role in mobilizing the public opinion of Assam against such move by the Muslim League government.[2]

How BJP made inroads into the Assamese ethnic identity process would require elaborate analysis; however, it would suffice to say that their approach to the immigration-induced identity process in Assam is marked by three distinct phases. The first phase may be described as 'Immigrants vs Nationals' during the Assam Agitation period from 1979–1980 onwards. The second phase is *Jati-Mati-Bheti* or 'Last Battle of Saraighat' from 2014 onwards. The third phase may be broadly classified as 'Clash of Civilisation and Culture' from 2019–2020.

During the Assam Agitation, the BJP leadership under A. B. Bajpayee, L. K. Advani and Arun Shourie provided all ideological and logistical support to the movement. In its Bombay session, BJP suggested that the post-1971 batch of foreigners should be deported. However, the party hastened to add that the case of bonafide refugees would be considered based on Government of India's policy pronouncements.[3] In a report in the *Indian Express* dated 25 August 1980, a strong supporter of Assam agitation, A. B. Vajpayee, made a clear distinction between the infiltrators and refugees. Although BJP considered the Assam Agitation as a clash between 'immigrant's vs nationals', they espoused the cause of the Bengali Hindus in Assam as per policy preferences of the Government of India and the persecuted Bengali Hindus did not come under the rubric of 'immigrant'.

The 2014 general election and, more particularly, the 2016 State Assembly election in Assam may be dubbed as the 'regionalisation' phase of BJP, which is away from its traditional Hindi–Hindutva–Hindustani base. The party conceptualized a 'rainbow coalition' whereby various ethnic-regional political parties were incorporated

---

[1] As cited in Bhuyan and Barpujari, *Political History of Assam*, 267. See *Assam Tribune*, 31 January 1941 and also 10 October 1941.

[2] Ibid., 265–66.

[3] Chhabra, *Assam Challenge*, 106.

into the NDA alliance.[4] According to Professor Udyon Misra, BJP's victory in Assam

> ... was the result of the BJP's success in garnering the support of regional forces like the Asom Gana Parishad, the Bodoland People's Front and the Rabha, Tiwa and other plains tribal organisations .... There was no Hindutva agenda as such in these elections and the emphasis was clearly on preserving the identity and culture of the indigenous people of the state in the face of rapid demographic changes triggered by infiltration from neighbouring Bangladesh'.[5]

BJP was successful in mobilizing the insecurity of the indigenous people of the state that emerged on account of the unbridled explosion of East Bengal origin Muslims. BJP very adroitly popularized the notion that the nationality, land and hearth (euphemistically called— *jati, mati and bheti*) are in danger and dubbed the 2016 election as the 'last battle of Saraighat'.[6]

From 2019–2020 onwards, on the eve of State General Election in the state in 2021, BJP has been increasingly focusing on the dictum of 'Clash of Civilisation' whereby the irreconcilable clashes between the Assamese and EBOM have been highlighted. This drift from identity dimension of indigenous people to a clash of civilization discourse has caused serious apprehensions among those people who put Assamese identity issue as 'foreigner's versus nationals' rather than problems of 'Hindus and Muslims'. Many indigenous and regional groups have started highlighting upon how BJP has been diluting the basic philosophy of Sankardeva in the name of Hinduization and saffronization. Professor Apurba Baruah urges that through the existing political process, there has been an effort to impose North and South Indian Hindu cultures that even look down upon fish-eating Brahmins

---

[4] Later on, a new platform known as Northeast-Democratic Alliance (NEDA) was created on 23 May 2016 to provide a platform to various ethnic and regional political parties of the region. Subsequently, the first conclave of NEDA was held in Guwahati on 13 July 2016, which was attended by various regional leaders, including the Chief Ministers of BJP and other regional parties of the region.

[5] Misra, 'Victory for Identity Politics, Not Hindutva in Assam', 20.

[6] The essence of the 2016 election is reflected in Sethi, *The Last Battle of Saraighat*.

in Assam.[7] There has been a gradual displacement of the Vaisnavite Bhakti and Shakti traditions of Assam with a more ritualistic and con-secrated version of Hinduism. There is an upsurge of rituals like *jogya, bhumi pujan, and havan* for almost all government functions which were previously conducted with *naam kirton-songkirtaan, borgeet, satriya* dances or through *saraswati bandana*. It is not that there were no Vedic rituals before; however, previously, it was all in the private domain or as the practice of a group away from the state glare; suddenly, there is a huge recognition of religious practices with a great amount of government sanctity. The ritualization of Namami Brahmaputra[8] by bringing priests and *purohits* from central India was viewed as a part of new emerging cultural politics in Assam. The people of Assam revere the Brahmaputra as *mahabahu* (mighty) in sync with a great song of Dr Bhupen Hazarika. The Brahmaputra is considered to be a male river and was never worshipped or deified the way it was done through state-sponsored rituals. Even within the precincts of the historic Kamakhya temple, the procession of *naga-sadhus* is a rare phenomenon during the Ambubachi Mela in the way it is seen today.

The maintenance and nourishment of Vaisnavite Hinduism and practices of other nature-based faiths are crucial for Assam as all other religious and cultural groups in the state are acquainted with this pluralistic model of religion where one could find a representation of all sections of society, including the Muslims and other downtrodden sections of the society. Assam does not want to compromise with this version of Vaisnavism as this is integrally embedded within the cultural essence of the Assamese nationality.

Assamese nationality, as we have argued in the previous chapters, has been maintaining its majority through a composite character of various subnational groups. However, the overall identity of this smaller nationality is in crisis as there is a numerical threat from EBOM. It is only through an understanding and hermeneutical discourse that

---

[7] Baruah, *Facebook Video*. Also see FB live 8 October 2020 at 12:40pm, www.facebook.com/apurbakumar.baruah.1/videos

[8] In tune with *Namami Gange* which was started for river Ganga, the Assamese people in Assam were not comfortable with such ritualistic celebration of *Namami Brahmaputra*.

both the contending groups can appreciate each other's concern. If EBOM appreciate the existential dilemma of Assamese nationality and address it in true earnest, there is no reason why they should not be considered as a part of the Assamese nationality. Already, there is awareness among the progressive section of EBOM regarding the challenges posed by population explosion and land encroachment.

However, denial of any potential problems on the part of EBOM and branding of Assamese nationality as 'xenophobic' and 'intolerant' would halt such an assimilation process. It may perhaps be stated that the increasing assertions of EBOM, particularly from the Miya Muslims,[9] have added further complications to the whole identity conundrum. Some of those initiatives of EBOM that enhance the insecurity of the Assamese people are the formation of 'Miya-Sahitya Parishad' and Assamese Miya Parishad, development of Miya Poetry as a distinct genre and the latest is the demand for the establishment of Miya museum on the eve of 2021 election.[10] Interestingly, such assertions have not come from Barak valley Muslims or the Sylheti and the indigenous Muslims of upper and lower Assam. It is the newly emerging middle class of Miya Muslims and the politicians belonging to those areas who have become increasingly assertive. While Assamese nationality has already welcomed EBOM as 'neo-Assamese', increasing assertions reminisce the trajectory of Muslim politics in the pre-independence period and that causes insecurity to the Assamese

[9] Although Miya Muslims denote EBOM, more specifically they are meant to be those residing in the lower and central Assam Brahmaputra valley areas, particularly in riverine char areas. However, to say that the Miya Muslims are concentrated only in the Char areas of Assam is a myth as they have been moving to other parts of Assam (like Upper Assam) for livelihood, manual work, education, etc.

[10] Miya Museum has been demanded by MLA of Baghbor Sherman Ali and other minority members of Congress in October–November 2020. They argue that the proposal was passed by the standing committee on Art and culture of Assam Assembly on 24 March 2019 in which there were certain BJP and AGP members. However, the suggestion that was made by the standing committee was for the 'char-chapori' people which denote not only East Bengal Muslims but also people living in other 'Char' areas such as Majuli. It may be added here that the 'chapori' is the traditional occupational place for Nepali graziers and other tribal communities such as 'Mishing". For a definition of char-chapori' areas, see PhD thesis Rizvi, *Political Participation and Voting Behaviour Women and Politics in the Char Areas of Assam*. http://hdl. handle.net/10603/245569

nationality. As we have argued in the sixth chapter, the emerging Miya elites and politicians hardly focus on those socioeconomic and human development indices that are holding them back. Hardly the new elites of EBOM talk about the population explosion, lack of family planning and other scientific means of education and Muslim women empowerment. The result is that no longer can the riverine areas cater to the needs of the community, and the burgeoning population move out to other parts of Assam in search of land and livelihood where they come in clash with indigenous community's resources. It is precisely such populations' explosion; literary, political and cultural assertions; and their march to other parts of Assam that push the Assamese nationality in search of the security provider. Smaller, fragmented regional political parties are no longer viewed as the platform for protecting a cohesive Assamese identity the way it was conceptualized in the post-Assam Agitation phase. BJP in Assam and the region has been gradually accepted as a political party that can confront such attack on the foundation of broad Assamese nationality at the behest of EBOM. Prasanta Rajguru, a senior journalist and former chief editor of popular Assamese daily *Amar Asom* argued that right from the moment of the formation of AIUDF in 2006, the indigenous populations of the state were highly apprehensive about their expansion. Since then, *Khilonjiyas* (the sons of the soil) were in search of a force against the increasing political assertions of the Bengali origin Muslims in the state. From 2006 onwards, this platform was provided by Congress until the place was filled up by a more uncompromising BJP in 2016.[11] However, at the behest of BJP, this political manoeuvre was not completely in sync with the inward-looking regional narrative of the Assam Agitation period. As a result, many *jatiyatabadi* regional organizations did not feel happy at BJP's bonhomie with Bengali Hindus and newly enacted citizenship Act of 2019. Nonetheless, BJP's entry into all the social bases of Assam was nearly complete except the Muslims.[12]

This book is not a typical historical chronicle. It tries to view how the politics of history has determined contemporary identity politics

---

[11] Rajguru and Asom, *Khilonjiyar Shakti*.

[12] For details on how BJP/NDA has entered various social bases of Assam, see, Sharma and Tripathy, 'Assam-2019: NDA Deepens Its Dominance', 23–25.

in Assam. It tries to analyse how a massive immigration process had started at the beginning of the century. What were the reactions of the Assamese leaders and how was the issue debated and discussed from the 1920s till the 1940s in state legislative councils and assemblies? The book devotes a notable portion of the book to the role played by the Muslim League and its leaders like Syed Saadulla and Maulana Bhasani. What was their ideological stand on Assam and their design to make Assam a part of Pakistan? Finally, the book devotes a significant portion of two important current debates: NRC and CAA-2019. Both the issues have been discussed within their historical contexts.

Going beyond conceptual definition, the book is the first of its kind that tries to analyse the growth and nature of Assamese nationality and, in the process, questions some of the underlying assumptions on identity and religion, as highlighted by the Leftist–Marxist scholarship. I argue that both NRC and CAA-2019 are the unresolved legacies of the Partition. The current debate on NRC and CAA-2019 hardly takes into account the historical contexts under which these issues are unfolding in today's context. Going beyond commentary and rhetoric, our analysis on NRC and CAA-2019 may perhaps be cited as the first academic effort to analyse the twin issues from historical perspectives.

There is a general uneasiness among scholars to talk about the plight and rights of the Bengali Hindus. A sizeable portion of Bengali Hindus has been rehabilitated in Assam in the post-independence period. There was a vibrant debate about undesirable immigration and displaced Hindus and other minorities in the Indian Parliament in the late 1940s and the early part of 1950s. Somehow, those discussions and issues related to the Bengali Hindus in the context of Assamese identity have been dodged over, and only one dimension is over-highlighted that there was huge resistance towards Bengali Hindu settlement in Assam. But this is a half-truth, only one side of the story. The stalwarts and protectorates of Assamese identity forcefully argued for the rights and rehabilitation of the displaced Bengali Hindus both in the Constituent Assembly debates and also in the Indian Parliament debates, and all this was a part of protecting the Assamese and Indian identity. Glossing over these discussions would constitute a serious omission of contemporary history. Dr Jayanta Kumar Ray, formerly

Centenary Professor of International Relations, Calcutta University, and former Vice-Chairman, Maulana Abul Kalam Azad Institute of Asian Studies, said:

> While discussing migration from Bangladesh to India, it is politically as well as ethically important to distinguish between refugees, i.e. Hindus, and infiltrators, i.e. Muslims. Circumstances of the 1947 Partition, assurances given by top-ranking political leaders of India to Hindus staying on in Pakistan (including East Bengal), and an uninterrupted squeezing out of Hindus from East Bengal/East Pakistan/Bangladesh since 1947 in contrast to the care with which Muslims are safeguarded in the secular-democratic polity of India, a contrast that is even compatible with the appeasement of, or blackmail by, minorities (mainly Muslims) in India—sustain this categorisation of migrants from Bangladesh into refugees and infiltrators.[13]

Gaurishankar Bhattacherjee, a prominent Gandhian and a communist leader, was a four-time MLA of Assam Legislative Assembly.[14] Professor Akhil Ranjan Dutta writes,

> Gaurishankar Bhattarcharyya for almost three decades from 1950 to 1970 was one of the most vocal, dominant and respectable members in the Legislative Assembly. He was truly a conscience keeper in Assembly ... for long 21 years in the Assembly [he] played the role of a historian, legal and constitutional expert, proponent of the rights of the peasantry and the downtrodden ... tak[en] together he was the symbol and sentinel of the mass aspirations of the diverse communities of Assam.[15]

Here, the opinion of such a noted Gandhian on Bengali Hindus is significant because there is an impression given by the CAA protagonists that the issues of Bengali Hindus were repugnant to the interests of the Assamese. Gaurishankar Bhattacherjee's opinion on Bengali Hindu refugees and their settlement in the state is significant to quote here:

> Many Bengali refugees have been given shelter and rehabilitation in Assam. I hope government will not become very harsh and push them forcefully

---

[13] Ray, 'Migration from (East Bengal/East Pakistan) Bangladesh to India', 36.

[14] In 1952 and 1957, he was elected as the Member of CPI; later, he was elected as an independent candidate.

[15] Dutta, *The Conscientious Statesman: Gaurishankar Bhattacharyya*, xxi–xiv.

... when we apply the constitutional and legal provisions we must also look into the humanitarian and practical dimension ... it has to be within the parameters of law ... while resolving the foreigner problem, one can't look at the illegal migrant and refugees from the same prism. If we settle the illegal migrants, it will jeopardise Assam's identity and India's security will also be under threat.[16]

A lot of scholars argued in favour of regularization of Hindus Bengalis in the state. Sanjay Hazarika had pleaded:

[A]s for the new exodus of Hindus from Bangladesh, they are true refugees, they are not migrants. They are as traumatised, frightened and brutalised as refugees in any other part of the world and this has been seen especially since the new government in Bangladesh took over.[17]

As I have argued in Chapters 4 and 5, rehabilitation and resettlement of the Bengali Hindus remained an important factor in contemporary Assam's politics. Somehow, many scholars writing on Assam do not feel it polite to talk about the burning issue. The Assam Agitation was a platform where the issues regarding Bengali refugees were discussed with contradictory standpoints both by AASU and the Government of India. In his book about the Immigrants (Expulsion from Assam) Act, 1950, Prafulla Kumar Mahanta has stated that

it is not at all difficult to read the Act between the lines. The Act openly encouraged free entry for a particular religion or community on the pretext that they were victims of Application of Citizenship Laws in Assam, ... in secular India the Hindu East Pakistanis were permitted to settle as refugees and the Muslim East Pakistanis were thrown out.[18]

Here, apart from the government's[19] stand, it would be noteworthy to gauge the initiative of some nationally reputed NGOs who were committed to resolving the Assam Agitation issue. B. G. Verghese, a

---

[16] Bhattacherjee, *The Agony of Indigenous People*, 16.

[17] Hazarika, 'Illegal Migration from Bangladesh', 30.

[18] Mahanta, *The Struggle in Assam*, 37–38. For details, see the chapter on 'Application of Citizenship Laws in Assam'.

[19] To understand the Government of Assam and Government of India's stands on the refugee issue, please see chapters four and five of this book.

friend of Assam, and others from the Gandhi Peace Foundation visited Assam and made the following proposals:

1. Foreigners should be detected based on the Constitution and existing laws. In doing so, the NRC 1951 and the 1952 electoral rolls and other relevant papers shall be accepted as documents for detection. An account shall be taken of those who could not be enumerated in the 1951 Census because of the communally disturbing situation.
2. Foreigners found to have entered Assam between 1951 and 1961 shall be conferred citizenship as a matter of course.
3. Foreigners of Bangladesh origin who entered Assam after 25 March 1971 shall be liable to deportation.
4. A humanitarian view may be taken in deserving cases of persons who are foreigners and who had entered Assam between 1961 and 25 March 1971. Their names shall, however, be deleted from the electoral rolls.
5. Persons who have been admitted to Assam from East Pakistan/ Bangladesh and who are eligible under the policy instructions issued by the central government or in respect of whom some commitment exists from Government that they should be treated as refugees shall be granted citizenship.
6. Those eligible for Indian citizenship by marriage, etc., under the Citizenship Act shall be favourably considered for grant of citizenship.
7. Efforts will be made to distribute the residuary number of foreigners, especially the 1961–25 March 1971 category, among other states so that Assam does not have to bear the burden disproportionately.

Thus, the Gandhi Peace Foundation (GPF) made very explicit suggestions for those persons who were eligible under the policy instructions issued by the central government and in respect of whom commitments had been made by the government that they would be treated as refugees.[20] GPF went to the extent of accepting other relevant

---

[20] Chhabra, *Assam Challenge*, 104–105.

documents besides NRC, 1951 and the 1952 electoral rolls. Besides, the Leftist parties were the staunchest supporters of the Bengali Hindu minority issue. It was argued:

> Amongst the political parties, only the leftist made their position unequivocally clear on the issue .... During debates in Parliament, apart from the Congress-I, leftist MPs would unfailingly recall the National commitments to the minorities left stranded in East Pakistan consequent on Partition and attribute their flight to India to recurring communal disturbances in that country. In Assam, the lefties groups were seen as deriving their support from the Bengali community and their espousal of the cause of the migrants was regarded as a sinister move to consolidate the position of the CPM. Since the CPM held sway in West Bengal and Tripura, its support for the Bengali community settled in Assam was suspected as part of a grand design to carve out portions from Assam to form a Greater Bengal.[21]

Gopal Krishna drew attention to the issue in the following manner:

> To concede that the Assamese have a serious case, does not, however, diminish the legitimacy of the Bengalis, who are among the most injured people in the sub-continent. Their misfortune has its source in the partition of India and the consequent division of Bengal. Remember that in 1947, the partition of India was reluctantly accepted by the Congress in order to protect Assam from the not so tender mercy of 'Muslim Bengal'. The price of that decision has been paid dearly, in the main by the Hindus of East Bengal. When forced out of their homes by the majority community in East Bengal/Bangladesh, the victims sought shelter in Assam Tripura and West Bengal. The latter two have accommodated between two-thirds and three-quarters of the Hindu refugees, while the rest found a new home in Assam.[22]

Many Assamese politicians adopted a soft stand towards the Bengali Hindus to counter the balance of the burgeoning growth of EBOM. Nibaran Bora argues that given the massive inflow of Muslim immigrants from East Bengal, Mahendra Mohan Chaudhury rehabilitated maximum refugees from 1957 to 1971.[23] Jyotirmoy Jana also argues

---

[21] Ibid., 104. To see how leftist political parties and organisations vouched for the cause of the Hindu refugees, please refer to the appendix of chapter five.

[22] *Times of India*, 9 March 1983.

[23] Bora, 'Mohendra Mohan Chaudhury amulotoei sarbadhik bhoganiar punorbarshan hoisil', 1, 3 and 10.

that Chaudhury did this to counter the massive scale of Muslim immigrants from Bangladesh.[24] Not only in post-1960s and 1970s, but also in various phases of its contemporary history, the Assamese nationality developed alliances with various ethnic and religious groups in order to maintain its ascendancy. The Assamese nationality was never in majority by exclusive reliance on its caste-Hindu groups. It is through alliances and coalition that 'Assamese-ness' has been maintained. The Assamese nationality never considered migrants from South India, Marwaris, Biharis, Nepalis and tea-garden people as immigrants, which was officially accepted by the British administration. This accommodation was never accorded to the immigrants of Mymensingh. Although this restriction was officially lifted in the 1940s by the Muslim League government, the Assamese nationality once again fought for its supremacy in the census of 1941 when the Muslim League government decided to put the tribal as a separate category from the Assamese Hindus.

It was precisely in such circumstances that on the eve of Pandu Congress, Rajendra Prasad who became the President of India made an elaborate plan for bringing Hindus from the Chapar district of Bihar. Ramesh Chandra Kalita argues that this was done to maintain the domination of Hindus. Kalita says:

> The 85 percent of immigrants that immigrated into Assam were Muslims and hence there was created an environment of communal conflict. There was a possibility of Hindus being minority from the viewpoint of population composition in Assam. In order to remain the majority of Hindus, Dr. Rajendra Prasad (who became President of India later on) introduced a scheme to let the Hindus of Bihar to migrate into Assam which was responded to by the Assamese middle class. His autobiography provides information on how he introduced a scheme of migration of Hindus from Bihar to check Muslim immigration from Mymensingh and East Bengal.[25]

Although we quoted this statement in an earlier chapter, it is worthwhile to repeat what Rajendra Prasad had said,

---

24 Jana, 'Andolan Aru Motantor' 174.

25 Kalita, 'Prabajankarir Samasya Aru Asom', 28.

I sounded the Assamese on this subject and they welcomed it. They told me that they liked the Bihari labourers and did not like the people of Mymensingh, whose treatment of the local population was far from satisfactory. Some thought it better to have the Hindus of Bihar than the Muslims of Mymensingh. The communal feeling was uppermost in man's minds then and Assam was no exception. They welcomed the idea also because by themselves the Assamese were unable to bring the land under the plough. But the influx of Muslims from Mymensingh was upsetting the population ratio, and the Assamese wanted to retain a majority in the Brahmaputra Valley. The influx from Mymensingh could be counted only by allowing the Bihar Hindus to settle down on the land.[26]

Thus, in retrospect, it could be safely argued that Assamese nationality maintains its distinctiveness and numerical majority through alliances. The issue of 'Assamese-ness' did not become a critical issue from the 1950s until the 1980s; however, from the period of Assam Agitation, the protection of Assamese culture and its distinctiveness has become a major variable in recent times. This perhaps is the most important reason why the CAA/CAB agitation from 2016–2019 could not cross beyond certain points in Assam. Although the agitators claim to have represented more than 59 organizations, one could hardly notice the mass participation of ethnic and indigenous groups of Assam in the said agitation. In the absence of those ethnic communities, the CAA agitation has remained a limited AASU-centric caste-Hindu protest which wants to drive away foreigners, whose character of had changed since 1985.

However, while regularizing the Hindu Bengalis till December 2014, it may be mentioned that the act of granting citizenship to foreigners, be they Hindu or Muslims, needs to be frozen forever in a state like Assam. Granting of citizenship cannot be an open-ended option for a state like Assam, which has received perhaps the highest number of illegal migrants in the post-Independence period. Besides, Assam's density of population has been alarmingly increasing with heavy pressure on land and forest reserves.[27]

[26] Ibid.

[27] As per the 2011 census, the population density of Assam stands at 497 per sq km in comparison to 382 per sq km national average. In some immigrant-dominated areas,

As shown above, the book has tried to fill up such important gaps in the study of citizenship and immigration. Whereas there are a substantial number of books on the pan-India Muslim League, very scant attention is devoted to the study of the provincial Muslim League in Assam. No serious effort has been made to look at its ideology, functioning and leadership. Although there is huge scope for further studies, nevertheless our effort may be considered to be pioneering in terms of understanding the Muslim League and its nature of activities in Assam. The book will also serve as a reference book to the students of social sciences to learn about the contemporary history of the region in an evolutionary trajectory. Perhaps one of the core facets of the book will be the utilization of huge primary data from various archival sources. In fact, we could perhaps utilize only 50 per cent archival and historical data, and a separate book may be published containing those primary data and resources in the future. Nevertheless, along with primary data, current available theoretical and other analytical literature, journals, PhD theses and newspapers in various libraries of India were consulted to arrive at factual accuracy.

Bibliography

Assam Tribune, 31 January 1941.

Baruah, Apurba Kumar. *Facebook Video*, 22 October 2020, www.facebook.com/apurbakumar.baruah.1/videos.

Bhattacherjee, Gaurishankar. *The Agony of Indigenous People* (in Assamese. *Bhumiptrar Mormo Bedona*). Guwahati: Jyoti Prakashan, 2015.

Bhuyan, A. C., and S. K. Barpujari. (eds.). *Political History of Assam*, Vol. III. Guwahati: Government of Assam, 1980.

Bora, Nibaran. 'Mohendra Mohan Chaudhury amulotoei sarbadhik bhoganiar punorbarshan hoisil' (Maximum Number of Refugees were Settled During the Time of Mahendra Mohan Chaudhury), *Agradoot*, 9 September 1981.

Chhabra, K. M. L. *Assam Challenge*. Delhi: Konark Publishers, 1992.

Dutta, Akhil Ranjan. (ed.). *The Conscientious Statesman: Gaurishankar Bhattacharyya*. Guwahati: Dr Subrata Sharma, 2015.

Hazarika, Sanjay. 'Illegal Migration from Bangladesh: Problem and Long-term Perspective'. In *Illegal Migration from Bangladesh*, edited by B. B. Kumar. New Delhi: Concept Publishing Company, 2006.

the number is exceedingly high. In Kamrup (Metro) 1999; in Dhubri 1171; in Nalbari 764; in Nagaon 711; in Barpeta 633 and so on.

Jana, Jyotirmay. 'Andolan Aru Motantor' (Assam Agitation and Difference of Opinion). In *Asom Andolan: Pratisruti Aru Phalasruti*, edited by Hiren Gohain and Dilip Bora. Guwahati: Banalata Publications, 2007.

Kalita, Ramesh Ch. 'Prabajankarir Samasya Aru Asom: Anandaram Dhekiyal Phukanar Para Gopinath Bardaloi Loike'. In *Asom Andolan: Pratisruti Aru Phalasruti*, edited by Hiren Gohain and Dilip Bora. Guwahati: Banalata Publications, 2007.

Mahanta, Prafulla Kumar. *The Struggle in Assam: Foreigners vs Indian Citizens*. Delhi: Vikash Publishing, 1986.

Misra, Udayon. 'Victory for Identity Politics, Not Hindutva in Assam'. *Economic & Political Weekly* 51, no. 22 (28 May 2016): 20–23.

Rajguru, Prasanat, and Amar Asom. *Khilonjiyar Shakti*, 21 May 2016. Guwahati.

Ray, Jayanta Kumar. 'Migration from (East Bengal/East Pakistan) Bangladesh to India'. In *Illegal Migration from Bangladesh*, edited by D. B. Kumar. Delhi: Concept Publishing Company, 2006.

Rizvi, Tabassum. *Political Participation and Voting Behaviour Women and Politics in the Char Areas of Assam* (Introduction), PhD Thesis, http://hdl.handle. net/10603/245569.

Sethi, Rajat. *The Last Battle of Saraighat: The Story of the BJP's Rise in the North-east*. New Delhi: Penguin Books, 2017.

Sharma, Dhruba Pratim, and Vikash Tripathy. 'Assam-2019: NDA Deepens Its Dominance'. *Economic & Political Weekly* LIV, no. 34 (24 August 2019): 23–25.

Times of India, 9 March 1983.

About the Author

Nani Gopal Mahanta is a professor of political science at Gauhati University, Assam, India. He was formerly Head of the Department, Political Science, and Registrar (2018–2019), Gauhati University. Dr Mahanta is currently the Director of the Centre for South East Asian Studies, Gauhati University, which was established by the Government of Assam to facilitate research and people-to-people contact as part of the Act East policy. His research interests include India's Northeast and Southeast Asia, peace and conflict resolution, human development and security, insurgency, ethnicity and identity politics. A Jawaharlal Nehru University (JNU) alumnus, Dr Mahanta was a Rotary World Peace Fellow at the University of California, Berkeley, from 2002 to 2004. As a World Peace Fellow, he travelled to various parts of the world, including Europe and South Asia, for his internship and empirical work. Dr Mahanta has published extensively in national and regional newspapers and journals and has authored several books. He regularly participates in debates and discussions on multiple issues in the state and nation on various platforms, including television and print media. He was felicitated with the Education Research and Development Foundation (ERDF) Excellence Award in 2009 for creating public awareness about civic and social rights and responsibilities. He is actively associated with several policymaking bodies of the Government of Assam. He is currently a member of the State Innovation and Transformation Aayog (SITA). He has provided consultancy services to the Department of Education, Government of Assam, Secondary Education Board of Assam (SEBA), Cotton College and others. He is the President of Governing Body, Handique Girls College—the oldest women's college of Assam. He served as the President of the Northeast India Political Science Association (NEIPSA) from 2014 to 2018.

Dr Mahanta has delivered lectures, upon invitation, at various prestigious world forums, such as the Rotary International World Peace Symposium in Chicago, United States, in June 2007, the Second World Peace Symposium in Birmingham (United Kingdom) in September 2008 and the Rotary International World Peace Symposium held in Bangkok, Thailand, in May 2013.

Dr Mahanta was a visiting fellow at the Peace Research Institute Oslo (PRIO), Manohar Parrikar Institute for Defence Studies and Analyses (MP-IDSA). His book *Confronting the State: ULFA's Quest for Sovereignty* was published by SAGE Publications in 2013. He has edited several titles in English and Assamese. His hobbies include playing badminton and popularizing the game. He has been the Vice President of the Assam Badminton Association for the last 5 years, and he is the President of Hatigarh Indoor Stadium, which was built as part of a community initiative to popularize badminton and table tennis in Guwahati city. Born into a Vaishnavite Satriya family in Sivasagar, Assam, he is a connoisseur of 'Naam Prasanga' and the Satriya ethos.

Index